HAMILTON COUNTY
TENNESSEE

WILL BOOK 1
1862–1892

James L. Douthat

Heritage Books
2024

HERITAGE BOOKS

AN IMPRINT OF HERITAGE BOOKS, INC.

Books, CDs, and more—Worldwide

For our listing of thousands of titles see our website
at
www.HeritageBooks.com

A Facsimile Reprint
Published 2024 by
HERITAGE BOOKS, INC.
Publishing Division
5810 Ruatan Street
Berwyn Heights, MD 20740

Originally published 1996

International Standard Book Number
Paperbound: 978-0-7884-8856-6

HAMILTON COUNTY, TENNESSEE WILL BOOK 1
1862 - 1892

Welcome to the world of the first Will Book that has survived for Hamilton County, Tennessee. This volume has made a long and strange journey to get into print. Several years ago, Tom Williams loaned me about 850 pages of the hand written copy of the W.P.A. version of this Will Book. On the cover of the box was written, "339 of the 559 pages copied". This meant that about one-third of the volume was not copied. We determined that if we were going to transcribe this volume, we wanted to do the whole thing and not just the first two-thirds of the book.

The next problem was to find the original. It was not found in the place where it should have been in the warehouse of county court materials. They started with Volume 3 and up. The probate court nor the county court office yielded any results. It had not been microfilmed as are all other records for the county. In a second visit to the probate office, I just said, "I guess I have the only remaining copy of the book and that is only two-thirds of the original." The secretary said, "Wait a minute!" and then disappeared back through the office to return in a moment with the volume in hand. She remembered that it was laying on the bottom shelf of a storage room. The probate judge ordered this microfilmed immediately. As I started to leave, the secretary ask if the others that were back there were needed. We then located an index to wills and the first will book for the old James County. This latter was the oldest surviving piece of material for that county since they have had several fires in their court houses. Each of these three volumes were microfilmed. Both of the will books have now been completed in their transcription.

The next decision was to abstract or full text the transcription? We opted to make a full text transcription which is longer and more costly, but the end results is well worth the efforts.

We have made ever effort to cross check names that were in doubt as to their spelling and in many cases, the will has more than one spelling of the name in the same body of material. We do note that but leave the spelling as presented in the original.

In the index, we have indexed both the surnames with given names and also the place names and names of companies where given. This latter makes the material more useful in a historic sense than just the full name index.

Just the reading of many of these wills tells volumes about the people and the times as presented in a first hand manner. We hope that you will find all of the material of interest and not just the one or two entries for your family.

James L. Douthat
Signal Mountain, TN
1996

Page 1 - blank

Page 2

HENRY GOTCHER

The last Will and Testament of
Henry Gotcher

I Henry Gotcher of the County of Hamilton and State of Tennessee, Planter, I make and publish this my last will and Testament, hereby revoking and making void all former wills by me at any time heretofore made. And first I commend my Spirit into the hand of God who gave it, and my body into the hands of my legatee to be intered at the place and in the manner and form which they may choose; and to such wordly estate as it hath pleased God to intrust me with, I dispose of the same as follows.

First, I direct that all my debts and funeral expenses be paid, as soon after my decease as possible out of any monies I may die possessed of or may first come into the hands of my executors any portion of my personal estate that may first come into the hands of my executors, or should the ravage of that war that is upon us so destroy my personal estate that it is not sufficient to answer that object, then out of my real estate that may first come into the hands of said executors.

Secondly, I give and bequeath unto my beloved wife Margaret Gotcher as her dower in real estate all that tract of land, and part of Ferry during her natural life which I got possession of by my intermarriage with her. Said land and part of Ferry lies in Rhea County, Tennessee and is well known as her dower in the real estate of her former husband William Hutchison, deceased.

3rdly. I direct that all my personal property which may remain after the payment of my debts as above named be divided equally between by beloved wife as above named and my beloved Sons, and daughters [i.e.] W. P. Gotcher, J. L. Gotcher, Nancy Towny, Betsey Ann Allen, Temperance Hancock, Jemima Varnell and Martha Johnson, except that my beloved wife have two hundred dollars more than either of them and the wooden furniture which she brought down here except it be destroyed. Said two hundred dollars to be taken out of the part that is coming to Betsey Ann Allen; which will leave her two hundred dollars less than either of her brothers & sisters.

Fourthly, I direct that all my real estate in this County be equally divided between my beloved sons and daughters as above named [Page 3] either by private sale among themselves, or at public out cry as they may choose.

Fifthly, I direct that the portion of my estate both real and personal that shall fall to my beloved daughter Betsey Ann Allen be kept in the hand of my executors & kept on interest as far as can be safely done untill the heirs of her own body shall arrive to the age of twenty one. And that the same be given to them as each one shall arrive to such age winding [sic] an equality amongst them, except such part of her own portion as her own separate and single necessities may from time require to be given to her this I direct to be done, and further direct that one fourth part coming to each of her children be kept back in the hands of my executors untill the youngest of her children become of age as above in order that in the final winding up of the business equal divisions may be made between them all, if however my beloved daughter Betsey Ann Allen meet with the misfortune to loose her husband then and in that case I direct that all her portion be given to her or such part there of as may remain in the hands of my said executors.

I do here by make ordain and appoint my beloved sons W. P. Gotcher and J. L. Gotcher and my beloved sons-in-laws Harrison Hancock & J. H. Varnell executors of this my last will and testament; in witness whereof I Henry Gotcher the said testator have to this my will written on one sheet of paper, set my hand and Seal this 16th day of June A.D. 1862.

Test: R. N. Varnell
          J. P. Varnell
          L. C. Moreland
          J. T. Gillespie

A True Copy
R. H. Guthrie, Clerk

[Page 4]

JOHN POE

The last will and Testament of
John Poe, dec'd

I, John Poe, do make and publish this my last will and Testament, here by revoking and making void all other wills by me made.

First, I direct that my funeral expenses, and all my debts be paid, as soon after my death as possible out of any money that I may die possessed of, or may first come into the hands of my Executors.

Secondly, I give and bequeath to my wife Rebecca

one milk cow, and my daughter Nancy one cow and they Rebecca and Nancy to have wagon and oxen, also two hundred and fifty dollars each and my son James Calvin Poe to have one hundred and Sixty dollars besides the amount which I owe him, my Son John L. Poe have one hudnred dollars, and all the other children fifty dollars each. Also, I want my wife and my daughter Nancy to live on the land, and have the rents of said farm untill August eighteen hundred and Sixty Seven; then the land to be sold to the highest bidders then the proceeds to be divided as aforesaid and if the proceeds Should fall short or over reach the Sums, then to be divided in proportion to the amount specified, Also all other loose property to remain in the care of my wife and Nancy, then to be sold when the land is sold.

Lastly, I do hereby nominate and appoint Christian E. Shelton, my Executor in witness where as I do to this my will, Set my hand and Seal this 3rd day of May Eighteen hundred and Sixty four.

John X Poe {Seal}
his mark

Signed Sealed and published in our presence, and we have subscribed our names hereto in the presence of the Testator this 3rd day of May 1864.
Green B. Stone
Hugh A. Boyd

A True Copy
R. H. Guthrie, Clk

[Page 5]

ELIZABETH LEWIS

The last will and Testament of
Elizabeth Lewis

In the name of God, Amen. I, Elizabeth Lewis of the County of Hamilton in the State of Tennessee, being of Sound mind and deposing memory and being satisfied that I must shortly depart this life, do by these presence make ordain, and publish this my last will and Testament, revoking all former wills by me made.

Item. I wish all my just debts and burial expenses paid as soon as convenient.

Item. I give and bequeath to my two daughters, Martha Jane Lewis, and Charity M. Lewis, and after their death to the heirs of their bodys all the right, interest,

claims and demand that I have, or may have in all the lands of which my Father William Swafford died seized and possessed of lying in Hamilton and Meigs County in the State of Tennessee that my father willed to me.

Item. All the rest of the personal property monies &c if any on hand at my mother Nancy Swafford's death, willed me by my father, William Swafford, I wish to be equally divided between all my lawful heirs.

In witness whereof I have here unto set my hand and seal this 7th day of February 1864.

Elizabeth X Lewis {Seal}
her mark

Signed, sealed and acknowledged and published in our presence as her last will revoking all others.

Thomas B. Smith
C. C. Turner

A True Copy
R. H. Guthrie, Clk

[Page 6]

ELISHA KIRKLIN

Elisha Kirklin Dec[d]

The last will and Testament of Elisha Kirklin, Deceased.

I Elisha Kirklin, Sen[r] of Hamilton County, Tennessee, do make and publish this my last will and testament hereby revoking all former wills by me made.

1st - I give and bequeath to my wife Susan Kirklin the land now occupied by myself on the home tract including the mansion house, out buildings & lots, with full control of the Spring, and an equal portion of the timbered land on the tract - the cleared land estimated at about eighty acres - also, my lot of one and a half acres lying near the mineral spring, where D. J. Rawlings now lives -my negro man, John, Four beds and furniture and all the other house hold and Kitchen furniture - all land and personalty as before described to be held by for and during the terms of her natural life, and no longer.

I also give and bequeath to my said wife, absolutely, a childs part of the ballance of my personal estate.

2nd - To my children, Eliza J. Rawlings, Malinda Shirly, Ephraim H. Kirklen, George W. Kirklin, Elizabeth C. Evans, Nancy Kirklin wife of my son Elisha Kirklin, Jr., Mary Smith, Allen J. Kirklin, William H. Kirklin, and Martha J. Kirklin. I give and bequeath all the rest, and residue of my estate to be held by them equally, share and share alike; as well the realty as the personalty, subject to the conditions & limitation hereinafter made. To my sons I give their portion absolutely, subject only to deductions for advancements; except my son Elisha, and what I had intended for him I hereby give to his wife Nancy Kirklin during her life, and after her death to her children by said Elisha, and in default of children living at her death, then to the said Elisha [Page 7] But the portion of my daughters, Eliza J. Rawlings, Malinda Shirly, Elizabeth C. Evans, Mary Smith and Martha J. Kirklin, I give for them sole and seperate [sic] use and benefits; not subject to the control or to be liable in any manner, for the debts or liabilities of the husbands of either of them.

In making the division amoungst [sic] my said children so as to give them equal shares in value as hereinafter provided; advancements which I have made to any of them shall be charged as so much of their portion already received by them, entiting the others to be first placed on a equality with them.

Such advancements are charged in my own hand writing in my general book of accounts on pages 46, 47, 48, 49, 50, 51, and 52-53, 54, and it is my will and desire that nothing be accounted on advancement to any of them, only as there charged by myself; and that the amounts as there charged shall constitute in all cases, the sums with which they are chargeable respectively to be deducted from their portion hereafter to be received by them, lands or other estates whichI have heretofore given or conveyed to them, shall not be accounted as advancements - my intention being, that my property as left at my death, and the advancements as charged in my book at said pages of 46,47, 48, 49, 50, 51, 52, 53 and 54, - shall consitute the whole which is to be taken into account in making the division amongst my said children.

The interest in remainder, in the property which I have given to my wife during life, I add to the portion of my children as heretofore given, with the same limitations and conditions in all respects.

I wish my real estate to be divided specifically by alloting a portion to each by commissioners and not be sold for the purposes of division; and in case the personal estate going to anyone of my children is insufficient to meet the charges for advancements, there the ballance shall be taken from the real estate of such legatee by the commissioners of partitions, and be added, at their valuation, to the share, or shares of those entitled.

I appoint my sons Ephraim H. Kirkin and my friend Thomas G. McFarland [Page 8] Exe-cutors of this my last will & testaments.

In witness whereof I have hereunto set my hand and seal the 19th day of July 1856.

Elisha Kirklin {Seal}

Signed, sealed & published in the presence of the testator, and each other at the testators request as his will.
Geo. D. Foster
James A. Whiteside

I make and publish as a codicil to my fore going will - 1st In partitioning my land, I wish the portion alloted to my three children, Allen J., William H., and Martha J. Kirklin, to be laid off adjoining each other and the portion of my son William H. Kirklin to be laid off as to include the house I now live in, not to interfere however with the life estate therein of my wife, and in the general allotment which shall include the land given to my wife during life, a reasonable allowance shall be made by the commissioners in favor of those who get the land so included by the life estate. The reasonable allowance to be in the land, and not in compensation otherwise.

In case my wife does not by herself occupy & use the one and a half acre lot at the mineral spring it shall be rented out by my executors, during my wife's life, and the proceeds divided equally amongst my three children, Allen J., William H., and Martha J. Kirklin, but she to have the privilidge if she should at any time wish to live there, to occupy the same herself. In selecting horses. she may take two mules instead of two horses.
19th July 1866.
Elisha Kirklin {Seal}

Signed, sealed and published in our presence, and witnessed by us in presence of the testator & each other.
Geo. D. Foster
James A. Whiteside

[Page 9]

ELBERT A. GLASS

Nuncupative Will of Elbert A. Glass, dec[d]

The nuncupative Will of Elbert A. Glass of the County of Hamilton, Tennessee, made at the residence of John G. Glass in said county about the middle of the month of September 1863, he having made his residence with said John G. Glass.

The said Elbert A. Glass being impressed with the belief that he would not live long, then being in bad health and his last will called upon John H. Glass, and Mary E. Glass specially to witness said nuncupitive will which is as follows:

First, the said Elbert A. Glass willed and bequeathed to his niece Mary Elizabeth Hogue, all his household and kitchen furniture of every kind, and all his jewelry of every kind and <u>discription.</u>

Second, he directed that all his just debts be paid, and for this purpose he said there was debts enough due him.

Third, He directed willed and bequeathed the remainder of his property equally to the said Mary Elizabeth Hogue, Sydney A. Hodges and his nephew, Elbert A. Glass, a son of Lewis Glass, share and share alike.

Fourth, If the nephew Elbert A. Glass should die before a distribution should be had under this will, then and in that case he directed that the remainder of his property, disposed of in the third clause should be equally divided between Mary Elizabeth Hogue and Sidney A. Hodges.

This will was reduced to writing on the 5th day of February 1864. Elbert A. Glass having died on the 3rd.

Witnesses:
J. G. Glass
M. E. Glass

A true copy
R. H. Guthrie Clerk

[Page 10]

SIMON BECHTEL

Will of Simon Bechtel deceased.

State of Tennessee }
Hamilton County   } S.S.

In the matter of the nuncupative will of Simon Bechtel late a private soldier of the 79th Regiment of Ohio Volunteers in the Service of the United States.

On the third day of February in the year of our Lord One thousand eight hundred and Sixty five, the said Simon Bechtel Private Soldier of the Army of the United States as aforesaid, being in <u>extremis</u> in his last sickness at General Hospital for the sick of the army of United States, Numbered two at Chattanooga in the County of Hamilton, and State of Tennessee of which he had been an inmate for over twenty days did request Burnhard Eckstein, undersigned to go for witnesses, to attest his last will, and testament and thereupon Surgeon John B. McPherson having been procured and also the undersigned, Joseph Wetherell, and George M. Hoover, Ward Masters of said

Hospital arriving the undersigned Enoch Rushbeing present from the time said Simon Bechtel desired Witnesses to his will the said Simon Bechtel did then and there in the presence of all of said named parties did declare his last will and testament as follows, to wit:

Said Surgeon John B. McPherson asked him the said Bechtel, whether he had any relatives in the County? to which said Bechtel replied in the negative by shaking his head, in the manner usually done to signify <u>NO</u>. The said McPherson then asked the following questions. Have you a wife? Have you any children? Have you father or mother? Have you brother or sisters? Have you any uncles or aunts? to each and all of which questions the said Bechtel answered as he had to the first one; by shaking his head in the manner generally done to signify No. - The said McPherson then asked, Is there any one present to whom you wish to leave your property? In answer to this said Bechtel assented by nodding his head in the manner usually done to signify yes and by pointing towards the person of Frederick Shoaf then present in the tent with the undersigned - the said Surgeon McPherson then laid his hand on said Frederick Shoaf and asked said Bechtel [Page 11] Is this the man? in answer to which the said Bechtel again replied affirmatively by nodding his head in the manner usually done to signify yes. The said McPherson then asked. Is there no one else you wish to have a part of it? to which last question the said Bechtel replied in the negative by shaking his head in the manner done to signify No - The said Surgeon McPherson then asked said Bechtel. Is this man to have all of it? to which said Bechtel again replied in the affirmative by nodding his head in the manner usually done to indicate yes.

The said McPherson then asked "Don't you want me to have some of it? - to which said Bechtel replied in the negative by shaking his head in the manner usually done to signify No.

The said Surgeon McPherson then asked said Bechtel "Have you no friends or relatives anywhere to which you wish to leave any of your property?" to which said Bechtel replied in the negative by shaking his head in the manner usually done to signify No. - more decidedly [sic] than to any former question, with reference to leaving any portion of his property to anyone other than the Said Frederick Shoaf - The said Surgeon then questioned said Bechtel, as to his property as follows, "Have you one thousand dollars?" Have you two thousand?" "Have you five thousand? Have you ten thousand?" Have you fifteen thousand?" to each of which questions Said Bechtel replied affirmatively - by nodding head in the manner usually done to signify yes.

Said McPherson then asked him "Have you sixteen thousand?" to which Said Bechtel replied in the negative by shaking his head in the manner usually done to Signify No." The said Surgeon then asked "Is any of this in gold?" "Have you a thousand dollars in gold?" "Have you two thousand?" "Have you five thousand?" to all of which questions the Said Bechtel replied in the affirmative, by nodding his head in the manner usually done to Signify yes. He was then asked if this fifteen thousand dollars were in bank in Ohio, to which he replied in the same manner - after questioning him about his gold & other money, Said Surgeon McPherson agained [sic] asked If he wished the said Shoaf to have all this money, to which Said Bechtel again replied in the affirmative by nodding his head in the manner usually done to Signify yes.

At the time the Said Simon Bechtel [Page 12] pronounced the foregoing will he was of Sound and disposing mind memory and understanding.

Reduced to writing and signed by us this 20th day of February A.D. 1865.

"The words "then aske" interlined after 13th line of 2nd page before Signing"

J. B. McPherson
Act. Asst. Surg. U.S.A.
J. Wetherell
Enoch Rush
George M. Hoover
Burnhard Eckstein

Proven in open Court
March 6th, 1865

A true copy
R.H. Guthrie Clerk

PATRICK GARDINER

The last Will and Testament of
Patrick Gardiner Dec

The last Will and Testament of Patrick Gardiner, made at Chattanooga Tennessee on the 3rd day of January A.D. 1865 hereby revoking all previous wills.

I Patrick Gardiner do make and publish this my last Will and testament hereby revoking all former Wills.
I will and bequeath to my brother Michael Gardiner and my Sister Eliza Gardiner, all the property of every kind and discription of which I may die Seized and posessed, in trust nevertheless for the benefit of my children John and Clara Gardiner, and direct that my funeral expenses be paid out of the first money coming to the hands of Said Michael and Eliza Gardiner, and I also direct that the said Michael Gardiner and Eliza Gardiner

use the property hereby bequeathed to them in trust to the best advantage, retaining the lands and the principle in any monies that may come to their hands, and apply the rents and profits of the real estate, and the interest of the money to the Support of my said Children till they arrive at maturity - and also to provide for their education as far as the means will allow and after they become of age to continue to pay them or the survivor the rents and profits of the lands and interest upon the money till their children Shall arrive at maturity when the whole estate shall be surrendered to their Said Children and the trust hereby created Shall cease.

2nd As all the lands for which I hold deeds [Page 1] in my own name and all the notes and evidences of debt I hold in my own name are the joint property of my said brother Michael Gardiner, and the estate of my deceased brother Timothy Gardiner and myself, it is intended that one third of the Same is disposed of by this Will

In Witness whereof I have hereunto Subscribed my name in the presence of these Subscribing witnesses, they having been called specially to Witness this my last Will and Testament. This 3rd day of January 1865.

Patrick Gardiner

Andrew Warren
Andrew Quigby
The foregoing Will was proven in open court at its May Term 1865

R. H. Guthrie Clerk

VINCENT F. ALLEN

The last Will and testament of
Vincent F. Allen deceased

I Vincent F. Allen, formerly Vincent Faller, and formerly of Spitgwold near Newstadt? in the providence of Schwargwold Grand? Dukedom Baden, Germany, and now a resident citizen of the City of Chattanooga in the County of Hamilton and State of Tennessee, in the United States of America, do made [sic] and publish this my last Will and testament.

1st It is my Will and desire and I do hereby direct that after my death; that all my property of every kind, and discription, including all my personal property, and that part of lot No. 40 on Market Street in the City of Chattanooga Tennessee designated as the Second South twenty feet, running back one hundred and ten feet, and the Same now occupied by myself as a Silversmith Shop, be Sold, either at public or private Sale as my executor hereinafter named Shall think best, and that the proceeds bee applied first to the payment of any just debts I may owe.

2nd I will and bequeath to my two Sisters Rosa Faller and Mary Schworer, both of the place discribed in the Caption to this will all the remainder of the proceeds of Said Sale, Share and Share alike.

[Page 14]

It is my will and desire that if my Sister Mary should be dead before this will is executed, that the portion hereby given to her should go to her Children, to be divided equally between them, and if Rosa Faller Should be dead then that all the property hereby bequeathed Shall go to my Sister Mary, and if she be dead then to her Children.

3rd If my sister Rosa Faller should have been married, and afterwards died leaving any child or children living, at the time of the execution of this Will, then it is my will and desire that that portion hereby given to her shall go to such child or children.

4 I do hereby appointe G. L. Maurer of Chattanooga Tennessee the Executor of this my last Will and testament, and direct that no Security be required of him for the fulfilment of the trust hereby reposed in him.

V. F. Allen [Seal]

Signed and Sealed in our presence this 28th day of May, 1865.

We having been called on by Vincent Fallen to specially Witness the Same.

R. Henderson
Jacob Kunz

The foregoing Will was proven in open Court at its July Term. 1865

R. H. Guthrie Clerk

JOHN G. GLASS

John G. Glass Deceased & C

The last Will and Testament of
John G. Glass

I John G. Glass of Hamilton County Tennessee, do make and publish this my last Will and testament, hereby revoking all former Wills.

1st I hold a lien by deed of trust from Elbert A. Glass to William F. Ragsdale for a tract of land in Hamilton County, Tennessee [Page 15] for discription of which Said deed of Trust is refered to.

It is my Will and desire that Said tract of land be Subjected to Sale to Satisfy the debt Secured by Said deed of trust, and bid in by my representative, provided Said land Should not bring at Such Sale more than the debt interest and cost, and in case Said land should be purchased by my representative, then that title be maid by Said trustee, William F. Ragsdale to Said tract of land to a trustee; in trust nevertheless for the use and benefit of my wife Mary E. Glass during her natural life, and at her death that the title to Said land be vested in my two youngest children, John Bell Glass and Willy Blount Glass. But in the event Said land should bring in more than the Said amount herin before specified, then, and in that case, I will and direct that the proceeds of Said Sale be applied to the Support and maintainance of my Said Wife and two children, John and Willy, and to their Education.

2nd I purchased a tract of land of Alexander Cooper, and paid him four hundred and fifty dollars of the purchase money, leaving four hundred and fifty dollars unpaid, for which I executed my note and took bond for title. Cooper is unable to make a good title to Said tract of land, I therefore direct that if Said Cooper will refund the four hundred and fifty dollars paid him, and interest thereon from time of payment, and surrender my note, that the contract for the purchase of the land be recinded, or if he will procure and make good title to the one half of Said tract of land adjoining the land of W. W. Anderson, it may be taken in lieu of the purchase money and interest already paid, and the contract recinded for the remaining half.

3rd I hold a note on F. Jordan of Madison County Alabama, for Six hundred and fifty dollars given about the 1st day of August 1862 and due about the 1st day of August 1864 Which note was burned with my residence, during the Battle of Missionary Ridge in November last.

I direct that Said note be collected as early as it can be done, and it is my Will and desire that the money when collected be applied to the [Page 16] support and maintanance of my Said Wife Mary and the said Children John and Willey.

I also held claims on the County of Hamilton Tennessee for one thousand and eighty dollars which were also burned, which I wish collected as early as possible, and will and direct that Said money when collected be applied to the support and maintainance of my Said Wife, Mary E. and the support maintainance and Education of my Said Children John and Willy.

I also hold a note on A. M. Johnson and _____ Rowlin for one hundred dollars due the 1st day of January last which was also burned With my house, which I wish collected and applied to the support and maintainance of my Said Wife Mary E. and the two Children John and Willy.

4th I will and direct that all my real estate, so far as is practicable be rented out to the best advantage, till my youngest child Willy Blount Glass arrived at the age of twenty one years, and then that all my property not heretofore disposed of be divided equally amoung all my Children, Share and Share alike - And I will and direct that my wife Mary E. occupy as a home for herself and two Children the house and lot in Chattanooga Tennessee recently purchased of Dr. Milo Smith, my present residence, and that She So continue to occupy the Same during her natural life.

5th I will and direct that any debts I may owe be paid out of the funds herin set a part for the Support and maintainance of my wife Mary and the support maintainance and education of the two children John and Willy, and I will and direct that all the pay that may be received from the Government of the United States for my negros, all of which ..[page burned].. the money paid as damages to my property of every discription by the United States, be also applied to the support and maintainance [sic] of my Said Wife and Children John & Willy, and the education of the two children, and I also will and bequeath to my Said Wife Mary all my household and Kitchen furniture.

6th I do hereby constitute and appoint Richard Henderson my Sole executor, of this my last [Page 17] Will and testament.

Signed and executed in presence of the follcwing persons who are specilly [sic] called to witness the Same March 21st 1864

J. G. Glass

Robert Smith
Thos. K. Wornacut

REV. HIRAM DOUGLASS

Rev. Hiram Douglass, Dec[d]

The nuncupative Will of
Hiram Douglass, Deceased

State of Tennessee)
Hamilton County)

We George W. Arnett and George W. Rider, were present during a part of the time of the last illness and at the time of the death of the Rev. Hiram Douglass, who died at the residence of Mr. Logan, at Charleston, Tennessee, on the 24th day of June 1865.

During the time of his last illness, even up to the time of his death, he was in perfect possession of his mental faculties - A few days previous to his death, he said that his will and desire was that all his property both real and personal (after the payment of all just debts) that he owned at the time of his death, should be used for the benefit of his wife Mary C. and his minor Children, until the youngest child arrived at age, at which time, after Supporting his said wife, Mary C. & rearing and educating his said minor Children, he wanted his real estate, and whatever of personal effects then on hand belonging to said estate to be divided amoungst all his children & he requested and desired us to See that his wishes and desires in this regard should be fully carried into effect.
July 4, 1865

G. W. Rider
Geo. W. Arnett

Sept. 4th
1865   Proven in open Court R. H. Guthrie, Clerk

[Page 18]

W. F. CARPER

W. F. Carper, Dec[d].

The County Court ats. October Term. 1865 - Ordered that Elizabeth Carper Executris of the Will of W.F. Carper, deceased, was permitted to have the certified Copy of said will recorded.

I William F. Carper of the County of Hamilton, State of Tennessee, Planter & Farmer, do make and publish this my last will and Testament, hereby revoking and making void all former Wills by me at any time heretofore made.

And first, I direct that my body be decently intered in the apple Orchard, on my own premises, where my mansion house stands, in a manner suitable to my condition in life, and as to such worldly estate. as it hath please God to intrust me with, I dispose of the Same as follows.

First, I direct that all my debts and funeral expenses be paid, as soon after my death as possible, out of any moneys that I die possessed of, or may first come into the hands of my executors from any portion of my estate real or personal.

Secondly, I hereby vest in the hands of my beloved wife, Elizabeth W. Carper, all my estate both real and personal, giving her the same power and control over the Same that I myself have always had, during her life time or widowhood, with the following instructions, that is to say, after raising and educating my beloved sons and daughters, Sarah Jane, Joseph H. Margaret M., William Alexander, Harriet Angeline, as they become of full age or is married, that such portion She, my beloved wife, Elizabeth W.Carper, whom I do hereby make, ordain, and appoint sole Executrix, of this my last will and testament, may see fit to give them, be recorded in a book by her for that single purpose, in order that, on a final distribution of all my estate, that each of them may have their lawful right.

Thirdly, I direct that at the death or intermarriage of my said wife either that all of my estate real & personal Shall then be disposed of as the law directs the case of intestates and on final divission among my Said Sons and daughters that special regard be had to the amount that any one or all of said Sons and daughters may have received from their mother, after their raising and education.

In witness whereof, I William F. Carper the Said Testator have to this my will, written on one sheet of paper set my hand and Seal, this 8th day of August in the year of our Lord, One Thousand Eight-Hundred and Fifty Nine.

William F. Carper [Seal]

[Page 19]
Signed, Sealed & published in the presence of us, who have subscribed in the presence of the Testator & of each other.

A.W. Moon
Henry Gotcher

State of Tennessee)
Hamilton County)

I George W. Arnett Clerk of County Court of Said County, do certify that the foregoing is a full, complete, and perfect copy of a paper writing, which was admitted to probate by said Court as the last Will and Testament of William F. Carper, Dec^d. as the same remain on file and of record in Said Court.

Witness my hand, and the Seal of said Court, at office in Harrison the 6th day of October, 1859.

George W. Arnett Clerk

WILLIAM RUNYAN

The last will and testament of
William Runyan Deceased

In the name of God Amen. The eighteenth day of October in the year of our Lord Eighteen hundred and Sixty one. I William Runyan of the County of Hamilton and State of Tennessee. Gentleman, being through the blessing of God in a sound state of mind and memory, but calling to mind the frail tenure of life, and that it is

appointed to all men once to die, do make and ordain this my last Will and Testament, that is to Say principally and first of all, I recommend my Soul in to the hand of the Almighty God who gave it me. The disposal of my body I leave to the entire discretion of my friends. With respect to my worldly estate I give and bequeath and dispose of it in the manner and proportions following. First I give and bequeath to my son William Ellis Runyan, the North half of eighty acres of land, being the west half of the North East quarter of Section 15 Township 2 and Range 2 west of the Basis line, and also give him the North half of the South west quarter of Section 15 Township 2 and Range 2, and I also give him forty acres of land in the North East corner of the North East quarter of Section Sixteen, Township 2 West of the Meridian, and I give and bequeath to my Son James K. Polk Runyan the South half of eighty acres of land being the West half of the North East quarter of Section fifteen (15) Township 2, and Range 2 West of the basis line, and I also give him the South half of the North West quarter of Section 15 Township 2 and Range 2, and I also give him the remaining 120 acres being a part of the North East Quarter of Section Sixteen Township 2, Range 2 West of the Meridian line, and the same aforesaid William Ellis Runyan, and James K. Polk Runyan, when they attain the age of 21 years, or narrys they are to have made to them each one of them a Warranty deed to the above described Land, by the proper Executor, and all of the above described Land in both cases, being and lying in the County of Bradly and State of Tennessee. I give and bequeath to my dearly beloved wife Malinda the residue of all my lands and perishable property, or cash, during the course of her natural life, and widowhood, if She Should mary the second time, then she is to have only an equal share with all my heirs, and at her death all of the remaining property of mine or hers to be equally devideed with and between all of my heirs except the remaining lands, which William E. Runyan and James K. Polk Runyan, is not to have a Share, except the above described lands, which I have already given them, is this my last will & testament but William Ellis Runyan, and James K. Polk Runyan they are to have an equal share of the personable property cash & C. with my heirs equally at the proper time.

And I therefore ratify and confirm this & C. no other to be my last will and testament. Witness whereof I have hereunto Set my hand & Seal the day, and, year above written.

William Runyan

Signed Sealed published pronounced and declared by the said William Runyan as his last will & testament in the presence of us the Subscribers.

J. L. Sears
M. A. Southerland

The foregoing will was provin in open court this 6th day of November 1865.

R. H. Guthrie Clerk

Bill of Costs Clerks fee	$1.25
Court Isaac Suclers summoning	
2 wit	.50
Witness James L. Sears;	
1 day 75 = 40miles travel &C	2.35
Mary An [sic] Henkle 1 day 75	
40 miles travel &C	2.35
Justice T. J. Weir 2 Sup-15	6.45

[Page 21]

J. H. BAKER

The last Will & Testament of
J. H. Baker, Dec[d]

I James Harvey Baker of the County of Hamilton and State of Tennessee, being in my right mind, and being desirous of Settling my worldly matters, myself, while in my proper mind I do here write this my last will and testament.

First, I want all of my just debts Settled out of my effects.

Secondly, I give and bequath to Phebe Caroline Baker my beloved wife all of my effects, that remain after my just debts are all settled.

In testimony whereof I hereunto Set my hand and Seal this 3rd day of January 1866. Also I hereby appoint M. H. Conner my Executor, to carry out this my last will and testament.

Signed in the presence of the following

James Harvey X Baker
his mark

Witnesses
W. R. Hainey
Hiram Hainey
A. L. Stulce

Probated at the February Court 1866

R. H. Guthrie Clerk

THOMAS W. SPICER

Thomas W. Spicer, Deceased

The last will and testament of
Thomas W. Spicer Dec[d]

In the name of God Amen.

I Thomas W. Spicer of the Town of Harrison, Hamilton County, State of Tennesse, being of Sound mind and memory, considering the uncertainty of this frail and transitory life, do therefore make, ordain and publish and declare this to be my last will and Testament.

That is to say first after all my lawful debts are paid and discharged, the residue of my estate real and personal I give bequath and dispose of as follows viz. To my Nephew John A. Smith my little Riffle gun; and to Wm. C. Davis I give my gold Spectacle; and will and bequath to Miss Bell Jack my sorrel colt, and I will and bequeath the remainder of my effects real and personal to the three children of Stephen Decatur Spicer. Likewise I make constitute and appoint Peter Mounger to be my Executor [Page 22] (without bonds) of this my last will and Testament hereby revoking all former Wills by [me] made and request my Said Executor to take charge of all my effects and property, collect all my debts, and settle up all debts and claims Justly due by me.

In witness whereof I have hereunto Subscribed my name and affixed my Seal this 18th day of June 1866.

T. W. Spicer (Seal)

Attest

T. H. Ruddy
C. H. Smith

Proven in open Court the 2nd day of July 1866, and ordered to be recorded and filed.

R. H. Guthrie, Clerk

JAMES GORDON

James Gorden, Deceased

State of Georgia)
Walker County)

In the name of God, Amen, I James Gordon of Said State and County being of advanced age, but of Sound mind and disposing memory, knowing that I must shortly depart this life, deem it right and proper, both as respects my family and myself that I should make a disposition of the property with which a kind providence has blessed me. I do therefore make this my last will and Testament, hereby revoking and annulling all others by me heretofore made.

First I desire and direct that my boddy be buried in a decent and Christian like manner, suitable to my circumstances and condition in life. My soul I trust shall return to rest with God who gave it, as I hope for Salvation in the merits and atonement of our Lord and Savior Jesus Christ.

2nd I desire and direct that all my just debts be paid without delay by my Executors hereafter named and appointed.

3rd I give bequeath and devise to my beloved wife Sarah lot of land Number two hundred and eighty and in the ninth District and fourth Section of originally Cherokee now Walker County known as the Crawfish Spring lot all the rights members and appertainances to said lot of land in any wise belonging.
[Page 23]

4th I give and bequeath to my beloved wife, Jess, a negro boy twenty nine years old, Ellen a negro girl about twenty four years old, and her two children to wit Esex - a boy about six years old, and Sarah a girl about three years old, and all the farming tools belonging to Said farm Blacksmith tools & waggons & four milk cows & calves & two mules & one horse & thirty head of stock hogs and fifteen head of Sheep & all the household and kitchen furniture, and one years support of provissions of all kinds and one thousand dollars cash, all the above named property I give and bequeath to my beloved wife Sarah for and during her life time, only after death the whole property to be Sold and equally divided among my lawful heirs the property devised and bequeathed in the above articles to my wife is full extinquishment of her whole right of Dower in my real and personal Estate.

5th The residue of my property both real and personal wherever and whatever it may be, I wish sold at public outcry and the net proceeds equally devided amoung my children (to wit) Thomas M. Gordon, William L. Gordon, Mary F. Caldwell wife of Leonatus M. Caldwell, Elizabeth M. Lee wife of James M. Lee, James C. Gordon, Cicro N. Gordon, Sarah Jane Fletcher wife of Joseph Fletcher deceased. If my Son William L. Gordon should wish the undivided half of what is known as the John P. Alexander farm lying & being in Catoosa county now owned by me the other half by messrs. Lee & Gordon, at the price of ten thousand dollars the price paid for said half tract, he is to have the priviledge of doing so without exposing said lot of land to Sale, Said purchase money to be subtracted from his part of my Estate.

6th I hereby appoint Thomas M. Gordon Trustee or Guardian for my daughter Sarah Jane Fletcher above mentioned to remain and take charge of her part of my estate, and to hold it in trust for her and the heirs of her body. Should She die without leaving any heirs of her body, then Said amount of my estate to be distributed equally amoung my other heirs above mentioned, I desire

that my Said daughter Sarah Jane shall receive a sufficiency of said fund for a comfortable living as her necessity may Require it and hereby empower the Said Thomas M. Gordon to use his discretion in the amount of funds paid out in relieving her necessities.

7th It is my will that each one of my heirs above named is to be accountable to the estate for the amount they have received heretofore.

8th I hereby constitute and appoint Thomas M. Gordon [Page 24] and James M. Lee Executors of this my last will and Testament.
January 21st, 1863

James Gordon (Seal)
Signed Sealed declared, and published by James Gordon as his last Will & Testament, in the presence of Said Trustee at his special instance & request in the presence of each other this 21st January 1863.

Thos. H. Hunt
F. M. Glass
W. B. Patillow
M. M. Phillips

State of Georgia)
Walker County)

I, T. W. Cobb ordinary in and for the County and State aforesaid do hereby Certify the foregoing is a true and correct copy of the last Will and Testament of James Gordon deceased late of said County as the Same appears on file and of record in my office.

In testimony I have hereunto set my hand and affixed the seal of the Court of ordinary for Said County of Walker this March 4th, 1863.

T. W. Cobb Ordinary
Recorded in Book 2 Page 435, 436, and 437 June 20th, 1866.

James M. Anderson
Ordinary

Presented to the County Court of Hamilton County Tennessee on the 1st Monday & 6th day of August 1866 with the foregoing Probate & C and ordered to be recorded & C.

R. H. Guthrie, Clerk

[Page 25]

JACOB CAPEHART

Jacob Capehart, Dec[d].

I Jacob Capehart of the City of Chattanooga County of Hamilton and State of Tennessee, of sound mind but in feeble health. In view of the uncertainty of life, and the certainty of Death Do make subscribe unto and hereby declare this my last Will and Testament;

1st - Let my boddy be decently Burried, after my demise.

2nd - I give and bequeath to my beloved wife Elizabeth Capehart, all my property Real and personal including Ready money on hand and all that may be due or owing previous and Household and Kitchen furniture subject to her use and control during her natural life, and at her death to my Daughter Rosanna Ann Five Beds and Bedding and to my Daughter Margaret Elizabeth, Four Beds and Bedding - the Remainder of the Household and Kitchen Furniture to be equally divided between my two Daughters Caroline and Adaline and my Son Quinton, share and share alike, that portion decending [sic] to my said Daughter not subject to the marital rites of their Husbands.

4th [No No. 3] - after the Demise of my wife, the Real Estate to be sold and the proceeds to be equally divided between my aforementioned Five Children or the Survivors of them, their heirs in all cases to be Representatives of the Parents; this 3rd October, 1856.

Signed and Sealed

Jacob Capehart

In Presence of

Joseph Ruoks
Jno. S. Brewer
Proven in open Court at the January Term 1867

R. H. Guthrie Clerk

[Page 26]

JOHN COWART

John Cowart, Dec^d

The last Will and testament of
John Cowart Dec^d

I John Cowart of Hamilton County, and State of Tennessee; do hereby make and declare this to be my last Will and testament, as follows, to wit,

After the payment of my funeral expenses, I desire all my just debts to be paid.

I give and bequeath to my wife Cynthia for and during her natural life one third of my real estate, including my dwelling house and out houses. I also give and bequeath to her during her natural life, all my Slaves - also the household and Kitchen furniture and farming tools, and implements.

It is also my desire that She Shall have all my Stock of horses, cattle and hogs, and so much of my bacon, lard and hay as she shall consider necessary for a years support of herself and family.

And whereas there is a written contract between myself and Madison Williams in relation to a part of my tract of land - Now I desire that Said Madison Shall have and enjoy the use and benefit of Said land, according to the terms of Said written contract, until my youngest child Shall arrive at the age of twenty one years - and in case of the death of Said Madison Williams, before expiration of Said term, it is my desire that his wife Jane, who is my daughter, shall have the benefit of Said written contract for the unexpired term.

I further will and desire that on my youngest child arriving at the age of twenty one years, that all my real estate, except my wife's interest in the Same herein bequeathed to her (if she shall then be living) Shall be Sold, on a credit of one two and three years credit, in equal annual instalments, and that the proceeds thereof shall be equally divided amoungst all my children, or the heirs of Such if any of them may be dead - my children amoungst whom I desire partition thus to be made are Jane Williams & Lemuel, Thomas, John and Slater Cowart. Such of my effects as is not above bequeathed, I desire my executors herein after named, I desire may be sold at public or private Sale as they deem best to the interest of my estate. And the rest and residue of my estate, after the payment of my debts as above directed, I desire may be equally divided amoungst my children above named, or their heirs if any of them should be dead. I hereby nomimate and appoint my friends [Page 27] Samuel Williams and William J. Standifer executors of this my last will and testament -

It is further my will and desire that my wife Cynthia Shall have power to Sell the above Slaves bequeathed to her, and pay over of the proceeds for Such Sale to my executors -

I also nominate and appoint my friend Richard Henderson an executor of this my last will and testament, jointly with my executors above.

John Cowart (Seal)

Executed by the testator in our presence, and by us witnessed in his presence, and at his request, this 6th day of March 1862.

A. C. Carroll
William Grant Sr.

Probated February Court 1867

R. H. Guthrie, Clerk

[Page 62]

WILLIAM DUNN

William Dunn, dec[d]

The Nuncupative Will of
William Dunn, Dec[d].

Probated May Term 1867

The last will of William Dunn, who was a citizen of Hamilton County Tennessee, and who died in the city of Chattanooga on the 31st day of March 1867, that is to say:

1st I desire my funeral expenses to be paid, and all monies owing to me to be collected, and all my just debts fully paid.

2nd The residue of my property, money goods Chattlis and effects of whatever character or description, including a package on deposit in the First National Bank at Chattanooga, Tennessee after the payment of my just debts, I desire to be delivered to the Rev. H. V. Brown, Catholic Minister at Chattanooga, to be disposed of by him according to his directions here to fore given him by me. And the Said H. V. Brown is constituted and appointed my Executor to carry out this my last Will in pursuance of the aforesaid instructions.

The above written instrument contains the last Will of the Said William Dunn, as it was published and declared by him to us, who were present at the making thereof, and especially requested to bear witness thereto by the Testator himself. Said will was made in his last Sickness in his room at the Kaylor house in the city of Chattanooga Hamilton County Tennessee where he has been personally residing for more than ten days. And we here state that we are in no wise interested in Said Will. That it was reduced to writing within ten days from the making thereof and that the Testator did not require the Said H. V. Brown his Executor to give bond as such. And we hereto subscribe our names and respective places of residence as witnesses to the same done in the City of Chattanooga on this 2nd day of April 1867.

J. B. Nicklin Jr. (Seal)
Chattanooga, Tennessee
Miles O'Reilly
Chattanooga, Tenn.

[Page 29]

ALEXANDER BOYD

The last will and testament of
Alexander Boyd, dec[d]

State of Tennesse)
Hamilton County)

I Alexander Boyd, being of sound and perfect mind and memory, do make and publish this my last Will and Testament, in manner and form folling.

First, I will that all my just debts, and claims be paid out of my effects. I do give and bequeath the remainder of my effects to my daughter Eliza Ann, wife of Robert L. McNabb to be paid to her as she needs it, - and desire that W. C. Wilson and Thomas B. Wilson, have three years from this date to pay their notes, by paying interest on it. I do hereby appoint Thomas Boyd my executor of this my last Will and Testament. In witness whereof I have set my hand and affixed my seal this the 2nd day of July 1867.

Alexander X Boyd (Seal)
His Mark

Signed Sealed, published and declared by the above named Alexander Boyd to his last Will and Testament, in the presence of us who have hereunto subscribed our names as witnesses in the presence of the testator.

T. H. Roddy
J.H. Swisher

Admitted to Probate the 5th day of August 1867, and ordered to be recorded and filed.

R. H. Guthrie Clerk

[Page 30]

PRICILLA BEAR

Pricilla Bear, Dec[d].

In the name of God Amen.

I Pracilla Bear of the County of Hamilton and State of Tennessee, being sick of boddy but of sound mind, and deposing memory, do made and publish this my last will and Testament in manner and form as follows.

first I will to my son John, the upper side with the mountain house, also my daughter Hannah one set [?] to John and lisabu [?] the lower end and with an equal divide in the land but I hold possession until my death this first December 1866.

Pricilla Bear

Witnesses

Jonathan Smith
D. K. Kimbrough

Probated in open Court the 7th day of October 1867.

R. H. Guthrie Clerk

HARRIET HALE

The Nuncupative Will of Harriet Hale, a woman of color who died on the ___ day of September 1867 (about the middle.)

In consideration of the love and affection She bore to E. M. Hale of Chattanooga Tennessee, The deceased in our presence bequeathed, and gave to Said Hale during her last illness all her property consisting of one horse a small field - about one acre of oats and about Seven acres of corn, a few potatoes, and a small quantity of cotton, being all the personal property of deceased. Said Hale took care of deceased during her last illness, and one condition of her bequest was that he should take all she had, pay her just debts and keep the ballance. Deceased was of sound mind when the bequests was made.

The foregoing was reduced to writing the 2nd day of November 1867, was read over and fully understood by us and is true in every particular and we certify deceased Seemed anxious that the bequests herin set forth be carried out and that a doctor bill She owed Dr. G. A. Gowin should be paid.

J. C. McRoy
Elizabeth Hembree

Attest:

E. Newby

Sworn to and subscribed before me the 2 Day of Nov. - 1867.

E. Newby, J.P.

[Page 31]

SAMUEL POE

The Last Will and Testament of
Samuel Poe Dec^d.

In the name of God, Amen.

I Saml. Poe of the County of Chattooga, and State of Georgia, being of sound mind and memory, being desirous to settle my worldly business, do make and publish this my last will and testament hereby revoking all wills by me heretofore made.

Item 1st I give and bequeath to my beloved wife Jane Poe all my plantations I now hold and where I now live, with all the improvements - These lands designated No. 141-149-176 in the 6th District, and 4th Section in said County - together with all the appertainances thereunto.

Also all my living Negroes, together with their increase if any - also my livestock, such as Horses, Mules, Cattle Hogs Sheep and bees, also waggons, Buggys Threshers, Blacksmiths tools, and all farming utensils, also all the household and kitchen furniture. All the just debts that may be held against me at the time of my death, must first be paid out of my estate. Should there be money, notes or accounts left, on hand, such notes, money or accounts I give to my wife. All the above property I give and bequeath to my wife Jane Poe during here natural life or widowhood - and in case She marries all the above property reverts back to my Estate at the time of her marriage, except two of the choice Negros be hers during her life, and at her death, it is my wish for the said two Negros to revert back to my estate, and at the death of my wife all the property be sold and equally devided between my Grand Children, except a sufficient amount to bury my wife, and erect a tomb over her grave, the above property to be sold by the Court - The children alluded to is the Children of A. W. Poe dec^d - and Mahaly, Catherine, Christopher - the money put on interest by the Court, and given to the heirs as they arrive at the age of twenty one years. Signed Sealed and published, and declared to be my last Will and Testament, this July 2^d 1861.

Samuel Poe

We the undersigned do hereby certify that the foregoing was signed by the testator as the last will and testament in our presence, and that we signed the same in his presence at his special instance & request, and in the presence of each other on this sheet July the 2^d 1861

L. B. Strange
A. K. Rhinehart
George W. Clemmons J.P.

[Page 32]

Georgia)
Chattooga County)

I Saml. Hawkins Ordinary in & for Said County and State, hereby certify that the above and forgoing, is a true and correct copy of the last will and testament of Saml. Poe dec^d as appears on file in my office.

Given under my hand and Seal of office this Feby. 28 - 1868.

Saml. Hawkins

(Seal)

Probated and filed in my office March 2^d 1868
R. H. Guthrie, Clerk

[Page 33]

J. E. C. RICE

The Noncupative Will of
J. E. C. Rice deceased

We John B. Weaver and L. Y. Green certify that John E. C. Rice, during his last sickness, and a short time before his death, called upon each of us to witness the following nuncupative Will, said Will being in the following words:

I desire my Executor to pay all the just debts which I owe out of any money or property may have.

I desire that all my property of every Character, and kind, remaining after my debts are paid, shall vest absolutely in my mother Sarah E. Rice, and that she dispose of the same as she may see proper.

I desire that my executor prosecute all suits that I may have in the Law or Chancery Courts.

I nominate and appoint John B. Weaver my Executor, and desire that he execute this my will as directed. This November 18th - 1867
J. B. Weaver
L. Y. Green
Probated May Term 1868
R. H. Guthrie Clerk

[Page 34]

THOMAS C. HAWLY

Thomas C. Hawly, Dec[d].

The last Will and Testament of
Thomas C. Hawly

I give to my Executrixes or the survivors of them, all my estate, real and personal, to be held and disposed of as follows.

1st - To pay all my debts, with such means belonging to the Estate as they may deem most judicious.

2nd - To set apart to my wife Sarah, for the support and maintainance [sic] of herself, my daughter Mary Eliza, and my son Thomas Orville, so long as they may remain with her unmarried, all my estate real and personal.

3rd - At the death of my wife all my estate real and personal shall be divided equally between my daughter Mary Eliza and son Thomas Orville.

4th - Should my children mentioned above die, or either of them, before marriage, and without issue, my daughter Martha Anderson and her bodily heirs shall be entitled to their portion of my estate, real and personal.

5th - I give to my executrixes or Survivors of them full power to rent or lease at their disention [sic], any or all of my estate, real or personal.

6th - I appoint my wife Sarah and my daughter Mary Eliza Executrixes of my will and Testamentary Guardian of my minor son Thomas Orville, and exempt them from bond and security for a discharge of the trust -

This 27th day of September 1865
Thomas C. Hawly
Witnesses:
J.W. Finly &
J.S. Gillespie

Admitted to Probate May Term 1868 and ordered to be recorded & filed
R. H. Guthrie Clerk

[Page 35]

SARAH MOORE

Sarah Moore, Dec[d].

The last will and Testament of
Sarah Moore Deceased

I Sarah Moore, do make and publish this as my last will and Testament hereby revoking and making void all other wills by me at any time made.

1st - I direct that my funeral expenses, and all my debts be paid, as soon after my death as posible [sic] out of any moneys that I may die possessed of, or may first come into my Executors.

2nd - I give and bequeath to my daughter Malinda Moore two cows two hogs and two bedsteads, Two Feather beds, and necessary bed clothing for same, and one little Bureau & table, and a reasonable amount of other vessels and furniture, about the house, then she Malinda Moore, have a right to live and hold possession of the house where I now live & to have a reasonable amount of the incomes of my farm for to keep and support her, during her natural life time, unless she should marry; then the lands all to be sold and she Malinda Moore have an equal share of all my estate according to the foregoing apportionment.

3rd - Polly Standifer my daughter have one hundred dollars of my estate and no more.

4th - All the rest of my children have equal shares according to my directions, in this my Will. My deceased daughter Susan Housers childrens proportion to be laid out in land, to be selected by my executors, and they receive the income yearly, during their natural lifetime -

My deceased daughter Obedience Howards children have their proportion, as they become of age except two hundred dollars, which she received in her lifetime -

My daughter Sarah Chitwoods Children to receive their mothers proportion as they become of age, with a deduction of two hundred dollars, which she has received.

My deceased Sons Edward H. Moore children have their proportion as they become of age.

My deceased Son Nimrod Moore's Children receive their proportion as they become of age. -

My deceased James M. Moores son John, receives his proportion at twenty one years of age -

My son Richard J. Moore have his proportion. -

[Page 36]

My son Frederic J. Moore, have his proportion.
My son Peter P. Moore have his proportion.

I further desire that all my personal property be sold as soon after my death as posible [sic], that is not otherwise appropriated, and the farm kept up and cultivated and all the surplus funds put at interest until disposed of according to this will.

Lastly I do hereby nominate and appoint Peter P. Moore, and C. E. Shelton my Executors.

In witness whereof, I do to this my will, Set my hand and Seal this 13th day of May one thousand eight hundred and sixty seven.

Sarah Moore (Seal)
her mark

Test. L. C. Moreland
James J. Davidson

Probated Aug.3ᵈ 1868   R. H. Guthrie Clerk

[Page 37]

JAMES C. MITCHELL

James C. Mitchell, Decᵈ.

The last Will and Testament of
James C. Mitchell Decᵈ

I James C. Mitchell, being of Sound mind and memory do make, and publish this my last Will and testament, hereby revoking all other Wills by me made.

First - I give and bequeath my soul to God, who gave it, trusting in his mercy for a hapy [sic] immortality after death.

2nd - I give and bequeath to my wife Nancy Jane Mitchell all my land of which I am possesssed, to have and control, during her natural life if she remain my widow, if she should mary [sic] it is to fall to my children.

3rd - All the personal property, after paying my just debts and funeral expenses, to be used by my beloved wife as she may see fit, and she is hereby appointed my executrix without giving security.

4th - The water power to be left on the land.

Signed Sealed and delivered in our presence, and in the presence of each other, this 20th day of May 1868
James C. Mitchell (Seal)
his mark

Witnessed by
R. L. McNabb
T. C. Mitchell

Probated 2ᵈ November 1868
R. H. Guthrie Clerk

[Page 38]

WASHINGTON EVANS

Washington Evans's Will

I Washington Evans being in feble [sic] health and of sound mind and deposing memory make and publish this as my last Will and Testament.

1st - It is my will that all my Debts and funeral Expenses be paid out of the assets belonging to my estate.

2nd - To make as near an equal Division of my Estate as possible between my Son John and my daughter Louisa, I give and bequeath to my son John Evans my home farm on which I now reside containing about two hundred and ninety acres which I estimate at the value of four Thousand Dollars and charge said farm with a suitable support for my beloved wife Jane Evans during her Life or widowhood.

3rd - I give and bequeath to my daughter Louisa Selcer the lands purchased by me as the property of Lewis Shepherd or in case it should be redeemed, then she is to have the money for said Land which I estimate at two

Thousand Dollars - and to make her Equal with her Brother John I give her Two Thousand Dollars more out of the personal assets of my Estate - and should there be more of the personal assets of my estate - It is my will that it be divided equally between my said Son and Daughter and to carry out this my last Will and Testament I appoint my wife Jane Evans my Executrix.

Given under my hand and Seal this 12th day of November 1868.

W. Evans (Seal)

Witnesses
        H. L. Swan
        L.C. Moreland

State of Tennessee)
Hamilton County)

Personally appeared before me R. H. Guthrie Clerk of the County Court of said County H. L. Swan and L. C. Moreland the subscribing witnesses to the foregoing will who being duly sworn deposed and said they were acquainted with W. Evans the makeer of the same and that he executed said will in their presence and that he was of sound mind and disposing memory, in a proper condition to dispose of his Estate.

Witness my hand at office at Harrison the 17 day of November 1868.

R. H. Guthrie Clerk

(a true copy)

[Page 39]

SAMUEL McCALEB

Samuel McCalebs Wills

I Samuel McCaleb being of sound mind and mature judgement do make this my last will, revoking all others by me made so help me God.

First - I give and bequeath to Clemantine Flemmings and her heirs Sixty Two acres to be laid of[f] at lower end of my farm that is on the South West end of my farm adjoining Matocks farm, and with his line to have and hold the same her and her heirs forever.

Secondly - I give and bequeath to my Daughters Eliza McCaleb and Jane Gardenhire, one hundred twenty five acres of land to be so laid off to include all of my buildings where I live, commencing on Miss Flemmings line when laid off so running as to include that much land, one Hundred twenty five acres.

Thirdly - I give and bequeath to my Daughters

Mary Murphy and Elvira J. Allen the remaining portion of my farm which is one hundred and twenty five acres to be divided equally between them.

Fourthly - I give Eliza McCaleb all my fat hogs and my Stock hogs and all my Cattle except one Cow and Calf, which I give to my Daughter Clementine Flemmings.

Fifthly - I give and bequeath to Louisa L. Rea ten dollars.

Sixthly - I give and bequeath Adeson F. McCaleb fifty Dollars which is not to be paid to his guardian for three years.

Seventhly - I appoint William Murphy my executor to carry my last will, to do and perform all things necessary to be done to close up and settle business and I further authorize said William Murphy my executor that in the event in closing up the business of my estate that One Thousand Dollars can be raised to pay it to Elvira J. Allen and divide the sixty two half acres of my land between the other four Daughters above named.

In testimony of the above I herewith set my hand seal this 17th day of Nov. 1868

Samuel McCaleb (Seal)

"In the second line from the bottom of the above is underlined which is a part of this will"

[Page 40]

Signed Sealed in the presents [sic]
John L. Yarnell
James J. Thompson

WM. C. KING

Will of Wm. C. King, Dec^d.

Chattanooga, 2nd Febry, 1867

I wish my Sister Lou to inherit & possess any and all property moneys &c &c that I may own when I die. Given under my hand and Seal this day.

W.C. King

Endorsement on back of Envelope "Open when I am dead"

W. C. King

[Page 41]

ANDERSON REYNOLDS

Will of Anderson Reynolds

This Will and Testament of Anderson Reynolds of Chattanooga Hamilton County State of Tennessee.

I Anderson Reynolds of the County and State aforesaid do this Seventeenth day of July one Thousand Eight Hundred and Sixty will and bequeath all my personal and Real property effects money &c at my death to my wife Maria whose widow name was at the time of our marriage was Maria Thompson. To have the full use and possession of the same according to the best of her knowledge and at her death the said Personal and Real property efects [sic] money &c shall be equally divided amongst her and my Children or their heirs. The Children of the said Anderson Reynolds are John Reynolds, James Reynolds, Sarah Crabtree, Elizabeth Crawford, Ester Goin, Alti Gudsey, Almira Corruth, Mary Reynolds, Margaret Reynolds and the Children of my wife Maria are Lettice McCormick, John, Thomas, Sanders

Unto this will & Testament I this 17th day of July 1860 Set my hand and Seal

Anderson X Reynolds
his mark   (Seal)

George F. Brown
George Adlam
    Witnesses

State of Tennessee)
Hamilton County)
    Law Court of Chattanooga October Term 1868..
    Hon. William L. Adams Judge presiding &c
        Saturday October 24th 1868
           Contested Will

Mariah Reynolds	)
vs.	)
O. C. Goins	)
Esther Goins	)
John Crabtree	)
Sarah Crabtree	)
Heirs at Law and	)
Distributees of	)
Anderson Reynolds Dec^d.)	

Came the parties by attorys. and also came the same Jury to wit 1. E. M. Hale, 2. W. Bursell, 3. Patrick McGuire, 4. William Martin, 5. J. C. Gillespie, 6. John Hartman, 7. Danl. Kaylor, 8. A. Hulsea, 9. Hugh Magill, 10. P. [or T] M. Humphreys, 11. W. A. McCorkle, 12. B. F. Nevels who were on yesterday - elected empanelled and sworn to well and truly inquire and ascertain whether or not a paper writting [sic] purporting to be the last will and Testament of Anderson

Reynolds deceased who not having heard all the Evidence, the argument of Counsel and received the charge of the court, were permitted to separate until the meeting of this [Page 42] Court this morning 8 o'clock who now come and resume the further consideration of the Cause and after hearing all the Evidence the Argument of Counsel and receiving the Charge of the Court upon there [sic] oaths after mature deliberation say that said Paper writting [sic] is the Last Will and Testament of Anderson Reynolds deceased.

It is therefore ordered by the Court that the same be certified by the Clerk of the Court to the County Court of this County to be recorded in said County Court as the last will and Testament of the said Anderson Reynolds, Deceased as required by law and it is further considered by the Court that the Plaintiff recover of the defendants and there [sic] Surety all the cost in this cause for which an execution may issue.

State of Tennessee)
Hamilton County)
    I Chas. W. Vinson Clerk of the law Court of Chattanooga do certify the foregoing to be a true and perfect Copy of the Record in said cause and judgement of the Court and that the Enclosed is the Will.

Witness my hand at office in Chattanooga the 30th Dec. 1868.

C. W. Vinson, Clerk

[Page 43]

JAMES ILES

Will of James Iles, Dec^d
Proven Sept. Term 1868

I James Iles of the County of Hamilton and State of Tennessee do make and publish this as my last Will and Testament -

1st After all my just Debts are paid, That my beloved wife Elender Iles have during her natural life the farm on which I now live on, with all the proceeds of the same and she have all my personal property and that she dispose of the same or enough of it as will pay all of my debts, and if there is any remaining, she is to use it as seems best to her -

Second - It is my wish and desire also that my beloved Daughter Leanaher J. Iles be educated and maintained out of the proceeds of the Farm until she arrive at the age of Twenty one, if she marrys [sic] before that time it Stops and when she arrives at the age of twenty one or marrys [sic] before that time, it is my desire that for the love I have for her, that she have out of my property or the proceeds of the Farm - That she have one bed and furniture, one Cow and Calf and Sow and pigs, one bee stand and one Sheep. It is my desire that my beloved wife give her as near the amount as she can, that I gave my other Children, when they were married - It is also my desire if my beloved wife should die before my beloved Daughter Leanaher J. Iles arrives at the age of twenty one that my beloved Daughter L. J. Iles have the proceeds of my farm until she is twenty one or if she marrys before she arrives at the age of twenty one it stops. It is my will and desire that at the death of my beloved wife Elender Iles, that my lands be equally divided between my beloved Children John Iles or his heirs Nancy A. Elsea formerly Nancy Iles, Leanagher J. Iles or their heirs. It is also my desire that my beloved wife pay out of my property, the amount of a note executed by me and John Iles to J. H. Shipley, the dates and amounts I misremember, as my beloved son John Iles has paid me, to pay the whole amount of the debt. It is also my will at my death for the love I have for my son John Iles, that he have my Rifle Gun, which Gun my Executrix is not to take or numerate with the balance of my property - It is my desire that my wife have all the bounties and wages that is coming to me from the Government by the death of my two Sons and that she apply the same to the payment of my debts.

Lastly - it is my will and desire for the confidence I have in my beloved wife Elender Iles, she be appointed Executrix of this my last will and Testament & that she not be required to give security as executrix.

Given under my hand and Seal this 9th August 1868

James X Iles (Seal)
his mark

Attest - J. B. Thomas & James Barnes

[Page 44]

ROBERT DENNY

Robt. Denny's Will
Contested Will

John Denny)
Surviving Executor of)
Robert Denny, Dec^d.)
vs.)
H. C. Alexander & Wife)
Margaret Alexander)
William Fitzgerald & Wife)
Angaline Fitzgerald)
Woodson Fitzgerald & Wife)
Nancy Fitzgerald)
Heirs at law of)
Robert Denny Dec^d)

Came the parties by Attorneys and came the same Jury to wit 1. Isom Penny, 2. W. R. Massey, 3. Jesse S. Ragan, 4. John Gross, 5. R. C. McRee, 6. James Varner, 7. James Matthews, 8. W. R. Puckett, 9. William Hughes, 10. Wm. Poe, 11. F. A. Carden, 12. George Sively who were on yesterday empanelled and sworn to well and truly try the issue between the parties joined who not having heard all the argument of the Counsel and received the charge of the Court were permitted to separate until the meeting of the court this morning 7 1/2 o'clock, who now come and resume the further consideration of the cause and after hearing all the argument of Counsel & receiving the charge of the court, upon the oath do say they find the issue in favor of the Plaintiff, that the paper writting [sic] purporting to be a substantial Copy of the last will and Testament of Robert Denny Dec^d. is substantially a Copy of the last will and Testament of Robert Denny Dec^d. which Copy is in the words and figures following to wit -

I Robert Denny will and bequeath
First - that all just debts be paid.
Second - to enable my wife Jane to support herself in her declining years - I will that she have all my personal property money and land left after my debts are paid, during her natural life.
3rd - That after the death of my said wife Jane, it is my will that my two Sons John and Thomas Denny have all my personal property money and land, left by my said wife Jane.
4th - It is my will that my two Sons John and Thomas Denny for the consideration herein set forth, be charged with the maintenance of my step Daughter, Betsy Horn. And that my two Sons John and Thomas be my executors to carry out this my last Will and Testament.

Witness my hand and Seal this ___ day of _____ 1859.

Robert Denny Seal
Witnesses
Thomas Shirley &
Jane X Biggs
her mark

[Page 45]

And it is further ordered by the Court that the Same be certified by the Clerk of this Court to the County

Court of this County to be recorded as substantially a true Copy of the last will and Testament of Robert Denny Dec[d].

State of Tennessee

I Chas. W. Vinson Clerk of the Circuit Court of Hamilton County do certify the foregoing to be a correct Copy of the verdict of the Jury and judgement of the Court in the case of John Denny Ex. &c against H. C. Alexander and others at the June Term of Said Court as appears of record in my office.

Given under my hand and Seal of said Court at office in Harrison this 5th day of July 1869.

C. W. Vinson Clerk
By S. A. McKenzie D. C.

WILLIAM A. SPENCER

William A. Spencers Will

State of Georgia)
Walton County)

In the name of God Amen;

I William Anson Spencer of the county and State aforesaid being of sound mind and memory and considering the uncertainty of this frail and transitory life do therefore make ordain publish and declare this be my last will and Testament, that is to say

First - After all my lawful debts are paid and discharged the residue of my estate real and personal, I give, bequeath and dispose as follows, to wit,

Item 1st - To my beloved wife Mary Weir all my real, personal and mixed property viz. my half interest in the property known as the Crutchfield House and lot and Appurtainances thereto attached and the three lots lying Opposite the Crutchfield House and known as Sutler Town, all being and lying in the City of Chattanooga, Tennessee and my whole interest in fifty acres of land more or less known as the Dr. Hooker Place, situated sbout two miles from Chattanooga Tennessee near Missionary Ridge in the county of Hamilton and State last mentioned and my half interst in a lot fronting the Court House in the town of Maryville Blount County Tennessee, and known as the "Fools Corner or Block" also my half interest in One Hundred and Seventy Acres of land more or less, situated about two and a half miles from Maryville Blount County Tennessee, lying on the road to Tuckaluchy Cove, also my interest in a farm known as "Ghormely Place" lying on the little Tennessee River, in the county and state last above named, also my half interest in the

Houses and land of the place on which I now live, situated in the Town of "Social Circle," County of Walton and State of Georgia, also my half interest in the house we are now building and the land whereon the same is situated containing Seventy five acres more or less, and known as the Supper House land, also my half interest in the Steam Mill and Lot, and all the appurtainances belonging thereto situated on the north side of Georgia Rail Road near the Depot in "Social Circle" Walton County Georgia; also my half interest in a Steam Saw and Grist Mill and all the Machinery and appertenances thereto belonging, now leased to Flemings, Bates, Carter, and situated about three miles of Adairville, on the West side of the Western and Atlantic Rail Road in the State aforesaid also my half interest in all the Horses, Mules, Cattle, Hogs, Wagons, Carts, Drays, Hacks, Buggies, Harness and all farming Tools and implements of all kinds, as well as Carpenters and Blacksmiths Tools &c, and also my half interest in all the notes, accounts and credits belonging to the firm of W. A. & H. L. Spencer, likewise whole interest in my undivided notes accounts, Credits &c to have and to hold during her natural life or widowhood, and at her death or in the event of her Marriage, Namely, should she marry again then all my personal, real and Mixed Property, shall be equally divided into four equal parts and given as follows viz. one fourth to my wife Mary Weir, one fourth to my Daughter Mrs. Mary Eliza Butler (or in the event of her death to [Page 47] her son William Morgan Butler, or any other issue of her Body. and should Mary E. Butler and Children all die, then the Said Interest is to revert back to my Son Hedges Lindsey Spencer and the other half to my two Grand Sons, William Spencer and Charles Hedges Carter.) One fourth to my son Hedges Lindsey Spencer (and should he die without lawful issue, then his Interest to revert back to Mrs. Mary E. Butler and her children One half, and the other half to William Spencer and Charles Hedges Carter and one fourth to be given to William Spencer and Charles Hedges Carter my Grand sons, and in the event they die without lawful issue, then their Interest to revert back to Mary E. Butler and Children one half, and the other half to Hedges L. Spencer or his lawful Heirs.

Item 2nd - Now in the Event of the death of my wife Mary Weir, then all my personal and mixed Property, shall be divided into three equal parts, Namely, One third shall be given to Mrs. Mary E. Butler, one third to Hedges Lindsay Spencer, and One third to William Spencer and Charles Hedges Carter, and in the event of the Death of any one the Heirs just named and the Death of their lawful issue then their Interest to revert back to the surviving heirs as named in the first Item of this my Will.

Item 3rd - Provides that my wife Mary Weir has

the power at any time during her widowhood, with the consent of two thirds of the rest of my heirs interested to sell any and all property belonging to my Estate, whenever the interest of said heirs can be promoted by the disposal of the same, except the House and lot known as the Crutchfield House, and all its appurtenances thereto belonging, in the City of Chattanooga, Tennessee.

Item 4th - Further provided that my wife Mary Weir, has the power, with the consent of two thirds of the rest of my heirs interested to give from time to time, from the proceeds of the sales of the property last above named or from any other money that may come into [Page 48] her hands any time during her widowhood for the Education, Clothing, any other assistance that in her Judgment may be necessary for the benefit of any of my heirs herein named, and I also desire that there should be a correct account kept of all the monies disbursed for the purposes herein named, and at the final Settlement of my estate Respective amounts advanced by my wife Mary Weir for the benefit of such heirs shall come out of and stand as credit in behalf of my estate against the Interest of each one for whom the amount was advanced.

Item 5th - Likewise I make, constitute and appoint my son Hedges Lindsey Spencer to be my Executor of this my last Will and Testament, hereby revoking all former Wills by me made.

In witness whereof I have hereunto subscribed my name, and affixed my Seal this the Twenty-ninth day of May in the year of Our Lord One Thousand Eight Hundred and Sixty Seven.

William Anson Spencer
(Seal)

The above written instrument was subscribed by the said William Anson Spencer in our presence and acknowledged by him to each of us, and he at the same time published and declared the above Instrument so subscribed to be his last Will and Testament, and we as Testators request and in his presence have signed our names as witnesses hereto and written opposite our Respective names Our Respective places of Residence.

A. M. Colton, Social Circle
Walton Co. Ga.
Sterling Eckles, Social Circle
Walton Co. Ga.
C. H. Shipp, Social Circle
Walton Co. Ga.

Walton Court of Ordinary at Chambers June 8th 1869.

Personally appeared before me at Chambers this the 8th day of June 1869 A. M. Colton & C. H. Shipp, two of the subscribing witnesses to the within Papper [sic] writing pronounced as the last Will and Testament of William Anson Spencer, late of said County deceased, Who being [Page 49] duly sworn, Say that they together with Sterling Eckles, the other Witness, saw Said deceased sign, seal, publish and declare the within paper writing as for his last Will and Testament freely and voluntarily and with out any undue influence being exercised over him at the execution of said paper writing,and while said deceased was of sound and disposing mind and memory, and of sufficient testamentary capacity to execute a Will that they together, with Sterling Eckles, subscribed said paper; writing as Witnesses at the Special instance and request of Said deceased in his presence, and in the presence of each other, and that Said paper writing was executed the day and year it bears date.

A. M. Colton
C. H. Ship

Sworn to Subscribed before me June 8th 1869
Jessie Mitchell
Ordinary

Whereas I William Anson Spencer of the town of Social Circle in the County of Walton and State of Georgia have made my last Will and Testament in writing bearing date the Twenty Ninth day of May in the year of our Lord One Thousand Eight Hundred and Sixty Seven in and by which I have given my Executrix Mary Weir Spencer my Wife the power at any time during her Widowhood with the consent of two thirds of the rest of my heirs to sell any and all property belonging to my Estate, whenever the interest of said heirs can be promoted by the disposal of the Same, except House and lots known as the Crutchfield House and all its appurtenances thereto belonging in the City of Chattanooga and State of Tennessee.

Now therefore I do by this my [Page 50] writing which I hereby declare to be a Codicil to my Said last Will and Testament and to be taken as a part thereof do order and declare that my Will is that the property known and described as the Crutchfield House and all its appurtenances thereto belonging with the lots attached to the Same being the place whereon the Crutchfield House stood (and now recently destroyed by Fire) in the City of Chattanooga and State of Tennessee and more particularly described in Item 3rd the third of my former Will above named. That my Executrix have the same power by and with the consent of two thirds of the rest of my heirs interested to sell the property excepted in Item third of my former Will above mentioned & known and described as the Crutchfield House and Lots and all appurtenances thereto belonging, in the City of Chattanooga and State of Tennessee.

In witness whereof I have hereunto Subscribed my name and affixed my Seal the Eighteenth day of April in the year of our Lord One Thousand Eight Hundred and Sixty Eight.

Wm. A. Spencer (Seal)

Signed Sealed published and declared by the said William Anson Spencer as and for his last will and testament in the presence of us who at this Request of the said William Anson Spencer and in his presence and in the presence of each other have hereunto subscribed our names and Respective places of residence, as witnesses.

A. M. Colton, Social Circle, Walton Co., Ga.

Sterling Eckles, So. Circle Walton Co., Ga.

C. H. Shipp, So. Circle, Walton Co. Ga.

[Page 51]

Walton Court of Ordinary at Chambers June 8th 1869.

Personally appeared before me at Chambers this 8th day of June, 1869 A. M. Colton and C. H. Shipp two of the subscribing witnesses to the within Codicil or Suplement [sic] of the will of William Anson Spencer propounded this day for probate who being duly sworn say That they Together with Sterling Eckles saw said testator sign seal publish and declare the within Suplement annexed to said will as Codicil thereto freely and voluntarily and without any undue influence being exercised over him at the Execution of said Codicil and while said deceased was of disposing Mind and Memory and of sufficient testamentary Capacity to make a will that they together with Sterling Eckles subscribed said Codicil as witnesses at the Special instance and request of said Testator in his presence and in the presence of each other and that said Codicil was executed the day and year it bears date.

A. M. Colton
C. H. Shipp

Sworn to and subscribed before me June 8th 1869
Jessie Mitchell)
Ordinary   )

State of Georgia)
Walton County   )

I Jessie Mitchell Ordinary and Ex officio Clerk in and for said county Certify that the foregoing contains a true copy of William Anson Spencer - late of said county deceased, and Codicil thereto annexed together with the action taken upon the proof before the Ordinary at

Chambers June 8th 1869, that on the fifth day of July last first being a regular term of the Court of Ordinary for said County said will and Codicil were admitted to Record upon the propounding [Page 52] of said Will and Codicil for probate in Common form that Hedges Lindsey Spencer nominated therein as Executor duly qualified before me at said Term and to vest him full authority to Execute said Will I have duly issued to him letters testamentary annexed to said copy of said will.

In testimony whereof I the Ordinary have hereunto set my hand and Seal of Office June 5th 1869.

Jessie Mitchell
Ordinary and Ex officio
Clk. Walton County, Ga.

State of Georgia Walton County

By the Court of Ordinary of said County to all to whom these presents [sic] shall come greeting.

Know ye that on the fifth day of July in the year of our Lord One Thousand Eight Hundred and Sixty Nine the last Will and testament of William Anson Spencer late of said County deceased, was Exhibited in open Court it being a regular Term thereof in common form of law, proved and admitted to Record a copy of which is hereunto annexed on administration of all and singular the goods chattles and credits of said deceased was granted to Hedges L. Spencer, one of the Executors in and by said will named and appointed, he having taken the oath and performed all the requisites required by law. He is by order of said Court, and by virtue of these prsents [sic] legally authorized to administer the Goods, Chattels and Credits of the said deceased according to the tenor and effect of said will and testament, and according to law and he is hereby required to render a true and perfect inventory of all and singular the goods, Chattels and Credits of said deceased and appraised and returned to the [Page 53] Court a true and correct account to the said Court of his actings and doings yearly and every year until his administration is fully completed. In whereof and by authority of said Court at the Regular Term thereof I have hereunto Set my hand and Seal of Office This 5th day of July, 1869.

(Seal)   Jessie Mitchell
                  Ordinary of said County

State of Georgia)
Walton County   ) Ordinary's Office

Recorded in Book "A" Page 311 this the 12th day of July 1869.

Thomas Giles
D. Clk.

[Page 54]

JAMES M. DOBBS

James M. Dobbs' Will

I James M. Dobbs do make and publish this as my last Will and Testament, hereby revoking and making void all other Wills by me at any time made.

First - I will and desire that my funeral expenses and all my debts of every character and kind be paid as soon as possible after my death out of moneys that I may be possessed of at the time of my death, or if this is not sufficient my executor or executors are directed to sell my personal property at public or private Sale as they may deem expedient, and apply the proceeds to the payment of my debts, and retain the residue as hereinafter directed, and in the event my personal property is not sufficient to pay my debt, my executor or executors will sell a sufficency of my real estate to pay the residue of said indebtedness.

I desire my executor or executors to rent out the real estate, and apply the results and profits thereof to the maintainance clothing and education of the children of said Joseph D. Dobbs in the event their parents fail to maintain, clothe, and educate them in a proper and suitable manner.

My special desire is that the children be well educated. The amount expended for each child for its support and education is to be made a charge against it interest in my estate.

When the youngest child arrives at the age of Twenty one years, my executors will divide the property among the children [Page 55] subject to advancement or expenditures for their support and education; and in the event of the death of any of the children, with issue the issue will take the same proportion as the parent would if living. All my personal property will be converted into money in such manner as my executor or executors may deem best for the interest of the children of my son Joseph D. Dobbs, and the proceeds applied to their support, and education; next will be appropriated the rents and profits of my real estate; and if necessary my executor or executors, will sell a portion of the real estate; disposing of the least valuable of said estate first. In the event the parents of said children support them in a proper manner suited to their condition in life, and give them advantages of attending good schools; or places of education, the fund arising from the Sale of the personal property; and the rents of the real estate will be held for distribution when the youngest arrives of lawful age.

I desire my executor or executors to be the Guardian of the children of my said son Joseph D. Dobbs, especially in reference to their interest in my said estate both personal and real and if the parents of these children do not maintain them in a proper manner, and give them all proper opportunities to receive and education I desire my executor or executors and the Guardian of said children to furnish them with a support and means of education.

I nominate and appoint D. M. Key and S. A. Key my executors, and the special Guardians for the children of my said son Joseph D. Dobbs. And it is my expressed wish, and desire that they and each of them be relieved from giving bond and taking the oath required by the Statutes of the Sate. And in the event of the death, resignation or renunciation of either of them the surviving or remaining executor is directed to execute the trust herein reposed in both of them. [Page 56] I wish them or either of them to exercise their discretion and judgment in the general disposition of the property belonging to me, and to have and receive a reasonable compensation for their services as executors and guardians.

Signed sealed and published in our presence, and we have subscribed our names in the presence of the Testator.

This 13th day of May, 1869.

J.M. Dobbs (Seal)

Attest

Wm. A. McCorkle
Samuel Clem

JOSEPH NELSON

Joseph Nelson's Will

In the name of God Amen:

I Joseph Nelson of the County of Hamilton and State of Tennessee being in sound and disposing mind and memory (praised be God for the same) and being desirous of settling my worldly afairs [sic] while I have strength and capacity so to do make and publish this my last Will and Testament - that is to say:

1st - I give and bequeath to my worthy friends W. R. Gray and W. G. Thomas the whole of my real and personal estate; after paying all my outstanding debts. I also direct that the net produce of my real and personal estate heretofore men[t]ionied be disposed of by Auction, and sold to the highest bidder, and that the proceeds of such sale, with all other money due me be equally divided to the above named.

This 7th day of September 1869

Signed by Joseph Nelson as and for his last Will

HAMILTON COUNTY, TENNESSEE
WILL BOOK 1 - 1862-1892

23

and Testatment in the presence of us who in his presence and in the presence of each other and at his request have hereunto subscribed our names as witness.

Joseph Nelson (Seal)

W. J. Manning
J. A. Clement

[Page 57]

JOHN MULLINS

John Mullins Will

I John Mullins of the City of Chattanooga and State of Tennessee being of sound mind, memory and understanding do make publish and declare this to be my last will and testament hereby revoking and making void all former will and testaments and writing in the nature of last wills and testaments by me heretofore made.

My will is first that my funeral expenses and just debts shall by my executor herein after named.

It is my will that Father Bronn recover the sum of Twenty dollars out of such moneys as may come into the hands of my Executor for masses for my soul.

It is my will that my executor shall rais sufficient funds to pay off my debts by a mortgage on my house and lot on Carter Street in the City of Chattanooga, and rent the same on such terms as he may seem best.

I will and bequeath the said house and lot subject to the above incumberance to my Niece Mag Quin supposed to be in the County Kerry in Ireland, if she can be found, and in case she is dead, or cannot be found then I bequeath said lot as above to her brother Thad Quin, and in the event he cannot be found then to Michael Connor the son of my sister Mary.

And I hereby nominate and appoint my trusty friend Thaddius Brice to be the Sole Executor of this may last will and testament.

Given under my hand and seal this 27 day of February 1869

John X Mullins
His Mark

Signed sealed and declared by the said Mullins to be his last will and [Page 58] testament in presence of us who at his request and in his presence have subscribed our names as witnesses and in the presence of each other.

John J. Oshen[?]
James Sullivan
Miles O'Reilly

LUCINDA BLACKBURN

Will of Lucinda Blackburn

I Lucinda Blackburn of the County of Hamilton State of Tennessee being of sound mind and disposing Memory do hereby make and publish this my last will and testimony hereby revoking all Wills or Codicils thereto heretofore made by me.

First - I will and bequeath to my beloved niece Sarah Elizabeth Carver wife of D. H. Carver Lot No. - corner Fourth and Chestnut Street in the City of Chattanooga Hamilton County, it being the same upon which I now reside, also one Cow and one Heifer, together with all my household furniture of every description and character To Have and To Hold said property to the sole and seperate use of said Sarah Elizabeth Carver free form the control, liabilities, debts and contract of her said husband or any future husband she may have. It is further my will that the said Sarah Elizabeth Carver take care of my husband T. J. Blackburn during his life, and in the event she fails to do so then I will and bequeath that the property herein willed to her be charged with maintainance for and during the remainder of his natural life.

And I hereby will to said Sarah Elizabeth Carver - all the property of every description and character of which I may die possessed of, or that may belong to me at my death. And I hereby nominate and appoint the said Sarah Elizabeth Carver my executrix of this my last will and hereby waive bond and it is my will that she be not required to give bond as executrix.

In witness whereof I have hereto set my hand and seal this 30th day Jany. 1870.

Lucinda Blackburn (Seal)

Attest

T.K. Wornacut
M.H. Clift

[Page 59]

H. V. BROWN

Will of H. V. Brown, Deceased

I, Henry Vincent Brown Pastor of the Roman Catholic Church of Saints Peter and Paul in the City of Chattanooga and State of Tennessee, being of sound mind and body, but mindful of the uncertainty of human life, do hereby will and bequeath to Patrick A. Feehan of the City of Nashville (commonly known as the Roman Catholic Bishop of Nashville) all my real and personal property, consisty of lands, houses, money, notes, accounts, claims, books, furniture and effects of every kind of which I may die seized in trust for the following purposes viz: -

1st - For paying my funeral expenses. My debts should I owe any and procuring a decent monument to be placed over my remains.

2 - For two Masses of requeim to be celebrated in the cathedral one on the day of my burial and the other at the end of a month, and ten private masses to be offered by every Priest in the diocese as well as the solemn masses for the repose of my soul, such sum as he may judge proper & necessary.

3 - For a Christmas gift to my aged Father George Brown who lives in Churchville Monroe Co. N.Y. one hundred dollars per annum for the term of his natural life.

[No. 6 follows 3 in the book]

6 - To pay St. Marys Orphan Assylum near Nashville One thousand dollars or which I would prefer to invest the same to the best advantage & pay the income to the Assylum. This bequest to be provided for out of the Note of two thousand dollars unpaid principal due me from the diocease and given by Bishop Jas. Whelan.

5 - One thousand dollars for the purchase and improvement of a Catholic Cemetery in Chattanooga.

16 - All the remainder of my estate I wish to be devoted to the completion & decoration of the new Church I commenced building, provided compensation from Government for damages done thereto, or donations or any other resourse shall furnish means enough to accomplish the object. Otherwise I desire the present Chappel to be enlarged [Page 60] and that any fund which shall remain be securely & profitably invested and the income devoted to the education of Catholic Children whose parents or guardians may not be able to send them to school.

H. V. Brown ( )
August 21, 1867

I bequeath all my books, pictures, furniture, etc. for the use of my successor, the Parish Priest of Chattanooga who shall not sell or in any way dispose of the same, without the consent of the Bishop and Congregation:

My field Glass I will to James Crowley and my ivory Crucifix to his mother.

I wish to be buried in St. Mary's Orphan Asylum near Nashville, that the sisters and children may remember me and pray for the repose of my soul.

I appoint the above named Patrick A. Feehan and Joseph Ruohs of Chattanooga administrators of this my last will and testament, signed and sealed this 21st day of August in the year of our Lord 1867.

Henry Vincent Brown ( )

Witness
A. M. Johnson)
P. A. McKenney)

I was born in Berkshire Co. Mass. of Presbyterian parents, Feb. 24th, 1815.

Baptised & recd. into the Catholic Church by Bishop Miles at St. Rose's Convent Ky. April 5th 1840.

Went to Rome in 1844 - was ordained Priest in June 1848, & reached Nashville in the autum [sic] of that year.

4th - For the completion & suitable furnishing of the parochial residence which I am now (August 20th, 1868) building, according to the plans & specifications of R. W. Smiley, Contracting Carpenter, and prices named in his bid, with such grading, fencing, planting or shoveling & other improvements that may be necessary, the amount required whatever it may be.

7th - For the completion of the education of Stephen Henry King now a student at my [Page 61] charge at St. Vincent College Cape Girardeau, Mo. so long as he shall persevere in studying for the Priesthood the needed amount and these bequests is to take precedence of that in favor of St. Mary's Orphan Asylum.

Schedule of my property and Liabilities Aug. 20th 1868.

5 - 20 Bonds		4800
Cash note of Bp. Whelan		
due from his successor	2000--	
Cash note of Daniel Crowley		
secured by real estate	616.98	
Interest on same to		
Sept. 18th 1867	259.12	
Cash note of Sims &		
Hamilton due Oct. 25, 1867	500--	
Cash note of Patrick Fitz-		
gibbons over due	80--	
Cash note of D. Kaylor and		
Mulligan due Oct 23rd 1867	200--	
Cash in bank in gold	334.50	
Premium on same at 40 pr.ct.	133.80	
Cash in Bank in Silver		
$33.50 pre. $11.75	45.25	
Due from Chancery Court		

expended in repairs on
Crowley's House   <u>1737.15</u>
    5906.80
    <u>4800.</u>

Amount of Cash & Cash Assets   10,706.80
Morrison's Note   <u>400</u>
    11.106.80

Doubtful Claims
Kelso & McDonald Note
   $500 Interest $350.00   850
   (See copy amongst notes in
box) (Kelso died insolvent)

I loaned Mrs. Julius Carpens[?]   100
I took for security a note on
   J. G. Walker for $555.00 but
   I suspect it is owrthless
In 1864 or 5 E. E. Jones of
   Nashville gave me his note
   for $200.
   I rec'd. from him 50 copies
   of Fr. Ryan's Oraltons at
   $12.50 leaving unpaid   187.50
   I have lost the note but Mr.
   Jones will not deny it.
Thos. L. Fornicks Note   143--
Interest for 9 years (Mr.
   F. is an honest man)   68.22
I loaned Wm. Maker (deceased)
   $150.00 Ten years ago   150.00
   Interest 10 years   90.00
James Lynch of Atlanta
   as Administrator, a constable
   has the note and Daniel Hogan
   the receipt
    <u>738.72</u>

Amount from other
   side   <u>850.00</u>
Total amount of
   doubtful debts   1588.72

[Page 62]

Real Estate
1 Lot on Second St.
   next to Union Alley   400.00
I own 20 feet by 400
   along the south of   presented
   the church lot north   300.00   to Bishop
Value of Real Estate   400.00
unsold

Debts due for Real Estate
   sold on account

From Andrew Warren
   besides interest   416.30
From Marcellus Bettus   265.00
From Dr. Ames Im-
   provement purchased
   from him to be
   credited until
   reimbursed by rents   716--
Due from Mrs.
   Catherine Kane   9.50
Do. from Mrs. L.
   Crowley   <u>86.50</u>
Amount of good debts   1,754.99

Value of Reast estate   400.00
Cash & Cash assets   <u>13,574.30</u>
Aug. 20th 1868   17,029.29

[written in red ink across entries]
   <u>I am not strong</u>
   <u>enough to examine</u>
   <u>the balance on</u>
   <u>this page"</u>

Liabilities
Note to Daniel Hgan[sic]
   dated Aug 28, 1861   792.40
Six years interest   285.26
Thos. Crane for money   650
   deposits
Thos. McMahan   <u>671</u>
    2,398.66

Net value of estate
   without bad debts   14,630.63
Bad or doubtful   <u>1,588.72</u>
   Grand Total   16,219.35
To which may be
added about 900.00
worth of Books and
furniture.

[Note written in red in between the lines]
     "I intend to write my will as soon as possible.
Should I never be permitted to so do, the above will
furnish to Bp. Feehan & Joseph Ruohs a sufficiently clear
knowledge of what I will & bequeath.
           H. V. Brown
           Aug 20th 186<u>7 & 8</u>

Omitted

I owe the Crowley Estate, or Mrs. Crowley for two years rent of the Crowley House with which I paid my board, at $300.00 per annum 600.--

I am to pay Mrs. Crowley $25.00 per month for my board only from May 20th, 67.

Wm. Palmer bought a lot from me in 1854, for $300.00. I have not heard from him in several years. Should he appear, he will be entitled to his purchase money, or any lot I may have unsold, not exceeding 100 feet front.

[Page 63]

Anthony Jacquet bought a lot for $200.00 in 1853 or 4. He went to France & told me if he never returned I might have the lot for the Church. I have sold it & should he come back & claim, let him have the purchase money.

MINERVA N. THOMAS

I Minerva N. Thomas being of sound mind & disposing memory do make & publish this my last will & Testament hereby revoking all others by me at any time made.

1st - After the payment of my just debts and funeral expenses I do will and bequeath to my son William McFadden Thomas all my property both real and personal as well as all moneys which I have in the bank or elsewhere.

2^d - In the event my said sone shall die before he arrives at the age of 21 years & without issue, I then will and bequeath all my aforesaid property & money to T. J. Latner as trustee for the use of the Baptist Church & Sabbath School of the Baptist Church in Chattanooga Tennessee.

3^d - I hereby appoint my trusty friends Foley Vaughn, P. D. Sims & O. H. Wayne Executors of this my last will & testament.

Minerva X Thomas
her mark

Signed sealed & acknowledged in presence of us who witness at the request of the testator & in his presence.

J. H. Weaver
J. W. Humphries

Probated 7th day of November 1870
J. H. Hardie Clerk

[Page 64]

MORNING JOHNSON

State of Tennessee)
Hamilton County) In the name of God Amen

I Morning Johnson widow and relict of James Johnson deceased of said County and State aforesaid being of sound mind also of advanced age, and knowing that I must shortly depart this life, deem it right and proper both as regards my family and myself, that I should make disposition of the property that a Kind Providence has blessed with do therefore make this my last will and testament. That is to say that I have paid my oldest son William Johnson a resident of Meigs County, Tennessee his share of his Father's estate amounting to Three hundred dollars also my oldest daughter Mary Jane Hunter has been paid the amount three hundred dollars also my son James Johnson has been paid the amount of Three hundred dollars also my daughter Mary Watkins has been paid the amount of three hundred dollars also Harriet Jane Watkins has been paid the amount of three hundred dollars also Franzina Johnson has been paid three hundred dollars also Eliza Johnson has been paid Three hundred dollars also Alta Johnson has been paid One Hundred and fifty five dollars her part of my estate. Also Sarah Johnson has been paid Two hundred & fifty Dollars her share of my estate.

It now remains that I should make some provision for my son Thomas H. Johnson who has never yet received any thing from his Fathers estate. It is my will and desire that he support me as he has done for many years and that he have in addition to his share of his father's estate the amount of his claims against me and also what he may pay out for me and my support during my lifetime and also my stock consisting of one bay mare and one cow and heifer also all my household and kitchen furniture except a few things hereafter mentioned which is to be given to my daughter Alta Burke.

Morning X Johnson (seal)
her Mark

Signed, Sealed, declared, and published by Morning Johnson as her last will and Testament in the presence of us the subscribers who subscribed the [Page 65] same with our names in the presence of the said testatrix, and in the presence of each other this march 21st 1870.

George W. Turner
Barnett Parker

Probated 5th Decr ₁₈₇₀
J. H. Hardie Clerk

MATERSON ESTILL

Know all men by these presents [sic] that I Materson Estill of Chattanooga in the County of Hamilton and state of Tennessee in ill health but of sound and Disposing mind and memory do make and publish this my will first and last. And as to my worldly Estate and all the property real and personal or mixed of which I shall die seized and posesed or to which I shall be entitled at the time of my decease I devise bequeath & dispose thereof in the manor following to wit first my will is that all my just debts & funeral Expenses shall by my Executor hereinafter named be paid out of my estate as soon after my decease as shall by them found convenient.

Item - I give devise and bequeath to my beloved children Materson Estill & his sister she not being named when last I saw her all my real Estate and personal Property after the funeral expenses and just debts are paid.

I give and bequeath all of my property as above stated to my son Materson Estill and his sister to be for there benefit forever Armstead Lewis Executor in testimony whereof I the said Materson Estill and I have subscribed my name and affixed my seal this 5 day of Dec. 1870.

Signed sealed & published & declared by the said Materson Estill as and for his last will & testament in the presence of us what his request & in his presence and in presence of each other have subscribed our names as witnessed thereto.

A. P. Melton   (seal)
H. Houston   (seal)
Hervy X Smith   (seal)
  his mark

Probated January 4, 1871
J. H. Hardie Clerk

[Page 66]

CASPER JOACHIM BLEWEL

The State of Tennessee)
Hamilton County   ) City of Chattanooga

I Casper Joachim Blewel of the City County and State aforesaid being of sound Mind and disposing Memory yet weak in body and knowing the uncertain Tenure of life do make and publish this my last will and testament.

First - I commend my spirit to God who gave it.
Second - I desire my body decently buried.
Third - I will and direct all my just debts and funeral expences paid as soon as practicable after my death.

Fourth - I will and bequeath to my beloved wife Magdalena Blewel Speciffically the proceeds of sale of Two Acres land more or less sold by me to Thomas Rohner lying in Grundy County Tennessee in what is called the Swiss Colony and described in Banns Map, for the sum of Eighty five dollars and writings were executed for the same which are now in the hands of Henry Sowderegger for safe keeping who lives in said County and Coloney and if the said notes are not paid without sale then the said land is to be sold and the proceeds of sale paid over to my said wife Magdalena Blewel or if the land has to be taken back then I devise said land to her in fee simple with all ints. acrued & to acrue Thereafter.

Fifth - I give and bequeath to my said wife absolutely and forever Three Thousand Fracs with all interest accrued and to acrue Thereon until received by my said wife now in or should be the hands of Baptist Blewel in Solo Thwen Switzerland in the Village of Erscheville and all the rights powers & convoemamces necessary are hereby bequeathed to her inforce collect and receive the same be the said Francs money or investments if any of the same wherever situated.

Sixth - I will and bequeath all my Household and Kitchen and other furniture which I may die seized and possessed of as well as all debts and other effects of every character kind and discription of which I may die seized and posessed of in law or equity to my said beloved Wife Magdaleana Blewel.

Seventh - I hereby nominate constitute and appoint Jacob Kunz of the City of Chattanooga County of Hamilton and State of Tennessee Executor of this my last Will and Testament hereby revoking all other Will or Wills or Codicils heretofore made by me.

[Page 67]

In witness whereof I have hereunto Signed my name.
In presence of the Witnesses hereto.
M. Block and D. C. Trewhitt June 18th 1871
Casper Joachim Blewel (Seal)
Signed and acknowledged by the testator in our presents

& of each other on this the 13th day of June A.D. 1871

M. Block

D. C. Trewhitt

Probated on the 6th July 1871

J. H. Hardie Clerk

THOMAS HARRINGTON

Know all men by these presents that we John Litener and Richard Harris both of the City of Chattanooga, County of Hamilton, and State of Tennessee were personally acquainted with Thomas Harrington of said City, County, and State in his life time. That on or about the tenth day of June 1871 being especially required by the said Harrington we bore Witness to his (the Said Thomas Harrington's) last Will and Testament, which was by him in our presence and we being then and there in the presence of each other Solemnly declare to be as follows.

I want my wife Mary Harrington to have my House and lot, deeded to me by John Litener and all other property I have. My boys are all grown, and are able to take care of themselves and I want my wife to have my property.

This declaration was made by said Harrington while in his right Mind, and on his death bed in his last Sickness. It was also made in his the Testators House where he had been residing for many Months previous to the time of his so making his Will. The said Testator further requested John Litener one of the said witnesses to see that the provisions of his said Will were Carried out, Makeing said Litener his Executor. On Testimony whereof we have hereunto set our hands and Seals this 28th day of June 1871

his

Richard X Harris (Seal)

mark

John Litener (Seal)

Attest

H. M. Wiltse

Probated 6th day July 1871

J. H. Hardie, Clerk

[Page 68]

MARSHALL W. GREEN

State of Tennessee

Hamilton County

In the name of God Amen.

I Marshall W. Green of the county and State aforesaid being Satisfied that my time of departure is at hand but being at the same time of sound mind and disposing Memory do hereby publish and declare this writing to be and contain my last will and Testament.

Item first - I give and bequeath my soul to Almighty God.

Item Second - After the payment of my just debts I give I give and bequeath all my property boath real and personal to my Beloved Wife Jane during the term of her natural life and after her death I give and bequeath said property to the Children of my Brother Leb. Green to be eaqually divided between said Children. In witness whereof the said Marshall W. Green hath hereunto set his hand and Seal this 8th day of June in the year of our Lord 1871.

M. W. X Green

his mark

Signed Sealed published & declared by the said Marshall W. Green to be his last Will and Testament in presents of the undersigned who have subscribed our names as witnesses thereto in presents of the testator and presents of each other the day and year above written.

A. P. Green

W. H. Murdoch

J. (or I) Hington

The forgoing Will was proven in Open Court 7th day of August 1871.

J. H. Hardie Clerk

NIMROD PENDERGRASS

In the name of God Amen.

I Nimrod Pendergrass of the County of Hamilton in the State of Tennessee Being now feeble in Body but of sound and disposing Mind and Memory and knowing the uncertainty of life and the certainty of death do make and Publish this my last will and Testament revoking all former Wills by me made.

Item 1st - It is my will and desire that all my just debts and funeral expences be paid that I be buried in a good respectable manner suitable suitable to my property and circumstances.

Item 2nd - I give and bequeath and devise to my Grandson James A. Pendergrass and his heirs or assigns

Son of my Son John Pendergrass all the property boath [Page 69] boath real and personal as well as all chases in action or right of action money &c of which I may die seized and possessed of or have a right to in any way at my death except the sum of one dollar which I will to my son Jesse Pendergrass and one dollar to my son Hiram Pendergrass and one dollar to my son John Pendergrass and one dollar to my son Nimrod Pendergrass and one dollar to my Daughter Martha Riddle formerly Martha Pendergrass and one dollar to my son Jefferson Pendergrass and one Dollar to my son Nathaniel Pendergrass heirs and one dollar to my Daughter Anne King heirs.

Lastly hereby appoint my and ordain my said Grandson James A. Pendergrass my Executor to execute this my last Will and Testament and he is hereby excused from giving Bond & security for the performance of said trust.

In Witness whereof I have hereunto set my hand & Seal this 28th day of December 1967.

Nimrod X Pendergrass
his mark

Signed sealed and acknowledged and Published in our presents and in presents of each other to be his last Will and Testament revoking all former Wills and we have at his special Instance & request, signed our names as Witnesses thereto this 28th day of December 1867.

John Roark
W. L. Hutcheson

The foregoing will was proven in open Court on the 19th day of August 1871

J. H. Hardie Clk. Co. Court

LORI A. KING

Chattanooga, Tennessee
Friday Morning 3 o'clock 23 day of June 1871
Be it known that I Lori A. King a Citizen of the County of Hamilton and State of Tennessee having on yesterday afternoon met with a serious accident from which I am advised by my Physician I may die and being now of sound mind and disposing memory desire to make known to my friends and Testators in this my last will and Testament what disposition I possess both real and personal. That is to say I want my property disposed of just as my Brother Will would have done he would have given to Mary G. King the Daughter of Brother John King [Page 70] and her Heirs forever. As I am unable to write from the effects of my injuries I ask Dr. P. D. Sims and

Mr. James M. Trigg who are present to witness this Will for me.

Witnesses;   P. D. Sims
                  J. N. Trigg

Probated in open Court Sept. 4, 1871
            J. H. Hardie, Clerk

WILLIAM LOWE

Know all men by These presents that I William Lowe of Chattanooga in the County of Hamilton and State of Tennessee Being in ill health and of sound and disposing mind and memory do make and publish this my last Will and Testament hereby revoking all former Wills by me at any time heretofore made.

As to my worldly Estate all the property real personal or mixed of which I shall die seized and possessed or to which I shall be entitled at any time of my deceased I devise and bequeath and dispose thereof in the manner following to wit.

First - My will is that all my just debts and funeral expenses shall by Executors hereinafter named be paid out of my estate as soon after my decease as shall by them be found Convenient.

Item - I give, devise bequeath to my beloved wife Sophia Lowe Six Hundred Dollars in lieu of her dower to be paid out of my Estate as soon after my decease as shall by my Executors found convenient.

To my son John Lowe who having been provided for heretofore by way of a farm in Summertown Michigan, I give the Family Bible as a momento of my love and affection.

I give and bequeath the remainder of my estate Phoeba Mariah, Mary Ann, Sarah Edward, Frank, Edith, Benjamin and Isabella Lowe to be divided eaqually when Isabel the youngest is of age.

Lastly I do appoint J. P. McMillian & Wm. Crutchfield to be Executors of this my will and testament.

In testimony whereof I the Said William Lowe have to this my last Will & testament contained on one sheet of Paper subscribed my name and affixed my Seal this the fifth day of July in the year of our Lor One Thousand Eight Hundred & Seventy One.

William Lowe (Seal)

Signed Sealed & published & declared by the said William Lowe and for his last will and testament in the presents of us who at his request in his presents and in the presents of each other have subscribed our names as witnesses thereto.

D. R. Grafton   )

Tho. H. Payne   ) Witnesses
Chas. Sundaqust   )

[Page 71]

PHILOMON BIRD

I Philomon Bird do make this my last Will and Testament.

First after paying all my Just debts and Expences I desire and Will that Guss Bird Son of Mary Gardenhire and Sam Bird Son of Wicker have all my property of any kind and caracter real personal and mixed. If either of them should die without lawful Issue before me his issue shall have what he should have received under This Will. But if either of them should die without such issue before or after my Death the survivor or his issue have his Share of the Estate.

Second - I appoint My Friend D. M. Key My Executor with power in him to appoint his successor and desire that he be required to give no Bond nor Security as such Executor and I desire that he be paid a Compensation of Two Thousand Dollars for his services as such, and Such Other Compensation as the Court having jurisdiction thereof may determine he is entitled to for Special.

This 20th day of July 1871
                Philomon Bird
Test

John P. Long
S. A. Key

The foregoing Will was Probated in Open Court Monday the 9th day of October 1871.
                J. H. Hardie, Clerk

PERMELIA THOMPSON

I Permelia Thompson wife of M. D. Thompson being of sound Mind and disposing Memory and having first obtained the Consent of my said husband, do make and publish this my last Will and Testament, hereby revoking all other Wills previously made by me.

First - It is my Will and desire that my husband Michael D. Thompson, should after my death, have and use all my personal property, and should have the use occupation and rents and profits arising from any and all real Estate I may die seized and possessed of, but my Piano Forte is excepted, and disposed of as hereafter Specified -

I Therefore give and bequeath to my said husband M. D. Thompson all the personal property of which I may die seized and possessed, absolutely, except said Piano [Page 72] which I give and bequeath to my infant daughter Ada A. Thompson.

Second - I give and bequeath to my said husband M. D. Thompson all the Real Estate I may die seized and possessed of in Trust, the rents and profits to go to him absolutely, and he is to have full control and management of the same and enjoy the products, rents and profits during his natural life, and at his death it is my wish that my said lands or their proceeds if sold sooner under the provisions of this Will, shall go to my three children Ada A., William H., and Michael Dean, Share and Share alike, and my Executor herein afer named is hereby clothed with full power to Sell, and Convey any or all of my lands on such Terms as he may see proper, and hold the Principal in Trust for my three Children, who shall at his death take said principal without interest.

And I hereby appoint my said husband Michael D. Thompson Executor of this my last Will and Testament, and it is my wish and desire that no security shall be required of him, in the Execution of the Trust reposed by the terms of this Will.

In Testimony whereof I have hereunto set my name this 22nd day of August 1871.
                Permelia Thompson
Witness -

We the undersigned have witnessed the execution of the foregoing will, at the special request of Mrs. Permelia Thompson the Maker, with whom we are personally acquainted, and certify that she signed it in our presence and that we have signed our names hereto in her presence, and in the presence of each other, date above. We also certify that the above will was written in the presence of the Testatrix.

Jane H. Ford
R. Henderson

The foregoing will was proven in open Court 1st day January 1872.

                J. H. Hardie
                Clerk

[Page 73]

WILLIAM G. SINGLETON

William G. Singleton's Will
In the Name of the Benevolent Father Amen.
I William G. Singleton of sound Mind Memory

being Mortally wounded, and desirous of arranging & disposing of my worldly affairs, do for that purpose and with full knowledge make ordain and publish this as my last Will and Testament, hereby revoking any and all former Wills by me made. The last one especially, the same is on record at Knoxville, Tennessee.

First - I will and direct that the amount due me from E. G. Eaton & Co. be expended first in paying all funeral expenses and all expenses attendant on this my last sickness - The residue of said debt if any be left, I will and direct shall be applied to the payment of any costs or labor Necessary to prosecute John Johnson, my Murderer. -

Second - I will and direct that all my Real Estate in the City of Chattanooga County of Hamilton and State of Tennessee shall be given to Eva Ransom daughter of Perry and Rebecca Ransom in said City to have and to hold to the Special use, benefit & behoof of said Eva Ransom -   Third - I will and direct that all of a certain Judgment recovered by me against Haley, Montieth & Co. of Chattanooga, and by them appealed to the Supreme Court of the State of Tennessee if decided in my favor after paying the fees of attys. or costs incidental & necessary in the prosecution of said Johnson shall be given to said Eva Ransom my intention being to make her my sole Heir, subject to no dominition except as herein stated.

Fourth - Having utter and full confidence in my friends Dr. J. H. Vandeman and E. G. Eaton I do hereby constitute and appoint them my Executors of this my last Will and Testatment, and do enjoin upon them to faithfully carry out the directions of this my will.

Fifth - I give, and bequeath unto my Cousin William Singleton, as resident of the Dominion of Canada, all and everything, Choses in Action &C property real and personal belonging to me in said Dominion of Canada except the portion of my Fathers Estate in Canada, to which I am heir, and authorize & direct him to take immediate possession and control of the same.

Sixth - I give and bequeath unto my Cousin Alice [Page 74] Singleton, all and everything real or personal Choses in Action &C to which I am heir from my Fathers Estate, or in which as such heir I have any interest or may have. This is intended subject to her own Control, and for her own use, benefit & behoof -- And enjoining on my executors again to faithfully and strictly carry out the intentions I have herein expressed, I do make and ordain this and sign the same as my last Will and Testament in the presence of my friends J. M. Johnson and F. S. Wolf.
          W. G. Singleton (Seal)
Feb. 12, 1872
Attest
     J. M. Johnson
     Francis[?] S. Wolf

Ben S. Nicklin

The words "and the payment of the balance that my be due of my last sickness if there should be any balance due" were interlined before signing, and are a part of this my last Will, and I hereby release Moses Stewart from any indebtedness to me, and direct my Executors to receipt him in full.
          W. G. Singleton (Seal)
Attest
     J. M. Johnson
     Francis [?] S. Wolf
     Ben S. Nicklin

Proven in Open Court 23rd April 1872
          J. H. Hardie, Clerk for County

JAMES MATHIS

State of Tennessee   )
County of Hamilton   ) I James Mathis being of sound Mind, and at my residence, do make this my last Will and Testament.

First - It is my will and request that all my just debts be paid, and that my remains be decently burried and that the expense thereof be paid -

2nd - It is my will and request that my beloved wife Melissa Mathis, have all the produce on my premises, to gether with all Household furniture, Wares and Chattles appertaining for the use of herself and my Minor Children, and that all other perishable property of which I am possessed be sold in [Page 75] such manner and such Terms as my Executor shall in his Judgment deem best, and out of the proceeds thereof my Executor shall purchase a good farm animal, Mare or Horse for the use and benefit of my said wife. -

3rd - It is my will and request that my real land estate be not sold til twelve months after my deceased and if any Statuto provisions will permit my Executor to privately sell my landed estate, that he do so at any time upon such terms, as he shall deem best in the premises. -

4th - It is my will and request after the payment of all just debts to gether with the necessary expenses and reasonable Consideration of Compensation retained My Executor to take the remainder, and with said means purchase my beloved wife a parcel of land, fertile, reasonably level with timber and water in a healthy location, and take the title in the name of my beloved Wife Melissa Mathis during her natural life time, and at her decease land to be sold, and the proceeds equally divided among my Children.

5th - It is my will and request that my Executor collect all debts, [burned] demands and notes to which I am entitled by Contracts -

6th - It is my Will and request, and I appoint West Shelby my Executor of this my last Will & Testament and I do hereby revoke all other Wills by me made.

In Testamony whereof I hereto set my hand this the 13th day of November A.D. 1871.

James Mathis (Seal)

Witnesses
A. Sively
E. H. Schrimsher

Proven July Term 1872

J. H. Hardie, Clerk

PETER CONRY

Chattanooga Oct. 9th, 1872

The last will and Testament of Peter Conry.

Leave to my wife, and Children, all my property namely Three Houses and two lots, together with Eight hundred and fifty dollars in Crutchfield & Kings Bank, all Debts to be paid out of this property.-

Peter X Conry
his mark

Witnesses -
Thos. Crean
Patt. McNally
P. McGuire

Probated in Open Court Oct. 17, 1872
J. H. Hardie Clerk

[Page 76]

JOHN M. WADE

John M. Wade's Will

My health is bad, I write this for the benefit of my wife if I should die. I will all my property to my Wife her left time, to do as she thinks best, to school and raise my Children.

I give her the power to pay and collect debts.

I want this will to stand during her life time and at her death, then divided among the Children -January

15th, 1873.

John M. Wade

Probated in Open Court
10th April 1873

J. H. Hardie, Clerk

JOHN C. GILLESPIE

I John C. Gillespie of the City of Chattanooga Hamilton County being of sound mind and disposing memory hereby revoke and cancel all former will & codicils thereto heretofore made by me - and do hereby make and publish this my last will and testament.

1st - I will that all my funeral expenses and just debts be paid.

2nd - It is my will that my Executrix hereinafter named collect all debts and effects due me and the proceeds arrising therefrom be by her so far as necessary applied to the payment of my debts.

3rd - It is my will that my Exexutrix hereinafter name sell my farm in Hamilton County known as the Rogers place and apply the proceeds if necessary to the payment of my debts, and if not to the support of the family.

4th - It is my will that my farm in Rhea County Tennessee known as a part of the Uchee old fields be kept rented out by my executrix until my youngest child arrives at the age of twenty one years or if a female marries previous to that time, and the proceeds arising therefrom so far as necessary for that purpose be applied by said Executrix first to the education of my younger children and the remainder if more than sufficient for the purpose will be applied to the support of the family.

5th - It is further my will that my said executrix hereinafter named take charge of all my other real and personal estate wherever the same may be situated or found and rent, lease, or sell [Page 77] the same as she may in her judgement deem best for the interest herself and my children, and the proceeds arising from the rent or sale of same will be by her invested as she thinks most to the interest of my children and herself, but she will not sell the farm above mentioned under item fourth in Rhea County, but all the other lands belonging to me she will have the full control and management of and may and has full power to lease sell convey or give such portion to any one of my children as she may deem right and proper so that all my children are made equal in the final division of my property hereinafter mention.

6th - It is my will on the arrival of my youngest child to the age of twenty one years or previous marriage if a female that all my property of every character be equally divided between my children and my beloved wife Margaret J. Gillespie, share and share alike, she taking a childs part, and should my executrix prior to the final division give off any of my estate to any one of my children they will only receive as much as makes them equal with the rest including the amounts previously received by them.

7th - I will and bequeath to my beloved wife Margaret J. the Gold watch she now wears and all the household and kitchen furniture owned by me.

8th - It is my will that in the event my wife Margaret J. Should marry again that her trust and power as executrix under this will cease and this will carried out by some one else.

9th - I hereby nominate and appoint my beloved wife Margaret J. Gillespie sole executrix of this my will and Guardian of my minor children in whom I have the utmost confidence and she will not be required to give bond or security as such executrix or Guardian, the same being hereby expressly waived.

Witness my hand and seal in the presence of J. S. Gillespie and W. H. Clift who were by me specially called to bear witness to the fact of my making signing and publishing this my last will and Testament this the 5th day of July 1873.

J. C. Gillespie (Seal)

Witnesses
J. S. Gillespie
M. H. Clift

Probated 4th August 1873
J. H. Hardie, Clerk

[Page 78]

RANSOM SWAN

April 27th 1873
Hamilton County, State of Tennessee

Believing that death is near at hand, I Ransum Swan of the County and State above named, desire while in the full possession of my mental faculties to make my last will and testament, disposing of my worldly effects in such manner as may be most advantageous to my son Munroe Swan as follows. I will and bequeath all my worldly effects to my son above named, he being my sole heir. I do further appoint Enoch Fluker of the County of Hamilton and state of Tennessee as my agent to take charge of all my property and effects and do will and

direct that the said Enoch Fluker as my agent, do proceed to pay all of my just debts out of said property and effects. I further desire that the remainder of my property after said debts shall have been canceled be held and preserved by said Enoch Fluker until such time as my son Munroe Swan shall be of suitable age to attend school, and then I most especially will and direct that all of said property and effects remaining be solely appropriated to the education of my son Munroe Swan, and I do hereby appoint said Enoch Fluker as guardian of my son Munroe Swan a minor, in all of the above matters, and I further desire that said Enoch Fluker direct the education of my son above named when he shall have arrived at a suitable age to attend school, and I do further desire that said Enoch Fluker may direct and control the moral training of my son and heir, so far as it may be in his power to do. And now having made the above will and testament in regard to my worldly effects, I commit my soul to the great first cause who gave it.

Ransom X Swan
his mark

Haddon P. Redding
John F. Kincheloe
Geo. W. Wells

Probated in open Court August 7, 1873
J. H. Hardie, Clerk

[Page 79]

SALLY HUMPHREYS

State of Tennessee)
Hamilton Coutny   )

I Sally Humphreys being of Sound mind and disposing memory, do make, publish and declare this my last will and Testament, hereby revoking and annulling any and all former wills which may have heretofore being made by me.

Firstly - I desire and direct that all my just debts be paid by my Executor hereinafter named and appointed, out of any moneys that may come into his hands as such Executor.

Secondly - I give and bequeath to my nephew Lewis Shepherd all the property of whatever discription or kind, all notes, debts Choses in action, rights and credits of which I may die seized and possessed, or may be entitled to, together with all money which I may have, at the time of my death.

Thirdly - I do hereby nominate, constitute and appoint Lewis Shepherd Executor of this my last Will and Testament - hereby relieving him from the necessity of giving bond and Security for the faithful discharge of his debts as executor.

Made and published as my last will and Testament on the 12th day of August in the year of our Lord one Thousand Eight Hundred and Seventy three.

Sally X Humphrey {Seal}
her mark

In presence of
J. F. Mee
Margaret Shepherd

Probated in open Court 1st day of September 1873.

J. H. Hardie, Clerk

[Page 80]

HUGH McGILL

Last Will of Hugh McGill

In the name of God Amen -

I Hugh McGill of the County of Hamilton in the State of Tennessee, being of Sound mind impressed with the fact that life is uncertain and being desirous to settle my worldly affairs while I have health and Strength, do make and publish this my last Will and Testament, hereby revoking all Wills by me, at any time heretofore made and after committing my Soul to God who gave it, my worldly affairs and Estate I dispose of as follows.

1st - I will to my three grandchildren - Maloy Long, Balam Long and James Long, children of my deceased daughter, Sarah Jane Long the sum of five dollars to be equally divided between them.

2nd - I will to my two grandchildren Mary Ellen McGill and Robert A. McGill, children of my deceased Son Alexander McGill the sum of Five Dollars to be equally divided between them.

3rd - I will to my daughter Harriet N. Neighbors the sum of five dollars.

4th - I will to my daughter Elizabeth Eidson the sum of Five Dollars.

5th - I will and devise to my two sons Columbus L. McGill and Monroe R. McGill in fee simple, to be equally divided in value between them, and to be immediately entered upon and enjoyed by them at my death, but not to be sold during the life time of my wife Rebecca McGill, my home tract of land upon which I now live, situated in the 4th Civil District of Hamilton County, Tennessee, containing two hundred and thirty acres more or less, adjoining the lands of John Tittle, Frank James and others, and the said Columbus L. and Monroe R. McGill, in consideration of Said devise are herein required to Support, maintain and take care of in a decent and comfortable manner, my beloved wife Rebecca McGill and my unfortunate blind Son William J. McGill, so long as the said Rebecca and the said William J. or either of them may live. Said Support and maintenance being herein made a charge upon the land herein devised to the said Columbus L. and Monroe R. McGill in their possession and in the possession of those to whom it may decend from them.

6th - It is my will that my said wife Rebecca McGill and blind Son William J. McGill shall remain at the old homestead with my two Sons Columbus L. and Monroe [Page 81] R. McGill or with whichever of them may hereafter reside at Said homestead if they desire so to do, and to that end I desire and direct that Said tract of land herein devised to the said Columbus L. and the said Monroe R. whereon said homestead is situated nor shall any part thereof be sold during the lifetime of my said wife Rebecca - and the expense of their support and maintenance is to be shared equally by the Said Columbus L. and the said Monroe R.

7th - I appoint my two Sons Columbus L., Monroe R. McGill Executors to this my last Will and Testament.

In witness whereof I the said Hugh McGill to this my will, consisting of the foregoing seven clauses have set my hand and Seal this 3rd day of May 1872.

Signed Sealed published and declared by the above named Hugh McGill to be his Last will and Testament in presence of us who at his request and in the precence of each other have subscribed our names as witnesses hereto

J. H. Warner
H. H. Knox

Probated in open Court 1st day of September 1873.

J. H. Hardie Clerk

ALBAN MEREDITH

Last Will of Alban Meredith

I Alban Meredith do make and publish this my

last Will and Testament, hereby revoking all other Wills by me at any time heretofore made.

1st - I will and direct that all my just debts and funeral expenses be paid out of the first moneys that may come into the hands of my Executors.

2nd - I will and bequeath to my brother George Meredith my gold watch and chain - to Thomas James my ornamental encased table clock -and to Harman Drury the sum of One hundred and fifty pounds sterling.

3rd - I will and direct that all the balance of my [Page 82] estate of every scription be divided and disposed of to wit - To my brother George Meredith one half (1/2) in addition to the special legacy above named. To my brother Conway Meredith (1/4) one fourth and to Thomas James (1/4) one fourth in addition to the special legacy above named.

4th - I hereby nominate and appoint my brothers George and Conway Meredith Executors of this my last Will and Testament. And it is my Will and desire, that they be excused from giving bond as such Executors. This January 31st, 1874.

Alban X Meredith
his mark

Signed and acknowledged in our presence this 31st January 1874
W. A. Haskins
Walter McFarland

Probated in Open Court February 2nd 1874.
J. H. Hardie Clerk
County Court of Hamilton Co Tenn

SARAH E. RICE

Nuncupative Will of Sarah E. Rice, deceased.
Chattanooga April 6, 1874

We the undersigned being present at the bedside of Sarah E. Rice on the seventh day of November 1873 at her residence in Chattanooga - that being the day before her death - she in our presence requested that her property after her death should go to her daughter Minerva Fisher, and desired us to become witnesses of her wishes.

J. B. Weaver
Susan Rowden

Probated in Open Court
April 6th 1874

J. H. Hardie Clerk

TIMOTHY R. STANLEY

I, Timothy R. Stanley of the City of Chattanooga, Tennessee, knowing the uncertainty of life, and being infirm of body, but of sound mind and disposing memory, do make, publish and declare this my last Will and Testament in manner following that is to say:

First - I direct that all my just debts, including any notes or obligations I have given any of my [Page 83] children by way of advancements or otherwise, and whether bound by the Statute of Limitation or not, be paid out of my personal estate of which I may die seized and possessed.

Second - I give and bequeath to my beloved wife Maria P. Stanley in case she shall survive me, all my household and kitchen furniture, beds, bedding, books and other personal property (much of which was purchased with her own means) situated in the house in Chattanooga where we now reside, and also the carriage and harness, having full confidence in my said wife, that any reasonable request made of her by my children for any article or articles, which may posssess a special value to them by reason of association, will be cheerfully complied with by her.

Third - I am indebted to Isaac H. Tower of Boston in the sum of fifteen hundred dollars and interest, for which he holds my note, and which is secured by a mortgage upon the House & Lot in Chattanooga upon which I now reside. This debt I direct shall be paid out of my personal property and said House and Lot free from any lien or ---[burned]--- devise to my said wife in fee, not in dower, with full power to sell and convey, or otherwise make disposition of same I have already made to my said wife a deed to said real estate conveying to her a life estate only.

Fourth - In addition to the foregoing provisions made for my said wife I give, devise and bequeath to her a childs. I have in all the remainder of my estate, both realty and personalty, a life estate in the real property, but the personal to be hers absolutely.

Fifth - All the remainder of my estate, except what has been already disposed of, or may be disposed of under subsequent clauses of this Will, I give devise and bequeath to my four sons, Timothy W. Henry G., George R., and Charles E. Stanley, to be equally divided between them, and whereas I hold against them or some of them, notes given for advancements, it is to be understood that these notes whether barred by the Statutes of Limitations or not, are to be deemed and treated as assets of the estate.

Sixth - I have always designed to erect over the

remains of my first wife, burried in the [Page 84] National Cemetery at Chattanooga a suitable monument but have failed to carry my intention into effect. I expect to die in Chattanooga and I desire to be burried by the side of my wifes, and I direct that my Executrix and Executor hereinafter named, to erect over the grave of myself and my first wife, a plain, simple monument and the cost of same shall be the first charge upon my estate after the payment of debts.

Seventh - I hereby nominate and appoint my said wife Maria P. Stanley and my son Charles E. Stanley joint Executrix and executor of this my last Will and Testament. I desire that they be required to give no bond for the faithful performance of their duties. They shall have full power to effect a full settlement of my estate and to this end may sell and dispose of all property realty or peronsalty (except as this power is hereinafter limited) may execute deeds for sales of realty and do all things necessary to settle my estate, and make distribution of same, but as I consider my land upon Waldens Ridge in Hamilton County to be very valuable, and likely to be much more valuable hereafter, I direct that this land be not sold by my Executrix and Executor, unless it should become necessary for the payment of debts which contingency I do not think likely to arise.

Eighth - All deeds made for real estate shall be executed jointly by said Executrix and Executor if both shall qualify as I trust they will do, but either of them may at any time resign, and in case of such resignation, the other shall have full power to effect the settlement of my estate herein provided, including the power to make deeds.

Ninth - I leave to my children a name untarnished which I am confident they will preserve.

Tenth - All former Wills by me made are hereby revoked.

In witness whereof I have hereunto set my hand and seal this 10th day of January in the year of our Lord One thousand eight hundred and seventy four.

T. R. Stanley (Seal)

The above instrument consisting of one sheet and one page, was at the date thereof, signed, [Page 85] sealed, published and declared by the said Timothy R. Stanley as and for his last Will and Testament in presence of us who at his request, and in his presence, and in the presence of each other, have subscribed our names as witnesses thereto.

W. S. Marshall
Xenophen Wheeler

Probated in open Court July 13th, 1874.
J. H. Hardie, Clerk

MARGARET N. PICKETT

I Margaret N. Pickett do hereby make and establish and publish this as my last Will and Testament.

First - Out of any means of which I may die seized and possessed I desire my funeral expenses and all my just debts to be paid.

Second - I desire after the payment of said debts and expenses, all my estate of every kind and character, personal, real and mixed, to belong to my daughter Sarah Jane Light wife of James H. Light and to her Children fully and absolutely. It is my desire that if any of her children die leaving issue, that such issue inherit and hold what the parent would have held had she or he lived.

Third - I appoint S. A. Key the executor of this my last Will and Testament.

Given under my hand and seal this first day of January 1870

Margaret N. X Pickett (Seal)
her mark

Attest
D. M. Key
J. S. Gillespie

Probated in open Court
July 25th 1874

J. H. Hardie, Clerk

[Page 86]

JAMES STEVENS

Will of James Stevens

State of Tennessee)
Hamilton County   ) To all whom it may concern.

Know ye that I James Stevens, in the name of God Amen, being of sound mind and in proper exercise of all of my mental faculties, and believing that I must soon depart this life, and also being desirous of settling all of my worldly affairs, have this day made and published this my last Will and Testament, hereby revoking any and all former Wills and Testament that I may have hitherto made or published.

First - I commend my spirit back to God who gave it, and my body to its mother dust.

Secondly - I will that my executor shall, out of my estate, pay all just indebtedness, and after this, I will that the remainder of my estate shall be disposed of as follows towit. 1st, I will unto each of my three eldest sons, by name, John A. Stevens, James Stevens and Thomas R. Stevens the sum of five dollars, respectively. 2nd, The remainder of my property, consisting of the following described real estate to wit: One Lot or parcell of ground lying and being in the City of Chattanooga Hamilton County Tennessee described as follows, being Lot No. -- fronting thirty feet on Mill Street, and running back of uniform width the distance of one hundred feet bounded as follows, North by Mill Street, East by the property A. Irons, south on Alley and the lands of A. Branam, West by the property of Mrs. Sarah Manun, together with all appertenances belonging thereto, and rights I will and bequeath unto my son Wm. T. Stevens, to have and to hold unto himself his heirs and assigns forever upon the following conditions to wit. That the said Wm. T. Stevens shall furnish support and maintenance as well as a home in which to live to my dearly beloved wife Louisa Clementine Stevens and our daughter, Mary Stevens, so far and in accordance with the proceeds of said property or such as said proceeeds will allow, without the expenditure by the said Wm. T. Stevens, of any money otherwise acquired by him, so long as my said wife Louise Clementine Stevens shall remain unmarried after my death and in case she should marry again, then I will that all of said property shall go to the said Wm. T. Stevens, his heirs and assigns forever.

[Page 87]

3rd - I will that, all just debts which I now owe shall have been paid, the remainder of my personal property and choses in action shall go to the said Wm. T. Stevens, and become his property upon the condition herein before mentioned relative to the support of my wife and daughter Mary Stevens.

4th - I will that John Thompson be my Executor and as such take charge and dispose of my property and effects at my death, according to the foregoing directions, without bond.

In witness whereof I have hereunto set my hand and seal this the thirteenth day of July A.D. 1874

James Stevens (Seal)

Witness. this witnesseth, that wi F. E. Tyler a citizen of Chattanooga Hamilton County Tennessee and Orien Hulbert of Chattanooga, Hamilton County Tennessee, were present and saw the within named testator sign his name thereto, and heard him declare this to be his last Will and Testament. Also that we saw each other sign this Will as Witnesses thereto, in witness whereof we have this day hereto set our hand and seals.

F. E. Tyler (Seal)
Orion Hulbert (Seal)

Probated in Open Court
August 3rd 1874

J. H. Hardie, Clerk

[Page 88]

J. S. WILTSE

Will of J. S. Wiltse

I, J. S Wiltse of Chattanooga Hamilton County Tennessee, having good health and the full power of my reasoning faculties, for the purpose of making provision for a just and economical settlement of all my business affairs in case of my death, and for the purpose of directing the disposition of my property, do make, publish and declare this my last Will and Testament hereby revoking any and all former wills by me made. I am at the date hereof seized of the following described real estate and personal property which would constitute my assets in the event of my death. Though I may omit some items, the list here given will embrace the bulk of my property at this date--

Real Estate

1st - A Lot of ground 33 1/3 X 190 ft. on B. St in Block 3 Griffins addition, begining 200 feet south of Gilmer St. valued at $600.

2nd An undivided half of a house and lot on B. St., Lot 26 2/3 X 190 ft. adjoining the above Lot on the South valued at $1000.00

3rd - House & Lot on B. St. 40 X 190 ft. South of the above and adjoining, valued at $3000.00

4th - An undivided half of a house and Lot, 50 X 128 ft. on Poplar St. known as #3, valued at $1250--C. C. Corporation now owns the other undivided half of this and of the above house and Lot called 2nd in this list.

5th - One Lot 50 X 128 ft. immediately North of the above, being between 7 & 8 St. in Chattanooga, valued at $750.

6th - House & Lot 35 X 128 ft. immediately North of the above valued at $1200.00

7th - House & Lot, East 58 ft. of West 138 ft of Lot 50 Poplar St. valued at $1200.00

8th - The North East 1/4 of Lot 51 Poplar St. with 2 houses, valued at $2100.00

9th - Lot 5 E on Mill St. in Lewis and Spitzers addition to Chattanooga - valued at $250.

10th - Lot 3 in the Caroline Muller Block in Glass addition to Chattanooga valued at $500

11th - Lots 10-11-12 Sidney St. Glass' Addition to

Chattanooga, valued at $8000.00.

12th - 1/3 undivided interest in 7 Lots on Whiteside & Cowart Sts. in Vaughns Addition to Chattanooga - Robinson of North Ridgeville ___rom Co., Ohio has a deed to my [Page 89] share, but is obligated to recovery - Henry Wiltse and H. Z. Chapman own the other 2/3 interest - my share valued at $800.00.

13th - 140 acres of land in 15th Civil District of Hamilton county bought of C. H. Barlow and wife, valued at $1800.00

14th - 1 undivided half of N. 60 ft. of Lot 33 Chestnut St. valued at $750. J. P. Wilkinson owns the other half.

15th - 1/3 of 1818 acres on Waldens Ridge owned by N. H. Burt and myself - R. L. McNabb - my interest valued at $600.

16th - Lot 1 Blk. 1 in Roane Iron Cos. Addition valued at $1000.

17th Several entries, with N. H. Burt to Mountain Land, value unknown.

18th E 1/2 Lot 27 Chandlers Addition to Chattanooga on Clift St. - value $500.

19th Lot 50 X 140 ft. Cor. of Long and White Sts. bought of Cope & wife valued at $300.00

20th - 5 Lots 50 X 140 ft. each in James Addition purchased at Chancery sale of P. H. Floods property - valued at (total) $1000.

21st - W. 1/2 Lot 4 & N.W. 1/4 Lot 5 in James Addition on Sidney St. bought at Chancery Sale of P. H. Floods property - valued at $750.00

22nd - Undivided half of 9 acres on Lookout Mountain. J. P. Wilkinson owns the other half - valued at $275.00

23rd - Undivided 1/3 of 160 acres in Georgia Lot 127, 10 Dist. 4 Section - Mary H. Peabody & J. P. Wilkinson own the other 2/3 - value $100.00.

24th - Undivided half of fractional Lots 57 & 59 Poplar St. W. L. Duggar owns the other half - valued at $1000.00.

25th - Undivided half of a Lot on Market St. between 4 & 5 - East side Market - Duggar owns the other half - valued at $750.

Personal Property

1 - One Policy in New York Mutual Life
Insurance Co. $5,000.

2 - One Policy in North Western Life
Insurance Co. $2,500.

3 - One Policy in North Western Life
Insurance Co. $2,500.

4 - Household good & books at
House $1,500

5 - Cash value of Shares in Taylor
Gun $ 750.

6 - Law Library and office furniture $1,500.

7 - Horses, buggy, harness &c $ 600.

8 - Abstract of Titles $7,000.

9 - Notes and probably good
ass's about $2,500.

Total Personalty $23,850
Total Real Estate $27,625
       Total $51,475.00

[Page 90]

W. H. Pratt, my partner in business is entitled to a deed to one undivided half of my interest in real estate as above set forth - taking it subject to all incumbrances, he and I being now in equity equal owners of all of it, & equally obligated to pay the incumbrances, and all debts against Wiltse and Pratt, & against J. S. Wiltse except what J. S. Wiltse owes his father Henry Wiltse - reference is had to the books of Wiltse & Pratt, & the partnership contract - W. H. Pratt also owns half in like manner of the items of personal property from item 6 to item 9 inclusive.

I do not interfere with his firm under law as surviving partner but desire him to advise with my executors in regard to the carrying on of the business of Wiltse & Pratt, and the disposition of firm property - of course he need only counsel my executors & my will in the carrying on himself of the same business, only so far as it may effect the assets & liabilities in such a way as to effect my estate. In the disposition of my property my executors have discretionary power, & have power to sell & convey real estate - I give this general instruction that I want my debts & liabilities settled and interest and expenses stopped as soon as it can be reasonably done in the interest of my estate. I want my funeral expenses & all just debts paid out of my estate and except where I specially provide for cash payments or legacies, I would like so far as may be practicable, & expedient, my executor to judge, to have my brothers and sisters legacies bestowed in real estate, except Reuben Wiltse's who will probably be more benefited by money, according to its value at time of distribution, and according to the properties mentioned as willed or given to each herein -

but should want it to go to them unencumbered or at any rate so that they readily manage it to their own interest & without risk of loss or sacrifice. If part of my real estate should be sold & part unsold, it will be well to sell first improved property. If unimproved property is sold, I suggest fair terms of credit, and liberal advertising if sold at public sale in case of any property, & in this last case, a judicious subdividing of Lots &c. In case of my liabilities I have in some instances agreed to pay more than ten per cent interest. I authorize my executors [Page 91] to make good all such agreements up to date of my death. They can ascertain these instances from the books of Wiltse & Pratt. I want all creditors treated fairly and justly & I don't want any of them to be allowed if disposed, to take any unjust or inequitable advantage of my legatees - I am fully confident that out of my estate all I owe can be paid in a reasonable time if equity is done, and leave to my legatees an estate equal to or greater than the balance the foregoing schedule & the schedule of my liabilities.

I bind my executors to no particular course & require no sales of personal property or otherwise. My personal property not specially disposed of herein - may be, if found expedient by my executors divided among my legates or part of them, at fair valuations - I apprehend no ill feeling or undue love of property among my legates, & my executors may freely consult their feelings & wishes. The[y] will gladly concur in all property manner first to discharge my debts.

I leave it to my executors with my surviving partner, to make the very most possible out of my estate, & discharge it from debt.

I leave to them to make an equitable division between my property & W. H. Pratts property -- & if it is found expedient to use any of my personal money, to be realized from life insurance or otherwise, to discharge debts against the whole property, this of course will be taken into equitable a/c in the settlment.

In cases where I own, or Pratt and I own real estate with some other person or persons, I leave it with my executors to make either an equal division, or a division such as the Law provides, if agreement cannot be had. My executors will look closely to the evidence of accounts that may be presented after my death against my estate conferring[?] freely with my partner W. H. Pratt & having reference to the books of the firm of Wiltse & Pratt, but of course giving all claims a fair investigation-- unless specially provided to the contrary any precise amount given to any of my legatees, will be discounted prorata, should my estate fall short in the aggregate after paying out--and should it overrun, then a prorata will be added in like manner.

First - At my decease, after paying all my just [Page 92] debts and reasonable funeral expenses, one tenth of my remaining estate is to be devoted in due time, to religious, charitable & educational purposes -- my present mind would be that most of this go to the Chattanooga Congregational Church & Society, but this matter of the special application of this fund I leave to my Sister Sarah E. Wiltse. My executors will consult her on this point.

2nd - Policy #43881 for $2500. in the North Western Mutual Life Insurance Co. is to benefit of my sister Sarah E. Wiltse & it shall be hers, absolutely & unconditionally & hers, the money to be paid on it.

3rd - I give to my father Henry Wiltse five hundred dollars & my gold Watch.

4th - I give to my mother Mary A. Wiltse one thousand dollars, which I recommend her to use in travel & in such other ways as to contribute most to her personal comfort. I want her to have the money herself and control it and use it herself & enjoy it. I want her to select some article of my personal effects especially for herself to keep -- & I want her to have a large and neatly framed picture of myself, to be procured by my executors, out of my estate.

5th - I give my brother Reuben Wiltse all he owes me & five hundred dollars. I give to his wife Lydia five hundred dollars. I give to Sarah E. Wiltse in trust for the support & education of Reubens children, Flora, William, & the baby, or any to be in the future, fifteen hundred dollars to be applied at her discretion, liberally and carefully, holding not back on a/c of what she may think the law may require as between the children, but making it do most good as it is needed as the children grow -- doing first the duty nearest by.

6 - I give to my brother Ahiman[?] S. Wiltse whatever he may owe me personally and three thousand dollars. I want him to use it in improving himself in his general education, his profession, & in laying by something for the time coming.

7 - I give my sister Sarah E. Wiltse in addition to the twenty five hundred dollars hereinbefore provided for, the sum of five thousand dollars. If it is added to, the prorata [Page 93] will be on the whole amount. This cause on my part needs no explanation.

8 - I give my sister Sarah E. Wiltse in trust for brother Reuben and his family as she may see it expedient to help them a little from time to time to things necessary for their use and comfort - five hundred dollars --

9 - I give to my brother Henry M. Wiltse what he may owe me at my decease if anything & three thousand dollars.

10 - I give my sister Sarah E. Wiltse one thousand dollars in trust to be distributed among my friends,

acquaintances, Cousins, &c, when she may from time to time find worthy persons in need, & when a little help will do a great deal of good & give to the receiver a great degree of pleasure & comfort.

My executors shall not be required to give bond & shall have reasonable compensation for their services - besides fifty dollars each which I give them.

I nominate & appoint the following persons my executors.

Parks Foster
Xen Wheeler
Milo Pratt
Sarah E. Wiltse
G. M. Sherwood

Witness my hand and seal at Chattanooga Tennessee this 8th day of July 1873. Eighteen hundred and Seventy three.

J. S. Wiltse (Seal)

In presence of
A. L. DeLong
H. G. Brooks
A. J. Pratt

Probated in open Court August 31st 1874.
J. H. Hardie
Clerk

[Page 94]

ELIZABETH KOELING

Will of Elizabeth Koeling

In the name of God amen.

I Elizabeth Kaeling, realizing the uncertainty of human life and being of sound mind & memory do make & publish this as my last will and Testament.

1st - I will and bequeath unto my beloved sister Amelia Wilke all my estate, both real and personal that shall remain after the payment of all my just debts.

2 - I nominate and appoint Cyrus Snyder of Chattanooga Tenn my Executor to carry into effect This will and direct him to first sell either at Public or private sale as he may think best all my personal estate and if a sufficent amount is not realized therefrom to pay all my debts, then I direct him to sell Lot No. (1) (being the lot with the small house on it) in Block No. two (2) in Tade's Addition to Chattanooga Hamilton County, Tenn. - and if that shall be insufficient to discharge all my debts, then my said executor shall sell Lot No. 2 (Two) (being the lot with the large square house on it) in Block No. Two (2) in

Tade's Addition aforesaid on such terms as he may think best and the necessary proceeds, if any, he shall pay over to my said Sister - And in case a sale of any part of my said real estate shall be made by my said executor, he shall have & is hereby vested with full authority to execute a good & sufficient deed or deeds & transfer of the same. I justly owe the following debts at this date & none other.

To William Crutchfield $251 and int. for about two years.

Mrs. Kehoe about Sixty two (62) Dollars, Mrs. Chloe Henderson Six Dollars (6) to S. Geismer Bro. Seven & 50/100 dollars.

Witness my hand this 6th day of October, 1874.
Elizabeth Kaeling

Signed in presence of
Lewis Donneberg
E. Murphy

Probated in open Court Oct. 28th, 1874
L. M. Clark, Clerk

[Page 95]

JAMES ROGERS

Will of James Rogers

Know all men by these Presents -

That I James Rogers of the City of Chattanooga, in the county of Hamilton in the State of Tennessee, one of the United States of America.

Mindful of the uncertainties of human life, and realizing the stern fact that death must at length come upon all men, do make, publish and declare this my last Will and Testament. In words and figures following to wit:

I hereby make, constitute and appoint my brother Samuel Bradford Rogers, sole Executor of this my last Will and Testament. And I hereby authorize and empower him the said Samuel B. Rogers as such Executrix of this my last Will and Testament to settle and compound and adjust all accounts and debts which I may have coming to me whether by account, note or other evidences of indebtedness, and I desire and direct that my said executor may be permitted to administer on my said estate without being required to give a bond as is required in other cases by law. I next desire and direct my said executor to pay all the expenses incident to my last sickness, whenever that shall be, and to pay all expenses incident to my funeral. I next direct that out of the proceeds of my estate, my said executor shall pay all just debts which I may owe if there shall be any such at my death. Next, I hereby direct my said executor out of the proceeds of my estate to pay to my sister Anna Davis Rogers, supposed to reside in Abee Aoon South Wales The sum of one Hundred Dollars in Gold.

Next, I hereby direct my said Executor, out of the proceeds of my estate to pay to my Sister Elizabeth Ann Rogers also supposed to reside in Abee Aoon South Wales the sum of One Hundred Dollars in Gold.

Next, I hereby direct my said Executor out of the proceeds of my said estate to pay to my sister Ellen Bomford Rogers, also supposed to reside in Abee Aoon South Wales the sum of One Hundred Dollars in Gold. [Page 96]

Next, There as James Badge resident of Chattanooga Tennessee is now indebted to me in the sum of Fifty Dollars, now by this my last Will and Testament, I hereby omit and cancel said debt, and moreover, in addition to the cacellation of said indebtedness I hereby direct my said executor, out of the proceeds of my estate to pay to my said aunt Blanche Badge, wife of said James Badge, the further and additional sum of Fifty Dollars in Green Backs, and I hereby make the bequest which I am about to make in this my last Will and Testament conditioned upon the father payment of the several sums herein directed by me to be paid, making the payment of said sums a condition precedent to the taking by my residuary legatee hereinafter named of the property, goods and chattels herein by me to him bequeathed. But it is not my desire that my said executor and residuary legatee should be compelled to sell my property for the payment of said sums any sooner than shall seem best to him, but I make said sums chargeable upon my estate so that my said residuary legatee shall sell the same he will be compelled to pay the same.

Next, all the rest and residue of my estate of whatever description, whether real, personal or mixed, I hereby give, devise and bequeath unto my brother Samuel B. Rogers, now resident of Chattanooga, Hamilton County, State of Tennessee, whom I have also made the Executor of this my last Will and Testament. To witness the signing of this my last Will and Testament I have hereto called W. H. C. Brown, E. R. Dunning and H. B. Case, all of the city of Chattanooga, Tennessee and requested them to witness my signature to the same and they have signed the same in my presence and at my request as witnesses hereto and I have affixed my signature to the same this 26th day of January in the year of our Lord One Thousand Eight Hundred and Seventy five at the city of Chattanooga, State of Tennessee.

W. H. C. Brown
E. R. Dunning
H. B. Case

Probated in open court Feb. 17th 1875
L. M. Clark, Clk.
By J. S. Bell, D. C.

BURL JACKSON

Will of Burl Jackson Deceased
Chattanooga East Tennessee
November 19th 1874

To whom it may concern that this Lot is 60 feet 115 feet back and is be devided into two parts or lots. The north side of this said lot 30 feet front 115 feet running back is to go to Granville Jackson and in that if he ever comes to sell it or his lot he shall give his Sister Mary Stokes [?] $50.00. This lot south of the above mentioned 30 feet front 115 feet running back shall go to my wife Charlotte Jackson. This room south of the house also and the little room south East of the house she shall have as long as she remains my respectable widdow and if she ever comes to marry her husband shall take her out of this house and off this lot entirely never to return again for a possession and from off both lots of Granville lot and Charlotte's lot. Shall give Samuel Jackson $5.00 and if my daughter Mary Stokes husband [burned] die and She be knocked out of a home She Shall come and ocupy the room north west of the house with Granville and if Granville lives to see Christmas he will be 16 years and one month old and if Samuel Jackson should outlive Charlotte Jackson, Burl Granville or Mary Stokes he shall have the plat (To wit) House and property and if my son Burl Should ever come home after my death it will be as you please about that and to my daughter Mary Stokes. She must not think hard of my not giving or leaving her no more than $50.00. I have done well [Page 98] in doing that much as she went off and married and never consulted me about it also her husband took my Deed down to the first National Bank and pawned it for ($10.00) ten dollars and Mr. T. G. Montague notified me of it and I went and paid ten dollars and received [burned] if it had not been for his gentlemenly principles I would have lost my property and as it may concern my son Burl when and went away I was renting since I have bought this sized lot above mentioned this lot he need not say a word or come blowing about my Fathers property he left me at the age of 17, and went in the U. S. service against my will so I can't say any more than he come and pay as others pay but don't think I have forsaken him for that. I recognize him as one of the family and do treat him as the same as one of my sons.

So this is Testified solemnly to be my will.

                                Burl Jackson Sen.

Three responsable Witnesses
I witnessed this--
                David C. Edingburg
                James Williams
                James Carroll

Probated in open Court March 27th 1875
                        L. M. Clark, Clerk

DANIEL HOGAN

Will of Daniel Hogan deceased
Chattanooga, Tennessee
April 20th 1861

I Daniel Hogan a native of Ireland and a citizen of the United States being now sound in mind and right in Judgement and in good health but knowing the uncertainty of life and wishing to leave my temporal affairs in such a condition as to be settled with the least difficulty and according to my own wishes Amen.

1st - I wish to leave to the Holy Catholic Church all the property, Notes, and money which I possess in Tennessee for the benefit of said Church to use for charatable purpose with one reserve. That if Should any one of my Nephews now in [Page 99] Ireland or anywhere else would wish to join the holy priesthood of Jesus Christ and serve a humble servant of our divine master and not the means to fulfill his wishes I would wish the Bishop or his V.G. if they think him properly disposed for the holy ministry to help him in the accomplishment of his wishes. He at least ought to give his services in this State for some term of years. May God have mercy on my Soul through the blood of Jesus Christ and the intercession of the B.V.B.

Witness my hand and Seal
                        Daniel H. Hogan (Seal)

Witness
A. (or H.) D. Fagan
Charles Phemer

Probated in open Court April 3rd 1875
                        L.M. Clark, Clerk

MARY McMAHON

Will of Mary McMahon, Deceased
April 6th, 1875

I leave all of my property and money to the amount in The hands of Mr. John McMahon $135 in the hands of Mr. Green $100, in the hands of J. S. A. Crawford $29.00, in the hands of Doc Hooke $25.00, and whatever else may be owing to me do I leave to my Children to be disposed of according to the wish of Mr. John McMahon whom I wish to be Guardian for my children. It is my wish to leave Maggie and Julia to Mrs. McMahon and Minnie to Mr. Green, Anne to Eliza Mahoney of Chicago, and Jennie to John McMahon.

                                Mary McMahon

Attested by
        John McMahon
        William Green

Probated in open court April 14th 1875
                        J. S. Bell, D. Clerk

[Page 100]

MARGARET E. MYLECHRAINE

Last Will and Testatment of Margaret E. Mylechrane of Chattanooga, Tenn.

I Margaret E. Mylechraine make This my last Will.

I give, devise and bequeath my estate and property real and personal, That is to say:

A certain piece or parcel of ground lying and being in The city of Chattanooga, State of Tenn. where I now reside, being the West Forty (40) feet of the North One Hundred and fifty (150) feet of Lot No 36 on Branham Street in Griffins addition fronting forty feet (40) on Branham Street and running back Southwardly One Hundred and fifty (150) being the same purchased from E. G. Crawford & Elizabeth J. Crawford by me and all personal property now in my possession to my husband Thomas Mylechraine to have and to hold and to make use of The same as he may see fit, Chattanooga Tenn. Sept. 5th 1874

                        Margaret E. Mylechraine

Witnesses
E. M. Wight
W. T. Cate

State of Tennessee)
County of Hamilton) Be it remembered that on this 5th day of Sept. A.D. 1874 before The undersigned, a Justice of the Peace within or for The County of Hamilton, state of Tennessee personally came Margaret E. Mylechraine who being personally known to me to be the same person whose name is subscribed to the foregoing instrument of writing as the fact Thererto acknowledged That she executed The same of The uses and purposes mentioned in testimony whereof I have hereunto set my hand and affixed my seal at office in Chattanooga on the 5th day of September 1874.

> W.T. Cate, Justice of the Peace for Hamilton County, Tenn.

Probated in open Court May 14th, 1875
> L. M. Clark, Clerk

[Page 101]

REBECCA M. SMITH

Last Will and Testament of Rebecca M. Smith -

The State of Tennessee

To all whom it may concern--in The name of God amen--

I Rebecca Smith being of sound mind and disposing memory and knowing the uncertainty in lease of life - and desiring to dispose of such property as I may die seized and possessed of, do make and publish this as my last Will and testament hereby revoking all other wills by me made.

Item 1st - I resign my soul to God who Gave it, and my body to be decently buried.

Item 2nd - I specifically give and bequeath to my daughter Martha A. Smith absolutely the following articles of property, to wit: 2 (two beds) and bed clothing to each and one bed-stead one dozen or twelve dining chairs, one side board marble topped, and rocking chair cane bottomed, six Silver tea spoons, six Silver table spoons, one set of Silver knives and forks, the knives are Ivory handled, all my crockery ware and falling leaf table (cherry) all the kitchen furniture of every description including all tubs and buckets &c. One cow and calf, Mahogany table, and one Sofa, two small tables two wash-stands & washbowls and pitchers - The said Martha A. is to have choice of the said beds & bed clothing and

including a white Marsailles quilt and two pieced up quilts, one rose-bud, and the other Sassafras bud, two blankets and sheets and six comforts including also the bolsters and pillows to the said two beds and all pillow slips & bolster slips, and one bureau and looking glass attached to it, and also one leather trunk.

Item 3rd - To Frank Smith youngest son of John A. Smith I give and bequeath one bed two pillows - two sheets, two comforts & two quilts.

Item 4th - To Narcissa M. Guthrie wife of Lawson Guthrie I bequeath all the rest and residue of any Silver Spoons.

[Page 102]

5th - To Isabella J. Ellis I give and bequeath one large looking glass and one caine bottomed rocking chair now at her house.

6th - At my death I desire and enjoin it on my personal representative as well as on my children to see to it - That I am decently buried - a longside of my husband, Col. Joseph G. Smith, deceased and that both graves be walled round by one common fence or walling of rock, one foot high, and then Iron railing around it on top of the rock, with Iron door & lock & Key, all expenses of which in every particular, I will desire & direct to be paid out of my money on hands at my death and that may arise from rents of my land or sale of any property, not herein before specifically disposed of, and all such remainder or surplus of any money or proceeds of sale of any such property as I may die seized and possessed of after such funeral and grave expenses are paid as above described I give and bequeath to Kittie G. Smith - a small daughter of my son - John A. Smith - Said Kittie is now in the care, custody and control of L. Guthrie & his wife - Narcissa M. Guthrie - this bequest to include any money owing to me by note or account or otherwise.

My watch I will dispose of during my life. This will is to be in operation only upon my death - during my life I retain the right to dispose of or do as I please with all said properties and money & debts or any part thereof.

Lastly, I nominate and appoint John A. Smith my only son - my Executor of this my last Will & Testament and enjoin upon him to fully execute the same according to its letter and spirit.

In witness whereof, I have hereto set my hand & seal July 11th, 1874

> Rebecca M. Smith

Signed Sealed & acknowledged by The Testator in our presence and in the presence of each other on the 11th day of July 1874.

> D. C. Trewhitt

A. J. Trewhitt

Probated in open court July 28th 1875
L. M. Clark
Per J.S. Bell

[Page 103]

MARY BANKS

Last Will & Testament of Mary Banks,

State of Tennessee)
Hamilton County)   In the name of God Amen.

I Mary Banks being of sound mind and descretion and feeling that my earthly career is hastily coming to a close do make and publish this as my last will and testament hereby revoking and making void all others by me at any time made.

First - I direct that my funeral expenses and all my debts, if any I have be paid as soon after my death as possible out of any moneys that I may die possessed of or that may first come into the hands of my exector hereinafter named.

Secondly - I give will and bequeath to my dearly beloved husband Andrew Banks, my oldest son by a former husband George Wm. Colburt[?] my next oldest son by my second husband John Thomas Huff and my youngest son by my third Husband Charles Steven Metts my lot of land situated in the northeast part of Chattanooga containing an acre more or less bounded and described as follows to wit: lying immediately adjoining the east line of the Corporion of the City of Chattanooga, beginning at a stake on the east side of the east Tennessee Va. & Ga. R.R. on the top of the bank of a deep cut and where the corporation line of said City of Chattanooga crosses said railroad running thence North 20° East one hundred and Sixty four (164) feet to a stake; Thence South 70° east two hundred & Sixty five and one half (265 1/2) feet to a stake; Thence South 30° West one hundred & Sixty four (164) feet to a Stake and thence north 70° west Two hundred & Sixty five & one half (265 1/2) feet to the place of beginning, the same being the lot of land bought by me of George W. Gardenhire in the year 1867. This lot herein before described & set out is all the land I own in the world and I will give and bequeath the same by this my last will and Testament to my husband Andrew Banks and my three said children - John T. George W. & Charles S. as heretofore set out by former husbands to be divided between them equally share and share alike and of equal value. I further wish desire will and direct that each of said devises shall hold the said land in trust for each of the others to this extent, That none of them shall be allowed [Page 104] to dispose of his share during his lifetime but the same at his death Shall go to the Survivor or survivors equally, the same shall not be alienable or transferable during the life or lives of any of the devises but shall go to the survivor or survivors as above set fourth.

Lastly, I do hereby nominate and appoint my dearly beloved husband (in whom I have the utmost confidence) Andrew Banks, my executor to execute and carry out my wishes as expressed & set forth in the foregoing Will and because of the smallness of my estate & the confidence I have in the honesty and integrity of my Said husband it is my wish & I so direct that he be allowed to execute my last Will and testament without giving bond & security as the law directs. I do further nominate and appoint my said husband Andrew Banks to be Guardian of the estates of my said Three children herein before named and to have the care & custody of my two oldest sons George W. and John Thomas and because of the tender years of my youngest son Charles Steven it is my wish and desire & I so direct that Nancy Jones a woman in whom I have the utmost confidence shall have the care custody and raising of him. I further direct will and desire that Nancy Jones and my said Husband Andrew Banks shall neither of them be required to give bond either as guardian or executor. I do this because of the confidence I have in them & each of them and because I know them to be very poor persons & not able to give such bonds as the law directs and rather than that my poor little helpless orphan Children & my little property that has cost me so much hard labor should fall into the hands of strangers have willed as above.

In witness whereof I do to this my Will set my hand and seal this the 6th day of July 1875.
Mary Banks
Signed and published in our presence and we have subscribed our names hereto in the presence of the Testatrix this the sixth day of July 1875
Geo. T. White
Mary Tolliver

[Page 105]

MALINDA MORROW

Last Will & Testament of Malinda Morrow, Deceased.

State of Tennessee)

Hamilton County) I Malinda Morrow of said State and County being of advanced age and knowing that I must soon die, do make declare and publish this my last Will and Testament.

Item 1 - I hold one note on Lewis Jacob for the sum of one Hundred and twenty five Dollars ($125.00) besides interest given by him to me for real estate in Talladega Alabama also some other debts due me. These debts I give to my son Lewis Morrow but require that he shall pay my funeral expenses and Doctor Bills of of the proceeds when collected.

Item 2nd - I give to my son Lewis H. Morrow to my Grand Son William Morrow of Talladega County, Alabama and to the five youngest Children of my son Jacob Morrow all the residue of my property including my real estate in Talladega Alabama to be divided between them Share and Share alike. That is to day to Lewis H. Morrow One Third to William Morrow one third and to the said Children of my son Jacob one Third. The children that I intend to take this property are said Jacobs Three youngest children by his first wife to wit David, John, and Annie and his two children by his last wife to wit Laura and Emma.

Item 3rd - I contribute and appoint my son Lewis H. Morrow executor of this my last will and testament and give him full power to act in such manner as he may deem best for the interst of my estate in all respects and authorize him to sell and dispose of any part of my property in such manner and on such terms as he shall judge to be best for the interest of my estate but he shall not sell my said estate except his own one Third without and order of the court but said land shall be divided or partitioned - I direct that my said executor shall not be required to give any bond for the execution of this Will but the oath and Bond required by law are waived. Witness my hand and seal this 20 June 1875

Malinda Morrow (seal)

Signed sealed declared and published by Malinda Morrow as her last Will and Testament and we certify that we have signed the same as subscribing witnesses in the presence of the testatrix by her special request and in the presence of each other this 20th June 1875

E. M. Dodson
J. C. Calhoun
Robert Beeby

[Page 106]

MORRIS BRADT

Last Will and Testament of Morris Bradt Deceased
Chattanooga, Tennesee
Nov. 8, 1875

I Morris Bradt being of sound mind and composing memory, do hereby express and set forth this as my last will & testament. I desire that all my property shall be sold on a credit of Six & twelve month and the proceeds when collected shall be applied first to the payment of a claim due Louis Silberman of about one Hundred & Eighty five dollars ($185) Second to the payment of a claim due Joseph Ruohs of about Thirteen Hundred dollars and the remainder if any to be applied pro rata to the remainder of my creditors.

I desire that all dues to which I may be entitled from Societies or Lodges and all moneys due on life Insurance shall be paid over to my wife Julia Bradt to be used as she in here wisdom & judgement may see proper in supporting & maintaining herself and children. I desire and request that Dr. P. D. Sims Shall assist her in making out & forwarding such papers and giving such other attention as may be necessary in the collection of my life Insurance.

I hereby name and appoint Joseph Ruohs sole Executor of this my last will and Testament and desire that he shall not be required to give bond and security as such executor having full confidence in his ability honor and integrity in the discharge of said duties.

Morris Bradt

Signed in presence of
P. D. Sims
S. Rosenbaum
Thos. Webster

[Page 107]

D. A. KENNEDY

Last Will & Testament of D. A. Kennedy, deceased.

In view of the uncertainty of life and being desirous to settle & dispose of my worldly affairs I Daniel A. Kennedy of the City of Chattanooga and state of Tennessee being of sound mind and disposing memory, do make and publish this as my last Will and Testament hereby revoking & making void all other Wills and Codicils Thereto by me made at any time.

First - I direct that my funeral expences and all

my Just debts, if any, be paid as soon after my death as possible out of any moneys I may be possessed of or that may first come into the hands of my executor.

Secondly - I give and bequeath to my Sister Mrs. Cynthia J. Morrison wife of Joseph L. Morrison one fourth of all my Estate, real, personal & mixed (remaining after my funeral expences and Just debts are paid) wherever said estate may be situated and in the event of her death before me or my Sister Myra T. Edmondson then said interest of one fourth shall go to the heirs of Mrs. Morrison.

Third - I give and bequeath to my Sister Myra T. Edmondson wife of John Edmonson one fourth of all my estate real personal & mixed wherever situated remaining after my funeral expences & Just debts are paid.

Fourth - I give and bequeath the remaining half of my estate as follows: One Third of said half to my Nephew W. W. Kennedy One Third to my Niece Margaret Rowena Kennedy and the other Third of said half to my Nephew Thomas H. Walker. But in the event of the death of any one or all of said Last three named Devises without lawful issue of their bodies or by them lawfully begotten capable of inheriting. Then in such event it is my will that the interest of such an one so dying would have had he lived or had such issue shall go to my two Sisters Mes. Morrison & Edmondson or their heirs or the survivor & the heirs of the others in the event either of said Sisters should be dead at the time. It being my intention to have said interest go to my own heirs & relatives rather than to strangers who have no claim upon me or my bounty, said interests given to said Devises by this claim to be paid to them as herein after provided.

Fifth - It is further my will and desire that my Store House & lot on the corner of Market & Ninth in said City of Chattanooga Tennessee shall not be sold by my executor or disposed of until such time as my two Sisters Mrs. Morrison & Mrs. Edmondson shall advise and request [Page 108] the same but in the meantime it is my will that my executor herein after named take charge of said property & keep the same rented out and in renting the same he will give preference to Morrison & Brother, Should they desire to rent the same provided they and my two Sisters Mrs. Morrison & Edmondson & my executor herein after named who is a partner of the firm of Morrison & Bro. can agree upon the rent to be paid, but in the event said Morrison & Bro. should not desire to rent or the parties above named cannot agree upon the rental value all the property is to be rented to other parties then my executor has full power to rent same & collect the rents and he will pay one fourth of the rents received from said property to my Sister Mrs. Morrison or her heirs and three fourths to my Sister Mrs. Edmondson

who will retain one fourth of the whole rental received for the property & the remainder she will divide Equally between W. W. Kennedy, Margaret Rowena Kennedy & Thomas H. Walker but in the event of the death of either or all of said three last named devises without issue as provided in clause four then Mrs. Edmondson will devide the interest such an one so dying would have been entitled to had they lived, euqally between herself and Mrs. Morrison or the heirs of Mrs. Morrison.

Sixthly - It is my will that my Executor herein after named sell my Store House and Lot on the corner of Market and Ninth Streets above mentioned at any time my two sisters Mrs. Cynthia Morrison & Mrs. Myra T. Edmondson may advise or request the same sold or the survivors of them may so request the other property he will sell at discretion and in the event of the death of both before said sale said Executor is vested with discretionary power as to the time of selling same to the best interest of the devises herein before named and said executor is here by vested with the title to said property as well as to all other property belonging to my Estate & with full power to see and --- the same at the time and for the purpose above indicated and upon the sale of said property or any part thereof he will pay the proceeds thereof over to the parties above named as Devises in the manner & proportion stated That is to say one fourth to Mrs. Morrison or her heirs one fourth to Mrs. Edmondson or her heirs or Devises except the interest willed to W. W. Kennedy, Margaret Rowena Kennedy & [Page 109] Thomas Walker which said interest said Executor shall keep loaned out at the best rate of interest that can be obtained for it consistant with the security of the same & he will collect the interest on the same yearly or oftener if he deems best & pay the same over to Mrs. Edmondson who will divide the same between said Devises as provided for in relation to the rents of said property but in the event of the death of Mrs. Edmondson before a final distribution of said estate or the arival [sic] of said Devises of age & no distribution as to them can take place under this my will until they arive [sic] of age or have issue capable of inheriting as herein before proved. Then it is my will that my said executor pay over said interst or rents in accordence with provisions & directions herein before expressed or given to my Sister

Lastly - I do hereby nominate and appoint Robert Morrison my executor with full power to sell & convey said lot and loanes upon the hapining [sic] of the conditions herein before stated and as I have full confidence in my said Executor he is not required to give bond as Executor as required by law but the same is hereby expressly waived.

In witness hereof I do to this my will set my hand

and seal this the 16 of August 1875.

D. A. Kennedy [Seal]

Signed sealed & published in our presence and we have subscribed our names hereto in the presence of and at the request of the testator this the 16th day of August 1875.

W. O. Peeples
S. C. Peeples

[Page 110]

R. C. McREE, SR.

Soddy Oct 13,1873

I R. C. McRee, Sr. of the County of Hamilton and State of Tennessee being of sound mind and perfectly in my senses do ordain and declare this Instrument of writing to be my last will and Testament.

That first of all at my decease give and bequeath all my personal property and affects of every kind by first paying my debts if there should be any then the balance of all moneys or personal property to be equally divided to each of my four living children [to wit] N. J. Anderson, R. C. McRee, Jr., M. A. Roberts and M. B. McRee to be equally divided between them and their loving children, then I give and bequeath all the lands that I may have right to lying between Big Soddy Creek and Oposom [sic] Creek Mountain and Valley to be equally divided between N. J. Anderson & M. A. Roberts them or their children, then I give and bequeath to my two Sons R. C. McRee, Jr. and M. B. McRee all my lands that I have a right to below Big Soddy Creek to North Chickamauga Creek on the Mountain and in the valley to be equally divided between them so as to best suit what they already possess except a small moiety of land set apart for lifetime only to J. V. A. Craighead and his wife L. W. Craighead particularly described in my writing in their possession and then that M. B. McRee have the other half of the Soddy Island in Tennessee River No. 3 in the Ocoa [Ocoee] Dst by paying to his Brother and each of his Sisters or their children One hundred and twenty five dollars in all four hundred Dollars - And their Satisfactory advancements as there necessity required, by myself to all my Grand children that was the children of J. L. Reed by each of my daughters yet I wish if there be lands held by Clift & McRee above Sail [sic] Creek in the Valley, that my interest be sold by my

executors and equally divided between the Reed Grand Children and furthermore I do appoint R. C. McRee and M. B. McRee with all the right I have to do so my two Sons, my lawfull Executors to carry out to the letter under the laws governin [sic] the case this my last and only will.

Given under my hand and Seal the day and date above set.

R.C. McRee [Seal]

Witnesses:
Wm. Clift
R.B.Clift

No exception to be taken to the interlining of N. J. Anderson and M. A. Roberts nor to R. C. McRee, Jr. & M. B. McRee.

R. C. McRee, Sen.

Probated Feby 7th 1876

[Page 111]

DANIEL R. RAWLINGS

Will of Daniel R. Rawlings Decd.

I Daniel R. Rawlings do make & publish this as my last Will and Testament it being the only one I ever made & as my beloved wife Martha J. Rawlings has been mainly instrumental in making by her constant labour & industry what little property we have I appoint her my sole executrix & I do hereby give and bequeath to her the said Martha J. Rawlings, all the property of which I may die possessed of every kind Real Personal or Mixed all debts due or moneys, every thing of value. I desire that it all may be hers for & in her own name & for her sole use & benefit to be disposed of by her as she sees fit. I wish my executrix to pay my debts, as soon as possible after she qualifies now I desire it to be understood that my object in making this will is to give my wife the sole use & control of the property which she had made the greater part of herself in witness whereof I do to this my will set my hand & seal, this 17th day of May 1870.

D. R. Rawlings (Seal)

Acknowledged the above signature in our presence and we have subscribed our names in the presence of the testator this 17th of May 1870.

J. H. Warner

Jno. B. Nicklin Jr.

Probated Feb. 24th 1876

[Page 112]

CELESTIA SEMMES

Will of Celestia Semmes

I Celestia Semmes do make and publish this my last Will & Testament, hereby revoking all former wills by me made to, wit:

First - I will and desire that all my indebtedness of every kind be paid out of any money on hand at my death or the first that is collected after my death.

Second - I will and devise to my Sister Mrs. Matilda Brawner all my right title and interest either legal or equitable in and to the lot and improvements upon the same where Mrs. Matilda Brawner now resides, being Thirty-five (35) feet front of lot number Eleven (11) and Five (5) feet front of lot number Ten (10) on Georgia Avenue in Chattanooga Tennessee. Said Matilda Brawner to take The Same as her seperate estate free from The control or liabilities of her present or any future husband to her sole use and behoof with power to devise the same, treating and using the same as though She was an unmarried woman.

I also give and bequeath to the said Matilda Brawner all my personal property of every kind, situated in and about the building where she now resides consisting of Furniture Silver-pictures, my wardrobe &c &c. The personal property to be her seperate estate.

I will and bequeath to my brother - B. J. Semmes who now resides at Canton Miss. all moneys belonging to me with The notes or other evidences of indebtedness due or owing to me. There is money owing to me in Memphis, Tenn. from B. J. Semmes, who is my cousin and from Wm. Dowling and J. R. Ryan of Chattanooga Tenn. It is my intention that my brother have this money if collected at my death, or if not collected That he take The evidence of indebtedness. And my executor will transfer The evidence of indebtedness, to him if in existence at my death.

I nominate and appoint my brother-in-law P. A. Brawner, Esq. my executor. He will not be required to give bond and security as required by The Statute, and need not file an inventory of the property - but is only required to deliver to my Sister and brother The property herein devised to each of them.

Witness my hand and seal This 27th day of March 1875.

Celestia Semmes

Signed in the presence of and each of whom was called to witness the Same.
S. A. Key
W. R. Rankin

[Page 113]

I append the following as a Codicil to my will heretofore made. I desire to change the same to the extent of The bequest herein contained--I will and bequeath to my brother-in-law P. A. Brawner $337 to be taken out of the money due me in The hands of B. J. Semmes of Memphis. Also the further sum of $50.00 not embraced in my will which I hereby in all other rspects ratify & confirm to be disposed of by him according to instructions given him.

Celestia Semmes
July 3rd 1875

Probated March 27th 1876

JUDIAH MORROW

Will of Judiah Morrow

State of Tennessee)
Hamilton   ) Judiah Morrow, wife of Lewis H. Morrow of said County, do hereby make my last Will & Testament, hereby revoking all wills heretofore made by me.

Item 1st - I give to my husband Lewis H. Morrow and my daughter - Sophronia Morrow, all my property, real and personal in equal portions, the said Lewis H. Morrow to be charged with the payment of my debts and funeral expenses.

Item 2nd - If any executor is required I appoint the said Lewis H. and Sophronia my Executor and Executrix and they shall not be required to give any bond.

Witness my hand and seal this 1st April 1876.

Judiah X Morrow
her mark

Witness:
E. M. Dodson
Robt. Beeley
George Adlain

Probated June 7th 1876

[Page 114]

ALBERT BRAY

Last will and Testament of Albert Bray, Decd.

I Albert Bray of Chattanooga Tenn. realizing and believing that my life upon earth will soon be brought to a close and being of sound mind do hereby make & publish this as my last Will and Testament.

1st - I do nominate and appoint John Higgie (my personal friend) my Executor to carry my will and bequest into effect.

2nd - I direct my said Executor immediately after my decease to take into his possession all my property and effects of every description both real and personal, and to sell and convert the same into money within such time and upon such terms as my said Executor may deem best.

3rd - I further direct my said Executor to pay all my just debts, first and second to pay to Peggie Womble the sum of One Hundred Dollars and Thirdly - after reserving to himself a reasonable compensation for his time and trouble in the execution of his trust, to pay over the remainder to Lookout Lodge No. 10 Free and Accepted Masons of Chattanooga Tenn. to be used by said Lodge only for the purpose of the purchase of ground and the erection of a lodge building or Hall thereon.

4th - I further direct that no bond shall be required of my said executor.

Albert Bray

Signed & Sealed in presence of
C. Snyder
Kie Fredrick

Probated March 5th 1877

[Page 115]

JOHN J. CRONIN

Last Will and Testament of John J. Cronin, Decd.

In the name of God Amen.

I John J. Cronin, of the City of Brooklyn in the County of Kings and State of New York, being of sound and disposing mind and memory do make publish and declare this my last Will and Testament in manner and form following. That is to say--

First - I hereby nominate, constitute and appoint the Reverend James O'Birne Parish Priest of Saint Johns Roman Catholic Church is said City of Brooklyn, the Sole Executor of This my last Will and Testament--

Second - I give, devise and bequeath to my Executor hereinbefore named in trust nevertheless for the uses and purposes hereinafter mentioned and described all of the real Estate which I now own or of which I may die seized and which real estate at the date of this instrument consists of one block in the City of Chattanooga in the County of Hamilton and state of Tennessee, and which said Block part or parcel of land is more fully described in a certain deed of conveyance made by J. P. Muller and Caroline Muller his wife to John Cronin (This Testator) which said deed bears date the Sixth day of Oct. 1865 A.D. and was recorded in the Registers Office of Hamilton County Tennessee on the 27th day of April A.D. 1866. And also one lot piece or parcel of land situated lying and being at the corner of Third Avenue and Thirty ninth Street in the City of Brooklyn, County of Kings and State of New York, said lot being one hundred feet (100 feet) by Twenty five feet two inches (25 feet 2 inches) and I hereby authorize and empower my said Executor Reverend James O'Berne to see the aforesaid property situated at Chattanooga aforesaid "sold" upon the best possible Terms he can obtain and to invest the proceeds of such sale in building a residence upon the said lot of land on the Corner of Third Avenue and Thirty ninth Street in said City of Brooklyn for the use and benefit of my wife and children as follows: viz: my wife Mary Cronin is to have the free use of said building when erected as a home for herself and our children--the legal title to the property however to remain in my executor hereinbefore named during the life time of my wife and at her death my said Executor is to convey all the property then remaining in his hands to my children Mary Agnes Cronin, Hannah Maria Cronin and to such other child or children as may be herafter born unto my said wife and myself, said conveyance to my said children to be in fee simple to my [Page 116] said children their heirs and assigns forever. And in the event of the death of my said wife and all of my said children then said property is to be conveyed to my Sister Mary Manney.

Third - I give my Tool Chest and the Tools therein and thereto belonging to my Nephew Francis Manney.

Fourth - And all the rest residue and remainder of my personal property I give to my wife the said Mary Cronin to have and to hold the same to her own sole and personal use forever.

Fifth - My said wife Mary Cronins acceptance of the provisions of this will shall be in in lieu of dower.

Sixth - I hereby revoke any and all Wills by me heretofore made.

In witness whereof I have hereunto set my hand and seal this Second day of October in the year of our Lord One Thousand Eigth Hundred and Seventy four.

John J. Cronin (Seal)

The foregoing Instrument was at the date Thereof signed sealed published and declared by the said Testator as and for his last Will and Testament in the presence of us, who at the request of the said Testator and in his presence and in the presence of each other have hereunto subscribed our names as attending witnesses.

Patrick J. Keating, residing at 38th Street and 5th Avenue, Brooklyn, Kings County, New York.

Joseph Gleeson 3rd Av. & 30th St.

Jeremiah D. Mahoney 39 Street

[Page 117]

E. S. CARD

Last Will and Testament of E. S. Card, Deceased.
Soddy Tenn.
April 5, 1878

In the name of God Amen.

I E. S. Card of Soddy in the County of Hamilton State of Tennessee, Being mindful of my mortality, do this day, date above writen, make and publish this my last Will and Testament in manner following.

First - I desire to be decently burried in my burrying ground on Waldens Ridge. Also I give and bequeath unto my faithful Nurse Miss G. A. Payne the sum of One hundred Dollars, to be paid unto her within Two Years after my decease shall be expired.

Also - I give and bequeath unto my eldest son Edward the sum of six Hundred Dollars the same to be held in trust for him by my Son in law W. A. Anderson to be used for benefit of the said Edward; and in case of his decease any of the said sum of six Hundred Dollars remaining the said money or moneys to be eaqually divided among my Children or their Heirs.

Also - I forgive unto D. R. Grafton my son in law and his wife my Daughter Janney the sum of one hundred Dollars out of the principal of a Note which I hold against them.

Also - I forgive unto Gabriel Hoff my son in law and his wife Lottie my Daughter, one hundred Dollars out

of the principal of a Note which I hold against them.

Also - I forgive unto my son George the sum of one hundred Dollars out of accounts I hold against him.

Also - I forgive unto my son Charles P., the sum of one hundred Dollars out of a note I hold against him.

Also - I forgive unto my son William H. the sum of one hundred Dollars out of the principal of a Note I hold against him due Feb. 1879.

Also - I give unto and bequeath to my son in law W. A. Anderson and his wife Lizzie the sum of one hundred dollars to be paid out of the proceeds of the sale of my town property situated in Chattanooga.

Also - I give and bequeath to my beloved wife Rachael all the residue of my property both real and personal and all the benefits accrued from the same to have and to hold the same during her natural life and [Page 118] at her deceased to be equally divided among my children except my eldest Son Edward who is already provided for in this my last Will and Testament.

Also I direct my Executors to sell my property in the Town of Chattanooga and to hold the money. The proceeds thereof and to dispose of the same according to the directions of my beloved wife Rachael.

Lastly - I do appoint C. P. Card and W. A. Anderson to be the Executors of this my last Will and Testament.

In witness whereof I have hereunto set my hand and seal this 5th April A.D. 1877.

E. S. Card (Seal)

The above instrument of three sheets was now here subscribed by E. S. Card the Testator in the presence of each of us and was at the time declared by him to be his last Will and Testament and we at his request signed our names hereto as attesting witnesses.

J. M. Watson L. S.

Wm. H. Barnes

Soddy Tennessee

Codicil to the above Will and Testament - I E. S. Card anex this as my will in addition to the above.

First - That my eldest Son Edward in case he shall outlive his Mother shall have the additional sum of two Hundred Dollars to be placed in the hands of W. A. Anderson in trust for him. The same to be disposed of according to the provisions of the above Will and Testament in witness whereof I have hereunto set my hand This 5th April A. D. 1877.

E. S. Card S. S.

J.M. Watson L.S.

Wm. H. Barnes L. S.

[Page 119]

GILBERT VANDERGRIFF

Last Will and Testament of Gilbert Vandergriff
Decd.

State of Tennessee)
Hamilton County   )   I Gilbert Vandergriff of the State
and County aforesaid do make this my last and only Will
but revoking all others that might be proposed to be my
will.

First - I desire that all my just debts and burial
expences be paid out of my personal property.

Second - I give and bequeath to my beloved wife
Elizabeth all my property both real and personal during
her natural life and after her death my desire is that the
real estate and what property may be left be sold in some
way to bring the most money and in a way that it will
bring the highest price. Then out of the proceeds of said
sale I desire that my Daughter Sarah Vandergriff have
fifteen Hundred Dollars first out of the proceeds of said
sale.

3rd - I give and bequeath to Polly Ann Doolin
Jacob Vandergriff heirs, Margaret Scott, Jane Brown and
Hile Vandergriff, Jr. the balance of the proceeds of said
sale of said property to be Equally divided Shear and
Shear alike Jacobs heir to be one Shear and

Lastly - I appoint A. Selcer my Executor to carry
out the conditions of this will and to do all and everything
required in the premesis and after it being read in my
heiring I cordially approve the same this the 12 day of
April A.D. 1877.

I am now in my right mind and this is what I
always intended to do.

Gilbert Vandergriff

Signed in the presence of
R. M. Brown
E. R. Martin
Hamilton Adams

[Page 120]

W. P. ALLISON - WILL

Last Will and Testament of W. P. Allison Decd.

State of Tennessee)
Hamilton County   )   I William P. Allison of said State

and County being advanced in years and knowing that it is
appointed unto all men to die do make this my last Will
and Testament.

1st - I will and bequeath to my beloved wife Sarah
Allison all the property real and personal of which I may
be possessed at the time of my death wherever it may be
situated to have and use as her own and to dispose of as
she deems proper: it being my intention that she shall use
any part or the whole of said property for her support and
if any remains at the time of her death she shall make
such disposition Thereof as she chooses. She shall have
the right to collect all moneys due me and to sell any part
or the whole of my property real or personal and Shall not
be required to account to any one for the proceeds or any
part thereof.

2nd - I have sold certain lands in the State of
Georgia to Moses Long and Edward Howard and given
them my bond for title or payment of the purchase money.
These lands and notes are discribed, the bonds held by
said Long and Howard - It is my Will and I direct that on
the payment of the purchase money for said lands my
Executrix and Executor herein after named or the Survivor
of them shall execute proper deeds of conveyance to said
parties for said lands without any order of Court or other
expense.

3rd - I constitute and appoint my beloved wife
Sarah Allison and my son Seth M. Allison Executrix and
Executor of this my last Will and Testament. In case only
one of them should qualify or if either should die or resign
or refuse to act the other shall be vested with full authority
to execute the provisions of this Will: No oath or bond
shall be required of my said Executrix or Executor.

Wm. P. Allison (Seal)

Signed Sealed declared and published by W. P.
Allison as his last Will and Testament and we have signed
the same as witness at the special request of said W. P.
Allison in his presence and in the presence of each other
this 24th day of March 1877.

E. M. Dodson
J. M. Brown
J. M. Alexander

[Page 121]

HARVEY J. WILEY

Last Will and Testament of Harvey J. Wiley, Decd.

Fork Plain, July 29th 1876

This my last Will and Testament. I do appoint Sam T. Dewes of Chattanooga Tennessee as Administrator knowing him to be strictly honest. Any money I may have, I wish I my Sister Ellen to have One Hundred Dollars in cash. The rest of any moneys I may have on hand at time of my death I wish my mother to have; all of my property I wish sold and the money realized from it I wish used in purchasing a monument for my father, mother, myself and sister Ellen; A larger lot than my father has I wish purchased and my father taken up and put on as well as myself, the lot not to cost over One hundred Dollars; the money to be taken from the proceeds of my property sold I wish the deepest kind of a metalic Coffin to be bot for me. I do not wish my property to be sold at to great a sacrifice rather have it held for a short time say a year or two.

                                        Harvey J. Wiley

Probated Jany. 28th 1878

The signature to the above Will was proven by Lewis Schneider M. B. Parham and R. A. Giles, as shown by the minutes of the county court.

SAMUEL J. BOYCE

Last Will and Testament of Saml. J. Boyce, Decd.

I, Samuel J. Boyce of Hamilton County, Tennessee do make and publish this as my last Will and Testament hereby revoking and making void all Wills and codicils by me at any time made.

Item First - I direct that all my just debts be first paid.

Item Second - I give and bequeath one moiety of all the rest and residue of my Estate whatever and wherever to my beloved wife Mary E. Boyce to and for her absolute use and behoof forever.

Item Third, I give, bequeath and devise the other moiety of all the rest and residue of my estate whatever and wherever to my brother James P. Boyce to hold in trust for my children, Mary L. Bilderback wife of Rev. J. A. Bilderback, Latimer Boyce and James Spain Boyce, that is to say the shares of my said children respectively, either jointly or severally as he deems best in lands, stocks, or other goods. Estate, sell, leave or otherwise dispose of the same and reinvest the proceeds subject to like uses and trusts to and for the following uses and trusts, that is to say to permit my said children severally to take the rents and profits and net income of their said Estate allotted to them respectively until they shall respectively arrive at the age of thirty years if they live that long, and in case any one of them should die before arriving at said age then in trust for their heirs and when my said children shall arrive, or attain the age of thirty years in trust for them severally to and for their absolute use and behoof forever, Provided, that any sale of any part of the Estate allotted to any one of my said children, made for reinvestment shall be ratified and approved by the child whose Estate is affected if living and by his, or her Executor as Administrator if dead.

Item Fourth: It may be lawful and I direct that my executors, or survivor of them may be a joint deed sell, or otherwise dispose of any part of my Estate for the purpose of paying debts, or of affecting the partition thereof between my said wife Mary E. Boyce and my said children as herein before provide.

Item Fifth: The share hereinbefore devised to my said wife Mary E. Boyce shall be in lieu of Dower, years support and of all other claims upon my estate.

Item Sixth: Until the shares of my said wife and children can be apportioned to them and it shall be deemed by my Executor to the interest of my Estate to hold any part of the same undivided, it is my will and direction that my said wife Mary E. Boyce shall be entitled to one moiety of the actual income of that part of my Estate then undivided after deducting all expenses and that my said children shall each receive one sixth part thereof after deducting all expenses.

Item Seventh: My said Executor, or the Survivors of them may allot or set apart to my said wife or to either of my said children any part of my said Estate at a fair valuation to be approved by my said wife and children if living or by their Executors or [Page 123] administrators if dead.

Item Eighth: I nominate, constitute and appoint my brother James P. Boyce and my wife Mary E. Boyce Executors and my brother James P. Boyce, Trustee of this my last Will and testament and desire that they be qualified and serve without being required to execute a bond usually required by law.

In witness whereof to this my Will written in three pages of this sheet of paper, I do set my hand and seal this 11th day of August, A.D. 1877.

                                        Saml. J. Boyce (Seal)

Signed published and declared by the Testator as and for his last will and testament in the presence of us who in his presence and at his request and in the presence of each other have heretofore subscribed our names in the City of Chattanooga in the County of Hamilton and in the State of Tennessee this the day and year above written.

                                        J. C. Haselton

A. B. Paine
O. P. Fouts

[Page 123 con't]

MARTHA J. RAWLINGS

Last Will & Testament of Martha J. Rawlings,
Decd.

I Martha J. Rawlings of Hamilton County Tennessee being of sound mind and disposing memory, do make and publish this my last Will and testament, hereby revoking all others by me at any time heretofore made.

1st - I direct that my funeral expenses and all my debts be paid.

2nd - I give and bequeath and devise to Lizzie Patten daughter of Z. C. Patten an undivided one half interest in my farm in 5th Civil District of Hamilton County Tennessee, called my home place, also the North West corner of lot No. 30 on Poplar Street Chattanooga Tennessee fronting 35 feet on Poplar Street and running back eighty five feet and being the lot on which Z. C. Patten built a residence.

3rd - I give devise and bequeath to Elizabeth Tutt an undivided one fourth interest in my farm in 5th Civil District of Hamilton County Tennessee called my home place also that portion of lot 28 Poplar Street Chattanooga, Tennessee which lies immediately west of the lot on which Mrs. Tutt now resides, being fifty feet and running back to Mrs. [Page 124] Gaskills line: also a strip of Ground on the north side of lot No. 30 Poplar Street Chattanooga, Tenn. fronting 20 feet on Pine Street and extending back of Uniform width to the lot herein bequeathed to Lizzie Patten, so as to give Mrs. Tutt a passway to the rear of her lot.

4th - I give devise and bequeath to John G. Rawlings an undivided one fourth interest in my farm in 5th Civil District of Hamilton County Tenn. called my home place.

5" - I direct that the balance of what I may own of lot 28 Poplar Street Chattanooga Tenn. not herein disposed of shall be sold by my Executor for cash or credit as he may deem best and the proceeds by paid over to him in equal proportions to Elizabeth Tutt, Lizzie Patten and himself, to whom I give the same.

6" - I direct that the balance of what I may own of lot 30 Poplar Street Chattanooga Tenn. not herein disposed of, shall be sold by my Executor at such time for cash or credit as he may deem best, and out of the proceeds pay a debt of about $1000 - due Z. C. Patten,

any other debts I may owe and the expenses of the Administration of my Estate.

And the balance of the proceeds I direct to be loaned out or invested to the best advantage by my executor, and the income from said fund to be paid over by him to Elizabeth Tutt until her death or marriage and at her death or marriage the Executor will pay over the prinicipal of said fund in Equal proportions to Lizzie Patten, Elizabeth Tutt (if she be living & if dead to her heirs) and John G. Rawlings - to whom I give the same.

7" - I do hereby nominate and appoint John G. Rawlings Executor of this my last Will and testament to carry out the provisions of the same and request that he be not required to give bond and security as such.

8" - I do hereby nominate and appoint Z. C. Patten Testamentary Guardian and Trustee for Lizzie Patten to receive take charge of and manage the property and funds herein devised and bequeath to her.

9" - Until the sale of said portion of lot 30 Poplar Street Chattanooga Tenn. shall be sold by my Executor I direct that the rents accruing thereon after paying Taxes, Insurance and necessary repairs shall be paid over to Elizabeth Tutt by my Executor. This March Sixth 1878.

Martha J. Rawlings

Attest

L. Y. Green
W. T. Woodruff

[Page 125]

The foregoing Will & Testament was admitted to probate in the County Court of Hamilton County Tenn. March 15th (or 13th) 1878.

J. S. Bell, Dept. Clerk
County Court H. C. Tenn.

JANE P. DOTY

Chattanooga, Tenn.
Dec. 12, 1877

Be it hereby known That I Jane P. Doty being of sound mind and fully realizing the uncertainty of life do make this my last Will and Testament.

1st - For the love I bear to my husband D. M. Doty I will and bequeath a certain house & Lot situated in the village of McMinnville Tenn. on Spring Street & known as the homestead. Also a certain house & lot situated on the Sparta road in McMinnville, Tenn.

2nd - I Will all Notes, mortgages & personal property now held in my name to my husband for the benefit of my Children. Trusting in the will of him who careth for all I calmly await my change.

Jane P. Doty

Witness
    D. G. Curtiss
    E. E. Loomis

ELIZABETH ANN CONDRY

Will of Mrs. Elizabeth Ann Condry.

This my last Will and Testament of Elizabeth Ann Condry.

I Elizabeth Ann Condry being in feeble health but of a sound and disposing mind do make and publish this my last Will and Testament as follows, to wit:

1st - I will that all of my just debts be paid.

2nd - I give, grant and devise to George Condry (Colored) a boy that is now living with me, one black cow and calf, one sow.

3rd - I give, grant and devise to my beloved Nephew Azariah Poe all of my personal property, consisting of Horses, Cattle, Sheep, hogs, chickens, wheat, corn, Rye and oats and all of my house hold and Kitchen furniture.

4th - I hereby appoint W. C. Champion, Executor [Page 126] of this my last will and Testament with full power to carry out the provisions thereof.

I hereby revoke all former wills.

In testimony whereof I hereby sign this my last Will in the presence of these subscribing witnesses who witness the same at my request and in my presents.
Attest July 21st 1877   Elizabeth Ann Contry
                    (Seal)

We the subscribing witnesses to the foregoing Will certify that we saw the Testatrix sign the foregoing will and that we witnessed the same in her presence at her request.
July 21st 1877   G. M. Walker
             E. F. Bell

Filed April 10th 1878 for probate
             J. S. Bell, D. C.
Proven by one witness only - G. M. Walker

[Page 126]

ELIZABETH H. JACK

In the State of Tennessee S. S.)
and County of Hamilton   )

In the name of God Amen.

I Elizabeth H. Jack of the 3rd Dist. in said County and State being weak in body but sound in mind and fully conscious that I must shortly die, do make this my last will and testament, hereby expressly revoking all other wills by me made, viz:

First - I resign my Soul to God who gave it, and my body to the dust.

Second - Touching my worldly goods and effects real and personal I dispose of them as follows, to wit:

3rd - I have rented all my lands in said district & County to my nephew R. M. Stringer for the year 1878 including the houses and residence where I live and all building, erections & improvements on all said lands. This renting I hereby ratify and confirm.

4th - I wish all my just debts paid as soon after my death as convenient including all funeral expenses and Physicians Bills unpaid.

5th - I give & bequeath to the colored girl Rose now with me as much as three common bed quilts and comfortables - clothing for herself the present writer to be bought by my Executor and paid for out of first monies realized out of sales of property.

6th - I give and bequeath to my niece, Mollie Stringer, my side sadde.

7th - I give and bequeath to my nephew R. M. Stringer & niece Mollie Stringer jointly all my household and kitchen furniture including all beds, bedsteads, delphware, silver plater, [Page 127] spoons, knives, forks and every description of property or furniture connected with or belonging to in or about my home dwelling and kitchen excepting said quilts and side sadde, absolutely and forever, the said R. M. Stringer if he desires to do so can give to his sister Mollie his half of the Silverware. All the above bequests are specific.

I will and direct that all the rest and residue of personal property of every kind be sold by my Executor and out of the proceeds pay all my just debts.

8th - I will and direct that my Executor rent out my lands for the year 1879 until the rents shall when added to the rents of 1878 amount to a sufficent sum of money to erect an iron railing or fence around my grave which is to include the grave of my deceased husband James Jack by which I desire my remains to be deposited and also to pay to Rev. Thomas McCallie of Chattanooga

Tennessee as trustee for the benefit of the Presbyterian Church at Chattanooga, the present place of worship is now on Market Street between 6th & 7th in Chattanooga Tennessee the sum of Three (3) hundred dollars, and also to pay any portion of debts against my estate costs and charges of any kind that may remain after the proceeds of sales of personal property and all monies on hand and debts oweing to me or collected and applied to such indebtedness by my Executor.

9th - I will and devise all my real estate, situated in 3rd District in Hamilton County Tennessee, and also where subject to said renting aforesaid to my nephew R. M. Stringer, my niece Mollie Stringer & my nephew James C. Cobbs & John S. Cobbs, each taking one undivided fourth in all said land & real estate as tenant in common, the fee to rest at my death and actual possession taken when the monies are raised by the renting heretofore divested, which I believe ought to be with the end of the year 1879, this devise to include equitable rights and titles as well as legal, and any remainder of my estate real and personal, I give and devise to the said R. M. & Mollie Stringer & J. C. & J. S. Cobbs Share & Share alike, And, lastly I nominate & appoint James H. Ford Executor of this my last Will & Testament and he is not required to give bond & security as such Executor.

Witness my hand & seal Nov. 3rd 1877

Elizabeth H. Jack

Signed sealed & acknowledged in our presence & each of us and we [Page 128] each witness the same in the presence of the Testatrix at her request as her last will and testament this Nov. 3, 1877.

J. H. Van Deman

J. T. Stringer

[Page 128 con't]

H. D. MAY

The State of Tennessee

In the name of God Amen. I, H. D. May, of the County of Hamilton and State of Tennessee being in delicate health but of sound mind and disposing memory do make and publish this my last will and testament.

Item First - I desire all my just debts paid by my Executor as soon after my death as practicable.

Second - I own the house and lot where I & husband & mother now reside on Walnut Street in the City of Chattanooga Tennessee on the east side of said Street and between 2nd & 1st St. having purchased the lot before marriage and possessed of the same in fee and my husband being nearer and dearer in life to me than any other person, I desire him to have said property in exclusion of all other persons. I therefore devise to him Charles May the aforesaid house and lot and all erections and improvements thereon in fee simple - Coupled with this devise however, I request and enjoin it upon my said husband Charles May to provide a house and home for my mother, Martha G. W. Mooney for and during her natural life, should she be living at my death. He can either permit her to remain in the house herein devised with him or provide an other house for her to live in. My mother has means to live on of her own so that my husband is not charged with the costs of her support and maintenance.

Item 2nd - I also give devise and bequeath to my said husband Charles May, any and all other property real, personal, or mixed, including money choses in action and everything else of value to which I may die owner or have legal or equitable right to wherever situated.

And, I hereby constitute and appoint my husband Charles May, Executor of this my last Will and Testament, and he is expressly relieved of giving any bond or security as such Executor and the Courts of the County will not require it of him before assining him letters testamentary. The words "where I husband [Page 129] and mother now reside" interlined before signed.

In witness whereof I have in the absence of husband and mother & unknown to either of them signed my name to this my last will and testament. This May 11th 1877.

H. D. May (Seal)

This will was signed and sealed by the testatrix in our and each of our presence and we each signed our names to it in presence of the testatrix and in the presence of each other all at her request, she having first read and understood the same in our presence.

M. M. Trewhitt

Mary J. Trewhitt

Probated May 23rd 1878

THOS. J. CARLILE

State of Tennessee)

Hamilton County) Hereby revoking all former Wills or Codicils heretofore by me made I Thos. J. Carlile do hereby publish and declare that my last Will and Testament to be as follows, viz:

I hereby bequeath to my wife Marion A. Carlile all my property, real and personal of which I may die Seized and possessed after the payment of my just debts -

I hereby nominate and appoint my Said wife Marion A. Carlile to be the sole executrix of this my last Will and Testament, and Authorize and empower her to execute the same without the execution of any bond as required by law.

In testimony whereof I hereunto sign my name and affix my Seal this Tenth day of April A. D. 1876.

Thos. J. Carlile (S.S.)

Signed Sealed, delivered and published by the Said Thos. J. Carlile, as his last Will and Testament in our presence and we have hereunto at his request and in the presence of each other Signed our names and affixed our Seals as Witnesses thereto.

Walter C. Carlile (Seal)
Paul H. Ravesus (Seal)
Mary C. Haselton (Seal)

Probated and filed November 4th, 1878

T. A. Evans D. C.

[Page 130]

W. D. UNDERHILL

It is my Will, well Knowing the uncertainty of life, that all my property real and personal, and mixed, shall go to my Uncle E. P. Durando - I appoint him my Executor, and do require any bond of him when qualified to act. -
Thursday Morning Oct. 17, 1878.

W. D. Underhill (Seal)

Signed Sealed and published in our presence and we have Subscribed our names hereto in the presence of the testator Oct. 17, 1878.

E. M. Eaton
Frank Kelly

Will filed & probated Nov. 9, 1878

JAMES B. NORRIS

The following is my last Will and testament. I commend my Soul to God, my memory to Chattanooga -

1st - I wish all my debts to be paid.

2nd - My watch to be given to my Father and after his decease to my brother in law J. H. Van Deman.

3rd - My Copy of Byron to my Sister Joe.

4th - My Pocket Book to Willie Neauseur and my Shirt Studs.

5th - My Keystone to Dr. Van Deman also my Medical Books &c.

6th - My Copy of Shakespeare and also of Tennyson to my Sister Mrs. Scofield.

7th - My Phi Beta Kappa key to Miss Annie Tower.

I will and bequeath all my Real Estate and personal property to my dearest loved Sister Rebecca as she may deem best - I desire that my bedroom furniture be given to my loved Sister Florinda.

I hereby Will my case of Instruments to Dr. Long. I wish that Dr. Van Deman act as my Executor without bond.

Jas. B. Norris

Chattanooga Tenn. Aug. 30th 1878.
Witnesses

D. P. Henderson
M. S. Long

Will probated and filed Dec. 2nd, 1878

[Page 131]

LUCY C. SPENCER

Will of Lucy C. Spencer.

In the name of God Amen -

I Lucy C. Spencer of the Town of Hartford the County of Hartford and state of Connecticut being of Sound mind and memory, do make and publish this my last Will and Testament.

First - I will that all my debts and funeral charges by paid.

Second - I give and bequeath to my beloved Stepdaughters Delia S. Crandall and Abby A. Cheesebro, and to their lawful heirs the whole of my estate, to be equally divided between the two - In testimony whereof I hereunto Set my hand and Seal, and publish and decree this to be my last Will and Testament in the presence of the Witnesses named below, this nineteenth day of February in the year of our Lord One Thousand eight hundred and sixty eight.

Lucy C. Spencer (Seal)

The within instrument was Signed Sealed declared and published by the Said Lucy C. Spencer as and for her last Will and Testament, in presence of us, who at her request, and in her presence and in presence of each other have Subscribed our names as witnesses hereto.

H. H. Hayden
Lucretia L. Hayden

Charlotte E. Hayden
All of Hartford

Chattanooga Oct. 15th 1878

I hereby certify that the within Instrument was this day taken from an envelope, the Seal of which was broken by W. I. Crandall in my presence & in presence of Ruth A. Austin & Charles A. Austin, and that the within page of writing is all the writing contained in said envelope at time of breaking the Seal as above mentioned.

J. A. Austin

Filed and probated Dec. 4, 1878

[Page 132]

KATE WELSH

Will of Kate Welsh -

Hereby revoking all former Wills or Codicils by me at any time heretofore made - I do hereby make publish and declare my Last Will and Testament to be as follows.

After payment of my just debts and the expenses of my funeral I will and bequeath to my two Children - Hannah Cain and William Welsh to each an undivided one half, all my property real and personal absolutely forever.

I have two other children John Enright and Margaret Enright who are now fully grown and capable to take care of themselves. The small amount of property I leave is required for the support and maintenance of the two younger children - I hereby nominate and appoint my friend William Colter as the Sole Executor of this my last Will and Testament this December 19th 1878.

Kate X Welsh (Seal)
her mark

Signed and published in our presence and we have subscribed our names hereto in the presence of the testator this 19th day of December, 1878.

M. J. O'Brien
C. P. Jones
Tomlinson Fort

Filed Jan. 11th 1879 & probated 11/1/79.

AUGUSTUS P. GREEN

Will of A. P. Green

State of Tennessee)
Hamilton County   )

In the name of God Amen.

I, Augustus P. Green of the State and County aforesaid being of advanced age but of sound mind and disposing memory knowing that I must shortly depart this life, deem it right and proper, both as respects my family and myself, that I should make a disposition of the property with which a kind providence has blessed me - I do therefore make, ordain and declare this my last Will and Testament, hereby revoking and annulling all other or former wills, which may have been made by me.

Item first - I desire and direct that my body be buried [Page 133] in a decent and Christian like manner suitable to my condition and circumstances in life - My Soul I trust shall return to rest with God who gave it as I hope for Salvation through the merits and atonement of the blessed Lord and Savior Jesus Christ.

Item Second - I desire and direct that all my just debts be paid without hindrance or delay to my creditors by my executors hereinafter named and appointed.

Item Third - I give bequeath and devise to my beloved wife Mary Ann all the property both real and personal of which I may die seized and possessed to her own proper use, benefit and behoof for and during the term of her natural life or widowhood only.

Item Fourth - I desire and direct that in the event of the death or marriage of my said wife Mary Ann My executor herinafter named take charge of the property bequeathed in the third item of this will, and sell the same at public or private
Sale, and at Such time as may be deemed most conclusive of my legatees and devisees herein after named provided a reasonably fair price can be realized for said property.

Item Fifth - I give and bequeath to my children Emiley J. Howard formerly Emily J. Green, Mary E., Sarah H., William T., and Samuel E. Green the proceeds of the Sale of my property as directed in the fourth item of this will, Share and Share alike and if my said wife Mary Ann, should marry again - I direct that she take a childs portion of the proceeds of the Sale of the property before mentioned. Should any of my said Children die leaving issue - I desire that the Share or Shares, the one or ones dying would have taken, go to such issue and be paid to regularly appointed Guardian or Guardians in case of minority. Should any of my children die without issue, I direct that his or her share [burned] the brothers and Sisters Share and Share alike.

I hereby nominate constitute and appoint my beloved wife Mary Ann Green to Executrx and my beloved Son Samuel E. Green to be executor of this my last Will and Testament.

                    A. P. Green (Seal)
[Page 134]

Signed Sealed declared and published by Augustus P. Green as his last Will and Testament in the presence of us the undersigned, who subscribed our names hereto in the presence of Said Testator, and at his special instance and request, and in the presence of each other. This Feb. day of 5th 1870.

                    E. J. Carter
                    J. M. Pratchard
                    S. H. Conner

Probated & Filed)
Jany. 11, 1879)
    March 1st 1871 William T. Green son paid me in Cash Two hundred fifty dollars, which he is entitled to the Same out of this will.

                    A. P. Green

    Feb. 1st, 1872 - William T. Green son paid me in cash one hundred dollars which he is entitled to same out of this will.

                    A. P. Green

    March 1873 William T. Green my son paid me in Cash one hundred & fifty dollars which is entitled to the Same out of this Will.

                    A. P. Green

                    T. C. LUMPKIN

        Holographic Will of T. C. Lumpkin

    Know all men by these presents -
    That I Thomas Crutchfield Lumpkin of the City of Chattanooga, County of Hamilton and State of Tennessee being fully in possession of my mind and mental equanimily and knowing the uncertainty of life and feeling and acknowledging the duty and responsibility resting on me to make a proper distribution or disposition of my worldly effects, to be carried out by my executor after my death, should the all wise Creator see fit to take me before I make a wiser and better disposition of the Said effects I do therefore duly appreciating the situation and acknowledging the duty resting on me, make the following disposition of all my property -
    First - After paying any and all debts that I may

[Page 135] owe, and also my funeral Expenses that may be necessary to give me a decent burial - I do then give and bequeath to my only living Sister Sallie Pope Stewart, all my property both real and personal of every description, to have and to hold in her own right and name, and the same not to be subject to the control or disposition of her husband - Jas. R. Stewart in any manner whatever - It is my intention to give every thing I have to my Said Sister Sallie for her sole and separate use, to dispose of as she thinks properly during her life and whatever remainder if any of said estate, at her death I desire that the said remainder be judiciously invested for the use of my said Sisters daughters known as Maddie and "Bink" or as Maddie and Mary, to be given to them when they marry or reach the age of Eighteen years - The property that I own and herein bequeath to my Said Sister and daughter is viz. one brick Storehouse and lot No. 71 Broad Street in the City of Rome, State of Georgia, Now occupied by Ayer and McDonald as a hardware Store - also an undivided one half interest in a 27 or 30 acre tract of land more or less lying on the outskirts of Said City of Rome, Ga., near and adjoining "Fort Jackson" owned by myself and Robinson family, also my set of law Books, my gold watch and chain and my room furniture &c., being all I own in my own right and Title worth mentioning.

    It is my desire that my property be so disposed of - I have not forgotten my Mother to whom I am really indebted and whose happiness and interest I greatly desire but I know she owns enough of the goods of this world to supply all her demands - nor have I forgotten my brother Samuel Cleage Lumpkin, but he is a man and more able to battle with the world than my said Sister Sallie, hence I have made the foregoing disposal of all I own to my said Sister Sallie for life. Remainder over to her two daughters named and such is my last wish and will and I do hereby appoint and request that Col. D. S. Printup [Pages 136 & 137 blank - Page 138] of Rome Ga. will act as my executor and that he will See that this my will my wishes, as they are herein expressed in this "Holographic Will" (wholly written by me) will be carried out in Spirit and in letter.

    Witness my hand and Seal this May 4th 1876 Chattanooga, Tennessee.

                    T. C. Lumpkin (Seal)
Endorsed
    "Holographic Will" T. C. Lumpkin - completed with due deliberation
Chattanooga Tennessee
May 4, 1876   T. C. Lumpkin

    I wholly assign this Property named in this Will to my mother Sept. 26 1878.

                    T. C. Lumpkin

Robert Axmaker
Sam Starling
Filed Feb. 3rd, 1879

MARY BOYCE BILDERBACK

Last will and Testament of
Mrs. Mary Boyce Bilderback

Hereby revoking all wills and codicils by me at any time heretofore made. I hereby publish and declare my last will and Testament to be as follows viz:

Item 1st - After the payment of all my just debts and funeral expenses - I will and bequeath to my husband Joseph A. Bilderback all of the remainder and residue of my estate real and personal, if he survives me and I leave no child or children me surviving and if I have any child or children me surviving and my said husband also surviving me then I will and bequeath one moiety of the remainder and residue of said estate to my said husband Joseph A. Bilderback, and the other moiety of said remainder and residue of my said estate to any such child or children to each an equal undivided interest.

Item 2nd - I nominate and appoint my said husband Joseph A. Bilderback as the Sole Executor of this my last will and testament. [Page 139] (word "debts" interlined before signing)

This Janry. 2nd 1879
Mary Boyce Bilderback
(Sealed)

Signed Sealed and published in our presence and we have subscribed our names hereto in the presence of the testator - This 2nd day of Jany. 1879.
Tomlinson Fort
J. P. McMillin
James Spann Boyce

Probated and filed Mch. 3rd 1879.
T. A. Evans, D. C.

JACOB FRIST

Will of Jacob Frist
Chattanooga
Hamilton County Tennesee
March 14, 1879

Unto all whom it may concern.

This the Last Will and Testament of Jacob Frist Sr. of Chattanooga Hamilton County Tennessee.
Being of Sound mind and in the presence of the witnesses affixed hearunto

I Jacob Frist Sr. of Chattanooga Hamilton County, Tenn.

Do will and bequeath all my Real Estate and personal Property to wit: One house and Lot situated on Carter Street - Chattanooga Tenn. and one Lot of Land situated in the 4th District Hamilton County Tenn. containing Eighty Acres more or less with all my personal Property money &c that remain at my death to my wife Mary Frist for her benefit during her life and at her death Should their be any Real Estate or effects remain to be disposed of by will of my wife Mary Frist - And furthermore I request that my wife Mary Frist be appointed Administratrix to my will without Bond.
Jacob Frist

Witnessed
G. F. Brown
Henry W. Richard

Filed & probated May 7, 1879
T. A. Evans D. C.

[Page 140]

THOMAS ROBERTS

Will of Thomas Roberts

"And in hopes wounts have to make nary nother one"

State of Tennessee County of Hamilton.
In the name of God - Amen.

I Thomas Roberts of Said State & County being of advanced age & knowing that I must shortly die, deem it right & proper that I should make a disposition of the property that I may be possessed of at my death. I therefore make & declare this writing to be & contain my last Will as Testament.

Item 1st - I desire and direct that my body by buried in a decent & Christian like manner, Suitable to my circumstances & condition - My soul I trust will return to God who gave it - as I hope for eternal Salvation through the blessed Lord & Savior Jesus Christ.

Item 2nd - I give & bequeath to my beloved daughter Milly Matilda Roberts, widow of William Roberts deceased during her natural life & to be equally divided at her death amongst all her children, fifty acres of land in the south East corner of the South West fractional quarter of Section Eleven, third fractional Township - Fourth Range west of the Basis line in Ocoee District including the present residence of Said Milly Matilda Roberts, Said fifty acres of land bounded on the West by Reuben Wesley Roberts lands & on the south by land in possession of John C. Roberts.

Item 3rd - I have heretofore given to John C. Roberts my son, one hundred acres of land, being part of the fractional quarter bequeathed to Milly Matilda Roberts & part sold to my Grandson Reuben Wesley Roberts, on certain conditions mentioned in the agreement between my said son John C. and myself which writing is of record: now it is my wish and desire that said John C. shall not inherit or be entitled to any more of my property until all my other heirs have received as much as the said John C. Roberts.

Item 4th - I give and bequeath the remainder of my property except one bedstead and feather bed and furniture which I will bequeath to Milly Matilda Roberts, to the heirs of my Son Reuben Wesley Roberts Deceased & to the heirs of my two deceased daughters to wit - Tempy Marilda wife of William Lovelady deceased & Cynthia [Page 141] Anna, wife of William Compton Deceased, all residing so far as I know and believe in the State of Arkansas.

Item 5th - I give and bequeath to my daughter Milly Matilda Roberts one bedstead & one feather bed and furniture, in addition to the life time use & enjoyment of the fifty Acres of land bequeathed to her in Item Second.

Item 6th - In bequeathing the remainder of my property in Item fourth - I intend what shall be left after the payment of my just debts & funeral expenses are paid out of said remainder.

Item 7th - I hereby constitute and appoint my beloved son John C. Roberts, Executor to this my last Will & Testament.

Given under my hand & Seal this 24th day of April 1873.

                              Thos. Roberts (Seal)

Signed, Sealed, published & declared by the said Thomas Roberts as his last Will and Testament in the presence of us the subscribers, who subscribed our names hereto in the presence of Said Testator & in presence of each other, this 24th day of April, 1873.

    W. R. Wilson
    T. S. Howlett
    Thos. G. McFarland

Filed and probated August 4, 1879
           T. A. Goans, D. C.

[Page 142]

SAMUEL H. COREY

Last Will & Testament of Samuel H. Corey Decd.

State of Tennessee)
County of Hamilton)   I Samuel Harvey Corey being of Sound mind and aware that I may die, do hereby make the following as my last will and testament as my last desire. -

I desire that Thomas W. Crutchfield shall by my sole Administrator and executor of any and all effects real and personal to receive any and all moneys due me from any one including a $2000 Two Thousand dollar policy on my life as a member of the ancient Order of United Workmen, that he shall then pay all lawful and just debts against my estate, and that the residue shall be retained by him or invested by him for the benefit of my Two Children Richard Sparks Corey my only Son and Jennifer Frank Corey my only daughter to be disposed equeally between each of them.

In addition to property referred to the property of my deceased wife consisting of House & Lot on 8th St. in the City of Chattanooga Tenn and due bills and notes from R. D. Williams my late wife's Brother who resides in Jacksonville, Alabama - amounting to some Fifteen Hundred Dollars more or less, are included in this request, and it is my desire that Thomas W. Crutchfield my Sole Executor and Adminsitrator take full and absolute charge of said real Estate and personal property and to dispose of as he may deem proper for the interest of my Children.

I concur with my late wifes last request that N. J. Crutchfield shall be the guardian of my daughter Jennie and T. W. Crutchfield in conjunction with his mother Mrs. N. J. Crutchfield shall be the guardian of my son Sparks, bespeaking for them that they shall be to them a Father and Mother to the Orphans.

I desire that T. W. Crutchfield be qualified [Page 143] as my Sole executor and administrator without Bond.

Dated this Eleventh day of February A. D. 1879 at Chattanooga, Tenn.

           Samuel H. Cory

Subscribed and acknowledged by Mr. S. H. Corey as Signed by him for the full purposes and interests therein contained this Feb. 11, 1879 at Chattanooga, Tenn.

H. H. Sneed
John A. Lee, Sr.
E. Weber

Filed & probated Oct. 14, 1879

Entered on Record Book E No. 4 pages 265 & 266.

HASTEN POE

Will of Hasten Poe
I Hasten Poe do make and publish this my last Will and Testament.

First - It is my last will and desire that Asariah Poe have the Two Hundred & fifty Acres of land already conveyed to him by Deed and no more.

Second - I desire and will that Thomas Windham and the heirs of William Windham have the two hundred & forty Acres heretofore conveyed to them by Deed and no more.

Third - It is my will and desire that my daughter Elizabeth Condray have Six Hundred Acres of land Bounded on the North and South by the lands R. A. Hunter holds & claims, on the East by James & Isaac Lewis and on the West by the lands of Clift & McRee for and during her natural life.

Fourth - It is my Will and desire that my grand children W. H. Poe - H. H. Poe - J. H. Poe - Sarah E. Putnam formerly Sarah E. Poe and James A. Poe have the Several tracts of land heretofore conveyed to them by deed and in addition thereto I will and desire that at the death of my daughter Elizabeth Condray they have the remainder interest in common and in fee Simple in [Page 144] and to the Six hundred Acres given by me to her in this my last will.

In witness whereof I have on this the 25th day of July 1873 hereunto Set my hand and affixed my Seal in the presence of the subscribing witnesses who have also witnessed the same in my presence and in the presence of each other.

Hasten X Poe
his mark

Witness
William R. Mysinger
S. C. Hickman

GEORGE WILSON

I George Wilson of Chattanooga, Tennessee - being of Sound mind & disposing memory and conscious of the uncertainty of life, do make and publish this as my last Will and Testament.

1st - I desire all my just debts and funeral expenses to be first paid out of my effects.

2nd - I desire that my brother Hugh Wilson of Green Point, N. York, shall have one third of my Estate which shall remain after the payment of all my debts and funeral expenses, and expenses incident to the adminstration of my Estate.

3rd - I desire that my brother William Wilson of Brooklyn, N.Y. shall have one third of the residue of my Estate after the payment of my debts, funeral expenses & costs incident to administration as above stated. This to be paid to him by my Executor hereinafter named upon condition that my said brother William shall visit me at Chattanooga during my lifetime or within a reasonable time from this date, he having been notified of my present illness, and in the event of his failure to do so, then it is my will and desire -

4th - That my Sister Isabella & my father and mother all residents of Boggside Cottage Dunkreeneely [?] Post Office County Donegal Ireland shall have all the rest and residue of my Estate after paying the debts, costs, expenses and legacies herein before named including the legacy to my brother William in the event of his failure to visit me in obedience to the summons this day sent to him.

5th - I desire that my body shall be decently [Page 145] buried in the Confederate Cemetery at Chattanooga, Tennessee among my former comrades.

6th - I hereby nominate and appoint James W. Kelly and James McCann of Chattanooga Tennessee as Executors of this my last Will, and I desire them immediately after my death & burial as aforesaid, to sell all of my property and effects of every description for Cash, believing that money would be of more real assistance to the legatees herein before named, and I wish my said Executors to ascertain whether or not my Said brother William has complied with my wish that he visit me, herein before mentioned except the first to my brother Hugh.

In witness whereof I have hereunto set my Signature in the presence of witnesses at Chattanooga Tennessee This 31st Dec. 1879.

George Wilson (Seal)

Signed and sealed and acknowledged in our presence & we each witness the Signature at the request of the Testator & in the presence of each other.
J. A. Caldwell
Jno. G. Rawlings

Eugene C. Shelton

Filed and probated Jan. 9, 1880

[Page 146]

SARAH ANN COOPER

Will of Sarah Ann Cooper

I Sarah Ann Cooper of Chattanooga Hamilton County Tennessee make this my last Will and Testament - I will and bequeath all my property real, personal and mixed to my Sister Jane Croff, Walbrook, Cosely near Bilston Staffordshire England, after first paying my funeral expenses and any debts I may owe.

I appoint James Spencer and George Byron my Executors either of whom may qualify and act - and I waive any bond rquired of them as Executor or Executors.

I desire that my executor or Executives will Send my Iron Trunk, once the property of the late William Croft to his mother the Said Jane Croft. My personal estate other than the above mentioned and real Estate will be sold upon Such terms as may appear most advantageous to my Executor or Executors, and the proceeds remitted to my Said Sister Jane Croft.

My Real estate is (75) Seventy five feet of ground on Mott Street, running back Two Hundred (200) feet on Lindsey Street, and also Forty feet (40) on Mott Street adjoining part of lots Numbers Five (5) and (7) in Chattanooga, Tenn.

In witness whereof, I have Signed and Sealed and published and declare this Instrument - or will and testament June 20, 1879.

Sarah Ann Cooper (Seal)

Signed Sealed and published in our presence and we have subscribed our hands hereto in the presence of the testator this the 20th day of June 1879.

Eliza T. Nagle
Sophrony Wilson

Filed & probated Mch. 3, 1880.

[Page 147]

SARAH A. LEIGH

Will of Sarah A. Leigh

The State of Tennessee

Remembering that the term of Life in this world is uncertain and that death is sure but the time thereof is certain - and being of sound mind and disposing memory - I do make and declare my last Will and testament to be as follows to wit -

Item 1st - I resign my Soul to God who gave it.

Item 2nd - I desire that after my death my body by buried in a manner corresponding to my property and condition in life, and in the manner of Christian burials.

Item 3rd - I direct all my debts to be paid, out of my property, which I may owe at my death, and which could be enforced against me at law.

Item 4th - I will, bequeath and devise all my personal property, monies, choses in action, bequests or gifts to me or coming to me by distribution or descent, from any one whether reduced to possession by me or not in my life time, so far as the law allows me to dispose of the Same by Will, however situated owing or being, to my children of my body born - Share & Share alike, the children or grand children of deceased children, to take such shares as their parent would have taken, if such parent had have been living at my death.

Item 5th - In like manner I will and devise to the Same Said Children and grand and great grand children, all the real Estate I may die owner of in law or equity, they to take respectively in quantities, and in manner as directed in Item 4th as to personal property, the device includes specially the House and Lot I now own on Cherry Street between 4th & 5th Streets in the City of Chattanooga in Hamilton County, Tennessee and described as follows to wit.

Item 6th - I will and direct that immediately on my death, if any of my devises and Legatees be under twenty one years of age, that the Chancery Court of the County where the property is situated take jurisdiction of Said and distribute to same to those entitled under this will in the proportions to each [Page 148] as he, she or they may be entitled with all rents.

Item 7th - If at my death I leave no child living nor grand nor great grand children, then all my property real and personal shall go & vest in fee as tenants in common in my brothers and Sisters, and the children of such as may be dead Share and Share alike as to living brother & Sisters & children of deceased brothers & Sisters are to represent their deceased parent.

Item 8th - My will is that my husband whoever he may be shall have no part of my property either absolutely or for life, nor is he to touch or handle it in any way as husband, father, Trustee or in his own right or in any manner whatever, and if a Guardian or Trustee is to be appointed I desire some other person to act as such.

In witness wher_of_ I have hereto Set my hand and Seal this September 29th A. D. 1879.

Sarah A. Leigh (Seal)

Signed Sealed and acknowledged to be the last Will and testament of Sarah A. Leigh in our presence and in presence of each other and of the testator and we bear witness to the Same in the presence of the Said Testatrix at her Special request.

Mary J. Trewitt
Caroline Trewitt

Filed and probated April 13th 1880.

[Page 149]

CAROLINE M. VINEYARD

Will of Caroline M. Vineyard

State of Tennessee)
Hamilton County) This is the last and only Will made by Caroline Vineyard made this twenty Sixth day of August 1880-

First - I will to Winfield Scott Vineyard One hundred Dollars $100.00 to be paid to him by Margaret Mowbray Fitzgerald and Mary Lou Vineyard - And to Marg^t Mowbray Fitzgerald and Mary Lou Vineyard I will equal portions to the rest of the property known as one Lot West 52 200 feet with all improvements thereon - Said lot fronts on Mott Street and is registered in Book V pages 14 & 15 in Chattanooga Hamilton County State of Tennessee.

Caroline Marg^t X Vineyard (Seal)
her mark

Witness my mark and Seal this Aug. 26, 1880.
Harry Wilcox (Seal) Witness
Mrs. H. R. Bowers (Seal) Witness

Probated Sept. 6th 1880
Filed Sept. 6, 1880
Entered and enrolled on Record Book 4, pages 438 & 439.

[Page 150]

LUCIUS P. BRIGHT

Will of Lucius P. Bright.

I Lucius P. Bright, a citizen of Hamilton County Tennessee hereby make and publish this my last Will & testament, revoking all others by me at any time heretofore made -

1 - I will and bequeath to my brother J. D. Bright, my gold watch and chain.

2 - After the payment of all my just debts, and funeral expenses, I will and bequeath to my Brother William J. Bright all the balance of my estate of every kind, and description, whether real personal or mixed. I do this in consideration of the fact, that my Said Brother William has devoted the earnings of his past life to the support of our parents and the support and education of our younger brothers and Sisters, and in case of my death, this duty which I have heretofore shared with him, will fall on him alone, my object being to indemnify him for the past, and aid him in the future -

3rd - I hereby nominate and appoint my said Brother William J. Bright, Executor of this my will, with full power and authority to sell any or all of my property, either real or personal, and to make deed to Same, with full discretion, as to the time terms and manner of Such Sale, and I desire that he be exc_use_ from giving bond as such Executor & so direct. This April 9, 1879.

Lucius P. Bright

Filed Sept. 8, 1880

[Page 151]

ARMSTEAD LEWIS

Will of Armstead Lewis

State of Tennessee Hamilton County

I Armstead Lewis being in feeble health, but of Sound mind and disposing Memory and calling to mind the uncertainty of this transitory life - Do make this my last will and testament -

First - I desire that my Funeral expenses and all debt be paid as soon as practicable out of the proceeds of my personal property (not otherwise bequeathed) by my Executor hereinafter named -

Second - I give and bequeath to Martha Spann in consideration of her kindness to me during my sickness (18) Eighteen Acres of land to include all in the following boundry beginning at the S. E. corner of the S. W. Quarter of Section 26, Township 2 Range 5 West of the

Basis line, being corner to the House Camp ground and Shelton Lands. Thence N. 70° W. to a stone Thence N. 20 E. to the E. T. Va. Ga. Railroad. Thence Eastwardly along said Railroad to the line between me and the House Camp Ground Lands - Thence S. 20° W. to the beginning corner. This includes the Homestead or Building that I now occupy and is a part of my Homestead Tract. I also give and bequeath to her One White Counterpane, 2 Pillows and one Mule.

Third - I give and bequeath to G. W. Timmons 1 Small Feather Bed - 1 Mattress 1 Knotty White Counterpane.

Fourth - I give and bequeath to William Spann all of my Books.

Fifth - I give and bequeath to my Brother Granville Lewis Heirs of Nashville 100 acres of land, being the remainder of the Lands conveyed to me by Campbell Wallace by deed of Record in the Registers Office of Hamilton County Book W, page 679 & 680 - and by G. W. House Et Als by deed not yet registered after taking out the 18 acres heretofore mentioned and 1 1/2 Acres given by me to Lewis Camp Ground.

Sixth - I give and bequeath to the Heirs of my beloved Sister Sallie Lewis my House [Page 152] and lot in the Town of Chattanooga Tennessee except thirty front feet - I desire that my Executor sell the thirty feet and apply the proceeds to the payment of my debts, provided the property already set aside for the purpose is not sufficient, the overplus from the proceeds of Said Sale I desire if any to be paid over by my Executor to my said Sister Sallie's heirs.

Seventh - I desire that after paying my funeral Expenses and all my debts, that the remainder of my personal property be divided equally between my brother Granville and Sister Sallies' Heirs.

Eighth - My wife Sarah having more than Seven years ago committed adultery and abandoned me I desire and so will and devise that she shall take no part or lot of my Estate by dower or otherwise commending her if by chance if she should yet live to repentance for her great crime against me -

Ninth - I hereby nominate and constitute and appoint William Lewis of Chattanooga Tennessee my Sole Executor of this my last Will and Testament on this the 19th day of February in the year of our Lord 1878.

Armstead X Lewis
his mark

Witness   H. J. Springfield
               James M. Davis

The foregoing instrument was Signed

acknowledged and published in our presence by Armstead Lewis as his last Will and Testament and we have there unto signed our names as subscribing witnesses in the presence of and at the request of the Testator and in the presence of each other This the 19th day of February 1878.
H. J. Springfield
James M. Davis

Probated and filed Jany. 7th 1881

Enrolled on Record No. 4 pages 523 & 524

[Page 153]

DELIA S. CRANDALL

Will of Delia S. Crandall

Know all men by these prsents - That I, Delia S. Crandall wife of Washington I. Crandall of the City of Green Bay County of Brown State of Wisconson, being of a sound deposing mind and memory do make and publish this my last Will and Testament.

First - I give and bequeath to my beloved daughter Julia S. Crandall five hundred dollars ($500), if she is Twenty one years of age at the time of my death, is unmarried or has married with my appropation. If she is not Twenty one years of age when this will takes effect and remains single until said age, she shall have legal interest from her eighteenth birthday on the Sum of Five hundred dollars, said interest to be paid to her semiannually, and the Said five hundred dollars shall be paid to her on her twenty first birthday; or if She marries after this will take effect with the approbation of her father, before she is Twenty one years of age the said sum of five hudnred dollars shall be paid to her on her wedding day and interest cease with the payment thereof.

Second - I give and bequeath to my beloved daughter Molly S. Crandall five hundred Dollars ($500) upon the same terms conditions and benefits set forth in my first bequest.

Third - I give and bequeath to my beloved daughter Lucy S. Crandall five hundred Dollars ($500), upon the same terms conditions and benefits set forth in my first (1) bequest.

Fourth - I give and bequeath to my beloved daughter Martha S. Crandall five hundred Dollars ($500) upon the same terms conditions and benefits set forth in my first bequest.

Fifth - In case I have other children born to me

of either Sex after this will is Signed and Sealed I give and bequeath to each such one the Sum of Five hundred Dollars upon the Same terms, conditions & benefits set forth in my first bequest.

Sixth - Circumstances in regard to the younger children may occur, when the Executor might deem it proper to give the benefits of the intended bequests an earlier date than mentioned above on account of their Education, in which case some discretion may be exercised; but the object of these bequests is to give my children a Marriage Dower beyond a doubt.

Seventh - I give and bequeath to my beloved husband [Page 154] Washington I. Crandall all the rest and residue of my estate, personal & real or property that may be in my name at the date of this will or that may accrue thereon thereafter.

Eighth - In case the residue of my estate, after the several legacies to my children, does not amount to ($5000) five thousand dollars, the separate bequest to each of my children may be reduced in the proportion of one dollar to ten dollars of the residue given to my husband so that the proportion of $500 each to $5000.00 to him shall be preserved, provided my husband does not marry again, the bequest to each of my children shall be five hundred dollars; if my whole estate amounts to five thousand dollars $5000.

Ninth - In case my husband as above named should die before myself the testator, this Will and Testament is revoked and becomes null and void.

Tenth - I appoint and ordain my husband Washington I. Crandall Sole Executor and Trustee to hold and carry out the provisions of this my last Will and Testament.

In testimony whereof I have hereunto set my hand and Seal and publish and declare this to be my last Will and Testament in the presence of witnessees named below this 27th day of January in the year A. D. 1870 Eighteen hundred and Seventy.

Delia S. Crandall (Seal)

Signed, Sealed published and declared by the Said Mrs. Delia S. Crandall as and for her last will and Testament in the presence of us who at her request and in her presence and in the presence of each other have Subscribed our names as witnesses thereof & thereto.

Rosa Burkhart (S.S)
Lucy G. Spencer (S.S.)
W. H. Norris Jr. (S.S.)

Probated January 4, 1881
T. A. Evans, D. C.

[Page 155]

R. W. CORBIN

Will of R. W. Corbin

Knowing how uncertain life is, and wishing to leave my property shoudl I die as I would have it could I live - I now write my orders in its disposion. The law makes the best will but I wish to make a little alteration.

First - I want my debt and funeral expenses paid.

Second - My life is insured for the benefit of my children, this Sum I desire to be charged to them as part of their Share of all my property.

Third - I give to my daughter Marion a lot I wish charged to my daughter Mrs. Marion Simpson at Two hundred & fifty dollars as part of her interest.

Fourth - I make the above Statement that these different sums in making an equal division of all shall be deducted from their whole interest.

Fifth - the law provides for my wife, but she if she thinks proper may take a child's part, and I leave it to her to break up housekeeping or do as she may think best. I make no distinction in my children they are all to share alike those now living and should any more be born to us.

Sixth - I leave to my grandchild Johnson Corbin an equal share with the rest of my children conditionally, have a guardian appointed who must give good Security, to take charge of what may be due her, and should she live to be of age or marry then the amount shall be paid over to her. Should she die before maturity or marriage then the money or property to revert back to my wife and children.

Witness my hand & Seal this 10th day of September 1873.

R. W. Corbin

Chattanooga Tenn.

My life is insured for the benefit of my first wife & children but my wife dying, I am her heir and I bequeath the same to my present wife Mary A. & her children this 15th day of April 1874.

R. W. Corbin

I have given Louisa E. Woodward my daughter a lot which must be charged to her in the disposition of my effects at Two hundred an fifty dollars ($250).

R. W. Corbin

Test-   [Page 156]
         John M. Brown
         L. M. Clark

Codicil

If any grand child after marrying should die without issue then the property to revert back to my wife & children.

R. W. Corbin

Endorsed

"Memo made by
R. W. Corbin"

Filed and probated April 4, 1881
T. A. Evans, Dep. Clerk

[Page 157]

ALLEN C. BURNS

Will of Allen C. Burns

Knowing the uncertainty of life, I desire now while still in the full possession of health and my mental faculties to make my last Will and Testament.

To my dear parents I give a support as long as either of them may live in amount and manner as follows - To my father James O. Burns I give a yearly allowance of ($360) Three hundred & Sixty dollars, to be paid to him in Quarterly installments so long as he may live. And to my mother Mrs. E. D. Burns the Same amount and in the Same manner - Say ($360) Three Hundred & Sixty Dollars every year in Quarterly installments So long as she may live. If there be not enough of money or personal effects, then let my real estate be sold -either in part or whole as may seem best to my executors in order to raise money to furnish my parents the allowance as stipulated above.

To Mrs. Ellen N. Burns my dearly beloved wife - I give the remainder of my property of every kind, class, character or description in fee simple to her and her heirs forever.

As will be seen by the above - I do not contemplate that my wife shall come into the possession of my property until my parents both shall have departed this life.

I hereby appoint James N. Trigg, Tom Crutchfield and W. D. Van Dyke all or either of them to execute and carry out the provisions of this my last will and testament.

This 26th October 1871.

Allen C. Burns

Attest

J. N. Trigg
J. F. Slover Jr.

Edgar McKinney

Filed and probated May 19, 1881.
T. A. Evans, D. C.

[Page 158]

BENJAMIN C. BUFORD

Will of Benjamin C. Buford

State of Tennessee)
Hamilton County)   I Benjamin C. Buford of Said State and County, being of sound mind and disposing memory make this my last Will-

1st - I desire that all my just debts be paid-

2nd - I give and devise unto my brother William F. Buford and unto the Children of my brother John L. Buford all my property both real and personal - to be shard as follows to wit: The Said William F. Buford shall have one halk of said property, and the other half of said property shall be equally distributed among the said children of my said Brother John L. Buford.

3rd - It is my desire that my Executor pay the notes given by me for the purchase money of store house and lot on Market Street Chattanooga Tennessee belonging to me and in which I now have a stock of family groceries, as they may fall due, and to this end I authorize and direct my Executor to keep all of my said property together for the purpose of paying said notes, until they are fully paid. I further authorize and direct him to continue my present business as grocer merchant, until the time of payment of the last note of said notes, shall have elapsed - when said notes shall have been paid, all my said property shall be distributed as directed in Second section of this Will -

4th - I nominate and appoint my cousin Milton H. Matthews Executor of this my last Will - and it is my desire and request that he act as such, without giving bond of any character whatsoever.

5th - It is my desire that my said Executor be paid a reasonable compensation for his Services as Executor, and for conducting my business as grocer merchant as herinbefore directed.

In witness whereof I have Signed and Sealed and published and declared this Instrument as my last Will at Chattanooga, Tennessee.

Benjamin C. Buford (Seal)

The said Benjamin C. Buford at said Chattanooga

Tennessee on said seventh day of May Eighteen Hundred & Eighty one Signed and Sealed this Instrument and published and declared the same as for his last Will - And we at his request and his [Page 159] presence of each other have hereunto written our names as subscribing witness.

C. P. Gorce
A. J. Stoops
M. H. Brooks

"Endorsed"

Filed and probated June 6th 1881 & enrolled on Record No. 4 pages 576, 577.

[Page 160]

MATTY WORTHEY

Last Will and Testament of Mrs. Matty Worthey.

I Matty Worthey being of Sound mind and disposing memory and knowing the uncertainties of life do make publish and Establish this my Last Will and Testament.

1st - It is my will that all my just debts by paid -

2nd - I hereby bequeath and devise to my beloved husband Samuel H. Worthy all my property of every kind and nature whatsoever and whereever situated, particularly Lot 2 Block 4 Stantons Spring Addition to Chattanooga Tenn. conveyed to me by T. G. Montague & others.

3rd - I hereby appoint nominate and constitute my Said husband the Executor of this my last Will and testament - This 2nd August 1881.

Mattie Worthey

Signed, Sealed, published, pronounced and declared by the Said Matty Worthey as and for her last Will and Testament in the presence of us & who in her presence & at her request, and in the presence of each other have hereunto subscribed our names as witnesses.

A. Reynolds
Jesse Blanton

Filed Sept. 5, 1881
L.M. Clark Clerk
per T. A. Evans, D. C.

For probate see Record No. 4 page 605

[Page 161]

Z. T. HUNNICUTT

I, Z. T. Hunnicutt of the City of Chattanooga do make and publish this my last will & testament.

1st I directd that my body be interred properly, and the expense be deducted from my property.

2nd I direct that all my debts be paid as soon after my decease as possible.

3rd I direct that my goods be sold at private sale and the money be placed in the hands of my Executor hereinafter appointed for the use of my only child Eva Hunnicutt, as also all of my cash and monies received from outstanding accounts due us and amounts due from my brother D. M. Hunnicutt living at Nashville I also authorize my Executor to get my shot gun now with W. E. DePorte at South Pittsburg & hold the same for the use of my beloved daughter Eva do also my gold watch from Mr. Kirby's to be held by him for the same purpose & to the same end.

4th I direct that my Executor out of my money pay to my Sister Mrs. Kate Pfrumer one hundred and fifty (150) dollars. And to my Sister Mrs. M. E. Locke Fifty ($50.00) Dollars in consideration for services rendered me. Also to my Sister Mrs. Kate Pfrummer I give & bequeath all my household furniture.

5th I do further authorize my Executor to compromise the difference between Dr. Frayer & myself as to the note which I hold of W. Alexander to the best possible advantage & the proceeds resulting therefrom to be placed with the rest of my property & money & to be used for the Same purpose.

6th I direct & request that Mr. Charlie Wright act as my executor & carry out to the best of his ability the letter of this my last Will. It is my wish no bond be required of my executor above appointed.

7th I give my daughter Eva Hunnicutt to the keeping of my Sister Mrs. Dronce Baker living at Bakers Station Tennessee hoping that She will kindly treat her, give her a good education & bring her up according to her proper Station in life and bring her up in the Catholic Religion.

I witness whereof I Z. T. Hunnicutt have to this my last Will & Testament Set my hand & Seal this 4th day of November 1881 [Page 162] in the presence of & before the Subscribing Witnesses.

Z. T. Hunnicutt (Seal)

Witnesses:
W. L. Horan
Charles H. Gorman
P. A. Browner, Jr.

Files & Probated Nov. 7th 1881
T. A. Evans D. C.

GEORGE CARROL BROWNE

Last Will & Testament of George Browne.

Chattanooga, Tenn.
Sept. 30, 1881
In the name of God Amen -

I, George Carrol Browne - William St. Chatta. Tenn. being in Sound mind and memory do hereby make, publish, and declare this to be my last Will and Testament, hereby revoking all former wills by me at any time heretofore made.

1st - I order and direct my Executor as soon after my decease as practicable to pay off and discharge all the debts, dues, and liabilities that may exist against me at the time of my decease.

2nd - I give and bequeath to my respected friend and Housekeeper Mrs. Mattie Butterworth who has nursed me long and faithfully through a severe illness, my House and lot on Wm. St. and all personal property of every description.

George Browne

Witness
A. J. Hicks
J. T. Tippins

Filed and probated Nov. 7, 1881
T. A. Evans D. C.

[Page 163]

J. P. ROBERTS

Will of J. P. Roberts

Soddy Hamilton County Tenn.
To all whom it may concern
I hereby authorize R. F. Roberts to collect all notes or accounts I have here in Tennessee and in case of my death before any of my children are of age or competent of doing for themselves. It is my request that the Said R. F. Roberts act as their Guardian and that he have Power to collect and Settle any and all of my business here or elsewhere, and to appropriate the Same to the use of my wife & children, as he may think best and

proper under Such circumstances as may exist, given under my hand and Seal this the 10th day of October 1879.
J. P. Roberts

Attest
M. B. McRee
J. A. Anderson

Filed and probated Dec. 7, 1881
T. A. Evans D. C.

[Page 164]

J. P. McMILLIN S^r

Will of J. P. McMillin S^r.

I, J. P. McMillin S^r. being in ordinary health and of sound mind in view of the uncertainlty of life, & the certainty of death do make this my last Will and testament.

1st - I give & bequeath to my sone James P. McMillin Ten thousand dollars ($10,000.00) as follows

Cash already advanced	$ 3000
Abel B. Beeson's Note which I hold for (with trust)	3000
Chas. W. Vinson	4000
	$10000

2nd - I give and bequeath to my son D. Cal McMillin Ten Thousand dollars ($10,000.00) as follows

D. Giles & Co. Note which I hold with trust for	$ 6000
C. P. Robertson's Note with trust which I hold for	4000
	$10000

3rd - I give and bequeath to my daughter Ann Cravens McMillin Ten thousand Dollars ($10,000) to be paid to her out of the remainder of my Estate, when she arrives at the age of twenty years or to be placed at interest or invested for her benefit to be provided for my Executor unless she should marry sooner, in which event it shall be paid to her provided She marries a man that is likely to take care of & not Squander it (my executors and the survivors of them to be the Judges) otherwise to remain in the control & Supervision of my Executors & the survivors of them & loaned out at interest or invested for her benefit. At the demise however of Said Executors and the last of them, it shall be given into her own control and management.

4th - I give & bequeath to my dear wife Nancy Jane McMillin all the remainder of my Estate of every kind & description, lands & benefits, Notes with their trusts, accounts & monies on hand or on deposit, to be hers for and during her natural life, that she may have & maintain a home that shall be a common resort & bond of Union to the family - With power to sell, exchange, purchase, reinvest, lease, rent, sue or otherwise dispose of at pleasure, or when thought to be advisable with the consent & advise of her Co-executors, or at least one of them, so that there shall be a majority of the three in favor of the proposed transaction - At her death Same with accumulations or remainder thereof to be equally divided between our children Share & [Page 165] Share alike - Or to the children of deceased parents. That is to say if any one or more of our children should die before She does, then that portion that would have fallen to that Son or daughter shall go to their children provided they have any, and if they should have no children then one half of Said portion shall go to the widow or Husband as the case may be, & the balance shall be equally divided among the living of our children and their living children as above indicated.

5th - I charge my said wife with the raising maintenance & education of our daughter Ann Cravens until she attains her majority & becomes possessed of the above bequest or the interest & profits arising therefrom and I charge her also with the burial Expense & the payment of my debts which are very small.

6th - I hereby appoint my sons James P. and D. Cal and my wife Nancy Jane my Executors and Executrix of this my last will & testament - No bond to be required of them or either of them.

The C. P. Robertson Note having been paid to me, Since the foregoing was written - it will therefore be necessary and I hereby direct that the amount of Four thousand dollars be made up to D. Cal McMillin in Notes, money & otherwise.

In the name of God Amen. Chattanooga Tenn. In the A. D. 1881 July 24th.

M. P. McMillin Sr.

In presence of and at Testator request
J. W. Elder Jr.
C. P. Robertson

Filed May 1st 1882

Probated May 1st 1882 in Record Book No. 4 pages 707-708 & 709

L. M. Clark Clerk
per T. A. Evans, Dep. Clerk

[Page 166]

JOSEPH WILLIAMS

Will of Joseph Williams, Deceased

I Joseph Williams being now of Sound Mind and disposing memory, and knowing the uncertainty of life, and being desirous to fix up all my worldly affairs before I die make this my last Will and Testament.

First - I will my Soul to God who gave it.

And Second - that all my debts and funeral expenses be paid out of my property Real and personal after which I give and bequeath to my beloved wife Dianer Williams on condition She takes care of me while I live and pays the taxes on same one hundred by fifty feet fronting fifty feet on Gilmer Street and running back of uniform width one hundred feet, being part of a lot of land conveyed to me by G. A. Clark on the 31st of December 1869, and the South East corner of Block twelve in Griffins Addition to Chattanooga in Hamilton County Tennessee, and it is my will that my Said Wife Dianer be her own Executor without Bonds. I have reserved fifty feet off the back end of the above described lot for the purpose of Selling it, but if I should not Sell it while I live, then it is my Will, that my wife have it as the other above described part of Said lot - this 7th day of August 1875.

Joseph X Williams
his mark

The foregoing Will was read to and Signed by Joseph Williams by making his mark, as his last Will and Testament this 7th day of August 1875 in our presents.

J. H. Light
M. R. Thurman
J. C. Rowden
A. G. W. Pucket

Probated May 1st 1882 - See Record No. 4 pages 711 & 712.

[Page 167]

DORCAS A. RUSSELL

Will of Dorcas A. Russell

I, Dorcas A. Russell of the City of Chattanooga

Hamilton County Tennessee do make and publish this my last Will and Testament.

I give devise and bequeath my Estate and property both real and personal as follows that is to say - To my two daughters Margaret Russell and Jennie T. Brown both of Chatanooga Tennessee described as follows -

The South half of lot No. 45 on Cyprus Street in said City, and fronting on said Cyprus Street 50 ft. and running back of uniform width on the North 160 ft. and on the South 180 feet to Section line, bounded on the South by M. J. O'Brien's lot - Being the Same house and lot where I now live -

I also give and bequeath to my Said two daughters Margaret Russell and Jennie T. Brown, all my house furniture in said house and on Said lot hereby bequeath, and all my personal property of every kind and description, consisting mostly of one Cow, house furniture and cooking utensils - I give it all to them absolutely. -

I nominate and appoint Thomas C. Russell of the City of Chattanooga Executor of this my last Will and Testament, and he is excused from and not required to give bond as such Executor.

I hereby revoke all Wills by me heretofore made.

In witness whereof I Dorcas A. Russell, the above named testatrix have hereunto set my hand and Seal on this 12th day of Jan. 1881.

Dorcas X A. Russell (Seal)
her mark

The said Dorcas A. Russell at her said home in Chattanooga Tennessee on 12th day of Jan. 1881, signed and Sealed this instrument and published and declared the same as and for her last Will and Testament and we at her request and in her presence, and in the presence of each other have hereunto written our names [Page 168] as Subscribing witnesses.

M. M. Hope
Rosina Karsten

Endorsed

Filed June 5, 1882
L. M. Clark Clerk
per T. A. Evans D. C.

Probated June 5/82
L. M. Clark Clerk
per T. A. Evans D. C.

[Page 169]

WILLIAM MOWBRAY

Will of William Mowbray, Deceased

Suffolk County -- Be it remembered that at a Surrogates Court held at and for the county of Suffolk November 23, 1875 - Present Henry P. Hedges, Surrogate, the last Will and Testament of William Mowbry late of the Town of East Hampton in Said County deceased was duly proved before the Said Henry P. Hedges the Said Surrogate as a valid Will of Real and personal Estate, which Will and proofs are as follows -

"In the name of God Amen"

"I William Mowbray at present residing in the City of New York but being about to resume my residence in the State of Tennessee, being of sound mind and memory and considering the uncertainty of this life do therefore make ordain publish and declare this to by my last Will and Testament as follows, that is to say.

I give, devise and bequeath all the real and personal property, estate and effects I may own or possess, at the time of my decease, subject to the payment of all my just debts and funeral expenses to my brother Thomas H. Mowbray, of the City and state of New York his heirs and assigns forever.

And I do make constitute and appoint my Said brother Thomas H. Mowbray, Sole Executor of this my last Will and Testament, hereby revoking all former Wills made by me -

In witness whereof I have hereunto Subscribed my name and affixed my Seal this tenth day of September 1867.

William Mowbray, L. S.

The foregoing Will was Sealed and Subscribed by the Said William Mowbray, at the end thereof, in the presence of Each of us, he at the same time declaring the same to be his last Will and Testament, and we at his request in his presence, and in the presence of each other have hereto subscribed our names as witnesses.

Chas. Judson - No. 16 Union Square New York
Chas. A. Davidson - 264 Bowery New York City
Wm. H. Heyburger - 226 Washing St. New York City

[Page 170]

Suffolk County Surrogate Court)
In the matter of proving   )
the last Will and Testament   ) Suffolk County

of William Mowbray Decd.   ) State of New   York
        Oliver Mowbray of Stamford in the State of Connecticut being duly sworn by and before his Honor Henry P. Hedges Surrogate of the County of Suffolk deposes and says - That the instrument now produced and offered for probate is the last Will and Testament of his brother William Mowbray late of Say Harbor deceased - That the Signature thereto attached is the Signature of said William Mowbray, and that he is well acquainted with the Signature of Said Testator.
        That Said William Mowbray on the 10th day of September 1867, the date of Said Will was 50 years of age and was of Sound Mind - That he is well acquainted with the Signature of the Witnesses to Said Will, Charles A. Davidson and William H. Heyberger personally and had known them for many years - That the Signatures of the witnesses to Said Will are the true Signatures of said Charles A. Davidson and William H. Heyberger respectively and that the Said William H. Heybeger is now deceased, that he died in the Spring of 1875 in the City of Brooklyn, and that the said Charles A. Davidson is a non resident of this State, being a resident of Chattanooga in the sate of Tennessee.
        Oliver Mowbray
Sworn to before me this 26th day of October 1875.

Suffolk County Surrogate Court
In the matter of proving)
the Last Will and Testa-) Suffolk County
ment of William Mowbray)
Deceased
        Be it remembered that on the 23rd day of November in the year One Thousand Eight Hundred and Seventy five before Surrogate Henry P. Hedges, Surrogate of said County, personally appeared [Page 171] Charles Judson, who being by the Said Surrogate duly sworn and examined, doth depose and say, that the deponent was well acquainted with William Mowbray deceased; that he was present as a witness, and did see the Said William Mowbray deceased, subscribe at the end thereof of the instrument now produced and shown to the deponent, purporting to be the Last Will and Testament of the said William Mowbray deceased, bearing date the 10th day of September in the year one Thousand Eight hundred and sixty Seven, that Such Subscription was made by the Said Testator in the rpesence of this deponent, that the Said Testator, at the same time declared the Instrument so Subscribed by him to be his last Will and Testament, whereupon this deponent Signed his name at the end thereof, at the request of Said Testator, and that the Said Testator at the time of executing and publishing the Said last Will and Testament, was of full age, of sound mind

and memory, and not under any restraint - This deponent further Says that Chas. A. Davidson & William A. Heyberger whose names purport to be signed as Witnesses to Said Will were present at its execution with this deponent, and the said testator & at the request of the Said Testator and in his presence Signed their names as Such Witnesses in presence of this deponent and that the Said Signatures purporting to be the Signatures Severally of the Said Davidson and Hyberger are genuine, and in the proper handwriting of each - That the testator Signed his name to said instrument and declared the Same to be his last Will & Testament previous to the Signatures of any of these Witnesses thereto but did so in the presence of all of them & at the time of the execution of Said Instrument.

        Charles Judson

Suffolk County - It appearing from the proofs duly taken in respect to the Last Will and Testament of William Mowbray deceased, that the Said Will was duly executed, and that at the time of the execution thereof, the Said William Mowbray was in all respects competent to devise real Estate and not [Page 172] under any restraint, the Said last Will and Testament and the proofs and examinations taken thereon are hereby recorded, Signed and certified by me this 23rd day of November 1875.
        H. P. Hedges, Surrogate

        At a Surrogates Court held at the Surrogates office in Bridgehampton in and for Suffolk County on the 23rd day of November 1875 -   Present Henry P. Hedges Surrogate
In the matter of   )
proving of the Will)
of William Mowbray)
Deceased   )
        This matter having been duly adjourned to this day and place, and Thomas H. Mowbray the executor in Said Will named, having appeared as Special Guardian for William Des Rochers, John Des Rochers and Oliver Des Rochers, minor heirs at law and next a kin of Said deceased and no one else appearing.
        Ordered that further proof be now taken and on taking and filing proofs Showing the due execution of Said Will, and the Surrogate being Satisfied that Said Will was duly executed, that the Testator at the time of making Said will was in all respects competent to devise real Estate and under no restraints, and that Said Will is genuine and valid - Ordered that Said Will be admitted to probate as a valid will of real and personal Estate, and that the Same together with the proofs and examinations taken thereon be recorded in the Office and that Letters testamentary of

Said Will be issued to Thomas H. Mowbray the Executor in Said Will named.

H. P. Hedges Surrogate

State of New York)
Suffolk County   )
Surrogates Office)   I James H. Tuthill Surrogate of the County of Suffolk in the State of New York do hereby certify that I have compared the annexed copy of the last Will and Testament of William Mowbray late of the town of East Hampton in Said County of Suffolk deceased and of the probate thereof and the decree [Page 173] admitting the Same to probate with the original record thereof now recmaining in Said Surrogates office and that it is a just and true copy of Such original record and of the whole thereof, and I further certify that as Such Surrogate I have no official Clerk.

Witness my hand and Seal of the Said Surrogate at Riverhead, N. Y. this 24 day of November 1880.

Surrogates   J. H. Tuthill Surrogate
Seal

State of Tennessee)
Hamilton County   )   The above copy of Will and certificate were filed 18th July 1881 at 2 p.m. entered in Note Book No. 2 page 259 and recorded in Book K Volume 2, pages 43-4-5-6.

Witness my hand at office in Chattanooga

H. C. Beck, Register

State of New York)
County of Suffolk) I James H. Tuthill Surrogate of the County and State aforesaid do hereby certify that the foregoing is a full true and perfect copy of the last Will and Testament of William Mowbray late of Said County Deceased, together with the proceedings had in said Surrogates Court probating and admitting to record Said last Will and Testament, having compared Said Copy with the originals now recorded and on file in my office and in my possession and under my controll as Such surrogate - I furthermore certify that Said Court is a Court of record having a Seal and full jurisdiction in matters of probate of Wills and the appointment and qualification of Executors that the record in this cause and the attestation of the foregoing copy of same by me as Surrogate are in due form of law and by the proper officer being the only judge or presiding magistrate of Said Court and my own Clerk having as Such the custody of the Seal records and papers of Said Surrogates Court -

In testimony whereof I have hereunto Signed my Official Signature and affixed the Seal of said Court at office in Riverhead this 1st day of September A. D. 1882

Surrogates   James H. Tuthill
Seal   Surrogate

[Page 174]

HENRY EVANS

Will of Henry Evans, Deceased

State of Tennessee Hamilton County
Circuit Court July Term 1882
Hon. D. C. Trewhitt Judge

Tuesday August 1st 1882

James W. Brown Jr.   )
    vs.   )
Bertha Evans by next)
friend Green Johnston)   Came the parties by their attornies, and thereupon the following July

1. B. F. Holland	2. A. A. William
3. F. A. Carden	4. Danl. Kaylor
5. Gilbert Vandergriff	6. M. R. Lust
7. R. H. Siveley	8. Thos. Crews
9. William Green	10. Charles Ward
11. W. R. Armor	12. Thos. Rose

good and lawful men who being elected tried and Sworn the truth to speak upon their issues found, who after hearing all the proof argument of Counsel & receiving the charge of the Court upon their oaths do find that the orginal paper dated June 11, 1882 in the declaration mentioned and which is in the words and figures following to wit -

Chattanooga Tenn. June 11 1882

I Henry Evans of the City of Chattanooga State of Tennessee being of Sound mind and memory declare this to be my last Will and Testament I give and bequeath to my Children Bertha and Frank equally my and my wife interest E. S. L. R. M. - The interest of which Shall take to School my children - The Executor will please Sell my Cow and young heifer and out of the money from Said Sale please pay Joe Johnson six dollars ($6.00) living near R. I. Co. Mills, and Samuel Collins my brother living at Tunnel Hill Ga. ten dollars and 75 cents ($10.75). I also owe Lary Mitchell living near Ooltawah Tenn. one hundred dollars ($100.00) I want Jenny McLamon to have two of my sow pigs - One to Miss Gray, the remainder to Mr. Green Johnson to make meat for the Children, the corn Sell a part of it, leave the remainder to feed the Children - The money from said Sale of corn shall be put in Bank. Pay Miss Dinah Gray the nurse for Services during Sickness, and last - I hereby constitute and appoint

Joe W. Brown Executor of this my last Will and testament revoking and annulling all other wills by me made, confirming this to be my last Will and Testament-

In witness whereof I Henry Evans have hereto Set my hand and Seal this Eleventh [Page 175] day of June in the year of our Lord One Thousand Eight hundred and Eighty two.

Henry Evans

Signed and declared by the above named Henry Evans as his last Will and testament in presence of us who at his request have signed as witnesses of the Same.
Chas. Riley, Dinnah Gray, Samuel Hoge by Denis B. Gorden is the last Will and Testament of said Henry Evans deceased, and the Jury aforesaid do further find that paper Styled a Codicil to the last Will & Testament of Henry Evans dated June 15 1882 in the declaration mentioned and in the words & figures following to wit

"Chattanooga State of Tennessee Hamilton C Co.

This day I will adde on my Will - If my children dies give the money to the E. Star Lodge 95 and my estate I don't want any one --- to have it but them.   My administrator J. W. Brown Jr.
Singled by me Soyd Henry Evans
Written by Chas. Riley Same Hodge Dina Gray Dr. Pear City Dr. June 15 1882 the year of Lord"

---- is not any part of the last Will & Testament of the Said Henry Evans deceased.

It is therefore considered by the Court that Said paper dated June 11 1882 as aforesaid is the Last Will and Testament of the Said Henry Evans Decd. in accordance with the finding of the Jury aforesaid and the Clerk of this Court will deliver Said orginal paper aforesaid to the Clerk of the county Court of Hamilton County Tennessee. to be recorded & administered and proceeded upon - together with a certified Copy of the record of their proceedings in the Cause - And it is further considered by the court that the Said paper Styled a Codicil as aforesaid is not any part of the last will and Testament of the Said Henry Evans, Deceased.

It is further considered by the Court, the parties consulted thereto, that the defendant Bertha Evans by her next friend Green Johnson recover of Joseph W. Brown Jr. Executor for the use of the parties entitled thereto all the costs of this cause, to be levied of the goods & Chattles in hands or that may come to his hands, to be administered belonging to his testator but, no execution will issue until further order of this court.

[Page 176]

And by consent and the agreement of all the parties and with the assent of the Court - Joseph W. Brown Jr. Executor or his Successor will pay reasonable Counsel fees to De Witt & Shepherd for their Services in behalf of the plaintiff & to W. L. Eakin for his services as counsel of Defendant in the cause out of the assets of Said Estate after paying all costs of Administration and Said Eakin agrees that his fee will not exceed One hundred dollars.-

State of Tennessee)
Hamilton County)   I A. R. Jones, Clerk of the Circuit Court in and for the County and State aforesaid do certify the foregoing to be a true and perfect copy of the judgement and order of the court in the case of Joseph W. Brown Jr. vs. Bertha Evans by next friend Green Johnson now of record in said Court.

Witness my hand and the Seal of Said Court at office in Chattanooga the 28th Sept. 1882
    Seal   A. R. Jones Clerk
                By C. W. Vincent D. C.

[Page 177]

MARY E. THURMAN

Will of Mary E. Thurman -

State of Tennessee)   I Mary E. Thurman of
Hamilton County)   the County and State aforesaid, being in Sound mind and memory, do make this my last Will and Testament.

First I will that all my debts and funeral Charges be paid out of my Estate.

Second I give and bequeath to Martha E. Thurman Lot No. 6 - Beginning on a pile of Rocks & Hickory pointers in A. M. Johnsons line & cor to Lot. No. 5. Thence 21° W about 25 poles along Said line to the corner of a four acre fraction laid down in McFarlands Jr. lott - Thence 70° E along Said fractional lot 54 poles to the Georgia State line Thence E with Said State Line to the middle of Chattanooga Creek. Thence down Said Creek to the corner of lot No 5 - Thence E about 230 poles to the beginning containing 45 Acres more or less and being in the 17th Dist of the County and State aforesaid, and being the lands set apart to me out of the Estate of my Father Elijah Thurman Decd as one of his Heirs.

Third I also give and bequeath to said Martha E. Thurman all my personal property, consisting of one Cow and Calf, one Feather Bed, bedstid and all the bed clothing and all other personal effects whatsoever.

But my intention is to give and bequeath the above property to the said Martha E. Thurman during her natural life and no longer. Thus I desire and so will that the real estate and personal property all and each decend and the ownership and title be vested in Mary Minerva Thurman Daughter of my Brother John Thurman.

I hereby nominate and appoint John Thurman the Sole Executor of this my last Will and Testament and authorize and empower him him to execute the same without the Execution of any bond as required by law.

In testimony whereof I hereto sign my name and affix my Seal this 10th day of October, 1882.

                    Mary E. X Thurman
                        her mark
Attest:
J. Foster Rogers
This will was Signed and Sealed by the Testator in our and each of our presence and we each Signed our names to it in the presence of the Testator and in the presence of each other all at her request she having read and understood the Same in our presence.
                    J. Foster Rogers
                    A. W. Poe

Filed Nov. 6th 1882
            T. A. Evans Dep. Clerk
Enrolled on record No. 5 pages 101 & 102
            T. A. Evans D. C.

[Page 178]

THOMAS D. McCORMACK

Will of Thomas D. McCormack

I Thomas D. McCormack of Chattanooga Tennessee do make and publish this as my Last Will and Testament, hereby revoking and making null all other wills by me at anytime executed -

First - I direct that my funeral expenses and all my just debts be paid as soon after my death as possible out of any money that I may die possessed of or that may first come into the hands of my Executors.

Secondly - I give and bequeath to my beloved wife Emma McCormack all the residue of my Estate after the payment of Said debts, including all the property real, personal or mixed of which I may die Seized or possessed, including my interst in the assets and business of the firm

of T. H. Payne & Co. and any other firm with which I may be connected -

Lastly - I hereby nominate and appoint my friend Z. C. Patten and my said wife Emma McCormack Executor & executrix of this my last Will.

In witness whereof I do hereto Set my hand and Seal This 10th November 1882.

                    T. D. McCormack

Witness
John G. Rawling
Eliel R. Warner

Signed, Sealed and published in our presence and we have Subscribed our name hereto in the rpesence of the testator and at his request. This 10th day of November 1882.

                    Eliel R. Warner

Filed and probated Dec. 4 1882
            T. A. Evans Dep. Clerk
See Record 5 pp. 112

[Page 179]

WILLIAM J. RAWLSTON

Will of Wm. J. Rawlston

The State of Tennessee -
In the name of God, Amen -
I William J. Rawlston of the County of Hamilton in the State of Tennessee having been blessed to live to a ripe age in life and blessed in some of the goods of this world - and of sound mind and disposing memory and knowing that at most I cannot live many years longer and desiring to avoid litigation or trouble about my property or effects after my death and to designate clearly myself the objects of my bounty, the person to enjoy it and the manner and proportion of enjoyment - Do make ordain and publish this as my last will and testament - hereby revoking and annulling any and all will or wills made by me at any former date.

First - I commend my Soul to God who gave it and pray its acceptance in peace -

2nd - That my earthly remains be plainly but decently buried.

3rd - That all my just debts be paid if any against me.

4th - I will, devise and bequeath unto my beloved

wife Martha Jane Rawlston all of my entire estate both real and personal let it consist in what it may of every kind and character, during her natural life - that she remain in peaceable and quiet possession of the same as long as she lives.

5th - I am now owner of the following land lying and being Situated in the first Civil District of Hamilton County, Tenn. and bounded as follows to wit - Beginning at the lower corner of Hacketts 300 acre Survey Thence down the meanders of the Tenn. River 260 poles to a White Oak on the River Bank near a point of Rocks that project into the River nearly opposite the mouth of Ooltewah Creek and corner to Johnson's line. Thence west 175 poles to a stake - Thence North 13° west 220 poles and thence to the beginning containing 200 acres be the same more or less.

6th - I devise to my beloved sons and daughters all the above described tract of land to wit T. W. Rawlston - Isabella Hodge - W. S. Rawlston - Elizabeth Watkins - John Rawlston - George Rawlston - James Rawlston - Mary Hixson and M. Virginia Rawlston; Share and Share alike equal as to No. of acres and I direct that my executor have the same laid off and set apart and equal as to No. of acres commencing at the River at the upper or lower end of the farm as he may deem best and proper so as to let each [page 180] lot of land run across the farm East and West so as to give each heir the benefit of timber and bottom land - I further will and direct that all of said heirs above named draw by No. in the usual manner of drawing for land, except my youngest Daughter M. Virginia Rawlston, who is now Single and living with us and caring for me and her mother in declining years - That my Executor Set apart to her separate and apart for her own use and benefit her No. of acres equal as to No. of acres with all the rest of the heirs, so as to include the dwelling house, all the out buildings, Orchard and apertenences and improvements thereon to her without her having to draw for it or pay to any other heir any further coinsideration therefore.

7th - I Will Devise and direct that all of my beloved children as above enumerated except M. Virginia as above stated pay from and to each other, when they now where their respective No.'s or lot of land lies, in money or otherwise, so as to make each heir equal in cash value in the lot of land so drawn by each of them as they can determine -

8th - I bequeath to, unto all of my beloved Children as hereto set forth and named in this my last will and Testament, all my personal property and effects of every kind and character that I may die Seized and possessed of, let it consist of what it may, Share and Share alike equally divided between them all.

9 - I hereby appoint my true and trusty Son Thomas W. Rawlston of Chattanooga Tenn. my Executor to execute and carry out this my last Will and Testament in all its bearings, in the true letter and Spirit of the Same, without Bonds.

In witness whereof I have hereunto Set my hand and seal as my last will and testament on this 16th of December A. D. 1882.

William X J. Rawlston
his mark (Seal)

The foregoing was at the date thereof Signed Sealed published and delivered by the Said W. J. Rawlston as and for his last will and Testament in the presence of us and each of us and we at his request and in his presence and in the presence of each other have subscribed our names as witnesses thereto the day and date above written.

Test Addison P. Hunter
James Brumley

Filed & probated April 11, 1883

[Page 181]

A. A. HYDE

Will of A. A. Hyde

I A. A. Hyde of Chattanooga Tennessee, being of Sound mind and disposing memory, but fully aware of the uncertainty of life, do make publish and declare this to be my last will and testament -

Item 1 - I hereby devise and bequeath all my real estate both real and personal to my well beloved wife Martha A. Hyde for her use and maintenance during her natural life intending thereby that she shall have the free use and enjoyment of all my property and the proceeds of Such Sales of real estate as may be sold by my Executor hereinafter named or shall be necessary for her comfortable maintenance and support.

Item 2 - If upon the death of my said wife there should remain any of my property real or personal, not used in the maintenance and support, such remaineder I devise and bequeath to my five Sons William A., F. G., F. S., Chas. R., and Albert E. Hyde Share and Share alike, and in case either of my Said Sons Should die before their mother, in Such case it is my will that the children of Such deceased son should inherit their further portion Share and Share alike.

Item 3 - I hereby nominate my Son F. S. Hyde as the Executor of this my Will and Testament and give him full power to wind up and Settle my estate granting him full power to make Sales of all real estate owned by me or in which I have an interest with others authorizing him to execute as such executor such releases acquittance deeds or other conveyances as shall be necessary and shall seem for the best interests of the estate, but he shall not Sell the homestead now occupied by me without the consent of his mother - nor shall his deed for the same be effectual to carry the Title, without she joins in the Same, and as I have no indebtedness of any account, to discharge, and have implicit confidence in the integrity and good judgment of Said F. S. Hyde - I desire that he shall not be required to give any bond for the faithful discharge of his duties as Executor.

A. A. Hyde

Signed Sealed published and declared to [Page 182] be his last Will and Testament by the Said A. A. Hyde this 7th day of November 1882 in our presence and we at the request of Said Testator and in his presence and in the presence of each other have Signed the same as witness thereto.

Mrs. Emma Clark
Xenophon Wheeler

Filed and probated April 4, 1883
L. M. Clark, Clerk

H. V. REDFIELD

Exemplified Copy of the last will and Testament of H. C. Reldfield from McKean Co. Pennsilvania.

Among the records and proceedings enrolled in the Registers Office of the county of McKean and Commonwealth of Pennsylvania is found a certain record of the last Will and Testament of H. V. Redfield deceased together with the proof taken on the probate of the Same and recorded in Register Docket "B" page 562 and is a follows to wit-

Copy of Relgisters Entry
In the Estate of H. V. Redfield Deceased
Will

In the name of God - I H. V. Redfield being of sound mind and memory do make and declare this to be my last Will and Testament -

First - I request the payment of all lawful debts as soon as possible -

Second - I desire & request that if my mother Should Survive me, that she have support from the proceeds of my Estate as long as She lives.

Third - I give and bequeath to Dr. William Byrne of Jasper - Marion County, Tennessee the Sum of One Hundred dollars.

Fourth - I give devise and bequeath to my beloved wife Nellie all the rest of my Estate real personal and mixed, she to have and to hold the Same to her heirs and assigns forever and with full power to Sell & convey any or all parts of it as her own property and thereby passing all the Title which I held during my lifetime.

Fifth - Having explicit confidence in my said wife I hereby appint her the guardian of my children [Page 183] and the execution of this my last will and testament without bail or bond being asked or given.

In testimony I hereunto Set my hand and Seal this 13th day of July 1880.

(Signed) H. V. Redfield (Seal)

Signed & Sealed and delivered by the above named H. V. Redfield as his last Will and Testament in the presence of us, who have hereunto subscribed our names at his request as witnesses thereto in the presence of Said Testator and of each other.

Witness (Signed) Delano R. Hamlin
(Signed) Byron D. Hamlin

Commonwealth of Pensylvania)
County of McKean)

This day before me John B. Bramley Register for the probate of Wills and granting letters of Administration in and for the County aforesaid personally came Byron D. Hamlin and Delano R. Hamlin the subscribing witnesses to the above Will, who been duly sworn according to law, do say that they were present and saw and heard H. V. Redfield, sign seal publish pronounce and declare the foregoing instrument of writing as and for his last will and testament and that at the time of so doing he was of sound mind memory and understanding to the best of their knowledge and belief, and deponents further say that the above will was made in the handwriting of and by said testator at Smethport Pa. on the 13th day of July A. D. 1880.

(Signed) Delano R. Hamlin
(Signed) Byron D. Hamlin
Sworn & Subscribed before me Nov. 21 1881

(Signed) John B. Brawley
Register

November 21, 1881 Affidavit of time of death of Decedent filed.

Same day Oath administered to executrix and letters Testamentary issued to her and copy of letters filed.

[Page 184]

GEORGE W. FORT

Certified Copy of Last Will and Testament of George W. Fort Deceased.

State of Georgia)
Bibb County)   In the name of God Amen.

I George W. Fort of the State and County aforesaid, being of Sound Mind and Memory do make ordain this my last Will and Testament hereby revoking and annulling all others by me heretofore made.

First - I give and bequeath all of my property both real and personal of whatever kind I may be possessed of to my beloved Mother Mrs. Martha L. Fort to have and to hold during her natural Life, and all income from Said property of whatever kind to be used by her as she may see fit or proper.

Secondly - On the death of my Mother Mrs. Martha L. Fort I desire and direct that all my estate and property be equally divided between my Sister Martha F., my Sister Catherine H., my brother Tomlinson, my brother Jno. P., my Sister Sallie F., my Sister Francis G. or their lawful heirs with the exception of the property left us by my Sister Julia E. Huegenin deceased, which property I desire and direct to divert back to the Estate of Edward D. Hugenin, deceased, and to be divided equally among my Sister Julia's Children viz: Martha F., Edward D., Leila V. and Julia D.

Thirdly - I further desire and direct that all of my property of whatever kind that may hereafter be allotted to my Sisters or either of them be settled upon them as a separate property not to be managed or controlled by them or their husbands if married but whatever income arising from said property to be paid to them by a trustee.

Fourthly - My brother Tomlinson and my brother John P. are hereby constituted Trustees for the management of said property.

Fifthly - During my Mothers lifetime it is my [Page 185] will and desire that she have the Sole and undivided management and control of my entire property or whoever she may see fit to appoint.

Sixthly - In the event of any one of my brothers or Sisters dying without issue, it is my desire that my property revert back to be divided equally among my brothers and Sisters or their heirs, and nothing in this my will shall be so contrued that the heirs of my Sister Julia shall in any manner receive any portion of my estate with the exception of the portion left me by Sister Julia as stated in the latter part of the Second clause of this my will.

Seventhly - It is my further will and desire that my Uncle Joseph D. Fannin be paid yearly the Sum of one hundred Dollars from the income of my estate during the term of his natural life.

Eighthly - It is my desire that my diamond breastpin be given to my brother Tomlinson my Gold Watch to my brother Jno. P. and my Silver Goblet to my Sister Frances G.

Ninthly - I hereby constitute and appoint my brother Tomlinson and my brother Jno. P. Executors on this my last Will and Testament this April 14th 1860.

Geo. W. Fort (Seal)

Signed Sealed and published by George W. Fort as his last Will and Testament in the presence of us the undersigned in his presence and at his request and in presence of each other.

L. N. Whittle
S. M. Whittle
Z. M. Whittle

State of Georgia)
Bibb County   )

Whereas I George W. Fort having written my last [Page 186] will and Testament and wishing to so change Said Will in relation to the property left me by my Sister Mrs. Julia E. Hueginin deceased and it is my Will and desire that my Sister Catherine H. have and hold during the term of her natural life or as long as she remains unmarried the property consisting of a house and lot in the City of Macon left me by my Sister Julia deceased, to hold as a home for my Sister Julia's children or my mothers children if they so desire to live in said house, In the event of the death or marriage of my Sister Kate, Said property to be and immediately revert back to be divided equally among the children of my Sister Julia.

I hereby appoint my brothers Tomlinson and John P. as my Executors to the Codicil of my last Will and Testament. This 14 April 1866.

Codicil -
State of Georgia)
Bibb County   )

It is my further Will and desire and I do hereby direct that there be given to my youngest Sister Frances G. the Sum of One Thousand Dollars in my Central Railroad Stock to have and to hold under the same conditions as are heretofore precribed in this my last Will and Testament and this Sum to be One Thousand dollars more than the rest of my brothers or Sisters in the Shape of Central Railroad Stock.

I do hereby appoint my brothers Tomlinson and John P. Executors to this Codicil to my last Will and Testament this April 14th 1866.

Geo. W. Fort (Seal)

[Page 187]

Signed and published by Geo. W. Fort as his codicil to his last Will and Testament in presence and our Signatures in the presence of each other this --

L. N. Whittle
S. M. Whittle
Z. M. Whittle

State of Georgia)
Bibb County   )

Whereas I George W. Fort wishing to annex another Codicil to this my last Will and Testament -

1st - That it was by order and desire that the clause originally written as the ninth was Stricken from my last Will and Testament - and is to form no part or parcel of Same -

2nd - It is my further will and desire that all property left me by my late Sister Mrs. Edward D. Huegenin - I bequeath to my mother Mrs. Martha L. Fort to have and to hold, to will and do dispose of as she may See fit, and all parts of my will in conflict with this Settlement are hereby annulled. My two brothers Tomlinson and John P. are appointed as Executors to this Codicil of my last Will and Testament.

Signed Sealed and published as Codicil to this my last Will and Testament - April 30, 1866.

G. W. Fort (L.S.)

Signed Sealed and published by Geo W. Fort as a Codicil to his last Will and Testament in our presence and we Signing in the presence of each other.

Maria McDonald
B. R. Doyle
J. D. Fannin

Georgia   )
Bigg County)

Before Wm. M. Riley ordinary of said County came in person John P. Fort and Tomlinson Fort Executors of the Last Will and Testament of George W. Fort deceased late of Said County and Lewis N. Whittle a Witness to said Will [Page 188] and two codicils of said Will and also Maria McDonald witness to third Codicil of Said Will, who being duly Sworn deposed and say that they Saw Said George W. Fort Sign Seal publish and declare the Said Instruments as his last Will and Testament voluntarily, freely, and without compulsion, and that he was of Sound disposing mind and memory and they Signed Said Will as Witnesses in the presence of the Said Testator Geo. W. Fort, and each others presence and in the

presence of the other Subscribing Witnesses.

L. N. Whittle
Maria McDonald

Sworn to & Subscribed in open Court before me this May 7th, 1866.

Wm. M. Riley Ordinary

State of Georgia)
Bibb County   )

I John A. McManus Ordinary of Said County & State do hereby certify that the Court of Ordinary of which I am Ordinary is a Court of Record, and by the laws of this State I am my own Clerk, having charge of the records & Seal of Said Court, and of the proceedings had thereon as Such -I further certify that the foregoing writing is a true copy of the last Will and Testament and Codicils of George W. Fort deceased as the Same was probated in Said Court and as it now appears of Record in the Office of the Court of ordinary of Said County and State - I further certify that my attestation as Clerk of Said Court is in due form.

In testimony whereof I have here to set my hand & affixed the Seal of said Court as said Blerk and ordinary hereof as aforesaid. This 22nd June, 1883.

J. A. Mc Manus
Clerk & Ordinary

Filed Sept. 4 1883
L. M. Clark Clerk per T. A. Evans Dep. Clerk

Admitted to probate Sept 3, 1883
L. M. Clark Clerk per T. A. Evans Dep. Clerk

[Page 189]

MARTHA L. FORT

Certified Copy of the Last Will and Testament of Martha L. Fort -

State of Georgia)
Bibb County   )

I Martha L. Fort of Said State and County, declare this to be my last Will and Testament -

Item 1st - It is my will that the house and lot on Jefferson Street in the City of Macon and all the furniture therein, that was bequeathed to me by the wills of my daughter Julia and my Son George, be sold by my Executors at either public or private Sale at Such time and place as they or either of them may see fit, and that the entire proceeds of such sale after deducting the necessary expenses thereof be divided equally among the children of my daughter Julia then in life, and if any are dead leaving child or children, said child or children to stand in and receive the Share of their deceased parent or parents.

Item 2nd - All the residue of my property of every kind, both in this State and the State of Tennessee - I desire to be sold at such time manner and place as my Executor or Executors may see fit, and the proceeds thereof equally divided, except as herinafter Set forth, among my children then in life and any of my children that may be dead leaving child or children, said Child or children to stand in the place of and receive the Share of their deceased parent or parents.

Item 3rd - Whereas I have advanced to my two daughters Martha F. Morgan and Sarah F. Milton Fifteen hundred Dollars each on March 1st 1875, I therefore will that my Executor and Executors deduct from the Share of each that would be due them under Item 2nd of this will, said Sum with interst at three percent per annum from March 1st 1875 up to the time of my death, at which time Such interest is to cease.1

Item 4th - Whereas my Son Tomlinson has done much Service to his Fathers Estate and to me, thereby benefitting his brothers and Sisters, for all of which [Page 190] he would not receive any compensation - I therefore give him the Sum of Five hundred Dollars from my estate in excess of any Sum due my other children or their decendants under this my Will.

Item 5th - The sum that will be coming to my grand daughter Lelah H. Tarver as one of the children of my daughter Julia - I wish to be received by her brother Edward in trust for her. I do not wish Edward to be required to give any bond or to make any report of his acts or doings to any Court, but he is to use the sum due his Sister Lelah for her benefit as his Judgment approves, and if he desires or thinks it best, he can turn it over to her and thereby be discharged from his trust.

Item 6th - Having confidence in my Executors hereinafter named I give the same power to one that I do to each or to both of them - They are authorized to sell either at public or private Sale any or all of my estate, at either public or private Sale and at Such time and place as they may think best without obtaining any order of any Court for said purposes and they are not required to make any return of their actings and doings in regard thereto to any court.

Item 7th - I hereby appoint my son Tomlinson Fort and my son John P. Fort as my Executors to this my will.

Witness my Signature this June 17 1882 A. D.
Martha L. Fort
Being called on by Mrs. Martha L. Fort with

whom we are acquainted to witness her signature to the above instrument as her Will we hereby certify that She Signed the above as her will in our presence and that we witnessed the Same at her request and in the presence of each other. This June 17th 1882 A. D.
J. M. Johnston
J.D. Fannin
Maggie Corkery

[Page 191]

State of Georgia)
County of Bibb)
Before me came J. M. Johnston named as a witness in the writing hereto annexed purporting to be the last Will and Testament of Mrs. Martha L. Fort of said County, and being duly sworn Saith that he with J.D. Fannin and Maggie Corkery at the request of Mrs. Martha L. Fort and in her presence did attest as witnesses the annexed writing as her will, the said Mrs. Martha L. Fort, that the same was signed and published by Mrs. Martha L. Fort in our presence as her last will - that she was at the time of said attestation and signed by herself, of sound and disposing mind and memory, that she executed the annexed paper voluntarily.

Subscribed and Sworn to before me this June 18th 1883.
J. A. McManus
Ordinary

State of Georgia)
Bibb County   )
I John McManus Ordinary of Said County & State do hereby certify that the Court of Ordinary of which I am ordinary is a court of Record and that by the laws of the State I am my own Clerk, having charge of the Records & Seal of Said Court, and of the proceedings had therein, as such I further certify that the foregoing writing is a true copy of the last Will and Testament of Mrs. Martha L. Fort Deceased as the same was probated in Said Court - and as it now appears of Record in the Office of the Court of Ordinary of Said County & State - I further certify that my attestation as Clerk of said Court is in due form.

In testimony whereof I have hereto Set my hand & affixed the Seal of said Court as aforesaid This June 22, 1883.
J. A. McManus
Clerk & Ordinary

Filed Sept. 4, 1883
L. M. Clark, Clerk

T. A. Evans, Dep. Clerk
Admitted to probate Sept. 3, 1883
T. A. Evans, Dep. Clerk

[Page 192]

JOHN RYAN

Will of John Ryan

In the name of God, Amen -

I John Ryan being of feeble body, but of sound mind, and bearing in mind that it is appointed unto all men, once to die - do hereby make and publish this my last Will and Testament, and do hereby revoke and make null and void any and all former Wills by me made or attempted to be made.

Item 1st - It is my will and desire that my funeral expenses and all my just debts be paid out -certain debts due me from William Cahill for a lot Sold by me to him or to his wife, should they not be collected in my lifetime - and if there is not enough to pay my funeral expenses and debts from these notes, then they will have to be paid with the proceeds of a vacant lot I own on Brannum Street in the City of Chattanooga Tennessee which I bought from Bridget Hughes.

Item 2nd - After the payment of the Expenses and debts aforesaid - I do hereby give and bequeath and devise all the remainder of my property, both real and personal, to Ellen Garvin, wife of Patrick Garvin, now residing on Whiteside Street in the City of Chattanooga Tennessee from the control of her present or any future husband - I do not wish her present or any future husband to have any control of any of the property she may receive from my estate in any way whatsoever - I am desirous of compensating her in some manner for the care and attention she has bestowed upon me in my old age.

Item 3rd - I do constitute and appoint Patrick Powers the Executor of this my last Will and testament.

Signed Sealed and published on this 4th day of August 1883 in the presence of the Subscribing Witnesses.
John X Ryan (Seal)
his mark

The foregoing will was signed in our presence and witnessed by us at the request of the testator.
Hugh McGovern
John Powers

Endorsed Probated Sept. 4, 1883. See record No. 5 pp. 253.

T. A. Evans D. C.

[Page 193]

SAMUEL DAVIDSON

Will of Samuel Davidson
Sept. 1883, this 30th day of

I, Samuel Davidson this day due give to Mary A. Davidson all of my property and Seine over to Setle aul of my detes and colex the Seam.
Samuel X Davidson
his mark

Test - J. C. Lewis
Jess Gann
H. J. Smith

Filed and probated Nov. 6th 1883
T. A. Evans, D. C.

[Page 194]

GEORGE H. HAZLEHURST

Will and Testament of
George H. Hazlehurst - Deceased

In the name of God Amen -

I George H. Hazlehurst of the City of Chattanooga State of Tennessee being of sound mind and memory do make and publish this my last Will and Testament.

I give devise and bequeath my estate and property real and personal as follows, that is to say -

Item I I will and desire that all of my just debts shall be first paid by my Executors hereinafter named and appointed.

Item II I give devise and bequeath to J. Nesbit Hazlehurst my son the sum of Four Thousand ($4,000) dollars, which shall be a first charge upon my Estate, subject however to the trusts and conditions hereinafter set forth in Item 4 of this my last will -

Item III I give devise and bequeath to my four children - J. Nesbit, Fannie W. - Sarah Harriet & Louise N. Hazlehurst all the residue of my Estate of whatever kind or description, whether consisting of personal real or mixed proeprty, which shall be equally divided among them share and share alike; but it is my will and desire that they shall have and enjoy the Same Subject to the trusts and conditions hereinafter set forth in the next item -

Item IV   I give devise and bequeath unto my Executors my true and tried friends Andrew J. Lane and Robert H. Plant both of the City of Macon Georgia all and every part of my Estate mentioned in the preceeding Items of this my will, to hold in Trust for the use behoof and benefit of my said four Children - It is my will and desire that my said Executors shall hold and possess all my said Estate, and that they shall have the full and perfect authority and power to manage and control my Said Estate in such manner as to them may seem right and for the best intersts of all of my said Children; and full power and authority is hereby expressly given and granted to them to lease sell and convey, and on such terms as they may think best, any part [Page 195] or all of my Said Estate, and to make deeds to the purchasers - They are also fully empowered to re-invest any of the proceeds of any Sale they may make in such manner as they may deem just, right, and to the best interests of my said children -

It is my will and desire that my said Executors shall expend such sums of money out of my estate as may be right and proper for the education, maintenance and support of my said children charging each childs share with amount expended in his or her behalf.

It is my will and desire and I so direct, that when my Son J. Nesbit shall arrive at the age of Twenty one years my said Executors shall turn over to him the part of my estate herein before given devised and bequeathed to him, and when my said son arrives at the age of Twenty one years I hereby leave it entirely in the discretion of my Said Executors whether or not to make division among my other children and power is hereby given them to do so or not as they may determine.   But in case they do so determine, I hereby will and direct that they shall select and have appointed the Guardian or Guardians for my Said Children, and they shall require of Said Guardian or Guardians good and sufficient bonds - But should my executors deem it best not to make said division when my son so arrives at the age of Twenty one years, I hereby direct and will that when my daughter Fannie W. arrives at the age of Twenty one years, my said Executors shall turn over to her her portion of my Estate hereinbefore given devised and bequeathed to her, and when she does so arrive at the age of Twenty one years the like power as above is given and granted to my said Executors to select and have appointed a Guardian or Guardians for the other two children, and turn their shares over to them or keep the balance of the Estate together as they may deem best -

As the other two children arrive at the age of Twenty one years my Executors will turn [Pages 196 & 197 blank - Page 198] over to them their parts of my Estate-

I now declare and will that power is hereby given and granted to my said Executors at any time after my Son arrives at the age of twenty one years to select and have appointed a Guardian or Guardians for the other three Children, and turn over to said Guardian or Guardians to share coming to each respectively upon said Guardian or Guardians giving good and sufficient bonds - My intention and meaning is that each child shall at all events receive his or her share upon arrival at the age of Twenty one years, and to give my Executors discretion and power at any time after my Son is of age to make full division among the other Children and select and have appointed a Guardian or Guardians for them to manage their Estates or to keep my Estate together as above directed until each Child arrives at the age of Twenty one years.

Item V - It is my will and desire and I hereby declare that the parts of my estate hereby given devised and bequeathed to my said daughters shall be for their Sole and separate use benefit and behoof free from the control of any husband they may hereafter marry, with full power to sell or dispose of the same in any manner after they shall arrive at the age of Twenty one years.

I hereby nominate and appoint my Said true and trusted friends Andrew J. Lane and Robert H. Plant, both of the city of Macon Georgia, the Executors of this my last Will and Testament and having the fullest confidence in their integrity and capacity - I hereby expressly excuse them from any bond and I will and desire that they shall act as the Executors of this my will without being required to give any bond as such Executors.
[Page 199]

In witness whereof I have signed and Sealed and published and declared this instrument as my Will at my residence on Gilmer Street in the City of Chattanooga Tennessee this the 9th day of October A. D. 1883.
Geo. H. Hazlehurst (Seal)

The Said George H. Hazlehurst at his said residence on Gilmer Street in the City of Chattanooga Tennessee on said 9th of October 1883 Signed and Sealed this instrument and published and declared the Same as and for his Last Will, and we at his request and in his presence and in the presence of each other have hereunto written our names as subscribing witnesses.
C. P. Goree
John Philan
N. Wingfield

Endorsed
> Filed Dec. 3, 1883
> T. A. Evans, Dept. Clerk

[Page 200]

JOSEPHINE C. HAZLEHURST

Last Will and Testament of
Josephine C. Hazlehurst.

I Mrs. Josephine C. Hazlehurst being somewhat feeble in health, but sound in mind, do now desire in case of my death to bequeath to my three daughters Fannie Wingfield, Louise Nesbit, and Sarah Harriet, this Lot, House and Furniture owned by me, held in my name and situated on the Corner of Gilmer & C. Streets in the Town of Chattanooga Hamilton County Tennessee.

This property to be held and divided equally between the three - And in case of the death of either one without an heir, it goes to the surviving Sisters or Sister -

I do this in consideration of my boys being better able to take care of themselves in the Battle of Life.

To this my last Will and Testament I set my hand and Seal this Seventh of June 1882.

Josephine C. Hazlehurst

At the request of Mrs. Josephine C. Hazlehurst and in presence of each other have subscribed our names as witnesses hereto
> Frances N. Nesbit
> Louise A. Wingfield

Endorsed
> Filed Dec. 3rd 1883
> T. A. Evans D. C.

> Probated Dec. 3rd 1883
> T. A. Evans D. C.

[Page 201]

HERMAN ZEIGER

Will of Herman Zeiger
I, Herman Zeiger of Chattanooga Hamilton County Tennessee - In the year of our Lord 1883 - Make this my last Will and Testament -

I give devise and bequeath my estate & property real and personal to my wife Caroline Zeiger as follows. That is to say

I will, devise and bequeath the following real Estate to wit - One lot or parcel of land that I purchased from Leonard Wolf & Jacob Trapp on Cowart Street Glass Addition in the City of Chattanooga Hamilton County Tennessee on the Twenty fifth day of June 1870 and the deed thereto registered in the Registers Office of Hamilton County in Book "T" pages 193 & 194.

I also Will devise give & bequeath to my Said wife Caroline another lot or parcel of Land a lot purchased by me from Kate Wolf of Louisville Kentucky on the 19th day of June 1882 fronting 45 feet on Cowart Street and running back of uniform width (150) feet and the deed thereto registered in the Registers Office of Hamilton County in Book "L" Volume 2 page 687 - I further will give devise & bequeath to my Said wife Caroline all the personal property that I may have at my death - And I further desire that she take possession of all my estate both real & personal without accounting to any person & Court for same.

I hereby constitute & appoint my wife Caroline Zeiger of Chattanooga Tennessee my lawful Executor without being required to enter into bond for the same as the bond is hereby especially waived of this my last Will. In witness whereof I have Signed and Sealed and published and declared this instrument as my will at Chattanooga this 9th day of November 1883.

Herman Zeiger

Jas. J. McGlohon
John Schentelmeir
Jas. S. Edsall

Probated Dec. 1883

[Page 202]

ELIZABETH HIXSON

Will of Elizabeth Hixson

Realizing the uncertainty of life I Elizabeth Hixson of the County of Hamilton and State of Tennessee make this last Will and Testament while in possession of sound mind and memory this 22 day of August 1881.

I bequeath all my personal Estate and all my household furniture, ready made goods and chattles and personal estate and effects whatsoever and wheresoever, unto my Son Franklin Hixson his heirs & administrators and assigns to and for his absolute use and benefit according to the nature and quality thereof respectively Subject only to the payment of my just debts, funeral and testamentary expenses and the charge of proving and registering this my Will and I appoint my Said Son Franklin Executor of this my Will and hereby revoke all other Wills by me at any time made - I the said Elizabeth Hixson to this which I declare to be my last Will and Testament Set my hand and Seal.

Elizabeth X Hixson
her mark

Signed by the Said testator Elizabeth Hixson and acknowledged by her to be her last Will and Testament in the presence of us present at the same time and Subscribed by us in the presence of the Said Testator and of each other.
Henry Barker
James F. Hixson

Filed and probated Feb. 4, 1884
T. A. Evans
Dep. Clerk

[Page 203]

LOUISA A. WINGFIELD

Will of Louisa A. Wingfield

I Louisa A. Wingfield being Sound in mind, tho' declining in health, do desire in the event of my death, to bequeath to my beloved niece Anna H. McDonald Twenty Shares Gas Stock, valued at one Hundred Dollars per Share being all the Stock I own in the Macon Gas Light and Water Company State of Georgia - in addition I also bequeath to Said Mrs. Anna McDonald the few pieces of Silver belonging to me, with request that all of which, both Gas Stock and Silver, in case Mrs. Anna McDonald dies without an Heir shall descend to my darling little Nieces Louise Nesbit and Sarah Harriet Hazlehurst.

To this my last Will and Testament I set my hand and Seal on this the 10th day of March 1883.
Louise A. Wingfield

At the request of L. A. Wingfield and in presence of each other the following witnesses do subscribe their names hereto:

Frances W. Nesbit
Geo. H. Wingfield

I bequeath no part of the above named effects to my dear boys, because [they are] too Small to be divided to any advantage and because I feel & believe they are better able to provide for themselves than their sisters would be.

L. A. Wingfield

Filed and probated March 3rd 1884.
T. A. Evans
Dep. Clerk

[Page 204]

MARY C. STRINGER

I, Mary C. Stringer of Hamilton County Tennessee being of sound mind and disposing memory, do hereby constitute and ordain this my last Will and Testament, disposing of all my property, both real and personal of every description.

First - It is my will that my brother R. M. Stringer have all my property both real and personal of every kind to his Sole use and enjoyment - and at his own disposal, except a certain amount of Money which I have set apart for my burial and funeral expenses, which my brother R. M. Stringer is requested to apply as I have instructed him.

Second - It is my will that should any other property come or anure to me by any means before or after my death than that I now possess That my brother, the said R. M. Stringer should have the Same, no matter what kind or Character the property may be.

Third - It is my Will that my brother the Said R. M. Stringer be Sole Executor of this my last Will and Testament, and that he be permitted to execute the Same without giving bond as is usually required by law -
This Augt. 11th 1883
Mary C. Stringer

Witness
T. W. Duggar
J. C. Edmondson

[Page 205]

PRESTON GANN

Will of Preston Gann

I, Preston Gann, being of Sound mind and disposing memory do hereby make and publish this as my last Will and Testament hereby revoking and making void all former wills by me at any time made.

First - I direct that my funeral Expenses and all my debts be paid as soon after my death as possible, out of any moneys that I may die possessed of or which may first come to the hands of my executors hereinafter named.

Second - I give and bequeath to my wife Susan Gann all my interst in the land known as the Flippo lands conveyed by William Flippo on the 30th day of August 1872 - Also I give to her the following personal property to wit - One Bedstead, and the bedding for the Same, She to Select any one she may desire - one ball faced horse about Six years old and one bridle and Side Saddle, also one Cow about three years old being the only one now owned by me, also one Sow and pigs, she to select the one she may want -

Third - I will and bequeath to my children Catherine Gann and William P. Gann all the property both real and personal of which I may die possessed except what I have given to my wife in Item Second.

Fourth - It is my will that all the stock, household and kitchen furniture except that mentioned in item Second be kept at the place where I now reside for the use and benefit of my said two children Catherine and William P.

Fifth - It is my will that all my property except the Home place if necessary be first Sold to pay my debts and my homeplace be left for my said two children Catherine and William P.

Sixth - I do hereby nominate and appoint Henry C. Hartman the Executor of this my last Will and Testament who will immediately upon my death or as soon thereafter as possible enter upon his duties as such, and if he finds it necessary to pay my debts to sell real Estate he may do so Except my homeplace - and he will not be required to give bond as my executor the Same being expressly waived.

In witness whereof I do to this my will set my hand and Seal this 18th day of [Page 206] March 1880
                    Preston Gann (seal)

Signed Sealed and delivered in our presence and we have Subscribed our names hereto in presence of the Testator by his request.
          This March 18th 1880
                    P. C. Hale
                    M. S. Brown

[Page 207]

E. J. MADDEN

Will of E. J. Madden

I E. J. Madden, being of sound mind and disposing memory, hereby make and publish this as my last Will and Testament, revoking any and all wills heretofore made by me.

I I will and direct that all my just debts shall be paid out of the assets of which I may possessed.

II I will and bequeath and give unto my beloved wife Julia Madden all my property of every description both real and personal of which I may die seized and possessed.

III I give to my Executrix, hereinafter named, full power and control of my property, to manage as she may think best selling such part of it as she may think best to raise funds to pay my indebtedness - giving her a discretionary power about manner, time and mode of sale, so as to make my effects realize the most to pay my few debts.

IV I hereby appoint My Beloved Wife, Julia Madden, as the Executrix of this my last Will and Testament, hereby relieving her from giving Bond and Security as such Executrix, also relieving her from advertising and making Public sale of my effects and from making settlements or returning inventories with the County Court requiring her only to sell my effects, or as much as may be necessary, as fast as she may deem proper and to apply the proceeds to the payment of my just debts.

Signed, sealed and published on this the 19th day of May 1884.

E. J. Madden

We the undersigned witnessed the foregoing will at the request of the Testator in his presence and in the presence of each other, and saw him sign and [Page 208] acknowledge the same on this the 19th day of May 1884.
          S. J. A. Frazier
          Jno. P. Long

Filed and Probated on Record #5 Page 392
          Filed June 29th 1884

[Page 209]

ALANSON C. SPOONER

Last Will and Testament of Alanson C. Spooner.

To all whom it may concern - Greeting: Know ye, that I, Alanson C. Spooner, of Chattanooga, Tennessee, in sound mind and memory and mindful of the uncertainty of human life, do make, publish and declare this my last Will and Testament, hereby revoking all former wills made by me.

I - I desire no legal administration of my estate, I expect to leave no debts against my estate and I expect my residuary legatee to pay the expenses of my last sickness and funeral, which I make a charge upon the amount to be received by widow and residuary legatee.

II - I have loaned my son in law Henry H. Souder the sum of Two Thousand and Eight Hundred dollars, which I will and direct shall remain as a fund for the support of my wife Alma F. Spooner and if she shall survive me, it is my will that she shall have and use so much thereof principal and interest, as may be necessary for her support and comfort during her life.

III - I hold a note of Thirteen hundred and thirty-five dollars and eighty cents against my son in law Halbert B. Case and my daughter Janie M. Spooner Case, bearing interest payable annually Within one year after my death. I hereby will and direct my said Son in law and daughter to pay to my daughter Ellen S. Hord, the sum of Six hundred dollars, and to my daughter Harriet E. Spooner Souder the sum of Two hundred dollars, which sums will be received in part payment of said note. In case my said son in law and daughter, shall have paid my portion of said six hundred dollars and said two hudnred dollars to me before my death, the same shall be deducted from the amount of the said Harriet and the said Ellen, the remainder of the note with the interest thereon, I will and direct shall be judiciously invested in the erection [Page 210] of a family vault, wherein the members of my family shall be placed after their decease and I make and empower my son in laws Halbert B. Case and Henry H. Souder as my agents to carry out this provision of my will.

IV - I hold one note for Four Thousand dollars, dated September 1st 1875 due on day after date, with interest, signed by my son in law J. K. Hord, also one note for One Thousand dollars, of the same date, due on demand with interest, signed by my Son in law J. K. Hord, both payable to me, also one note for One Thousand dollars dated July 12th 1876 and due 6 months after date with interest payable to the order of H. H. Souder signed by J. K. Hord and Ella S. Hord.

These notes I give, devise and bequeath to my daughter Ellen S. Hord, to my said daughter Ellen, a certain note for Two Hundred dollars, which is to me, by my Nephew A. C. Hord, and is given for rents for the plantation in Louisiana. I also give, devise and bequeath to my said daughter, Ellen, the sum of Six hundred dollars, heretofore directed to be paid to her by my son in law and daughter Halbert B. and Janie M. Spooner Case.

V - The residue of my property real, personal and mixed wherever situated, I give devise and bequeath to my daughter Harriet E. Spooner Souder, including whatever may remain of the fund set apart for my widow Alma F. Spooner at her death.

VI - All the bequests herein made to each of my said daughters are made as separate estates to each of them, to be free and unincumbered by any of the marital rights of either or any of their husbands, with power in each to sell, convey, devise, bequeath, use and enjoy the same as fully as if each was a fini soli.

[Page 211]

VII - I hereby will, direct, authorize and empower my son in law Halbert B. Case to deliver the notes aforesaid to my said daughter Ellen, and to transmit to her at the proper time, the money which I have above bequeathed to her.

Given under my hand and signed by in presence of Charles E. Stanley and Charles B. Freeman, whom I have called to witness the signing of this my last Will and Testament on this the 24th day of November 1881.

Alanson C. Spooner

Signed in our presence by Alanson C. Spooner who has called us to witness the signing thereof and we have signed the same as witnesses, in his presence at his request and in the presence of each other on this the 24th day of November.

Charles E. Stanley
Charles B. Freeman

Codicil: to my last will and Testament:

In my foregoing will I provided for the payment of a certain note and mortgage amnounting to the sum of Thirteen Hundred and Thirty Five dollars, which was given me by son in law H. B. Case & his wife and my daughter Janie M. S. Case.

Since the making of said will I have agreed to release my said son in law from the payment of said note and mortgage and from the payment of other claims in consideration of which relinquishment he has executed and delivered to me a deed, of his undivided one half interest in and to lot 7 Caroline Street on which my said daughter and son in law live and which deed is duly recorded.

Therefore I hereby will devise and bequeath unto

my said daughter Janie M. S. Case - as a separate estate, to her separate use and behoof, free from the marital rights of her present or any future husband, with power to use [page 212] sell and enjoy or bequeath, as fully, as if she were a feme soli - all my right, title and interest in and to said lot 7 Caroline Street in the City of Chattanooa, subject however to the payment, by my said Daughter, Janie, of the said sum of Thirteen Hundred and Thirty Five Dollars, in the manner and at the times and to the persons as directed in my said Will.

Given under my hand on this 17th day of March A. D. 1882 and I have signed this codicil in presence of F. E. Tyler and Milo B. Coulter, whom I have called to witness my signature and they have signed it as witnesses in my presence and in the presence of each other - the day last named.

Alanson C. Spooner

Signed by us in the presence of A. C. Spooner at his request and we have signed as witnesses in his prsence and in the presence of each other the 17th day of March 1882.

Francis E. Tyler
Milo B. Coulter

Filed June 9th, 1884
Entered on record #5 pages 395, 396, 397 and 398.

[Page 213]

MITCHELL QUEENER

Will of Mitchell Queener

I Mitchell Queener, being of sound mind and disposing memory but in failing health, do make, publish and declare this to be my last will and Testament.

I direct that my body be decently buried and that my funeral expenses and all my just debts be paid by my Executor, hereinafter named, out of money that may come to his hands belonging to my estate.

II After all my just debts and funeral expenses and the compensation of my Executor shall have been paid, I give the rest and residue of my estate to my Executor in trust for my friend Zed Lucas of Chattanooga Tennessee to be held and managed by my Executor for said Lucas, the Executor to keep the money at interest or invest it in real estate for the benefit of said Lucas, paying him the rents or the interest as the case may be.

I hereby appoint Lewis Shepherd Esq. to be Executor of this will and relive him of the necessity of giving bond and security.

Mitchell X Queener (Seal)
his mark

Signed, Sealed and declared in our presence and we have subscribed our names, hereto as witnesses, in the presence of each other of the Testator and at his request on this February 24th 1884.
A. J. Mahagan
L. M. Clark
C. H. Peabody
G. M. Sherwood

Entered of record in Book #5 Page 402

[Page 214]

TIMOTHY PAIGE

Will of Timothy Paige

I, Timothy Paige, of Chattanooga in the County of Hamilton, and state of Tennessee, being of sound disposing mind and memory, do make and publish this my last Will and Testament.

I I give and bequeath to Adeline Wells, the south half of lot number Thirty Five (35) on Chestnut Street, in Chattanooga, fronting fifty (50) feet on Chestnut Street and running back the full length of the block to Pine Street, supposed to be Two hundred and thirty seven (237) feet, more or less.

II I give and bequeath to Anna M. Wells, Sallie Wells and Katie E. Wells, my money and personally property, to be equally divided.

III I ordain and appoint Moses Wells, without security, as Executor of this my last will and Testament, all wills heretofore made by me I hereby revoke.

In testimony whereof I have hereunto set my hand and seal, and publish and declare this to be my last Will and Testament in the presence of the witnesses named below, this second day of
August in the year of our Lord One Thousand Eight Hundred and Seventy Nine.

Timothy Paige (Seal)

Signed, sealed published and delivered by the said Timothy Paige, as and for his last will and Testament in presence of us, who in his presence and in the presence of each other and at his request have hereunto subscribed our names as witnesses.

John L. M. French

G. H. Wells
James C. Wells

Filed July 19th 1884
Entered on record #5 Page 409

[Page 215]

LUCY A. THAYER

Will of Lucy A. Thayer

I, Lucy A. Thayer, of Chattanooga Tennessee, formerly of Boston, Massachusetts, do make, publish and declare this my last Will and Testament, thereby revoking all former wills:

I I direct that the sum of Ten Thousand Dollars ($10,000.00) be set apart out of the proceeds of any property of which I may die seized and possessed and placed in trust with the "Massachusetts Hospital Life Insurance Company" of Boston, Massachusetts, for the use and benefit of my daughter Mrs. Mary Montague, during her natural life and to be by her disposed of by will, at her death the interest and profits alone of said fund to be paid to her during her natural life, for her sole and separate use. The Corpus of the fund to remain intact during her natural life, to be by her disposed of by will, at her death, and in the event she should die intestate as to said fund I then direct that said fund, at her death, go to the heirs of her body, share and share alike, and if any of such heirs, shall have died leaving issue living at the time of her death, such issue shall take the share such heir would have taken if living, said fund and the interest and profits thereof, to be forever free from the control, debts, contracts and all marital rights of her husband and my Executrix, hereinafter named is directed and fully empowered to sell and transfer and convey any kind or portion of the property or estate of which I may die seized and possessed, as to her may seem best, for the purpose of providing said fund to be placed in trust as above directed.

II - All the rest and residue of my property and estate, real and personal, of whatever character and wherever situated, I devise and bequeath to my said daughter, Mrs. Mary Montague [Page 216] for her sole and separate use and to be forever free, from the control, debts, contracts and all marital rights of her husband, giving here full power to sell, convey, transfer, encumber or dispose of the same, without any instrictions or limitations in such manner, at such times, to such persons and upon such terms as she may deem proper and as fully to all intents and purposes as if she were a femi soli.

I appoint my said daughter Mrs. Mary Montague, sole Executrix of this my last will, without bond.

In witness whereof, I have hereunto set my hand and seal this 2nd day of February in the year of our Lord, one Thousand eight hundred and eighty four.

Lucy A. Thayer (Seal)

The above instrument was at the date thereof signed, sealed, published and declared by the said Lucy A. Thayer as and for her last Will and Testament, in the presenece of us, and we at her request and in her presence and in the presence of each other have subscribed our names as witnesses thereto.

W. S. Marshall   Chattanooga, Tenn.
J. H. Rathburn   "   "
Winthrop Barr   "   "

Filed August 12th 1884
Record Book #5 Page 414 & 415

[Page 217]

GORDON J. EMORY

Will of Gordon J. Emory

I will my property in the State of Tennessee, near Chattanooga and in Canada, to my Brother William T. Emory and his wife in trust for their children. The said William S Emory and wife to have the interest of the same during their lives. The same arrangement to take place in regard to Florida land.

Gordon J. Emory

March 18th 1884

D. T. Dodds, Witness

Appendix to said will, the power to sell all of said lands, is given to William S. Emory and Charlotte Emory, at any time they wish.

Gordon J. Emory

Witness D. T. Dodds
March 18th 1884

Filed and Probated Aug. 12th 1884
Entered on Record Book #5 Page 420

[Page 218]

E. J. COLLINS

Will of E. J. Collins

I, E. J. Collins, do make and publish this my last Will and Testament.

I desire that all my debts and funeral expenses be paid and the balance of my property I give and bequeath to Mrs. Honey, wife of John Honey, who lives on my place near Chickamauga Station.

I nominate and appoint John Honey to be Executor of this my last Will.

(no signature)

Witness Lewis Shepherd

Filed and Probated Sept. 1. 1884
Record Book #5 Page 422

[Page 219]

O. E. ROSS

Will of O. E. Ross

I, O. E. Ross, of the County of Hamilton in the State of Tennessee, of sound mind and disposing memory do make and publish, this my last Will and Testament hereby revoking all other wills by me at any time made.

I - I give and bequeath to my wife, Linda B. Ross, and to my children Gus B. Ross and Mary E. Ross and to any other children that may be hereafter born to myself and my said wife, to all the same as tenants in common, share and share alike, all of my right, title, interest and claim either legal or equitable in and to the houses and lots owned and on which Dr. Milton R. May of Athens, McMinn County Tenn. resided at the date of his death, situated in Athens McMinn County Tenn. and being the same property willed to me by the last Will and Testament of the said Dr. Milton R. May and to which said will reference is had for particular description of said property. I also will and bequeath to my said Wife and children share and share alike any and all other property real personal or mixed, wherever located of which I am now owner or which I may hereafter acquire or become possessed.

Given under my hand and seal this 9th day of August 1884 in the presence of T. M. McConnell and G. W. Vinson, who are called as witnesses to the same at my request.

O. E. Ross (Seal)

Attest:

T. M. McConnell
Geo. W. Vinson

Filed Oct. 6th 1884
Probated Oct. 6th 1884
Record in Book #5 Page 446

[Page 220]

JOSEPH PEARSON

Will of Joseph Pearson

I, Joseph Pearson, considering the uncertainty of human life, do make and publish this my last Will and Testament in manner and form as follows.

I - I give and bequeath to the children of Abner Pearson ($200.00) Two hundred dollars to be divided equally among them, having already given to children now living all I believe to be their just due. I now give and bequeath my real estate and all my goods, chattels and personal property of whatever nature to my beloved wife Nancy M. Pearson excepting the ($200.00) Two hundred dollars above mentioned and I hereby appoint Edward M. Brooks, Administrator of my estate, revoking all former wills by me made. In witness where of I have hereunto set my hand and seal this 8th day of October, 1884.

The above instrument consisting of one sheet, was now here at King's Point, Hamilton Co. Tenn., in the residence of the testator Joseph Pearson, signed by him, in the presence of these witnesses and was declared by him to be his last will and Testament and signed by us at his request.

A. J. Brooks,
    Residing at King's Point, Hamilton Co., Tenn.
    Perry X Irving
        his mark
    Residing at King's Point, Hamilton Co., Tenn.
    Edward M. Brooks,"   "   "   "
    Rebecca Morse "   "   "   "   "

I, W. H. Tilman, a Justice of the Peace for the 7th Dist. County of Hamilton State of Tenn. hereby affirm that Joseph Pearson is in a feeble condition by reason of sickness and that he acknowledged to me that the above marks were made for his signature to his last Will and Testament

William H. Tilman, J. P.

Filed Oct. 30th 1884
Record Book #5 Pages 472 and 473

[Page 221]

ALEXANDER McMILLAN

Will of Alexander McMillan

I, Alexander McMillan of Hamilton County Tennessee, forty years of age, being of sound mind and disposing memory do hereby make and publish this my last Will and Testament, hereby revoking all others.

First: I direct that my Executor shall out of my Estate pay all of my just debts, including funeral expenses, medical attendance and a fair compensation to my executor for his services in winding up my business.

Second: I will and bequeath two thirds of all my property, real personal or mixed or the proceeds thereof after making sales of the real estate and after paying the matter set out in the first clause, hereof to my brother William McMillan, now living near the Village of Drumnando chit Inverness shire Scotland.

Third: I will and bequeath the remaining one-third of my property to my youngest sister Elizabeth McMillan, of the above mentioned place.

Fourth: I hereby appoint Morris B. Powell executor, of this my last will and Testament hereby conferring on my executor full power, and authority to sell and convey any real estate, I may die siezed and possessed in such manner and upon such terms as he in his judgment may deem best and to do all other things necessary to be done under the law to settle up my Estate and to carry out the terms of this will:

Fifth: I direct that my Executor be allowed to serve without giving the usual statutory bond.

Witness my hand, seventh day of October 1884.

Alexander McMillan

Signed in our presence & by us in the presence of the Testator, at his special request, this seventh day of October 1884.

M. Cary
John Steele Jr.

Filed Nov. 24, 1884. Probated Nov. 24, 1884
Recorded on Page 485 & 486 Book #5

[Page 222]

Will of Alexander McMillan
Mission Ridge, Hamilton County, Tennessee

I, Alexander McMillan of Hamilton County, Tennessee, forty years of age, being of sound mind and disposing memory, do hereby make and publish thismy last will and Testament, hereby revoking all others.

[The will of Alexander McMillan is copied, word for word, as it appears on page 221. Date of probate, however, is omitted in this, also the words "Recorded on Page 485 & 486 Book #5"]

[Page 223]

MARTHA JANE ASHBURN

Will of Martha Jane Ashburn

In the name of God Amen:

I, Martha Jane Ashburn, being feeble in body, but of sound mind and disposing memory, and in view of the uncertainty of life and the certainty of death do make and publish this my last will and Testament.

Item 1st - It is my will and desire that all my just debts and my funeral expenses be first paid.

Item 2nd - It is my desire that my Executor shall see that my children are at good homes, where they will be properly and kindly cared for. My beloved Aunt Caroline Read has kindly consented to look after the welfare of the three younger children and I have placed them in her charge and prefer that she have the supervision of them during their minority, if she should live so long, but in the event of her death, then if the children should need the protection and care of my Executor I desire that it be extended to them. My beloved son Bernard is, I suppose at his Grandfather's Townes in Davidson County Tennessee. It is my desire that my Executor shall secure him a good home with some kind family, and that my said executor shall act as the Guardian of all the children, if he will. It is my desire that all my children be instructed in the rudiments of a good English education, but my means and estate will not allow that they be sent to expensive schools.

Item 3rd - After my death, I direct that my executor shall as soon as practicable, sell either Publicly or Privately as may seem to him most advantageous and in the most advantageous terms (all of which is left to his discretion) all my real estate situated in the Civil District of Hamilton County Tenn. and bounded by the lands of [blank] and others, being the same land inherited by me, from my [Page 224] Grandfather's estate Josiah M. Anderson's estate and more particularly described in the decree of Chancery Court of Hamilton County Tenn. vesting the title to the same in me, to which I refer for a more perfect description of the same and I do further direct that my said Executor shall reinvest the proceeds of said sale (except as here in after provided) in unimproved real estate situated within the corporate limits of the City of Chattanooga Tenn. taking the title to the same in his own name as Trustee for my four children viz: Bernard Townes, my oldest, and Icie F., Ida A., and Anderson T. Ashburn, my three youngest children, who, I direct shall share in the same and in the increased valuation thereof as tenants in common, but I also direct that no division of said real estate shall be made among them until the youngest becomes of lawful age that is to say of the age of Twenty One years.

Item 4th - There may not be sufficient personal assets beloning to my esate to discharge the debts and demands against it and also to meet accruing current demands to this end, therefore, I direct that my Executor shall set apart out of the proceeds of the sale of my real estate, the sum of One Thousand Dollars, which with any other personal assets unappropriated by him for charges against my estate, direct shall be loaned out at interest on undoubted security. Further, I direct that the said unimproved property when purchased by my said Executor, shall be leased or let to good tenants for a term of years (provided this can be done) but not to exceed the time when the youngest of said Children shall become of lawful age said tenant paying a stipulated ground rental quarterly or semi-annually.

I direct that the proceeds of these leases, and the interest on the fund [Page 225] loaned out be used for the payment of the current taxes and also to defray the necessary expenses of my said children but if the interest and rents be inadequate for this purpose, then I direct that the principal of the fund loaned out be drawn upon from time to time for what may be necessary and upon the youngest child becoming twenty one years of age, I direct that all my estate both real and personal shall be divided equally between my said children.

Item 5th - It is my wish and desire that my beloved Uncle William E. Anderson act as this Executor of this my last Will and Testament.

Given under my hand on this the 12th day of August 1884.

Martha Jane Ashburn
Signed and acknowledged in our presence.

William Rankin
B. B. Bennett

[Page 226]

MARIA SETTARI

Last Will and Testament - Maria Settari

To all to whom these presence may concern Greeting.

Know ye:

That I, Maria Settari of mature age and sane mind and being mindful of the uncertainty of human life and being desirous of settling all my earthly affairs while I am able to do so hereby make, publish and declare this my last Will and Testament as follows subject to the payment of my just debts. I hereby give devise and bequeath unto E. Richi my faithful friend, all of my property whether real, personal or mixed of every description whatsoever of which I may die possessed and seized.

I am led to make this bequest as a merited reward for kindnesses already shown and extended to me by said E. Richi and in consideration of the further fact that the said E. Richi has agreed to care for me and protect me as a son would do, during my natural life and to see that my remains are decently and neatly put away after my decease and this Will and Testament is made upon the condition that the said E. Richi shall continue to show & exercise a kind care of me and nurse and protect me during my said natural life and shall pay the expenses of my last illness and funeral expenses & all other debts which I may owe at the time of my decease.

I hereby revoke and annull all former wills by me made of whatever character.

In witness whereof, I have hereunto affixed my hand on this the 27th day of December A. D. 1879 In the presence of H. B. Case and H. F. Griscom, whom I have called to witness my signature and who have signed the same as witnesses at my request in my presence & in the presence of each other.

Maria Settari

The foregoing will was signed by Maria Settari in our presence and we have signed the [Page 227] same as witnesses, in her presence and at her request and in the presence of each other, on this the 27th Day of December A. D. 1879.

H. F. Griscom

H. B. Case

GEORGE RENWICK

Last Will and Testament of George Renwick Decd.

I George Renwick, of Chattanooga Tennessee being in feeble health, but of sound mind and disposing memory, do make and publish this my last Will and Testament, hereby revoking any will heretofore made by me.

First, I desire that all my just debts & funeral expenses, shall be paid in full as soon as possible.

Second, I give and bequeath to my beloved wife, Mary C. Renwick, all my property real, personal and mixed of every description and wherever situated.

Third, I will and desire that she shall for the present continue the business of Renwick & Trout in the same manner as if I were living, and until such time as it may be her desire to change the business.

Fourth, I hereby nominate and appoint my said wife Mary C. Renwick and my partner John Trout, Executrix and Executor of this my last will and testament with full power to execute the same. I excuse my said wife from the execution of a bond as Executrix of this will, and desire that her preferences and wishes shall control in winding up my business and in the management of the property herein bequeathed to her.

Signed, sealed and published at Chattanooga Tennessee This 26th January 1885.

George Renwick (Seal)

The foregoing will was signed, sealed & published in our presence and we have subscribed the same in the presence of the Testator of each other, This 26th Jany. 1885.

J. A. Caldwell
H. Berlin
Monroe Hilton

Probated Feby. 4, 1885

[Page 228]

R. B. McGAUGHEY

Last Will and Testament of
R. B. McGaughey Decd.

Indio Cala. Dec. 3 1883
To whom it may concern.

Knowing that I am fast declining with Consumption, I do make this my will. I will to my wife Lizzie G. McGaughey, all the effects and property whether real or personal that I own and possess, to have and hold same and dispose of as she may think best.

I do request of my wife Lizzie G. McGaughey, to educate and take care of my little girl Nellie Belle McGaughey and see that she never suffers for anything and in event my girl Nellie Belle McGaughey lives to be grown and marries I do request of my wife Lizzie G. McGaughey, to give her just so much property, as my wife in her judgment, may be able to spare and not cripple herself. I further request of my wife Lizzie G. McGaughey, in event my daughter Nellie Belle McGaughey, does not live agreeably with her husband to take my daughter Nellie Belle McGaughey, to her home and forever support and take care of her.

This will may appear awkward to the Court, but is the best I can do without any form.

R. B. McGaughey

Witness
G. O. Coffman

[Page 229]

DAVID. D. JONES

Last Will and Testament of D. D. Jones

Hereby revoking all Wills or codicils by me at any time heretofore made, I, David D. Jones hereby make publish and declare my last Will and Testament to be as follows.

Item 1st - My Executor hereinafter named shall out of my whole Estate first pay all of my just debts, my funeral expenses, purchase a lot in a Cemetery and erect a suitable monument over my remains.

Item 2nd - I desire the residue of my Estate to be applied, in manner and as is hereinafter prescribed, to the rearing, education, maintenance and support of my son Lattner Q. Jones, until he arrives at the age of Twenty Five years, at which time the residue, with its accumulations, shall be turned over to my said son, Latner Q. Jones upon his arrival at the age of Twenty five years, as aforesaid, to be held by him as an Estate in fee simple forever.

Item 3rd - In the event of the death of my said son Latner Jones before arriving at the age of Twenty five years, unmarried and without living issue him surviving, then and in that event, I will and bequeath the said residue of my Estate to my brothers and sisters, to wit: Mary Davis, wife of Price Davis, of the city of Liverpool in England, Jane Evans, wife of Enoch Evans, William Jones and Ann Hughes, wife of Joseph Hughes, all of Gyffylliog, Denbrightshire, North Wales, to each of my brothers and sisters an equal undivided interest as an Esate of inheritance in fee simple.

Item 4th - It is my will and desire that my executor hereinafter named, shall expend not exceeding Fifteen Dollars a month for the maintenance and support of my said son [Page 230] Latner Q. Jones from the date of my death, until my son shall arrive at the age of Eight years, provided, that in the event of sickness of my said son, Latner Q. Jones that such additional sum may be expended as shall be necessary to pay all reasonable expenses incident to said sickness and provided that so long as my said son Latner Q. Jones, shall remain with his mother my former Wife, then my executor hereinafter named, shall expend only so much as may be necessary for the clothing, schooling and Physicians bills of my said son.

Item 5th - It is my further will and desire that my Executor, upon the arrival of my said son Latner Q. Jones, at the age of eight years, shall in accordance with the terms of a decree of divorce between myself and my former wife, his mother, rendered at the May Term 1883 of the Circuit Court at Chattanooga, Tenn., shall take custody and control of my said son, Latner Q. Jones, and shall maintain support, clothe and educate him until he arrives at the age of Eighteen years, or if my said Executor shall deem it most to the interest of my said son, may continue his education until he shall graduate at some Institution of Learning and in the event upon the arrival at the age of Eighteen years or graduation, the consent of my said son can be obtained thereto, it is my Will and desire that my Executor shall apprentice my said son to some suitable person or corporation, a sufficient length of time to learn a trade.

Item 6th - It is my will and desire that my said son, Latner D. Jones, shall receive nothing from my Estate from his arrival at the age of Twenty one years until his arrival at the age of Twenty five years, at which time, my Executor shall turn over to him the residue of my Estate, with its accretions as hereinbefore provided.

Item 7th - It is my further Will and desire that my Executor shall act under the advice and consent of Tomlinson Fort Esq., and that my said Executor with the approval of said Fort, shall be authorized and empowered to sell and convey any portion of the Real Estate of which I may die seized and possessed or which may be acquired in pursuance of this, my Will, and apply the proceeds to carry out its objects and purposes and shall not be required to give any bond, unless upon the demand of said [page 231] Fort, my Executor, with the approval of said Fort, may tresspass upon the corpus of my Estate and if necessary, consume it all in the rearing and education of my said son Latner Q. Jones. But my said Executor shall be required to invest all surplus arising from the rents or sales of property after payment of my debts, funeral expenses, support, maintenance and education of my said son, in Real Estate in the City of Chattanooga Tennessee and in improvements and repairs placed thereon.

Item 8th - I hereby nominate and appoint David W. Hughes, as the execuotr of this my last Will and Testament.

Item 9th - I further Will and desire, that in the event of the death of said David W. Hughes, before the arrival of my said son at the age of Twenty five years, That said Tomlinson Fort shall qualify as Executor of this, my will, without giving any bond as such and in event of the death of said Fort, that said Hughes, shall be authorized to act under all of the items of this Will, without consulting any other person or persons, in as full manager as he and said Fort could have done, upon the death of said Fort.

This Feb. 12th 1884

D. D. Jones {Seal}

Signed, sealed and published in our presence and we have subscribed our names hereto in the peresence of the Testator

This 12th day of Feb. 1884
C. P. Jones
L. C. Martin
W. C. Ashley

Probated Mch. 2 1885

[Page 232]

HANNAH LAWRENCE

Last Will and Testament of
Hannah Lawrence, Decd.

I, Hannah Lawrence, being in sound mind disposing disposition do on this 11th day of October 1884 at Chattanooga in Tennessee make and publish this my last Will and Testament.

I am the owner of a note made to me by my brother Job Sackey, payable one year after the death of my Father Enos Sackey for Fifteen Hundred Dollars (1500$) and on my death it is my desire and Will that my funeral expenses, debts and liabilities be paid out of said note, upon which in consideration of the love and affection I bear to my Sister Jennie White of Indianapolis in Indiana I bequeath to her Two Hundred Dollars (200$) and for the same consideration I will and bequeath to my Sister Carrie Sellars of Indianapolis in Indiana Two Hudnred Dollars (200$) both amounts to be taken and paid them be my Executrix out of said note and for the love and affection I bear my sister Kate Hamilton of Chattanooga in Tennessee, I will the entire remaining interest in my Father Enos Sackey's Estate I bequeath the same to said Kate Hamilton.

And I constitute and appoint the said Kate Hamilton as the sole Executrix of this my will.

Mrs. Hannah Lawrence
Dr. H. Berlin
Mrs. S. B. Bennett

Signed, sealed, published and declared to be the last Will and Testament of the said Hannah Lawrence, in the presence of us who both together at the same time in the presence of the said Hannah Lawrence and at her request have hereunto subscribed our names as witnesses.

Mrs. Hannah Lawrence
Dr. H. Berlin
Mrs. S. B. Bennett

Witness
Wm. A. Freudenberg

[Page 233]

CYNTHIA FOUST

Last Will and Testament of Cynthia Foust, Decd.

I, Cynthia Foust, of the City of Chattanooga Tennessee, being in weak body but of sound mind and disposing memory and being desirous of disposing of such property as it has pleased an all wise providence to bestow upon me, in such way as to me seems right and proper, do make and publish this my last Will and Testament.

1st - It is my will and desire that my debts and my funeral expenses be first paid by my Executor hereinafter named, as soon as praticable after my death, out of any money or property of which I may die siezed and possessed.

2nd - I will and bequeath unto Edward S. Thompson, sometimes called Birdie Thompson son of Andy Thompson, the absolute, fee simple title to my house and lot upon which I now live on Fields Alley in the City of Chattanooga Tennessee, fronting 25 feet on Field's Alley and running back of uniform width 25 feet and being 25 feet square out of the North East corner of Lot 3 in Block 7 of P. & E. C. Foster's subdivision of Griffins addition to the City of Chattanooga.

3rd - I will and bequeath unto my sister Mrs. George Anderson all my personal property of any kind that I may die seized and possessed of.

4th - I hereby nominate and appoint W. M. Fields Executor of this my last Will and Testament.

Given under my hand and seal on this the 31st day of March 1885.

Cynthia X Foust
her mark

Signed, sealed, published and declared by the Testator to be her last will and testament in our presence and we witness the same at the testators request, in her presence and in the [Page 234] presence of each other.

This the 31st day of March 1885
attest

Wm. Fields
B. Moore
Harry X Morgan
his mark

JACKSON SMITH NO. 1

Last Will and Testament of Jackson Smith No. 1.

I, Jackson Smith No. 1 do make and publish this as my last will and Testament hereby revoking and making void all other wills by me at any time made.

First, I direct that my funeral expenses and all my debts be paid, as soon after my death as possible out of any moneys that I may die possessed of, or may first come into the hands of my executor.

Secondly, I give and bequeath to my wife Susan Jane, the remainder of my property and effects, after the expenses mentioned in the first clause is liquidated and all legal debts against my estate.

I do hereby nominate and appoint G. H. Jarnagin, my executor, in witness whereof I do, to this my will, set my hand and seal This 11th day of January 1885.

Jackson Smith No. 1 {Seal}

Signed, sealed and published in our presence and we have subscribed our names hereto in the presence of

the Testator.
            This 11th day of January 1885
                      Thos. Giffe
                      Henry Lacy

[Page 235]

DANIEL S. JONES

Last Will of Daniel S. Jones, Decd.

I, Daniel S. Jones being of sound and perfect mind and memory do make and publish this my last Will and Testament in manner and form following.

First, I give and bequeath unto my beloved wife Mary Jane Jones and her heirs a certain tract or parcel of land lying and being in Hamilton County Tennessee on the waters of Oppossom Creek Bounded and described as follows commencing on Black Oak corner on the shin bone ridge corner to Madison Varner and running with his line to the foot of Walden's Ridge thence north east with the foot of the ridge to Dan's Branch thence with the Branch south eastwardly to the old ford then a straight line to a Pine to the foot of the shin bone ridge thence South eastwardly to the old line thence with the old line to the beginning corner also after my debts and funeral expenses is settled all the perishable property that I am seized and possessed of I bequeath unto her the said Jane Jones and her heirs forever, whereunto I have set my hand and affixed my seal this the 10th day of February 1873.

Signed, sealed, published, and declared by the above named Daniel S. Jones to be his last Will and Testament in the presence of us who have hereunto subscribed our names as witnesses in the presence of the Testator.

                      D. S. Jones {seal}

Witnesses
A. T. Miller
Madison Varner

[Page 236]

NICHOLAS NOLAN

Last Will of Nicholas Nolan, Deceased

In the name of God; Amen.

I, Nicholas Nolen being of sound mind and feeling assured that I am now on my death bed and being desirous of adjusting and disposing of all my earthly concerns as far as possible do make this my last Will and Testament. Owing to my long continued bad health and misfortunes I have but little to dispose of but I desire of it in a manner that will do most good to those interested especially to my dear Wife and Children. I owe a few small debts, that I recognize as just and due, and wish if possible to be paid viz; I owe Pat Morgan about Ninety Dollars on account. I owe Pat Byrne an account of some two or three dollars. John Wolf about two dollars. I owe Casper Saffer about twenty cents & his brother George some two dollars & 50/100. There has been some considerable business done between Pat Powers and myself but I think he has been about if not fully paid. These amounts to the best of recollection are the only debts that I honestly owe.

There will be found on the Dockets of G. A. Wood Esq. J. P., Judgments against sundry persons in favor of Nolen & McCloud these Judgments are my property and McCloud really has no interest in them.

There is also a suit pending in the Chancery and Supreme Court in favor of Nolan Bro. & Bolin vs. H. C. Squires & Co. in which I have 1/3 interest these are about all the outstanding claims that I now remember of and I direct my administrator or executor to look after these claims and as soon as possible to pay my honet debts.

Realizing that my beloved wife Mary will have a hard time in caring for and supporting our numerous family [Page 237] seven children in all four of whom are under Twelve years of age I therefore give and bequeath to my beloved wife Mary the Homestead or House and lot on which I now reside situated on the corner of Williams and Eakins streets Chattanooga Hamilton County Tenn. together with all the improvements and apurtenances thereon together with all the household goods and furniture of every description now in said Home except one Piano which I specially reserve and bequeath to my youngest Daughter Anastasia now eight years of age and whom I desire if possible to have the advantages of a musical education such as her elder sisters have enjoyed at least. The above bequest is made to my wife Mary to have, to hold and use during her lifetime at her death I direct that the real estate and such other effects as not specially disposed of by her by will or otherwise shall be disposed of and equally divided between our beloved children or their heirs towit our Daughter Maggie now 18 years old, our Daughter Mary Ellen now 16 years our son John aged fifteen our son Nick aged eleven years our son Thomas aged nine years, our daughter Annie aged eight years and our son Joseph aged six years.

And I hereby nominate and appoint my beloved wife Mary as My sole Executrix to carry out and fulfl this my last will and Testament and I further direct and hereby empower my wife Mary as my Executrix. If in her judgment at any time before our youngest child shall become of age it be to the interest of all concerned she may sell and convey such Real estate and reinvest the proceeds thereof in other real estate for the benefit of the aforesaid heirs and I further direct that my wife Mary shall qualify as my executrix without bond.

Given under my hand and seal this the 1st day of August in the year of our Lord 1885.

Nick Nolan {Seal}

Witness
M. S. Cooper)attest
J. W. Fleck   )J. R. Harris
              Atty.

WESLEY C. YOUNG

Last Will of Wesley C. Young, Deceased.

I, W. C. Young farmer and fruit grower of the 5th civil district of Hamilton County Tenn. make this my last Will. I give devise and bequeath my estate and property real and personal as follows, that is to say, my farm located on Mission Ridge and described and bounded as follows on the North, East and West by the lands of N. Huddle and containing nine and one third acres (9 1/3) and fully described in a deed given by D. F. Dodds to me bearing date October 27, 1883. I also give devise and bequeath all my personal property and effects also desire and wish my wife S. J. Young to have full and complete control to transfer and reinvest or otherwise dispose of the property or any part of the same as she may wish. I further desire that at the decease of my wife the property as above decribed or the proceeds thereof shall become the property of my daughter Essey May Young.

I appoint my wife S. J. Young sole executrix of this my last will and Testament.

In witness whereof I have signed and sealed and published and declared this instrument at my will at my [Page 237] residence on the 17th day of August 1885.

Wesley C. Young {Seal}

The said W. C. Young at said residence on said 17 day of August 1885 signed and sealed this intrument and published and declared the same as and for his last Will and we at his request and in his presence and in the presence of each other have hereunto written our names as subscribing witnesses.

Witnesses
F. J. Bennett
Noah Huddle
O. P. Huddle

D.A. HARROVER

Last Will of D. A. Harrover Decd.
Chattanooga, Tenn.
Nov. 1, 1885

As I have good reason to think and feel that I shall soon be called upon to enter into eternal rest with the spirits of the just, I request my friend Richard Graves to have the following requests carried out after my departure.

I wish my Sister Margaret to take charge of my faithful old servant Harriett to give her the funds necessary to place her in proper condition to accompany her to her home in Washington, D. C. with her expenses paid to that point. I request him to have packed with care the set of furniture which I bought for her and delivered in Washington with any pieces that she may wish packed after she had conferred with my son in regard to certain articles of goods which I wish her to give to my daughter.

As my brother William gave to the family a good lot in Congressional Cemetery in Washington in which rests my wife [Page 240] and two of my children, I request a suitable marble shaft with the names of those resting there inscribed upon it also my own name when I shall be placed with them.

To my sister Elizabeth I give my shawl, to sister Mattie I give my clock to my brother Hiram I give my clothing, to Margaret I give my books and request her to aid my daughter in any way she can consistently in training her three fatherless boys.

After my affairs are justly settled whatever remains I wish equally divided between my two children Hammond and Sallie.

I pray God's richest blessings may rest upon them and that they may be just and kind to each other and that they may endeavor to train their children properly in the sight of God.

Any articles of household goods that my children may not want and my sister may designate I desire given to my faithful nurse, Mrs. Davis.

D. A. Harrover

Witnesses
G. W. Lacey
W. M. Cunningham

[Page 241]

N. J. GILLILAND

Last Will of N. J. Gilliland Decd.

Know all men that I, N. J. Gilliland of Chickamauga Hamilton County Tenn. being of sound mind and memory do make and publish this my last will and Testament to wit;

1 - I nominate and appoint my brother T. A. Witcher my sole executor and he shall not be required to give bond and give security for the faithful performance of his duties as Executor the same being expressly waived.

2 - I will and commit to the care and protection of my brother T. A. Witcher my two children James W. and Lady Blance Gilliland and appoint my said brother their guardian.

3 - I will and bequeath to my son James R. W. Gilliland one hair watch chain

4 - I will and bequeath to my daughter Lady Blance Gilliland one sewing maching the Wheeler and Wilson patent & my rings and Jewelry.

5 - To my brother T. A. Witcher herein appointed executor I will and bequeath in his capacity as executor & for the use and benefit of my said children James R. W. and Lady Blance Gilliland all other property real, personal and mixed of every kind character and description that I now own or may own at my death the said property or the proceeds of the sale of the same to be divided equally between my two children aforesaid.

6 - My said executor is fully authorized and empowered to convert into money for the use of my said children all my property herein conveyed or bequeathed to him in trust as executor either by public or private sale as he may think or otherwise to dispose of the same as he may deem best to the interest of my said children.

7 - I desire my executor and Guardian of my children to educate them and [Page 242] for the purpose of their education and support he is authorized to expend proceeds of sale of my property (if he deems it best to sell the same) for the purpose.

8 - Nothing in this will shall be so construed as depriving my executor of full power to dispose of my realty and personalty and all other property debts and accounts and closes in action as he may deem proper or from expending proceeds of same as in his opinion is best for the benefit of my children and particularly for their education.

In testimony whereof witness my hand at Chickamauga, Hamilton County Tennessee on the 11 day of July 1885.

N. J. Gilliland

The foregoing last will and testament of Mrs. N. J. Gilliland was signed by her in our presence and at her request after she had read and signed the same before us we hereunto signed our names as witnesses to the same in her presence and in the presence of each other at Chickamauga Tenn. July 11 1885
R. M. Robertson
R. S. Smith

[Page 243]

MALVINA SMITH

Last Will of Malvina Smith Decd.

I, Malvina Smith being of sound mind and disposing memory do make, publish and declare this to be my last Will and Testament.

1st - I desire to be decently buried and that my funeral expenses and just debts shall be paid out of the property, money, or assets which I may leave.

2nd - I give, bequeath, and devise to my two children Henrietta and Clarence all the property of every kind and character that I may die siezed and possessed of.

I hereby nominate and appoint Wm. Lewis colored and Lizzie Montague colored to be executor and executrix of my will and also testamentary guardians of my two children. I desire that they shall take charge of my property real and personal; the personal property they are to use in their discretion for the benfit of my children and they will rent out the real estate also for their benefit. It is my desire, that, if possible, the real estate of which I may die siezed and possessed be kept and preserved for my children and turned over to them upon the majority of the younger. If it shall become necessary in order to provide a support and education for my children to sell my real estate, my executors will apply to the Chancery Court of Hamilton County Tennessee for leave to sell such real estate, the proceeds of sale if a proper case shall be made to authorize a decree of sale by said Chancery Court shall be applied as far as necessary to the support and education of said children. My request is that my children be educated at the Public Schools of Chattanooga and that if possible my real estate be kept for my children. I think that my personal property and rents with what my children can earn ought to provide for their clothes and board. [Page 244]

Witness my hand and seal this Jany. 8 1885.

Malvina Smith {Seal}

Signed, sealed, and acknowledged in our presence, we having been requested to witness the signatures of the testatrix and become subscribing witnesses hereto and we here subscribe our names in the presence of the Testatrix and of each other Jany. 8, 1885.

Lewis Shepherd
Louis C. Gibbs

ROBERT A. GILES

Last Will of Robert A. Giles
March 22nd 1886

Chattanooga, Hamilton Co.
State of Tennessee

Unto all whom it may Concern.

This Last Will and Testament of Robert A. Giles of Chattanooga, Hamilton Co., State of Tennessee.

Whereby he Doth Will and bequeath to his wife, Sarah Jane Giles all his Real Estate, personal property, money &c. for her benefit and use during her life time; and at her death whatever Real Estate that was left as the property of R. A. Giles, will become the property of our Daughter, Cora Jane Giles to have and to hold as her Property for ever.

Furthermore I desire that my Wife, Sarah J. Giles, be appointed Adminstratrix to this Will without Bond.

R. A. Giles

G. F. Brown)
W. B. Wells) Witness

[Page 245]

KATIE VAN EPPS

Last Will of Katie Van Epps
The State of Tennessee

I, Katie Van Epps, being of sound mind and disposing memory do make, ordain and publish this to be my last Will and Testament hereby revoking any former Will which may have been heretofore made by me.

1st - I desire that my body shall be decently buried, and that all my funeral expenses and just debts be paid, if I owe any at the time of my death.

2nd - I give and devise to daughter Emily Scott, five acres of land including my dwelling house, out of the tract of land on which I live, the same to be laid off to her off the North side of my eleven acre tract, making the road in front of my house the northern line or boundary, beginning at a point where my land adjoins the Rickey tract of land thence running with the road to my north east corner thence with John Farris' line for enough to make the complement of five acres. Said 5 acres to be taken off the north end of my eleven acre tract.

3rd - I give to my grand daughter, Catherine Smith, two acres and a half of my said eleven acre tract to be laid off adjoining the five acre tract above devised to my daughter Emily and to run clear across the eleven acre tract from East to West, so as to make two acres and a half.

4th - I give and devise to my daughter Alsa Reed three acres and a half to be taken off the South end of my said eleven acre tract of land, to be run off so as to be bounded on the north by the tract above devised to have and to hold the same to her the said Alsa Reed for and during her natural life with remainder to her heirs as next of kin.

5th - I give to my grand daughter, Catherine Smith, my bed and bed clothing belonging to it, also one cow named Rose and her present calf and all her future increase, also a small watery table.

6th - I give to my daughter, Emily Scott, my cow named Mollie and her calf, and all her future increase. I also give her my large wash kettle.

7th - I give my daughter, Alsa Reed, a young heifer to be selected by her out of my stock on hand at my death.

[Page 246]

8th - I give my daughter Emily her bed and bed clothing including six quilts and a large white counterpane, also I give her my wagon and mule.

9th - I give my Jennet to Pompey Price and if he is nothing at my death then my grandon Joshua Reed is to have the Jennet

10th - I desire that all the rest of my property be equally divided between my daughter Emily Scott, and my grand children who are the children of Alsa Reed, my said grand children to take one share and my daughter one share.

11th - I appoint William Crawford to be executor of this will.

In testimony whereof, I have hereunto set my hand, this 26 day of March 1886.

Katie Van Epps

The foregoing will was signed and acknowledge before us by the testatrix and we were called by the testatrix, to witness the same, and we have hereunto subscribed our names as witnesses in presence of the testatrix,, March 26 1886.

Lewis Shepherd
Isom Brantley

B. F. DAVIS

Last Will of B. F. Davis

State of Tennessee, Hamilton County
Know all men by these presents now made while I am in my right mind, as my last Will and Testament.

That I wish Policy No. 62 of Presbyterian Mutual Assurance Fund of Louisville Kentucky changed as to the heirs of Bessie R. Allison and that the amount of same be paid direct to Bessie R. Allison herself for love and affection.

I make this change in my will, that the amount of said Policy may be paid to Bessie R. Allison without any litigation in the courts or any guardian or Administrator being appointed.

This Will revokes all other Wills concerning said Policy.

This 9th day of April 1886
B. F. Davis
Attest
J. M. Hale
E. J. McCroskey

[Page 247]

ROBERT SIMPSON

Last Will of Robert Simpson

In the name of God, Amen:
I, Robert Simpson of the County of Hamilton and State of Tennessee, do make and publish this my last Will and Testament.

Item 1st - It is my Will and desire that my funeral expenses, and all my just debts, if any, be paid with any money I may leave, at the time of my death, or with the first money that may come to the hands of my executors.

Item 2nd - I give and devise to my daughter, Eliza Ann Elizabeth McBryant wife of James S. McBryant, for her separate use and benefit alone, and free from the marital rights and control of her present or any future husband; the tract of land upon which the said James S. and Eliza Ann Elizabeth now reside, together with a tract of land situated in the 17" Civil District of Hamilton County, Tennessee, known as the "Donaldson place" purchased by me, as a part of the estate Lewis Shepherd: & a tract of land containing Eighty Acres known as the Darwin tract and conveyed to me by [line blank] free from the debts and liabilities of her present or any future husband except that the said James S. McBryant is authorized to with the absent of his wife, to sell the "Donaldson tract" of one hundred and sixty acres and "Darwin tract" of eighty acres and apply the proceeds of said two tracts of land to the improvement of the farm on which he lives and the comfort of his family, provided, however, that his wife will join in any conveyances that may be made of either tract, and my said daughter is not to receive any other part of my estate real or personal.

Item 3rd - I give and devise to my daughter Mary Jane Nayl, wife of Lamb Nayl, for her separate use and benefit and free from the control of her present or any future husband and from the debts and liabilities of her present or any future husband, and free from any right whatever her present or any future husband could acquire by reason of any marital right [Page 248] a tract of land situated in the 6th district of James County, Tennessee, adjoining the lands of E. C. Shelton, Wm. Julian, lands owned by the heirs of Dr. McKay, Chas. Grey and others, containing seven hundred acres, the same upon which the said Nayl now resides.

Item 4th - I give and devise to my two daughters, Sarah Catherine and Ephania Clemantine Simpson, jointly and in equal proportions for their separate use and benefit, free from the control, contracts, debts, liabilities and marital rights of any future husband, the tract of land upon which I now reside known as my "Homeplace" together with a tract of land conveyed to me by Joshua Jones and his wife [blank] Jones, being part of a tract of land formerly owned by T. M. McGhee, dec., lying upon the waters of South Chickamauga Creek, near the shallow Ford bridge in Hamilton County, Tennessee. I refer to all the deeds and title papers I hold for said land registered and unregistered, for a description of all the lands herein devised, but which are not present while this will is being prepared. I also give and bequeath to my two said daughteres Catherine and Ephania Clemantine, all the stock, including horses, mules, cattle, sheep, poultry, and all animals I may own at the time of my decease, they having already become the owners of the greater portion of the stock on my farm.

I also give and bequeath to them my wagon and farming implements and tools that may be upon lands devised to them at the time of my death, together will all my household and Kitchen furniture as well as all grain and provisions that may be on hand at my death, it being my purpose and will that they take the lands devised to them, with all the stock, grain, provisions, farming implements, tools and other articles heretofore bequeathed that may be on hand at my decease.

I also direct and it is my Will that my executors collect all debts due me in [page 249] any manner whatever and apply them with my money of which I may die possessed to the payment of my funeral expenses, debts and costs of administration and pay the surplus, if any, in equal parts to my daughters, Sarah Catherine & Ephania Clementine Simpson.

Item 5th - I authorize my executors to sell three small tracts of land conveyed to me by William Lafeny at private or public sale, as in their discretion may seem best, upon a credit of twelve or eighteen months, except the sum twenty percent in cash, and execute deeds therefore upon the payment of the purchase money, and apply the proceeds if necessary to the payment of my debts and divide the remainder equally between my said four children and if any child should be dead leaving children, her child or children will take the share that should have gone to the mother if living.

Item 6th - No one of my children is to be charged with any advancements, and should any crops be growing in the lands herein devised, at the time of my death, the respective devisees will take the crop growing upon the lands devised to them.

Item 7" - Should any one of my children herein named as a devisee contest this will or attempt by bringing a suit in any court, to render it nojutory, then such child or children will not take any thing under this Will and the share devised to that child or children will go to those who do not contest this will or the children of that child or children if she be dead.

Lastly - I nominate and appoint Thomas Wolly and James S. McBryant executors of this my last Will and Testament and earnestly request that they accept the trust.

Robert Simpson {Seal}

Signed sealed and published in our presence on this 27" day of June 1866.

W. L. Eakin
Alx. Richey

[Page 250]

MARGARET LATIMORE

Last Will of Margaret Latimore

State of Tennessee)
Hamilton County)

We, Eliza Cobb, Emeline Cobb and Hulda Chestnut, were present last evening at 8 1/2 o'clock on the 3rd day of July 1886 at the residence of David Cobb, before and at the time of the death of Margaret Latimore who was in perfect possession of her mental faculty, as appeared to us; said Margaret Latimore called upon bystanders, and especially upon the undersigned, to take notice and remember what she was about to say; when she said that it had been her intention for some time past, to make her will in writing, thereby to dispose of her property, but had neglected to carry her intentions into execution, and that now it was not practicable

That she wished us to understand that her Will and desire was that Mack Cobb, Hulda Chestnut, and Dave Cobb should have take and possess all of her estate, personal and real, of every kind and description to them, their own proper use, benefit and behoof.

Her real estate of 38 1/2 Acres situate and lying in McMinn County, Tennessee, 1/2 acre situate and lying in the city of Athens, Tennessee.

Her personal estate ($112.50) one hundred and twelve dollars and fifty cents now deposited in the First National Bank in the City of Chattanooga, Tennessee. That said property should be equally divided between her said children David Cobb, Mack Cobb, and Hulda Chestnut, and she desired that he son David Cobb would see to her wishes and desires in this regard well carried out; immediately after which she died.

This July 5th 1886 -

State of Tennessee)
Hamilton County) We, Eliza Cobb, Emaline Cobb, and Hulda Chestnut, were present on the 3rd day of July 1886, at 8 1/2 o'clock and at the time of the death of Margaret Latimore when she made her last request and Verbal disposition of the property and effects of the disceased of said County; and it is just and true in all its parts.

David Cobb
Emaline Cobb
Hulda Chestnut
Eliza Cobb

Sworn to and subscribed before me this 5th day of July 1886.

R. G. McRee, Judge

[Page 251]

JULIA SNODGRASS

Last Will of Julia Snodgrass

I, Julia Snodgrass, of the city of Chattanooga, Tennessee, of the age of 65 years, and being of sound mind and memory do make, publish and declare this my last Will and Testament as follows to wit: -

I hereby give, devise and bequeath all my property both real and personal, wherever situated, and of whatever kind, and nature to Huston Wilson and Willie Wilson, children of C. T. Wilson by his first wife;

And I hereby appoint C. T. Wilson executor of this my last Will and Testament, of whom no bond shall be required.

And I hereby revoke any and all Wills heretofore made by me.

In witness whereof I have heretofore set my hand and seal this 20th day of August 1886.

Julia Snodgrass {L. S.}

Signed and sealed by Julia Snodgrass and by her declared to be her last Will in our presence who have hereunto subscribed our names as witnesses in her presence and in the presence of each other at her request. This August 20th 1886.

J. Hodge McLean
Chattanooga, Tenn.
Harry W. Durand
Chattanooga, Tenn.

JOSEPHINE M. RICHARDSON

Last Will of Josephine M. Richardson

I, Josephine M. Richardson, wife of the late Thomas Richardson, Sr. both of the City of Chattanooga

and state of Tennessee, do declare this to be my last will and Testament hereby revoking any Will by me at any time heretofore made. I give and bequeath to my stepson Thomas Richardson and his wife Ellen M. my double tenement house on 4th street to hold during their natural lives, at their death if they leave no children the property to go to Hanona wife of my stepson Joseph G. Richardson.

I give and bequeath to Hanona wife of Joseph G. Richardson my house and lot on the corner of 4th and Lookout St. After the work on houses and lots are completed and my debts paid in order to make the division [Page 252] equal I give and bequeath to Hanona wife of J. G. Richardson my money, notes, real estate & interest in store I may possess at my death.

I bequeath to T. Richardson & wife 6 silver forks, 4 old family tablespoons, 6 teaspoons, 2 salt spoons, and three dessert spoons, the rest of silver to Hanona wife of J. G. Richardson. I leave to Tom his father's and mother's pictures in gilt frames also some pictures of his Cousins in port folio if he wishes to have them, to Hanona Richardson I bequeath all my household furniture including piano, pictures, all glass and Chinaware &c. at Nona's death I wish Josie Fry to have my piano, I bequeath to J. G. Richardson my dear husband's watch and chain at his death to go to Richie Fry. I also wish Richie to have his grandfather's leather trunk. I bequeath to Josie Fry my two sets of Amethyst jewelry when she is 18 years old. to Annie Joe Hay I leave my two gold bracelets.

I appoint my stepsons, Thomas and J. G. Richardson my executors not requiring them to give bond. This I do without being influenced by any party or parties at Chattanooga, Tennessee.

Nov. 22nd 1886
J. M. Richardson

Witness
G. W. Drake
L. C. Drake

I don't wish Tom to pay back the $191.00 his father lent him to pay on Mountain farm.

J. M. Richardson

[Page 253]

PENDER SATTELWHITE

Last Will of Pender Sattelwhite

I, Pender Sattelwhite, being of sound mind and

memory do make this my last Will and Testament.

Item 1 - I give to my granddaughter, Carrie Ware, all my personal property; one bed, one looking glass, three tables, six chairs, a pot and two irons, set of glasses and dishes, all the books, one trunk, one washstand, the wardrobe, one picture, some clothes.

And real property, she, Carrie Ware, is to have the following described property, 14 ft. fronting Third St. between High St. and Lookout St. the east line of this property running straight line south 112 ft. more or less, the west line running 38 ft. south, a uniform width, thence a direct west 16 ft. and then south a direct line 74 ft. a uniform width.

All this I give to Carrie Ware, my granddaughter, the balance of the real property is to be divided equally among the following named persons, all of which are my children.

Nelson Sattelwhite
Penina Kelly
Dolly Johnson
Margette Henry
Robert Sattelwhite

The remaining part of this real property after taking off Carrie's of which I shall die seize I hereby appoint as executive of this my last Will and Testament Nelson Sattelwhite, Executive.

Pender Sattelwhite {seal}

Witness
N. M. Mays
Geo. W. Sewell

This the 1st day of Feb. 1883.

[Page 254]

ANTHONY HANDMAN

Last Will of Anthony Handman

I, Anthony Handman, being of sound mind and disposing memory, but in feeble bodily health and of mature age, do make and publish this my last Will and Testament.

1st - I desire that all my just debts and funeral expenses shall be paid by my executor out of the first money coming to his hand to be administered.

2nd - I will and desire that my beloved wife, Margaret Handman, shall have, occupy and enjoy my house place on Chestnut & 3rd Streets in Chattanooga Tenn. for and during the term of her natural life - for a home for herself and such of her children and

grandchildren as may choose to remain with her. And thereafter it shall be and remain a Homestead for my son Alfred Handman, my daughter Addie Agness Handman and the four children of my daughter, Mrs. L. M. Bush to wit: - Alice, Maggie, Julius and Charles Edward Bush; and at the arrival at the age of twenty one years of the younger of said Children Of Mrs. Bush, then living, I desire that the fee simple title to said Homestead lot shall be vested in said parties in the following proportions: Alfred Handman one third, Addie Agnes Handman, one third; and said children of Mrs. L. M. Bush one third - And if any one or more of them shall have died, then the share of such to his or her heirs at Law: -

3rd - I give and bequeath to my said daughter Addie Agness Handman, the sum of six hundred dollars to be paid to her in cash by my Executor out of the first money coming to his hands out of which he can pay the same.

4th - I give and bequeath to my son, Alfred Handman, the sum of three hundred dollars, which sum is to be loaned out by my Executor and well secured until such time as said Alfred Handman may marry and then said sum of $300 is to be paid to him - but until he marries, my said Executor is to pay to him the accruing interest upon said fund. And I direct that said interest shall be collected and paid over to him quarterly or semi-annually.

4th - I give and bequeath to my said Grandchildren [Page 253] Alice Bush, Maggie Bush, Julius J. Bush and Charles E. Bush, each ($100.00) one hundred dollars said sums to be held by my executor and kept at interest, well secured, until they shall respectively arrive at the age of twenty one years at which time they shall respectively receive the sums due them - The accruing interest on each of these bequests shall be paid as collected to the guardian of said grand children to be used in the maintenance, education and support.

5th - I give and bequeath to my said wife, Margaret Handman, all the rest and residue of my property of every character and description wherever found and wherever situated.

I hereby nominate and appoint my son-in-law Kelly O'Rear Executor of this Will trusting that he will carry out my wishes as herein expressed.

In testimony whereof I hereto sign my name in the presence of the subscribing witnesses, at Chattanooga, Tennessee. This 15th day of Dec. 1886. "Addie" on 15th line first page, interlined before signing.

A. Handman {seal]

Signed, sealed and published in our presence and we have subscribed our names hereto at the request of the

Testator and in his presence and in the presence of each other - this 17th day of December, 1886.

Johana Fischer

J. A. Caldwell

[Page 256]

JOHN DONOVAN

Last Will of John Donovan

State of Tennessee) In the name of
Hamilton County   ) God, Amen

I, John Donovan, being in feeble health but of sound mind and memory - knowing the uncertainty of life and the certainty of death - do make and declare this my last and only Will and Testament.

Item 1st - I Will my Soul to God Who gave it, and my body to be buried in a decent, Christianlike manner -

Item 2nd - I want my funeral expenses paid.

Item 3rd - Any and all property - money and notes due me, which is not required to pay funeral expenses, I will and bequeath to my nearest relative and Kinswoman, at whose house I am now staying - Mrs. Ellen Clark, a daughter of my deceased brother.

In testimony whereof I have hereunto set my hand, affixed my seal, this 4th day of Dec. 1886.

Jno. Donovan {L. S.}

Signed, sealed and executed in our presence and at his special instance and request we have signed same in his presence and in presence of each other, 4th day of December, 1886.

Wm Cottes

Thomas Crean

[Page 257]

MARY BENTON

Last Will of Mary Benton

I Mary Benton, of Sewanee, Franklin County, Tennessee, being well advanced in years, and infirm of body, but of a sound and disposing mind and memory, so make and declare the following to be my last will and testament.

Item 1st - commend my body to the earth, in the hope of a glorious resurrection, and my soul to the mercy of God, through our Lord and Savior Jesus Christ.

Item 2nd - After the payment of my funeral expenses, and just debts (if there be any) I give, devise, and bequeath to my beloved foster child Mrs. Mary Benton Sevier, wife of Col. T. F. Sevier, of Sevier, of Sewanee, and to her children which she now has, or may hereafter have or to their legal representatives in case of death, all my property of every description both real and personal, consisting mainly of lands in Texas and land warrents [sic] and claims, all money that may be on hand at the time of my death; all notes, bonds, accounts, or claims at the time due, and owing to me, or thereafter to become due, to her and her said children jointly; all my wearing apparel, plate, furniture, books and other personal effects of every description at the time of my death, I give to the said Mary Benton Sevier absolutely to her own, and the foregiving devise and bequest, in both parts, to her sole and separate use. Should any of her children attain the age of 21 years, or marry and the said Mary Benton Sevier should desire to set apart to such child a portion she is hereby ivested [sic] with the power so to do, the same to be accounted for at the final division which I desire shall be made at the decease of the said Mary Benton Sevier.

Item 3rd - I give and bequeath to my beloved niece Mrs. Allinewa Dunlap, the sum of Five Hundred Dollars, the sum to be paid to her within a reasonable time after my decease at the discretion of my executor.

Item 4th - I desire to be buried at the cemetary [sic] at "University Place" Sewanee, and I request and direct that my executor will have the remains of my husband brought to Sewanee and buried by me side.

I hereby nominate and appoint my beloved and trusted friend Col. T. F. Sevier sole executor of this my last will and testament; and it is my desire if consistent with the law of the land that he be relieved from the necessity of giving bond and security as such executor. I hereby also make known and declare that it is my will that my said executor, with the consent of the said Mary Benton Sevier, in writing, shall have power and authority to sell and dispose and funds hereby devised and bequeathed, and reinvest the same or the proceeds of the same in other property which shall then be subject to the provisions of this will in like manner as the original funds or property.

In testimony whereof I have hereunto subscribed my name in the presence of witnesses this 29th day of July A. D. 1870.l

Mary Benton

Signed and published in presence of us witnesses this 29th day of July A. D. 1870

Jno. B. Elliot

Jno. D. Phelan

[Page 259]

SARA A. BALDWIN

Non Cuput [sic] Will of Sara A. Baldwin

On the 27 day of Jan. 1883, while in attendance on Mrs. Sarah A. Baldwin, then and there sick with pneumonia, she requested me to bear witness to the following disposition of her property.

She stated that she desired her property, being in houses and lots on Whiteside Street, and all other property of which she was then in possession, to be equally divided between her husband Wm. Baldwin and her daughter Maggie Baldwin. She further stated that she desired the sum of ($200.00) Two Hundred Dollars to be held from funds then in her possession, and placed in trust for her nephew, James Edward Isom, son of Wm. Isom decd. until such time as he reached the age of twenty one, and then to be turned over to him for his benefit and use.

The above statement was made by Mrs. Baldwin of her own free will and accord, and on what she expressed and felt was her death bed.

Her mind was clear and she made the statement in my presence and that of her husband at her own request. She died in about thirty six hours after making this statement.

I hereby certify to the facts as set forth in the foregoing statement.

W. F. Hope

Feb. 5th 1888.

[Page 260]

BARBARA M. KUHN

Last Will of Barbara M. Kuhn

In the name of God Amen

I Barbara M. Kuhn widow and a citizen of Chattanooga, Hamilton County being of sound mind and as I verrily [sic] believe on my deathbed, and wishing to dispose of my little world of possessions while in possession of all my faculties so as to properly reward those of my children and natural heirs who have stood by me, not only in prosperity but in poverty, in health and in sickness, and who have always been good and dutiful children.

I therefore make this my last will and testament.

I will and bequeath to my two sons J. K. Kuhn and J. H. Kuhn jointly all the household and Kitchen furniture, table ware and bedding, Carpets and all other personal property now possessed by me and in the house occupied by me and my said sons to wit, No. 310 Williams Street in the 5th Ward of Chattanooga, Hamilton County, Tenn.

And I further will and bequeath to my said sons J. K. Kuhn and J. H. Kuhn, all other personal property, goods chattels or judgements of which I may be signed or possessed at the time of my death or which may accrue to me or my estate after my death by reason of any suits in law or equity now pending in the courts in behalf of a suit instuted by me against my brother Joseph Ruohs for Dower Interest in certain property situated in Chattanooga, Tenn., in short I hereby will and bequeath to my said boys J. K. Kuhn and J. H. Kuhn all the property shares in [blank] and interests of all kinds of which I may die, signed and possessed of.

To the exclusion and disbarment of all other claimants pretended heirs or kin [Page 261] whomsoever and especially do I forever disinherit one George Saffer who married my daughter Mariah J. Kuhn now deceased, and his and her heirs from any benefits or inheritance in my property or effects, he having by his unnatual conduct toward me in my old age, not only forfeited all claims that natural blood or affection may have granted him and so having estranged his two children from me, those I do not feel bound to do anything for them. But to my sons J. K. Kuhn and J. H. Kuhn who have watched over me in sickness and health and as dutiful sons have anticipated my every want, provided for me in my old age, I bequeath all my worldy possessions.

Give under my hand at my home in Chattanooga Tennessee this the 25th day of May 1885.

Barbara X M. Kuhn {seal}

her mark

Executed and signed in the presence of

B. F. Bartles

G. Wm. Spiers

Attest   J. R. Hanes - Atty.

[Page 262]

JOHN PIERSON

Will of John Pierson

In the name of God, Amen.

I John Pierson being of sound mind and memory do hereby make, publish and declare this to be my last will and testament, hereby revoking and making void all former wills by me at any time heretofore made.

First - I order and direct my executors as soon after my decease as practable to pay off and discharge all debts due and liabilities that may exist against me at the time of my decease the amount must be paid out of my entire.

Second - I give and bequeath to my Son Thomas Carter Pierson a lifetime interest in all my property in Dade County Georgia especially my tan yard property deeded to me by Anna C. Grant with all improvisements thereon and at the decease of said Thomas C. Pierson the aforesaid property must go to the oldest son John Edward Pierson of said Thomas C. Pierson his heirs and assigns forever.

Third - I give and bequeath to my two daughters Mary Ann Irving and Hellen Turnell Pierson all the remainder of my estate of whatever description it may be, also all cash on hand and all amounts due me from any sorce [sic] whatever without any exception it must be divided between my two daughters above named in the proportion of Three Fifths to Mary Ann Irving and the remaining Two fifths to Hellen Turnell Pierson.

Fourth - I hereby nominate and appoint W. A. Spencer and George Burge of Chattanooga State of Tennessee as my executors to this will.

In witness whereof I have hereunto set my hand and seal this the 4th day of September 1885 at Chattanooga state of Tennessee.

                              John Pierson

[Page 263]

Witness   Adam Severin Jr.
               Joe Sullivan

Sate of Tennessee)
Hamilton County) Personally appeared before me, Edgar McKenny a Notary Republic [sic] in and for said County and State John Pierson the within named bargainor with whom I am personally acquainted and who acknowledged that he executed the within instrument for the purpose therein contained.

Witness my hand and seal of office this the 4th day of September 1885.
               Edgar McKinney
               Notary Public

State of Tennessee)
Hamilton County) The above deed and certificate were filed 9 Sept. 1885 at 8 a.m. entered in Note Book No. 3 Page 278 and recorded in Book S. Volume 2 Page 832 & 321. Witness my hand at office in Chattanooga.
       H. C. Beck Register

JOSEPH T. WILLIAMSON

Last Will of Joseph T. Williamson

State of Tennessee, Hamilton County

I Joseph T. Williamson of said State and county do make this my last Will and Testament hereby revoking all others by me hertofore made.

Item first - I give and bequeath unto my beloved wife Anna E. Williamson all property of every kind and description which I may own at the time of my death whether situated in this state or elsewhere to be hers absolutely and unconditionally.

Item Second - I constitute and appoint my said wife the sole Executrix of this my last Will and Testament and direct that she shall not be required to give any bond or security as such executrix nor shall she be required to report or account to [Page 264] any court for my estate or any part thereof or for the management thereof.

In testimony whereof witness my hand and seal at Chattanooga Hamilton County Tennessee March 24" 1881.
               Joseph T. Williamson

Signed sealed declared and published by Jos. T. Williamson in our presence as his last Will and Testament which we hereby witness as such at his special instance and request in his presence & in the presence of each other this the 24th day of March 1881 at Chattanooga, Tennessee.
               B. M. Hord
               T. H. Ewing
               John C. Griffiss

PENDER SATTERWHITE**

Last Will of Pender Satterwhite [sic]

I Pender Satterwhite being of sound mind and memory do make this my last will and testament.

Item 1st - I give to my grandchild Carrie Ware all of my personal property, one bed, one looking glass, three tables, six chairs, a pot and two irons, set of Glasses, and dishes, all the books, one trunk, one washstand, the wardrobe, one picture, some clothes.

And real property she Carrie Ware is to have the following described property, 14 ft. fronting third st and between High St. and Lookout St. the east line of this property running strait [sic] line south 112 ft., a uniform width thence a direct line west 16 ft. and then south a direct line 74 ft. a uniform width.

All this I give to Carrie Ware my grand daughter.

The balance of the real property is to be divided equally among the following named persons, all of which are my children.

Nelson Sattelwhite, Penina Kelly Dolly Johnson, Margetta Henry, Robert Sattelwhite.

The remaining part of this real property after taking off Carrie's of which I shall die sieze. I hereby appoint as exezutive [sic] testament Nelson Sattelwhite exezutive.

Pender X Sattelwhite**
her mark

** both spellings used in this will.

Witness
N. M. Mays
Geo. W. Sewell
This the first day of Feb. 1883

(Note - this is first found on p. 253 with a little difference in description of lot)

SARAH E. BUTLER

Last Will of Sarah E. Butler

The State of Tennessee
County of Hamilton

Know all men by their presents that I Sarah E. Butler of said County and state in consideration of love and affection and to restore to its proper place & name the title to the hereinafter described property the purchase having been made by my husband and the title taken in my name for the purpose of conveniences which do not

now exist. I do hereby will and convey to J. W. Butler of said County and State the following described property to wit - one lot of one hundred and thirty six feet on Gillespie Street, and two hundred and ten feet on Helen Street to the line [Page 266] between the said lot and the lot of old Mrs. Whitesides - the one hundred and thirty six feet on Gillespie Street line between Helen and Florence - all within the town of Chattanooga and County of Hamilton State of Tennessee being the home place on which we now reside to have and to hold to him said J. W. Butler his lines and assigns forever. Witness my hand this July 3rd 1886.

Sarah E. Butler

Attest
J. C. Hutcheson
Gary Pitman

State of Tennessee
Hamilton County

Personally appeared before me Julius Ochs a Notary Republic [sic] for said County J. C. Hutcheson and Gary Pitman with whom I am personally acquainted and have made oath in due form of law (and are personally acquainted with) have witnessed the signature of the above Sarah E. Butler to the above instrument and that they signed the same as witnesses at the time at her instance and request.

Witness my hand and seal this 7th day of August 1886.

Julius Ochs
Notary Public

State of Tennessee)
Hamilton County) The above deed and certificate were filed for record 7 Sept. 1888 at 1 p.m. entered in Note Book 5 Page 267 and recorded in Book M, Volume 3, Page 544.

Witness my hand at office of Chattanooga.
H. C. Beck, Register
Per J. K. Hodges, D. Reg.

[Page 267]

JAMES GOTHARD

Last Will of James Gothard

My Last Will and testiment [sic] this 19th April 1886 I desire and request that all of real and personal property be divided between my heirs as follows, that is to say that I request that my daughter Mary Thirmon and my son Larkin Gothard, and my son Ira Gothard, and my son John Gothard, and my son Lewis Gothard, and my daughter Arbel Olinger, and my daughter Maholy Morgan, and my daughter Margaret Rogers, and my daughter Ibby Horton and my daughter Nancy Coleman, and my daughter Elmira Shipley each have and receive One dollar of my effects at my death, and the entire remaining part of both real and personal property remain in the possession of my daughter Elizabeth Gothard to be controlled and used for the support of her and my Grandson Thomas Coleman who has lived and is now living with us, and the entire right title and interest in the aforesaid real and personal property to remain in her the said Elizabeth Gothard during her natural life time, and after her death I desire and request that the entire right title and interest be vested in my Grandson Thom Coleman to be controlled and converted to his own use at his pleasure and desire, provided however he the said Thomas Coleman remains with us or provides for our support during our natural lifetime given under our hand and seal this the day and date above mentioned.

James X Gothard {Seal}
his mark

Attest:　Peter Bolton
　　　　　Wm. Wiffiths

[Page 268]

J.C. EDMONDSON

Last Will of J. C. Edmondson

Being impressed with the uncertainty and the certainty of death and being desirous of disposing of the little property belonging to me in such way and manner as to me seems right and proper - I, J. C. Edmondson, being of sound mind and disposing memory, hereby make and publish this as my last Will and Testament, revoking all former Wills and testaments made by me.

First - I direct all of my just debts to be paid out of my assets.

2nd - I will bequeath to my beloved wife M. T. Edmondson, all my property both real and personal, during her natural life, to be used by her as she may wish.

3rd - I will and bequeath all my property not consumed in use, heretofore left to my wife during her life, upon her death, to my beloved niece Mrs. Rowena Smartt, and her two children Myra Smartt and George E. Smartt sharing equally. And if any other children shall

hereafter be borne to Mrs. Rowena Smartt, they shall take an equal share in said property.

I will and direct that J. P. Smartt and wife Rowena Smartt, shall be authorized to manage and control the [blank] property of said minors during their minority for their benefit during the minority of said children aforesaid. I authorize my wife M. T. Edmondson, J. P. Smartt & Mrs. Rowena Smartt or in case of death of either of them the survivors to sell and dispose and make title to any Real Estate [Page 269] of which I may die seized and possessed, when in their judgment they think best to do so.

5th - I hereby nominate and appoint J. P. Smartt as the executor of this my last will and Testament relieving him from giving any bond as such.

J. C. Edmondson

Signed and acknowledged in our presence and in the presence of each other and witnessed by us at the special instance of the Testator on this the 6th day of August 1883.

S. J. A. Frazier
Robert L. Coulter

HUMPHREY B. HEYWOOD**

Last Will of Humphrey B. Heywood**

I Humphrey B. Haywood Senior of Chattanooga Hamilton County Tennessee being of sound mind and memory do determine make and declare this to be my last Will and Testament as follows.

I give bequeath and desire my estate and property as follows:

All the Real Estate I own excepting one lot in Cleveland, Bradley County, Tennessee lies in Hamilton County Tennessee.

First - I will and direct that all my just debts by paid.

Second - It is my will that my funeral be plain and I direct that a lot having good natural drainage in Forest Hills Cemetery be purchased and that a tomb of solid rock [Page 270] and of proper dimensions be built thereon above ground with the floor above surface flow, my executrix to keep the cost of tomb within reasonable limits. I direct that the lot and tomb be paid for out of any money available - This I designate as a burial place for all the members of my families by both marriages.

Third - I direct that the following parcels of Real Estate be sold as soon after my decease as may seem to my Executrix most condusive to the interest of my estate to wit. A - the south half of the north half No. 4 Market Street Chattanooga Tenn. B - A lot in Weavers addition to Chattanooga Tenn. fifth ward fronting fifty feet on the south side of Missionary Avenue by one hundred and forty feet deep to an alley lays fifty feet east of the lot sold by said Weaver to Jos. Burton. C - About forty acres in the 16th Civil district of Hamilton County Tenn. purchased from Geo. Vandergriff Jr. and part from John F. Haigar all in one parcel. I direct that my executrix reinvest the proceeds of these sales to the best interest of my estate and that she make good and sufficient general warranty deeds to the purchasers. I also direct that my 130 acres in the third civil district of Hamilton County Tenn. purchased from Zion Grayn be sold at any time after my decease or that she may delay the sale thereof until my youngest living child shall attain the age of twenty years if she thinks it to be the best interest of my estate to do so that she reinvest the proceeds of the sale to the interest of my Estate or that if the sale be delayed until about the time my youngest living child shall attain the age of twenty years that they hold the proceeds for final distribution and that she make good and sufficient general warranty deeds to the purchasers.

[Page 271]

Fourth - I direct that as soon after my decease as practicable the sum of from twenty four to twenty seven hundred dollars be expended in purchasing material and building three neat and commodious houses on my lot No. Six Payne Street Chattanooga Tenn. and that when completed my executrix keep them rented to derive in part a support for my family by my second marriage. They may be paid for out of any money on hand or if necessary by the conversion into money of any of my notes or certificates of deposit and the proceeds of the converion used for the payment or to complete it.

Fifth - I give and bequeath to my wife Ruth the use and rents of the following real Estate until our youngst living child shall attain the age of twenty-two years - Lot No. 6 Payne Street Chattanooga Tenn. B - The north one hundred and three (103) feet of lot No. 14 High Street Chattanooga Tenn. C - The North east 1/4th of lot No. 9 High Street with offset and alley to Lookout Street Chattanooga Tenn. D - My 130 acres in third civil district of Hamilton County Tenn. until sold. I also give and bequeath to her the yearly interest or income accruing from any and all notes bonds and all other securities of any description or kind that I may have on hand and own at my decease or that my be at any time thereafter belonging to my estate until my youngest living child shall attain the age of twenty two years this income and rents to

be used by her in her support and the support & education of our children. I also give and bequeath to her for use in our family all my household and kitchen furniture tools live stock and all property of like kind [Page 272] whatever and direct that any of this for which she has no use in the family be sold and proceeds used in their support I will and direct hat she use our residence on High Street on lot NO. 14 said Street as a homestead for the family until our youngest living child shall attain the age of twenty two years.

Sixth - I will and devise to my daughters Ruth and Blanche jointly the rest residue and remainder of the North Fifty three feet of lot No. 14 High Street Chattanooga Tenn. extending back in a uniform width of fifty three feet to Spring Street with all the tenements and improvements thereon.

Seventh - I give and bequeath to my wife Ruth the use of the north East one fourth of lot No. 9 High Street Chattanooga Tenn. with ofset [?] and alley to be used by her as a homestead after my youngest living child shall attain the age of twenty-two years during the remainder of her natural life. At her death remainder estate to my son Humphrey B. Jr.

Eight - I give and devise to my son Humphrey B. Jr. the rest residue and remainder of the northeast fourth of lot No. 9 High Street Chattanooga Tenn. with offset and alley to Lookout Street. I also give and devise to him the North fifty fee of lot No. 6 Payne Street Chattanooga Tenn. with all the tenement and improvements on both lots.

Ninth - I give and devise to my said son John the residue or remaining portion of the said lot I own in said Cleveland Tenn. fronting about 80 feet on said Inman Street extending back north in a [Page 273] width of about 80 feet to the next street north but in trust and not otherwise for the benefit of my son Baldwin and I request and direct him to sell the same and reinvest the proceeds for the benefit of and to the best interests of the said Baldwin.

[No Tenth Paragraph]

Eleventh - I give and bequeath to my said son John the sum of one thousand dollars to be paid out to him outof the first moneys available after making the payments heretofore directed in this will.

Twelve - I give and bequeath to my said son John one thousand dollars to be paid to him in like manner as directed for his own legacy in item eleven but this one thousand dollars is given him in trust and not otherwise to be invested by him for the sole use and benefit of my son Baldwin.

Thirteen - I will and direct that when my youngest living child shall attain the full age of twenty two years all the Real Estate belonging to my estate and remaining unsold be sold and the proceeds be used in the final distribution also I direct that at this time all the property of any kind name or nature real personal or mixed then belonging to my estate including any money or any other assett [sic] or property be sold and converted into ready money and that all the money accuring be used for final distrubtion and that executrix make good and sufficient general warranty deeds to the purchasers of the Real Estate and further will and direct that the whole sum or fund thus accumulated be equally divided share and share alike among my wife Ruth and all my children living at this time my wife Ruth taking a childs share my children by the first marriage to share in the distribution.

Fourteen - The North East 1/4 of lot No. 7 High Street Chattanooga Tenn. and one acre and thirty-five poles of land in Hill City 3rd Civil District of Hamilton County, Tenn. were paid for with my money and deeded to my wife Ruth in the final distribution of this property acquired by her through its sale and remonstrated I request and enjoin upon her to divide the same among those of our children then living by the last marriage.

Fifteen -I will and direct that in the event of the death of either of my sons John and Baldwin by my first marriage that the estate and property he takes under this will go to the survivor of the two and that in the event of the death of anyone of my children Ruth Blanche or Humphrey B. Jr. that the estate and property that the one takes under this will go to the surviving two and in case that a second one die in the estate and property taken by that one under this will go to the survivor of the three; or children of the deceased devised if they have any. That portion devised to the two children of my first marriage to belong to them, and to be shared by them, and the property devised to the three children by my last marriage to be shared and inherited by them to the exlusion of the children of the first marriage. [Page 275] If at time my wife Ruth my executrix should deem it necessary to do so, she sell convey and make title to South 47 feet front of the north 103 feet of Lot No. 14 High Street, being a lot fronting 47 feet on High Streets and running back Eastward of the uniform width of 47 feet, a distance of 185? feet. If this sale should be made it will leave a space of three feet front on High Street between this lot and the lot devised to my two daughters Ruth and Blanche, under item 6th of my will. I devise these three feet front to said two daughters which will make their lot have a front of 56 feet instead of 53 feet on High Street.

I also give and bequeath to my wife Ruth for the use of herself and our three children until the youngest child arrives at the age of Twenty-Two years, the rents of any and all real estate, that may be acquired by my estate after my death. Also in addition to the provisions made in Item Fifth (5th) of this my will I direct that for the first year after my death, the sum of Three Hundred and Fifty dollars ($350.) be applied by my said wife to use of herself and our children, out any money on hand or available if at any time, until our youngest child arrives at the age of Twenty-Two years, the income provided in section or Item Five for the support of my family should fall below the sum of Eleven Hundred dollars yearly it is my will and desire that the deficit be made up to that sum out of any money on hand or available. All ordinary repairs or improvement such as paving side walks, damages [Page 276] from fire, storm or otherwise will be paid out of any money on hand or available.

Seventeenth - It is my will and desire that upon the final settlement and distribution of my Thirteen (13) in this my will that before said distribution is made my son Humphrey B., Jr. be paid the sum of Nine Hundred dollars and my wife Ruth the sum of Five Hundred dollars and this she will retain as her own property; after these payments are made, the residue will be distributed in the way and manner directed in said item Thirteen (13) which item is changed so far as provided for the payments of said two sums before distribution is made. Any devise or legated under this will who may contest the same shall be deprived of any and all the benefit intended to be given him or her under this will.

Eighteenth - I nominate and appoint my beloved wife Ruth my sole executrix of this my will and reposing the utmost confidence in her integrity and business capacity, it is my will and desire, that she be relieved from giving bond and security and taking the oath directed by the statutes. If my executrix should marry before our youngest child arrives at the age of Twenty-Two years it is my will and desire that her executorship terminate with her said marriage, and she will no longer have or hold and continue the management of my estate.

The words "after the lapse of eight years" in the 16th line of 2nd page stricken out before signing.

Witness my hand this 2nd day of February 1887 and signed by me in the presence of the witnesses whose signatures appear [Page 277] below who witness the same at my request.

Humphrey B. Haywood, Jr.

** both spellings used here

Witnessed by us in the presence of and at the request of the Testator H. B. Haywood who signed the same in our presence February 2, 1887.

E. R. Betterton
Geo. W. Martin
John Sullivan
S. A. Key

MAMIE KING

Last Will of Mamie King

I Mamie King being of sound mind and disposing memory and knowing the uncertainty of life and certainty of death do make and publish this my last Will and testament, hereby making & revoking void all other wills by me at anytime made.

First - I direct that my funeral expenses and all my debts be paid as soon after my death as possible, out of any monies that I may die possessed of, or may first come into the hands of my executor.

Secondly - I give and bequeath to my beloved Aunt Carrie Roberson, who raised me from a small child - the following described Lot on King Street in the City of Chattanooga Tennessee it being the property conveyed to my Mother Missouri H. King by Thomas B. Van Horn & Margueret [sic] Van Horn by deed executed 24th day of August 1868 and Registered in the Registers Office of Hamilton County Tenn. in Book "R" Pages 208-209 on the 10" day of October 1868 - It being the property I inherited from my mother Missouri H. King, described as follows to wit - The East half of Lot No. (9) nine in Chandlers Addition to the City of [Page 278] Chattanooga Hamilton County Tennessee and conveyed by Benjamin Chandler by Deed dated from June 12" 18_ which is Registered in Register office of Hamilton County, Tenn. in book P page 457.

I do hereby nominate and appoint Rev. Charles Scott my executor.

In witness whereof I do to this my last will set my hand and seal - This the Second day of April, 1887.
Mamie King

Signed and sealed and published in our and we have subscribed our names hereto in the presence of the testator - This the second day of April 1887.
Phillip Giminard
Wm. Washington
W. J. Clift

JOSEPH STAGMAIER

Last Will of Joseph Stagmaier

I Joseph Stagmaier being of sound mind though weak in body, do make this my last will & testament.

First - My assits [sic] consist of policy of 2000.00 in Cath. Knights of America also one thousand dollars or more due me by the firm for whom I have worked T. A. Snow & Co.

1. I direct my executor herein after named to pay my funeral expenses and all my just debts.

2. I give and bequeath my parish priest fifty dollars for Masses for my soul.

3. I direct my executor to divide the balance remaining between my Sisters Lizzie and Katie and brother Henry share and share alike.
[Page 239]

4. I appoint Rev. P. J. Gleeson executor of this my will and direct that he be relieved without bond or security.

Joseph X Stagmaier
his mark

Acknowledged above as his will in our presence -

Witness
John Schmit
Mary E. Mullery
Chattanooga Aug. 27, 1887

HOMER C. SQUIRE

Last Will of Homer C. Squire

In the name of God, Amen.

I Homer C. Squire of Knoxville Tenn. being of sound and disposing mind and memory, calling to mind the frailty and uncertainty of humane life, and being desirous of settling my worldly affairs, and directing how the worlds goods, with which it has pleased God to bless me, shall be disposed of after my decease, while I have strength and capability so to do, make and publish this my last will and testament, hereby revoking and making null and void all other last wills and testaments by me heretofore made, And first I commend my immortal being to Him who gave it and my body to the earth to be buried with little expense or ostentation, by my executor here in after named.

As to my worldly estate and all the property, real personal or mixed of which I shall die siezed and possessed or to which I shall be entitled at the time of my decease I devise bequeath, and dispose thereof in the manner following to wit <u>Imprimis</u> My will is, that all my [Page 280] just debts and funeral charges shall, by my executor hereinafter named, be paid out of my estate as soon after my decease as shall by her be found convenient.

Item I give, devise, and bequeath to My beloved wife Antoinette E. Squire all of my household furniture, money and all of my estate real, personal or mixed of which I shall die seized and possessed, or to which I shall be entitled at the time of my decease, I do this because I have implicit confidence in her, knowing that she will use all the faculties and power given her by Almighty God to raise our children up in such a manner that they will be Christians and useful citizens.

Lastly - I do nominate and appoint my beloved wife Antoinette E. Squire<u>s</u> to be the Executrix of this my last will and testament; and it is my desire that no bond whatever be required of her by the court having authority in the case.

In testimony whereof, I the said Homer C. Squire have to this my last will and testament subscribed my name and affixed my seal this twenty sixth day June 1874.
Homer C. Squire {S.S.}

Winesses
John H. Scarbro Knoxville Tenn.
T. A. Joye   Knoxville Tenn.

[Page 281]

JOHN C. ULERY

Last Will of John C. Ulery

I John C. Ulery of North Side Hamilton County and State of Tennessee being aware of the uncertainty of life and in failing health, but of sound mind and memory, do make and declare this to be my last Will and testament in manner following to Wit.

I bequeath all my property real and personal whatsoever and wheresoever unto my beloved daughter Catherine Stoop, her Heirs and Administrators and assigns. To and for her and their absolute use and benefit according to the nature and quality thereof respectively. Subject only to the Payment of my just debts Testament and funeral expenses and the charges of proving and registering this my will, and it is my will that my said daughter shall not be required to give bond, or security to judge of probate for the faithful execution of the duties of

executrix, and I desire that my daughter Catherine in her will make an equal division of all such property coming from my estate to her Heirs. In Witness whereof I have set my hand and seal this thirteenth day of July A. D. 1887.
John X C. Ulery
his mark

Signed, sealed, published and acknowledged by the as and for his last Will and Testament in the presence of us who in his presence and at his request and in the presence of each other have subscribed our names beneath as Witnesses thereof.
John Ashworth
Timothy T. Overshines) Northside Tenn.

[Page 282]

SAMUEL MARTIN

Last will of Samuel Martin Chattanooga, Tenn.
Nov 26, 1887.

It is my will that portion of my lot lying with of what is called the center apple tree about 16 feet north to tenth street be given to Samuel Martin my grandson his life time and also Thomas Martin my grand son, also my wife Elizabeth Martin and my sister Harriet Henry. To hold their life time, and at their death the same is to go to the estate of Samuel Martin.

2nd and all of the Lot lying south of what is known as the center apple tree be in charge of Margrett Gorman about 150 ft. south of what is known as center apple tree.

She is to collect all the rents and the rents must be used in keeping up the Taxs [sic].
Signed
Samuel X Martin
his mark

Signed before me this the 26th day of Nov. 1887
J. W.White, J. P.

Witnesses:
Julas X Gibson
his mark
M. H. Holder

[Page 283]

S. V. OGBOURNE

Last Will of S. V. Ogbourne

I, S. V. Ogbourne being of sound mind, memory and understanding make and publish this my last will and testament, hereby revoking and making void all former wills that may have been made by me.

1st - I give, devise and bequeath to my nephew W. D. Hill my house and lot on the corner of Adams and Bainbridge Sts. and my vacant lot joining the lot above mentioned and fronting on Adams Street, both lots being in the city of Montgomery State of Alabama and a farm containing about one hundred and forty (140) acres lying in Montgomery County, Alabama. I also gave to him the house hold furniture of every description and kind now in my house in Montgomery, Ala.

2nd - I give and bequeath to Nellie W. Flanders, daugther of J. P. Flanders my pianno which is now at the house of J. P. Flanders in Chattanooga, Tenn.

3rd - I give and devise to Dora Flanders wife of J. P. Flanders and my nice one dozen silver forks the smaller set which are now in the banking house of Farley, Spear and Co. at Montgomery Ala. one pair of china vases in the house devised to W. D. Hill.

4th - The remaining silver ware and a gold watch in banking house of Farley, Spear and Co. I give and devise to W. D. Hill mentioned in the first article of this instrument.

5th - I give and devise to Ettie W. Hill wife of W. D. Hill one diamond scarf pin, two family portraits of myself and husband who is dead.

6th - I give and devise to the said W. D. Hill a set of diamonds consisting of a breast pin and car rings which I direct him [Page 283] to sell and erect a monument over the graves of his second daughter Susie Ogbourne Hill, had she lived I would have given these diamonds to her.

7th - I give and devise to Mrs. J. P. Flanders a diamond ring being a cluster of small diamonds.

8th - I give and bequeath to Fred W. Hill a finger ring with a diamond (solitaire diamond).

9th - I give and bequeath to my sister C. T. Hill all my wearing apparel except a black silk velvet dress which I reserve to be buried in. I hereby nominate and appoint the said W. D. Hill my executor and authorize and empower him to carry into execution this my last will and he need not make bond which is hereby waived.

In testimony where of I hereto sign my name in the presence of T. J. Lattner and Thomas C. Latimore. This Nov. 26, 1887.

S. V. Ogbourne.

At the request of the above testatrix in her presence and in the presence of eachother we signed this will and witnessed the signature of the above testatrix when signed and delivered the same to us with the request that we sign the smae as witnesses. This Nov. 26th 1887.

X Thos. C. Latimore
T. J. Lattner

[Page 285]

DAVID CRAWFORD

Last Will of David Crawford
State of Tennessee)
Hamilton County   )

In the name of God, Amen.

I, David Crawford, colored, of said state and County, being of sound mind and disposing memory do hereby make and publish this my last will and Testament.

Item 1st - It is my desire that all my just debts be paid.

Item 2nd - I devise and bequeath unto my brother Prince Crawford all my property both real and personal and mixed of whatever kind and wherever situated of which I may die possessed or of which I may be entitled.

Item 3rd - I constitute and appoint my brother Prince Crawford the executor of this my will, and it is my desire and request that he be excused from giving bond as such and that he be not required to make any settlement of the said estate with the clerk of the County Court of said County or with any other power or office.

Item 4th - At my death, I direct my executor to give my body a decent christian burial.

Item 5th - I will to my wife Lizzie Crawford one dollar to be paid by my executor out of my estate after my death.

In witness whereof I hereto set my hand and seal this 17th day of March 1887.

David X Crawford {seal}
his mark

Signed and sealed by David Crawford in our presence and by him declared to be his last will and testament and we [Page 286] the undersigned in his presence and at his request and in the presence of one another have this 19" day of March 1887 as subscribing witness here signed our name

C. P. Goree
D. H. Bird

ALEXANDER BEATH

Last Will of Alexander Beath

I Alexander Beath of the City of Chattanooga and State of Tennessee declare this to be my last will and testament.

I give and bequeath to my wife Purleyell Beath all my Personal Property and household goods chattels and efects other than securities.

I give and Devise to my said wife the Note of C. W. Tenney of Iowa 1000, also all money due me in Wisconsin, also 80 acres of land in Obrian Co Iowa, also all money due me from Thomas Scott of Obrian Co Iowa, I give and bequeath all the above to my wife her heirs and assigns for ever.

I give and bequeath to my sisters two sons in Nebraska James B. Murray and Willie Murray 1000 each. I give and bequeath to my Niece Mrs. H. C. Hulse 1000, and to her second son Bruce Hulse 1000, to them and their heirs.

I give and bequeath to her oldest son Alexander B. Hulse my House and lot where I now reside on the corner of sixth and Pine Streets in the city of Chattanooga and State of Tennessee to have and to hold the same and to his heirs and assigns for ever.
[Page 287

I appoint Herbert C. Hulse of Chattanooga to be executor of this my last will, in witness whereof I, Alexander Beath have hereunto set my hand and seal this tenth day of January Eighteen hundred and Eighty Five.

Subscribed by the testator in Presence of each of us and at the same time declared by him to us as his last will and testament.

Alexander Beath {Seal}
Witness our hands this tenth day of January 1885.
A. J. Hulse
Sam Conn
James Mchann

BOSEN BOYCE

Last Will of Bosen Boyce
Boyce - Hamilton County, State of Tennessee

In the name of God - Amen

Be it known to all men by these credentials that this is my last will and testament. Of all my personal property that I now own and shall here after own after these papers are writen [sic], I do bequeath and give to my wife Pollie Boyce, to have and dispose of as she pleases -

And my Real Estate one acre more or less adjacent to the church property and that upon which the public school is built - the same I give and bequeath to my wife Pollie Boyce to have and control as she pleases my home place I give and bequeath to my Grand children Ida Wooden and Isaiah Wooden to own and be used for their advantage until they shall become of age and to be turned over to them to [Page 288] control and use as they see fit - What I leave and notes after my expenses shall have been paid the same do I give and leave to my Wife Pollie Boyce - and it my desire that W. H. Tilman be appointed to make a sittlement [sic] of my estate and humbly pray that this my last will and statement to be not made void.

To which I sign my name This 9th day of Nov. 1886 Eighteen Hundred and Eighty Six year of our Lord.
Bosen X Boyce
his mark
Witnesses
Perry X Irvin
his mark
W. H. Tilman

A. W. COLBY

Last Will of A. W. Colby
Sept. 18, 1887
Fairmount, Tenn.

Fully realizing the uncertainties of life and being in sound mind I do hereby make this my last Will and Testament for those herein mentioned.

1st - After paying all my just debts I bequeath to my beloved wife Lettie C. Colby the Hotel property known as the Waldens Ridge Hotel consisting of ten acres. Allso [sic] the farm purchased of Elisha K. Smith consisting of fifty seven acres more or less for her own individual and sole use.

2nd - I will to my wife Lettie C. Colby all my personal property consisting of money deposited in the bank of Chattanooga [Page 289] Tenn; notes and account all furniture books &c for her own sole use forever, and appoint I. F. Loomis A. W. Colby to act as executor without bond.

A. W. Colby

We the undersigned hereby certife [sic] that we saw Mr. Aaron W. Colby affix his name to the above instrument and have affixed our names in the presence of each other this 18 day of September 1887.

E. K. Smith)
J. M. Brown) Witnesses
D. G. Curtis)

ANDREW G. W. PUCKETT

Last Will of Andrew G. W. Puckett

I Andrew G. W. Puckett being now of my sixty eighth year of sound mind and disposing memory knowing the uncertainty of life and certainty of death disiring [sic] while I am in health to have all my worldly affairs settled before my death I therefore make and publish this as my last will and testament revoking all other wills heretofore made by me.

Item 1st - I will soul to God, who gave it.

Item 2nd - It is my will that all my just debts if I should have any at my death together with my funeral expences [sic] be first paid out of the assets of my estate.

Item 3rd - I will and bequeath to my beloved wife Nancy Lee Puckett the rents and proffits [sic] of all the Lands and lower lots that I may die seized and possed [sic] of after paying taxes and repairs, together with all my personal property of every kind except one pionner [sic] and Bed and Bedstead and furniture which will be by me disposed of in Item four, to have and use as her own and to dispose in any way that she may [Page 290] desire as I intend it to be hers and subject to her own use and disposal as she may see fit during her natural life.

Item 4th - I will and bequeath to my daughter Julia Cannon Puckett who is hereby adopt as my child and heir the pianner [sic] that I have bought and given to her and one good bed bedstaead and furniture and the one half of all the real estate I may die seized and possed [sic] of together with such other things as I may buy and give her here after, the other half of my real estate I will and bequeath to my Niece Elizabeth V. Vinson wife of C. W. Vinson said real estate lands and lots to be equally divided my daughter Julia Cannon Puckett and my niece Elizabeth V. Vinson if the same can be done value and satisfactory if not then it is my will that such parts as cannot be divided be sold to the highest bider [sic] on long time with intest [sic] bearing notes and the proceeds divided between them.

Item 5th - It is my will that if I should die before my daughter Julia becomes of lawful age or, if she marries after she has attained the age of eighteen which will be on the fifth day of November 1880 then and in that event she shall have all the personal property devised and bequeathed to her in item four of this my will. It is my will that she remain with my wife until she marries, or

until the death of my beloved wife who will retain the possion [sic] of all my real estate until her death, and then it is my will she shall have possion [sic] of and control all the real estate devised and bequeathed to her in item four of this will together with all appurtionances [sic] there on belonging with rents and proffits [sic] there on belonging during her natural life in remainder [Page 291] to the heirs of her body in fee, if she should have any fee from the control of or any life estate of her husband after her death, but if she should die without issue, then said real estate to revert back to my lawful heirs to be sold and equally divided between.

Item 6th - It is my will having full confidence in my beloved wife that she may carry out the provisions of this my last will and testament I hereby constitute and appoint her executor of said will and she will not be required to give any bond as such this 21st day of May A. D. 1878.

A. G. W. Puckett

Witness
J. S. Bell
C. W. Vinson
L. M. Clark

MILES MANN

Last Will of Miles Mann

Hereby revoking all wills and codicils by me at any time heretofore made I thereby make publish and declare my last will and testimony to be as follows.

First - I direct that my funeral expenses and all of my debts be first paid and that end authorized my executor hereinafter named to sell at public or private sale on such terms as she thinks best any part or the whole of the property of which I may die seized or to which I may be entitled.

Secondly - I hereby bequeath and give my wife Amanda all property real or personal of which [Page 292] I may die seized and possessed or which I may be or may become entitled.

Third - I do hereby nominate and appoint my said wife Amanda as my executrix and do not require her to execute any bond or make any reports to any courts as such.

In witness whereof I do to this my will set my hand and seal. This the 31st day of August 1887.

Miles Mann {Seal}

Signed, sealed and published in our presence and we have subscribed our names hereto in the presence of the testator and of each other. This the 31st day of August 1887.

The name above is the signature of Miles Mann now living at No. 413 Cherry St. Chattanooga, Tenn.
Tomlinson Fort
Harry J. Crawford
Clara X Hargrove
her mark

EMMA SMITH

Last will of Emma Smith

I Emma Smith being of sound mind do make and publish this my last will and testament hereby making all other wills by me at any time made. I give and bequeath to my children equally, to wit, Lucy Jones, Ida Jones, Roda Jones and Mamie Jones the house and lot and all house hold furniture where I now [Page 293] live share and share alike, said house and lot is described as follows to wit lying in civil district of Hamilton County Tennessee to wit: Lot No. 24 of McCulloughs subdivision of block 8 and [blank] of the Huddle farm as located and laid out and described in a plot and survey made for C. C. McCullough and of record in plot book No. one page 11 of the Register office of Hamilton County Tenn., And I hereby request, will and direct that the deed to said lot be made out and the title to said lot vested in my said four children above named, by W. H. DeWitt and M. M. Hope from whom I purchased said lot but who have not yet made and executed to me this deed. They are directed to make said deed to my said four children according to the terms and conditions agreed on by us.

My personal property of any kind and description I give to my four children above named equally after paying all my just debts and liabilities of every kind and description including my funeral expenses.

My property consists alone of my house hold goods, house and lot as aforesaid and some money in hands of Dr. W. T. Hope which he holds as executor of my dead husband.

I nominate and appoint Dr. W. T. Hope as my executor This 15" April 188_.
Emma X Smith
her mark
Witnesses
M. M. Hope, W. E. DeWitt, T. H. Smith

[Page 294]

JOHN M. GILLESPIE

Last Will of John M. Gillespie

I Jno. M. Gillespie, do hereby appoint J. A. Caldwell testatory Guardian of my son J. K. Gillespie and direct that he act as such without bond and be relieved from oath and not required to settle in any Court; And knowing the uncertainty of life and being now very sick in body but of sound mind, and desiring, in the event of my death, that my temporal affairs shall be wound up and settled without delay or expense, I make this my last will and testament.

I here by appoint J. A. Caldwell executor of this will and desire that he wind up and settle all my affairs as he knows I would have him do.

I hereby convey to the said J.A. Caldwell all my property, real, personal and mixed to be used and employed as herinafter directed -

I desire that my son John K. Gillespie have all the residue of my estate, after paying all debts and obligations and the legicies [sic] hereinafter mentioned - payable to him upon his arrival at 21 years of age.

All sums bequeathed to Presbyterian Church are to be paid to J. C. Griffiss Jr. and expended as directed by J. A. Caldwell. In addition to the provisions heretofore written by me and appended to my Insurance Policy in the Royal Arcanum, Chattanooga Council No. 137 - I desire the insurance money which may be collected thereon to be paid as follows -

First after the payment of five hundred dollars therein mentioned to the Orphans "Home' I desire to have paid two hundred and fifty dollars to the Associated Charities and Two Hundred and Fifty Dollars to the Womans Christian Association for use in erecting the Orphans "Home" Hospital - and any balance due said orphans Home on any subscription of two dollars per month for the year 188- next to Deacons of 1st [Page 295] Presbyterian Church or J. C. Griffis Jr., any balance due on my subscription to the expense fund and Pastors Salary of said First Presbyterian Church at Chattanooga, Tenn. - Next to Rev. J. W. Bachman Fifty Dollars - Next to William Blain col[d] who nursed me in my last illness a balance in full for said services (amount stated by Mrs. A. N. Watkins) and any other sum due him. I wish J. A. Caldwell to act as my executor, without oath or bond - and I desire him to keep my son John K. Gillespie with my brother George L. Gillespie who will look after his education and give him such attention as he needs.

I desire J. A. Caldwell to settle up all my business (as executor) as speedily as possible and without litigation except when absolutely necessary.

Witness my hand and seal at Chattanooga Tennessee This 16th April 1888.
John M. Gillespie
Attest

John L. Altee
James H. Altee

AMELIA DUDA

Last Will of Amelia Duda

I Amelia Duda wife of August Duda of the City of Chattanooga, being in feeble health but of sound and disposing mind do make this my last will and testament.

Item 1 I wish my body to be decently buried but in a plain manner, avoiding all display and extravagance in my burial.

Item 2 I owe Dr. Casset of Cincinnati twenty dollars, Dr. Williams eye physician also of Cincinatti ten dollars.

[Page 276]

Mrs. Constant Worlitzer Seven dollars, and a man named Strifer Conner Corner Walnut and Allison Streets nine dollars, this last item being for three months rent. These sums I wish to be paid as soon as possible.

Item 3 I appoint my husband August Duda executor of my will and guardian of my daughter Constance Duckintz, and relieve him from giving bond either as executor or as such guardian.

Item 4 I give to my husband three thousand dollars and the rent of my houses until my daughter becomes 18 years old after which time she is to have the rents, but this request is made on condition that my husband shall take care of support and educate my daughter. His obligation to support her to cease when she becomes 18 years old or sooner if she marries before that age and on the further condition that my father John Geiler, Sr. shall have a home in my house situated on Lindsey Street in Chattanooga.

Item 5 I give to my daughter Constance Duckintz all the property of which I may be the owner at the time of my death, including the Piano, Organ, my gold watch and clothes and including also all of my real estate both on Lindsey Street and on Chestnut Street in Chattanooga. She is to have said real estate in fee simple if she attains the age of 18 years. After she is 18 years old she may dispose of it by last will and testament. But if my said daughter should die before she attains the age of 18 years or marries then on her death my Lindsey Street property shall belong to my husband August Duda, and my Chestnut Street property shall belong to the children of my brother John Geiler in fee.

Item 6 The three thousand dollars given to my husband shall be paid to him after Constance becomes 18 years old - for the reason that I have no means of providing for its payment except by raising it on my property which I do not wish now to encumber. After she is 18 years old this sum may be raised on the Lindsey Street house. But if other means should be available then the house shall not be sold. It is a condition that this sum shall not be paid to my husband unless he accepts all the terms herein provided, and if he marries again he shall cease to be guardian for Constance and shall be paid five hundred dollars per annum from my death up to time of his marriage and no more, but if the property shall not be sold anyway until Constance is 18 My husband shall also pay the taxes and repairs on my proeprty and shall have the rents until Constance is 18 unless he marries again and if he marries the rents shall go to Constance. In case of his marriage $500.00 per annum shall not be payable until Constance is 18 years old.

Item 7 I request my daughter Constance to give to the First Baptist Church of Chattanooga two hundred and fifty dollars and to the Central Baptist Church of Chattanooga two hundred and fifty dollars whenever she can spare the money. My executor may allow her this sum or any part of it at any time when he has the money and shall be allowed credit then for notwithstanding the fact that she may then be a minor.

This is intended mainly as a request to Constance and not as a donation and shall not be enforced but only paid by Constance as a free will offering if she chooses to make the gift.

[Page 298]

Item 8 Being a Baptist myself I wish my daughter to be raised and educated in the same faith as far as possible.

Item 9 My father John Geiler Sr. is to have a home in my Lindsey Street home as long as he lives if he chooses and if he should be unfortunate and lose his own property then if necessary for any reason he shall be supported out of my Chestnut Street property until Constance is 21 years old when she will I doubt not take care of him if he is not able to take care of himself. The rents only to be used if necessary for that purpose during her minority.

Amelia Duda {Seal}

Mrs. Amelia Duda signed, sealed declared and published the foregoing paper as her last will and testament and we have subscribed the same as witnesses in her presence and in the presence of each other this 8th day of June 1888.

S. M. Dodson
John A. Moore

HARRY F. GRISCOM

Last Will of Harry F. Griscom

I Harry F. Griscom of Hamilton County, State of Tennessee, being of sound mind and memory do make and publish this as my last will and testament.

I give and all of my estate, real or personal of whatsoever character or wherever situated to my wife Fanny J. Griscom her heirs administrators and [Page 299] assigns for her and their use and benefit forever.

This estate consists among other things of a lot of land and residence where I now live in the third civil district of Hamilton County, Tenn. and of policies of insurance in the following life insurance company:

In the Mutual Life Insurance Company of Newark, New Jersey, $1,000.00: In the Suthern [sic] Mutual of Louisville, Ky. $1,000.00: In the Knights of Honor $2000.00: in the Royal Arcanum $3000.00 -

This together with all I now possess and all I die seized of, are included in the above devise and bequest to my beloved wife Fannie J. Griscom, whom I appoint sole executrix of this my last will.

In witness thereof, I Harry F. Griscom have hereunto set my hand and seal, this 10th day of September in the year of our Lord one thousand eight hundred and eighty seven.

                              Harry F. Griscom

Signed, published and declared by said testator, Harry F. Griscom, as and for his last will and testament in the presence of us, who at his request have signed as witnesses to the same.

    L. G. Walker x

    Charles H. Dyer x

[NOTE - These cross marks are used where the seal is usually indicated]

[Page 300]

DENNIS DONOVAN

Last Will of Dennis Donovan

Hereby revoking all former wills and codicils by me heretofore made I Dennis Donovan hereby make publish and declare my last will and testament to be as follows -

1st My executrix hereinafter named shall pay all my just debts and funeral expenses and erect a cheap monument at my grave.

2nd The residue of my estate I will and bequeath to my executrix hereinafter named to be held by her as testamentary Guardian of my only surviving child Alice Donovan the same to be expended by my said Executrix in such manner as she thinks best for the support maintanance [sic] and education of my said child, and authorize and empower her to loan the principal, taking good security from time to time and to expend if necessary both principal and interest for the purpose aforesaid, the balance if any to be paid to my said child on arriving at the age of twenty one years, or if my said child should die unmarried and without child or children before arriving at the age of twenty one years then to such person or persons as may at that time be entitled by the laws of Tennessee to interest any such balance if any.

3rd I appoint my sister Mrs. Ellen Clark sole executrix of this my last will and testament and authorize and empower to act as such and as Testamentary Guardian as herein upon act forth with out bond.

    This June 25, 1888

Signed sealed and published in our presence and we have subscribed names in the presence of each other and by the testator this June 25, 1888.

    W. B. Garvin   Mrs. Bishling Hoff
    Bridget X Hughes   Tom Fort
       her mark

JOHN FIELDS

Last Will of John Fields

John Fields of the Co. of Hamilton and State of Tenn. being of sound mind, memory and understanding, do make my will and testament manner and form following.

First, I give devise and bequeath to my wife Jane Fields, all my property whatsoever kind it may be, from this date to her death then the said heir, Amelia Fields will fall heir to all the property.

    This the 22nd day of Sept. 1888.

                              John Fields

Witness
Jas. A. Long
W. C. Lafarry

JOSEPH FRIEDELL

Last Will of Joseph Friedell
Chattanooga, Tenn. March 27/88

I Joseph Friedell, do hereby will and bequeath all my property both real and personal and cash on hand, to my dear wife Elizabeth Friedell, and I appoint her executor and administrator to my estate and I devise that she be not required to give Bond.

Joseph Friedell

Witness
Leo Staple [or Strahle]
Lizzie Stagmaier
Johanna Fisher
E. Scott

[Page 302]

THOMAS DAILY

Last Will of Thomas Daily

I Thomas Daily being in feeble health and knowing that life is uncertain do make this my last will and testament.

Item 1 I wish to be buried by the side of my wife in Forest Hill Cemetery in a decent and Christian like manner.

Item 2 I direct that the funeral expenses of my deceased wife and my own doctors bill funeral expenses and expenses of my persent sickness be paid. This is to include the money paid by E. M. Dodson for the lot in the cemetery amount of bill at Wassman's assumed by him, and undertakers bills.

Item 3 I give to E. M. Dodson as executor all the real estate and the personal effects also owned by me at the time of my death including the houses and lot on the corner of Williams Street in the city of Chattanooga devised to me by my wife. I direct that said E. M. Dodson shall sell said property as early as possible on such terms and conditions as he thinks best for the estate. Said Dodson is authorized to sell at private or public sale without any order of court, and shall convey said property by good and sufficient deed to the purchaser or puchasers in fee simple.

Item 4 Out of the proceeds of such sale my said executor shall pay off the items herein before specified and a reasonable compensation to himself as executor and whatever I owe him or the firm of which he is a member for legal Services and all that remains he shall pay over to my nephew Mortimer [Page 303] Sullivan son of my deceased sister Ellen O. Sullivan for the use and benefit of said Mortimer and his brother and sisters, children of said

Ellen O. The receipt of said Mortimer, shall be a sufficient legal discharge of my said executor. No bond is to be required of said Mortimer.

Item 5 I constitute and appoint my friend E. M. Dodson executor of this will and relieve him from giving any bond as such executor.

Item 6 My executor shall provide a suitable monument for myself and wife out of the proceeds of the property herein specified and directed to be sold, said monument to cost not exceeding five hundred dollars.

Thomas Daily

The above paper was signed declared and published by Thomas Daily as his last will and testament and we have signed our names hereto as subscribing witnesses at the special instance and request of said Thomas Daily in his presence and in the presence of each other this 9th day of May 1888.

M. H. Ward
J. B. Jones

[Page 304]

LOUISA N. DAILY

Last Will of Mrs. Louisa N. Daily

I Louisa N. Daily, wife of Thomas Daily make this my last will and testament.

I will and devise all the real estate of which I may die seized and possessed to E. M. Dodson Trustee in fee simple for the use of my husband Thomas Daily but subject to the following condition[s]; Said trustee is required to protect the property, collect the rents, make necessary repairs and pay the taxes and pay over the net income to my said husband, but neither the property itself nor the income nor proceeds thereof shall be subject to the payment of any debt existing against my husband, at the time of my death, nor shall any court have the power or right to subject said property, its income or proceeds to the payment of any such existing by execution, judgement or decree.

My husband and said Trustee are authorized to sell and convey said property in fee simple or otherwise and re-invest the proceeds in other property but on the same terms conditions and terminations as above provided and no change shall be made by which the property hereby divised [sic] nor that purchased with its proceeds shall be made subject to the payment of any debts existing at the time of my death. If any sale is made the proceeds may be paid to my husband at his option and when so paid this trust shall cease.

If the property is not sold in the life time of my husband he is hereby empowered to devise, bequeath and dispose of it in fee simple or otherwise by Last will and testament [Page 305] and the title shall vest according to such disposition, and this provision applies to any property purchased with the proceeds of such as I may die seized and possessed of; This 22, March 1888.

Louisa N. Daily

The foregoing paper was signed by Louisa N. Daily, and by her declared to be her last will and testament in our presence, and we sign the same as witnesses by her special request and in the presence of each other.

This ___ day of March 1888.
N. H. Ward
R. M. Meyers
J. E. Meachand

EDWIN W. JOHNSON

Last Will of Edwin W. Johnson

I Edwin W. Johnson do make and publish this my last Will and Testament, not having heretofore made any will.

I desire and direct that my funeral expenses and all my just debts, be paid, out of any money I have at my death or that may first come to the hands of my representative.

Secondly: I give and bequeath all my real estate both real and personal, to Mary A. Johnson, wife of my only brother Albert O. Johnson, free from the control of her present or any future husband and for and during her natural life upon the following conditions and not otherwise: That is to say She shall have the full use and control of and shall receive all the rents and profits derived from any and real estate of which I die seized & possessed in law or equity, and all such rents and profits derived from such real estate during her life shall become hers absolutely free from the control of her present or any future husband, and it is my intention that she take all my personal estate absolutely likewise free from the control and from any marital right of her present or any future husband with this condition alone: that is to say: Should any money or personal property she may receive from my estate, or its proceeds, of any nature whatever, remain in her hands at the time of her death, it shall be equally distributed among her children now born or that may

hereafter be born by her to my brother the said Albert O. Johnson; but this limitation is not intended to prevent Mary A. from using and disposing of said personal estate during her life.

Item Third I will and bequeath that at the death of the said Mary A. Johnson all my real estate shall descend in equal shares to the children she has or may hereafter bear to my brother Albert O. Johnson.

And I do hereby appoint the said Mary A. Johnson my executrix and do not require that she give any bond for the performance of her trust. She should immediate possession of my estate both real and personal and when she shall have [Page 307] paid my funeral expenses and my debts she is not required to make any further settlement of her administration, but shall hold and enjoy my estate in the manner I have directed in this Will.

E. W. Johnson {Seal}

Signed sealed and published by the testator Edwin W. Johnson in our presence and witnessed by us, at his request, on this tenth day of May 1881.
Fred F. Wiehl
W. L. Eakin

I Edwin W. Johnson do make and publish this codicil to my foregoing will and do affirm it in all things, except, as revoked, and herein modified.

And I do so far revoke and modify it as to devise and bequeath all my property, real and personal to my brother Albert O. Johnson and his wife Mary A. Johnson for and during their natural lives and to the survivor during his or her natural life upon the same terms and conditions contained in my foregoing and original will, giving to the survivor the same rights as I have given to the said Mary A. Johnson in said Will and upon the death of the survivor all the remaining property devised and bequeathed by me shall be equally divided among the children of the said Albert O. and Mary A. Johnson, provided the youngest child born to the said Albert O. and Mary A. shall have attained the age of twenty one years, but if both said Albert O. and Mary should die before their youngest child becomes twenty one years old, in that event the distribution of [Page 308] the remainder of my estate will be postponed until said youngest child arrives at twenty one years of age, and should any one of said children die before such distribution, the children of such child will take the interest of such deceased child under this will and I appoint said Albert O. Johnson one of my executors and he will not be required to give security for the discharge of such trust. Aug. 24th 1883.

The word not [blank] before the word security interlined before signed.

E. W. Johnson

Signed and published in our presence and witnessed by each of us, at the request of the testator Edwin W. Johnson who is the same person that signed the original and foregoing Will, Aug. 24th 1883.

W. L. Eakin
Alexander Ayre
Probated Nov. 12, 1888

T. KING ROSS

Last Will of T. King Ross

Lookout Mountain Tenn.
Hamilton County July 21st 1888

Know all men that T. King Ross being in sound mind and believing that Death is near make this my last Will and Testament;

All property Real or Personal belonging to me I give and bequeath to my Wife Mary Jane Ross for love and affection.

This does not include any prospective claims that I have and might have in the future except on one condition which will be made hereafter.
[Page 309]

The property is more particularly described as follows, half a block of Land more or less with a House Fixtures Plate Barn and Fence known as my Residence in El Paso Texas which I deeded to the said Mary Jane Ross some time ago and trust it so appears on the records.

One operating chair in the office of Dr. Justise Herein disclaiming any debt due him.

The Notes, Mortgages, against Jesus Eouillet and Dr. J. M. A. De Forgoso with interest for over a year at rate of one percent per month on $50.00 more or less.

One Note against Mr. and Mrs. A. H. Carter for $1000.00 with interst at rate of ten percent per annum for 16 months indorsed [sic] by Joseph P. Ross.

The forenamed property being in my Wife's name I simply take this occasion to mention the fact that it is the property of Mary Jane Ross. Further One fourth interest in the Lease, Fixtures in the Lookout Mountain House.

A one sixth interst in #2322 Michigan Ave. Chicago, Ills. and known in the family as belonging to myself, Brothers and Sisters. I would ask that this property be made productive, not less than 4 per cent being demanded above taxes.

Assessments, Insurance upon a valuation of $30,000, the interst to be paid to Jennie semiannually. I would advise a long lease.

This last being simply a suggestion not seeming to Dictate to my Brothers and Sisters, but should the property not be productive within two years, I would ask my Mother to have the proceeds derived from my interest invested in Guilt Edge securities, not [Page 310] to be vested in any corporation but a First Mortgage upon City property prefered [sic], Interest to be paid to Jennie semi annually $1600.00 more or less deposited in the Merchants Loan and Trust Co. Bank, Chicago Ills. I set aside for payment of the following named persons J. G. Burton in the neighborhood of $15.60, S. T. Dewees and Co. $4.00
T. A. Snow $10.00
T. H. Payne $7.50
Aull and Anderson, and Drennan for Meat and Ice during the last month.
H. O. Lane - 30 c
Wm. Campbell $8.60 in full
Euphrania Hopkins balance due her
And payment of my Funeral Expenses.

It is my wish that the plainest coffin without ornaments be provided, and my Body carried to Chicago and Burried [sic] in the Family Grave Yard.

That the funeral be conducted as economically as consistent with my Birth and Education. The balance if any be given to my Wife Mary Jane Ross to provide her with mourning.

Further known that all Debts due me from whatever cause including a note against A. T. Carlstrand for $75.00 indorsed [sic] by Wm. Peak for 80 days with interest.
Mrs. Hunt, $15.00
Mr. Hunt $30.00 money loaned
F. Hoffman for Professional services for his niece $20.00
Dr. F. H. Goodwin of Tucson, Ariz - $270.00
County Warrents 350 shares in the Nogates Mining and Smelting Co. and all other Debts due me in Arizona and elsewhere I give to my Wife Mary Jane Ross. Also my watch and Diamond shirt Studs and ring.
[Page 311]

To my mother, it is my sincere wish to have you give Jennie a Home, and treat her as you would your own child briefly accepting Jennie as a Daughter for the loss of a Son.

And it is my wish that she would live with my mother if practicable.

I can't express how desirous I am of this and it is only in the belief of the carrying out of these plans that I die easy and release all claims to the one sixth of one third interest in the estate of Tuthill King.

I will not say much of Jennies goodness except that the last Seven Years (our married life) in spite of sore trials, sickness, the dangers on the Frontier they have been the happiest of my life. Now Father, Mother, Brothers and Sisters Aunt Mamie and any one else who might be slighted, Good Bye.

T. King Ross

Witnessed

July 21st 1888
J. B. Linn
John J. Heelan

ROSA STATEN

Last Will of Rosa Staten

I Rosa Staten considering the uncertainty of life, and being sick and weak in body but of sound and disposing mind do make this my last will and testament hereby revoking all former wills by me at any time made.

I direct that all my just debts shall be paid and if the debts due me and [Page 312] the proceeds of the sale of my personal property be insufficient for that purpose my executor is authorized to sell my other estate or so much as may be necessary to pay said debts.

First I give and bequeath all my estate both real and personal to be equally divided between my Aunt Ella Thompson and her son (and my cousin) Frank Shindlebowers to have and to hold in fee simple forever.

Secondly - I appoint J. T. Lupton my executor to carry out the provisions of this will and direct after paying all my debts as herein before provided to sell the rest of my property both real and personal and divide the remainder equally between my Aunt and Cousin as hereinbefore provided.

Witness my hand Oct. 25th 1888.

Rosa X Staten
her mark

Signed and published by Rosa Staten as and for her last will and testament in the presence of us who in her presence and in the presence of each other have hereto subscribed our names as witnesses.

J. H. Abercrombie
C. F. Brown
Mattie Foust
J. T. Lupton

[Page 313]

MILES SHIELDS

Last Will of Miles Shields

Chattanooga, Tenn.

Augus [sic] 4th 1887

I Miles Shields of the City of Chattanooga Hamilton County state of Tennessee Do make this my Last Will and Testament.

First it is my just debts and all Charges be paid out of my Estate.

Item - I give devise all the Residue of my estate to Royhe Shields and I Miles Shields and Matildy Maning Son and my motherinlaw is to Receive $5.00 per month From Said Estate During Her Life Time To Be To Them and There [sic] Heirs Forever.

Item - I appoint and make The said Amos Manning Sturling Shields and Jinie Shields Executrix of This my last Will and Testament after my Death Millie Sheals Signed and sealed The Fourth day of Augus [sic] A. D. 1887.

Miles Shield {Seal}

Witness by Rev. Wm. Washington
S. X Luter   D. X Horehan
his mark   his mark

I Miles Sheals do also appoint Jack Haggie and Chas. Washington as Executrix for my motherin law to see that she get her $5.00 out of said estate during Her Life Time. This is after my Death Milles Shield. This is after my death Milles Shield.

State of Tennessee)
County of Hamilton) Before me, H. A. Brown, a Notary Public duly appointed, commissioned and qualified in and for the County and State aforesaid, personally appeared Miles Sheald [sic] of Chattanooga Hamilton County the within named bargainer with whom I am personally acquainted and who [Page 314] acknowledge[d] that he executed the within instrument for the purpose therein contained.

In Testimony Whereof I have hereunto set my hand and Notarial Seal at office in the City of Chattanooga Tennessee, on this the 10 day of Aug. 1887.

H.A. Brown
Notary Public

MARY J. STOUTEMYER

Last Will of Mary J. Stoutemyer

Morris Grundy Co., Illinois.
Friday Morning 6th February 1880

I, Mary Jane Stoutemyer do this day will and

bequeath all my property Personal and real estate to be equally divided between my sister Susannah Elizabeth Nelson, William Stockstill Winters, Lewis Jesse Winters, and Harrison Allison Winters. And that my Mother Susannah Winters shall have the use and benefit of said property above mentioned at her own option, during her natural life.

Mary J. Stoutemyer

Witness, A. G. Woodbury
  Do   J. H. Sampson

And that the same Mary J. Stoutemyer signed the above Instrument at Morris Grundy County Illinois and in our presence and that we Reside at Morris Grundy County Illinois.

[Page 315]

LAURENCE JOHN WOODHEAD

Last Will of L. J. Woodhead

I, Laurence John Woodhead do hereby make and publish this my last will and testament hereby revoking all other wills, if any, by me made.

I devise and bequeath to my beloved wife Adah Woodhead all my property be the same real, personal or mixed, of every kind and character and wherever located or situated - It is my intention that she take the absolute title to all my property, with power to sell, convey make title, and receive or collect the purchase money. I expect her to waive all rights of homestead and dower and trust to her affection and devotion to our children to see to their care and protection.

The real estate now owned by me, is described generally as follows - In Hamilton County Tennessee - One lot in Chattanooga on Doud Street, fronting about 55 feet on said Doud Street and running back to Kirby; one lot of land in the 10th District of said Hamilton County, containing (4 1/5) four and one fifth acres bounded South by the Harrison road and North by the Switch yard of the E. T. V. and Ga. R. R. Co. - West by Citico Furnace Co., and East by D. J. Chandler.

This real estate my said wife can sell rent or dispose of as she may deems best for the interest of herself and children but she has full authority to make title without resort to the courts.

All personal property is bequeathed to my wife absolutely. She can sell or retain it as she thinks best, or retain a portion and sell the residue.

I constitute my said wife Adah my executrix and desire that she be not required to give bond and security or take the oath required by statue.

Executed by me this 10th day of August 1888 in presence of F. M. Gardenhire, J. A. [Page 315] Conner and S. A. Key who are present and witness the same at my request in the presence of each other.

L. J. Woodhead

Witness
S. A. Key
F. M. Gardenhire
J. A. Connor

JAMES F. SHUMATE

Last Will of James F. Shumate

State of Tennessee
Hamilton County

I James F. Shumate do make and publish this my last will and testament, hereby revoking and making void all other wills by me at any time made.

First, I direct that my funeral expenses be paid as soon after my death as possible: out of any moneys that I may die possessed of, or may first come into the hands of my Executor.

Secondly, I direct that Benjamin F. Shumate and James L. Jackson to take charge of my body. I direct that my body be dressed in full dress suit, placed in a neat coffin, costs of which not to exceed twenty five dollars and by them taken to the Cemetery at Cincinnati Ohio there shrouded and cremated, my ashes to be given to my brother Benjamin F. Shumate to be diposed of by him as he may see fit, but under no circumstances must they be given to the custody of my wife. Should the Knights of Pythias desire to take charge of my remains and accompany to the Cemetery at Cincinnati Ohio let them do so; but do not ask or make any request of them to do it.

Thirdly, I give and bequeath to James L. Jackson my large rotory [sic] desk now packed at Bellefontaine Ohio also all paper weights, inkstands belonging to it which are either with the desk or packed in a box now in the custody of Benjamin F. Shumate. In the event I should die at the residence of James L. Jackson then all the furniture and household effects belonging to me in his house are to become the property of Emily S. Jackson.

Fourthly, I give and bequeath to my son Frank D.

my diamond shirt studs, my double case gold watch, gold watch chain, watch charm now on the chain, my large gold ring, all meddels [sic] swords, belts, uniforms and all equipment pertaining to the order of Knights of Pythias; but these articles herein mentioned must remain in the custody and care of Benjamin F. Shumate until my son Frank D. arrives of age; and in the event of Frank D's death before attaining majority, then said articles are to be the property of Benjamin F. Shumate.

Fifthly, I give and bequeath to my daughters Myrtle and Maye my home library of books at Urbana Ohio to be divided equally between them.

I give and bequeath to my son Frank D. my library of books at West Liberty and Bellefontaine Ohio.

Sixthly, I direct my executor to collect all insurance due on my policies and pay it to my children as they become of age, share and share alike as provided in the policies.

Seventhly, I direct that my executor to take the mortgage note I hold against Sarah McLoed have it cashed and pay to James L. Jackson such expense he may [Page 318] have incured [sic] during my illness on my account, and during such time as he had care of me; and I direct that my executor to take charge of all other notes or personal property belonging to me not herein mentioned and after paying all my funeral expenses to dispose of them for the benefit of my children as he may think best.

Lastly, I do hereby nominate and appoint Benjamin F. Shumate my Executor.

In witness whereof I do to this my will set my hand and seal.

This August 10th 1888

James F. Shumate

Signed sealed and published in our presence, and we have subscribed our names hereto in presence of the testator This August 10th 1888.
J. B. Ruck
W. L. Shumate

SABRA SNYDER

Last Will of Sabra Snyder

I, Sabra Snyder, of Chattanooga Tennessee, being of sound mind do make and publish this as my Last will and testament hereby revoking any and all wills by me at any time heretofore made.

I give and bequeath to my dear son Charles C. Snyder two notes and the proceeds thereof, executed to

me on 21" day of Feby. 1887 for $3500.00 each by Michael O'Grady bearing interest at 6 per cent per annum and secured by him on 85 acres of land in 3" civil district of Hamilton County Tennessee. But out of the [Page 319] proceeds of these notes there shall first be paid the sum of $2000.00, as evidenced by mortgage or deed of trust executed by me and my husband on our home place lot No. 30 Cedar Street, Chattanooga, Tennessee.

The interest on said $2,000.00 shall also be paid out of the proceeds of said notes.

Then all other debts of every kind and description which I may owe at the time of my death shall be paid out of the said notes and their proceeds, and the balance shall go to the said C. C. Snyder.

My house and lot, the place where we now live and being I believe Lot No. 30 Cedar Street, Chattanooga, togather with all the rents, buildings and appurtanances to the same belonging, I do hereby give and bequeath to my husband Cyrus Snyder for and during his natural life, but at his death this as well as all other real estate of which I die seized and possessed shall go to the legitimate children of my son C. C. Snyder by his present or any future wife share and share alike.

But the said Cyrus Snyder owning hereby a life estate in said real estate and being entitled to the proceeds of the same shall pay the taxes on the same and keep it in good condition and repair.

Should C. C. Snyder die before he receives the proceeds of said two notes then I direct that the same shall go to his legitimate children by his present or any future wife.

I nominate and appoint Cyrus Snyder my executor.
[Page 320]
In testimony whereof I have hereunto set my hand and seal this 23 day of Nov. 1887.
Sabra Snyder
Witness
W. T. Hope
Lucy Park

A. E. NEWMAN

Last Will of A. E. Newman

Know all men by these present [sic] that I, A. E. Newman, do hereby will and bequeath to my husband Thomas W. Newman all my right title and interest in two acres of land in the 17" [or 19] district of Hamilton Co., Tennessee situated at the foot of Lookout Mt. and near the depot of the Incline Rail Road, being the same land purchased by myself and E. K. Anderson from Lewis

Hicks on the 18" day of July 1883 given under my hand and seal this the 20" day of July 1887.

A. E. Newman

Witness

Watson Fisher) State of Tennessee
Adelia Ford) Hamilton County

Acknowledged before me William Street a Notary Public in and for said County at Residence of A. E. Newman No. 10 Missionary Ave. City of Chattanooga Tenn. this 20th day of July 1887.

William Street Notary Public

[Page 321]

CHRISTIANA SMITH

Last Will of Christiana Smith

I Christiana Smith alias Jones widow of Jessie Jones wife of Tom Smith solemly [sic] impressed [with] the uncertainty of life and the certainty of death and being of sound mind and disposing memory do make this my last will and testament hereby revoking all others.

1st I consign my body to the grave and my soul to the God who gave it.

2nd I desire all my debts if any paid out of any property I have at my death, and that my body be given a decent christian burial.

3 My present Husband Tom Smith has in no way contributed to my support in years, has been very cruel and wicked to me, and has been incarcorated [sic] in the Penitentiary for violating the laws of his country.

For a long time I have been in feeble health, and needing much care and attention.

For years I have been cared for, and kindly treated and in a great measure supported by Samuel Hoover, a hard working industrious man. Now in view of the many kindnesses I have had at his house, and as a small token of my appreciation of his kindness, I hereby give and bequeath to the said Samuel Hoover all the property of every kind real and personal that I may own at the time of my death to be his absolutely and unconditionally subject alone to the interest hereinafter bequeathed to Mary Henry.

3 Mary Henry has for some time lived at my house and taken care of me and I bequeath to her a home during her life on the premises and in the House that I may die seized and possessed of, and it is my will and desire that the said Samuel Hoover shall allow her [Page 322] the free and unobstructed use of enough of my residence to make herself a comfortable home during her life. I desire that she have this home free of any charge, and free from taxes and repairs.

4 I own Lot No. 18 Baldwin and Ellwells Allotment on Fortwood in Chattanooga Hamilton County Tenn. and being the lot I bought of Dudly Baldwin and J. J. Ellwell by Deed dated August 26, 1878 and Registered in the Registers office of Hamilton County in book Y of Vol. 1, pages 530-531 and a lot of Household and Kitchen furniture all in my house on said lot. All this I give and bequeath to the said Samuel Hoover subject to the life interest of the said Mary Henry togather [sic] with my other property and effects I may own at my death.

5 And having unlimited confidence in the said Samuel Hoover I hereby nominate appoint and constitute him executor of this my last will and testament and excuse him from giving bond as such.

In witness whereof I have hereunto set my hand and seal this the 27th day of March 1888.

Christiana X Smith
her mark

Signed in our presence and we attested the signature of the said Christiana Smith at her request Mch. 28, 1888.
Geo. T. White
Henry X Fields
his mark
Foyt X Bodget
his mark
Wm. X Conall
his mark

[Page 323]

I Christiana Smith alias Jones do hereby make the following codicil to the foregoing will. Samuel Hoover died on this day at my house from injuries received while in the services of the Chattanooga Rome and Columbus R. R. Co. and [I] desire to change my said foregoing will on account of his death and to give and bequeath and do hereby will give and bequeath all the property I have or may have at my death of every kind both real and personal to my friend Mary Henry, the same Mary Henry named in my will and to whom I therein gave a life estate, or a home for life it is my will and desire that at my death she have all my property of every kind, real personal and mixed. I do not leave my husband Tom Smith anything because he has been very unkind to me and failed to support me and has been convicted of a high crime. I desire that my body be given a decent Christian burial and that all my debts be paid and I hereby appoint the said Mary Henry (colored) executrix of this my last will and testament, the death of Samuel Hoover making it necessary to appoint some one else. And I also excuse the said Mary Henry from giving Bond as such executrix. Witness my hand this the 20th day of April 1888.

Christiana X Smith
her mark

Signed in our presence in the presence of each other and we attested the signature of the said Christiana Smith at her request.
This April 20, 1888
Geo. T. White
J. R. Downs

[Page 324]

LEWIS OWEN

Last Will of Lewis Owen

I Lewis Owen of the City of Chattanooga County of Hamilton State of Tennessee, hereby make and publish this my last will and testament revoking all wills if any heretofore made by me.

1st My executor herein named and appointed will first pay all my just debts of every kind out of the money on hand at my death if this is not sufficient he will sell first sufficient personal property to meet any balance - if the personal estate is not sufficient he may sell sufficient real estate to pay the remaining balance, exercising his judgment as to what realty he will sell.

2nd After the payment of my debts the residue of my property real personal and mixed wherever situated will be divided by executor as follows:

To my wife Julia Owen one third in value of my estate for and during her natural life, and at her death the remainder estate to my children or their issue either of them marry & die leaving issue living each taking an equal part the issue to my deceased child to take as the parent would if living.

The residue of my estate I will and devise to my children now living, or hereafter born, each taking an equal interest. In the event of the marriage of my child, issue of said marriage and death of said child, with issue living the issue will take the part the parent would if living.

I appoint and constitute A. J. Wisdom my executor, with full power to act in the premises. In order that my estate may be adjusted and settled up with as little delay and expense as possible. I authorize my executor to dispose of property [Page 325] in such way or manner as he may deem best for the interests of the estate.

He may sell at private or public sale and for cash or on time as he sees proper and deems to the best interest of the estate.

He has full power to settle and adjust all my partnership business of any kind, on the best terms that his judgment may dictate for this purpose he may sell my interests or buy the interests of other partners may compromise all or any matters of dispute and do everything necessary to settle up the business. In order that the purposes of my will be effectually carried out without any unnecessary resort to the cowits, I hereby vest the legal title of all my property real and personal in my said executor with full authority to sell any or all of said property real or personal upon such terms as he may deem best and receive the purchase money, or purchase money notes, and dispose of the same as indicated in this will.

He has the full and complete power to make and convey title to purchaser of any property, real or personal.

My said executor is hereby relieved from making bond and taking the oath required by statutes for executors.

Witness my hand and seal in the presence of witnesses this - day of Oct. 20 1882.

Lewis Owen {Seal}

Witnesses
Clem Tomlinson
Wm. B. Ragsdale
H. W. Clark
H. G. Hitchcock

[Page 326]

JULIA OWEN

Last Will of Julia Owen

I, Julia Owen, being of sound and disposing mind and memory, do make and publish this my last will and testament.

Item 1st - I will that my just debts and personal expenses be paid.

The residue of my estate, both real and personal, I devise to my three children Jennie, James and Wisdom, each taking one third. In the event of the marriage of any child, issue of said marriage and death of said child, with issue living, the issue will take the part the parent would if living. I appoint and constitute my father, A. J. Wisdom, my executor, with full power to act in the premises, without bond, in order that my estate may be settled up with as little delay and expense as possible, I authorize my said executor to dispose of any or all of my personal property, or any or all of my real estate on such time or terms as he sees proper, and deems best for the interest of the estate, and to re-invest the proceeds of said sales from time to time as in his judgment is for the best interest of the estate.

In order that the purposes of this my will may be effectually carried out, and without resort to the courts, I hereby vest the legal tittle [sic] of all my property, both real and personal, in my said executor, with full authority to sell any or all of said property, real and personal, on such terms as he may deem best, and secure the purchase money and notes given for the same and dispose of the same as indicated in this will.

He has full and complete power to make and convey title, to the puchaser, of any property, real or personal.

My said executor is hereby released from making bond and taking the oath required [Page 327] by the statutes for executors.

Witness my hand and seal in the presence of witnesses this 16th day of February 1888.

Julia Owen {SS}

Witnesses
F. F. Wiehl
T. O. Foust

MOSES PEARSON

Last Will of Moses Pearson

I, Moses Pearson being of sound mind and disposing memory do make and publish this as my last will and testament.

1st I desire my body to be decently buried 2 n d I desire all my just debts to be paid out of my property.

3rd I will and bequeath to Cornelia Taylor, who has nursed and cared for me in my last sickness all of my property of every description both personal and real property - including my barber outfit, chairs, looking glass &c - also a gold watch and two gold rings, my trunk and its contents also my house on West 9th St. on the lot of W. L. Duggar, and in short I give to said Cornelia Taylor every thing I have and own of whatever description, whether personal property or real estate and whether embraced in the above description or not - and she is to have the absolute title to all of said property.

4th I nominate and appoint said Cornelia Taylor executrix of this my last will and testament and I hereby [Page 328] excuse her from making bond or from making any report to the County Court.

In witness whereof I hereunto set my hand and seal.

This April 12th 1888

Moses X Pearson
his mark

We the undersigned witnesses saw the testator sign and acknowledge the foregoing will, in our presence and we signed the same in his presence and in the presence of each other -

This April 12th 1888 -

James W. White
Adline X Arnold
her mark
J. B. Frazier
Minnie X Day
her mark

J. P. WILKINSON

Will of J. P. Wilkinson

I J. P. Wilkinson of Chattanooga. Hamilton County Tennessee being now in the full possession of my reasoning faculties do hereby make, publish, and declare this instrument to be my last will and testament hereby expressly revoking all former wills and Codicils -

I give to my wife Eva M. Wilkinson Lot No. 85 Poplar Street in the City of Chattanooga, County of Hamilton and State of Tennessee the same fronting one hundred feet on Poplar Street and running [Page 329] back of uniform width to Cedar Street, and the three houses now thereon and all the improvements and appurtenances there unto belonging and which may hereafter be made and placed before the said property also one lot on Lookout Mountain being Thomas and Wilkinson plat - being in Hamilton Co., Tenn. Also one half interest in property on said Mountain, in said county which I own partly with W. R. Thomas the intention being to give to my said wife all of my interest therein.

Also all and any other real estate of which I may die siezed and all interest of whatever kind or real estate anywhere at the time of my death -

I also give to my said wife all personal property bills, notes, account choses in ensurance of whatever kind and all property and interest whatsoever which may belong to me at the time of my death.

I hereby appoint said Eva M. Wilkinson my Executrix with full power and Authority to execute this will and wind up the affairs of my estate as to her judgment may be best.

In testimony whereof I have hereto affixed my

signature and caused it to be attested in my presence by witnesses who have signed as subscribing witnesses at my request in my presence and in the presence of each other this 11th day of Febry. 1887.

J. P. Wilkinson

We the undersigned witnessed the signature of the above Instrument by J. P. Wilkinson at his request and have attested the same by signing our names hereto in his presence [Page 330] and in the presence of each other this 11th day of February 1887.

J. W. Butler
C. P. Becks [or Beeks]

MILTON WALKER

Last Will of Milton Walker

In the name of God Amen: -

I Milton Walker of Hamilton County Tennessee being of sound mind but somewhat feeble in body, knowing that it is appointed unto all men once to die; do make and publish this my last will and testament revoking my former wills if any.

Item First It is my will and desire that my just debts, if any, be paid out of any money that I may be possessed at the time of my death or that may first come to the hands of my executor.

Item Second I give and divise to my beloved wife Julie Walker the house and lot where I now live fronting (50) fifty feet on Wanison Street or road and running back one hundred and fifty feet along Ramsey Street, bought by me from Sam Ramsey but conveyed to me by Charles Stanley situated and being in a village formerly known as Stanleyville now called Churchville, in Hamilton County, Tenn. and adjoining a lot on which I now have a storehouse, and the same upon which I have erected a dwelling house stable and outhouse, for her natural life there.

Item Third I now give and bequeath unto my said wife all the house hold and kitchen furniture in my said house and on said lot at the time of my death togather [sic] with any live stock that I may have at the time of my death and all the personal property that I may own at the time of my death togather [sic] with all money that may be on hand or due me in any way including all debts of every nature that may be due me in any way whatsoever to be hers absolutely and to be used and disposed of as she sees proper.

It is my will that at the death of my said wife the said lot herein devised to her shall go to my two sons Abner and Grant Walker to have and to hold during their natural lives, share and share alike and at their death to become the property of their children begotten in lawful wedlock.

If either of them should die before my said wife then their living children shall take the share of their deceased parent.

Item Fourth I give and devise the lot on which my store house now stands fronting (66) sixty six feet on said Wanison Street or road running back south one hundred and fifty feet and adjoining the lot devised to my said wife to my said two sons Abner and Grant Walker for and during their natural lives and no longer and then to the children of my same two sons, in fee simple; and should either of my two sons die before I do, leaving children then such children will take the share intended [Page 332] for the parent if living. It is my purpose that my two sons and their children shall only take the reversionary interest in the lot devised to my wife Julia, and the lot on which my store house stands, and no part of my personal estate of any kind which is bequeathed to my wife the said Julia.

In testimony whereof I have hereunto set my name in the presence of witnesses this 5th day of December 1887.

Milton X Walker
his mark

Signed in presence of
W. L. Eakin
M. J. Eakin
Witnesses

Codicil to Will of Milton Walker

I Milton Walker, being feeble in body but of sound mind do make and publish this as a codicil to the only will I have heretofore made dated dec. 5th 1887 Witnessed by W. L. Eakin and M. J. Eakin.

I now revoke and change my said Will and that part of it contained in item 4 and do give and devise to my son Grant Walker to have and to take absolutely, without any restrictions thereon whatever, the lot upon my storehouse now stands, adjoining the lot devised by me to my wife Julia for life - said lot fronts (66) sixty six feet Wanison Street or road and runs back of uniform width one hundred and fifty feet. I am endebted [sic] to Charles Stanley in the sum of two hundred dollars purchase money on said lot [Page 333] and should I not pay said purchase money to said Stanley in my lifetime, then my said son Grant will take said lot subject to the payment of any purchase money due said Stanley on sad lot.

I do also bequeath to my said son Grant all the goods that may be in my store on the lot devised to him and all debts due the store and subject to any debts incured [sic] by me if any on account of the store. And I do hereby change my said Will so far as modified by this codicil but not otherwise.

In testimony whereof I have affixed my signature on this 18th day of January 1888.

Milton X Walker
his mark

Attest

W. L. Eakin
William X Baker
his mark
F. A. Morris

J. W. CHAMBERS

Last Will of J. W. Chambers

In the name of God Amen!

I John William Chambers of Chattanooga Hamilton County Tennessee well knowing the uncertainty of life and the certainty of death and being in failing health though of disposing mind and memory dc hereby make and publish this my last will and testament hereby revoking and annulling all others.

Item First I bequeath my body to the earth from whence it came and my soul to the God who gave it.

Item second To my dearly beloved wife Sara Elizabeth Chambers I give and [Page 334] bequeath all my personal property of every description including notes choses in action &c to be hers absolutely unconditionally and forever.

Item Third I also give and bequeath to my said Wife Sarah Elizabeth Chambers for and during her natural life all the real estate I die seized and possessed of subject to the bequeath hereinafter set forth in favor of my mother Sara Chambers.

It is my will and desire that my said wife have the use rent and profits of all my lands except the bequest in favor of my mother during her natural life, and that she have, and own, and controll [sic] the same as her separate estate free from marital rights and controll [sic] of any future husband, and free from his debts, contracts and liabilities. My real estate is located in Chattanooga Hamilton County Tennessee and consists of the following Houses and lots viz: Two houses and lots on McCallie Avanue [sic]; Two Houses and lots on Penelope Street; Two Houses and Lots on Vaugn [sic] Street; Two Houses and Lots on Tenth Street; Two Houses and Lots on Baldwin Street; Two Houses and Lots on Gilmore Street, and if I have omitted mentioning any real estate I own, or

may own at my death, I desire it to take the same course with that mentioned.

Item Fourth To my beloved Mother Sara Chambers I give and bequeath for her natural life the use, occupation and enjoyment of my Two Houses on Vaughn Street in the said City of Chattanooga Tennessee. It is my will and desire that she have the absolute controll [sic] of said Houses and Lots, as long as she may live and that she collect the rents and profits therefrom pay the Taxes thereon, keep said property in good repair, and keep the Houses insured and that at her death if my wife should be [Page 235] living that she have the use of said Two Houses on Vaughn Street during her natural life.

Item fifth It is further my will and desire that at the death of my wife, all my real estate go to my three children Proctor Hamilton Chambers, Maud Lillian Chambers, and Kate Lee Chambers unless my Mother is still living and in that event, I direct that my said children be given all my real estate except the Two lots on Vaughn Street, and that at her, my mothers, death my said children have these Two lots, But if my wife should die before my youngest child Kate Lee Chambers, now an infant, should reach the age of twenty one years, or in case of her, Kates, before she reaches the age of Twenty one years, if my wife dies before my then youngest child living reaches the age of twenty one years, it is my will and desire, that all my real etate be kept togather [sic] until my youngest child shall reach the age of Twenty one years of age.

I desire that no division or distribution of any land and estate will be made until the youngest child living reaches the age of twenty one years of age. And in the event of my wife's death during the minority of any youngest child, I hereby delegate to her the power to appoint a trustee, by will or deed, to take care of and manage said estate and keep it togather [sic] until my youngest child reaches Twenty one years of age, then to be equally divided between my three children or the survivors, or in the case of the death of any our living issue [Page 336] I desire that issue to represent their dead parent. During the life estate of my wife, it is my will and desire that she take care of the property, keep it in reasonably good repair, pay the Taxes and take care of the estate in remainder for the benefit of my children. It is further my will and desire, as I know it will be her pleasure to use the rents, profits and income from the property bequeathed my wife, and I hereby direct my said wife to use the income from said property, for her support, and for the support, education and maintainance of my said three children. I desire that they have a liberal education and I trust to my said wife to apply the income from my said property so bequeathed to her to give them as good an education as said income will afford. If she should die and said estate should be managed by a Trustee, the Trustee shall manage the estate for the same purpose, and to the same end, and divide the occretions [sic] equally among my children, or their legal representations, when the youngest reaches his or her majority. But in no event shall said property be divided or the children come into the enjoyment of said property during my wifes life.

Item Sixth I have my life insured for Eight Thousand Dollars in three insurance companies. As soon after my death as possible, I will and direct that my executrix collect all of said insurance money and pay to my mother a legacy of one Thousand (1000) Dollars. It is further my will and desire, that my said wife and executrix pay out of said insurance money all my debts, and especially pay off and satisfy out of said insurance money any and all [Page 337] encumbrances on any real estate, and I desire as far as I may do so to create said Insurance money and Trust fund for the payment of all my debts, and especially to pay off the encumbrance on my land. The rest of said insurance money after paying my Mother the said Sarah Chambers One Thousand Dollars, and paying my debts to belong absolutely to my said wife, to be used for the support education and maintainance of my said wife and children, and all bequests in this will in favor of my said wife and upon condition that the insurance money when collected is applied as herein directed by me.

Item Seventh: I hereby nominate constitute and appoint my dearly beloved wife Sarah Elizabeth Chambers, my true and Lawful executrix to carry out the objects of this my last will and Testament.

Item Eight I likewise hereby appoint my said wife Sarah Elizabeth Chambers Guardian for my three children during their minority, and having unlimited confidence in her, excuse her from giving a Guardian's Bond.

In testimony whereof I have hereunto set my hand in the presence of the subscribing witness [sic] who have attested the same at my request and in my presence and in the presence of each other This the 27th day of March 1886.

John W. Chambers

Signed in our presence and in the presence of each other March 27, 1886.
S. C. Peoples
L. M. Elder
T. H. Pitner

[Page 338]

J. W. CHAMBERS

Last Will of J. W. Chambers

Whereas, I, John William Chambers of Chattanooga Hamilton County Tennessee on the 27th of March 1886 in the presence of S. C. Peeples, L. M. Elder and T. H. Pitner did make and publish my last will and Testatment wherein I devised all my real estate. And whereas since making my said will I have sold the following described real estate devised in my will viz: Two Houses and Lots on Gillespie Street, Two Houses and Lots on Penelope Street, Two Houses and Lots on Tenth Street, Two Houses and Lots on Baldwin Street, and Two Houses and Lots on Vaugn Street all in Chattanooga Tennessee, the last two Houses and Lots mentioned having been by me devised to my beloved Mother, Sarah Chambers, for life; and whereas with the proceeds of the sale of said property I have bought the lot in Weihl and Pattens Addition to Chattanooga Tennessee upon which I have erected six cottages, said lot being on Weihl street and Harrison Avanue [sic] and have also built two Houses on my lot on Magnolia Street and one on Palmetta Street, all of said property being in Chattanooga Tennessee. Now in view of the premises I, the said John W. Chambers being of sound mind and disposing memory do make this my codicil hereby confirming my said last Will and testament made in March 27, 1886 as far as this codicil is consistent therewith and except as modified by this codicil.

Item first The two Houses and Lots on Vaughn Street devised to my mother in said will having been sold, it is my wish and desire that she, my mother, the said Sarah Chambers have the use, occupancy, benefit and enjoyment, during her natural life of my House on Palmetto Street, and the east House on Harrison Avanue [sic] and at her death said property to go as directed in [Page 339] my said will I direct that she, my said mother keep said property in good repair, pay the Taxes on the same and keep the improvements well insured in good and solvent companies for the benefit of my children named in the will. My mother will hold said Houses and lots precisely as she would have held the lots on Vaughn Street had they not been sold, the House and Lot on Palmetta Street and the east House on Harrison Avanue [sic] being substituted for the House and Lots on Vaugn Streets.

Item Second I desire and direct that my mother be paid one Thousand Dollars in money out of my life insurance money when the same is collected as provided in my said Will dated March 27, 1886.

Item Third It is my wish and desire that my wife Sarah Elizabeth Chambers take and hold for her natural life the said Houses and lot on Harrison Avanue [sic] and Weihl Street and other Houses built by me except those two bequeathed and devised my mother, upon the same terms, retrictions, powers, trusts, conditions and limitations that she takes and holds all my land mentioned in will and at her death said Houses and Lot to go as my said Will directs the rest of my land shall go. And I desire that my wife Sarah Elizabeth Chambers heretofore apppointed executrix of my last will and testament be and she is hereby appointed executrix to execute and convey out this my codicil as well as my will.

In witness whereof I have hereunto set my hand in the presence of the subscribing witnesses who have attested the same at my request and in my presence and the presence of each other. This the 21st day of February A. D. 1887.

J. W. Chambers

Signed in our presence and in the presence of each other this February 21, 1887.
Geo. T. White
W. H. Pitner

CHRISTIAN HOMAN

Last Will of Christian Homan

I, Christian Homan of Chattanooga, Tennessee do on this 11th day of June 1887 make the following as my last Will and Testament, to wit:

I direct that my Executrix pay all my just debts as soon as possible out of any money or other personal property (or proceeds of sale thereof) coming into her hands. And I give and bequeath all the money or other personal property I may die seized and possessed of to my beloved wife Amelia Homan hereinafter named as Executrix, subject to the payment of any debts I may leave unpaid, to be absolutely.

She is also to pay my funeral expenses out of said personal property.

I will, bequeath, and devise to my said wife, Amelia Homan during her widowhood or natural life (should she remain a widow after my death until she dies) all of my land or real estate, which now consists of a lot fronting 68 ft on 9th Street, where we live, and a lot fronting 300 feet on 9th Street, in Chattanooga, Tennessee.

She shall have full control and possession of all real estate I may die seized and possessed of, during her said widowhood, and shall be entitled, absolutely and in her own right, to all the rents and income that may be derived from said land or real estate.
[Page 341]

I will, devise and bequeath all my said real estate, subject to the interest willed to my wife therein as above provided, absolutely and in fee simple to my two children Leonora Amelia Homan and Frederick Charles Homan, share and share alike, each to have equal interest. And I

desire and direct my said wife to properly support and educate my said children during their minority, out of provisions made for her benefit in this Will.

I will and direct that my said executrix shall have full power and authority to sell and convey, or otherwise dispose of any of said real estate she may think proper at any time. She may sell any or all of the same. In case she sells any of said land the proceeds of sale shall belong to her during her widowhood and the remainder or corpus to my said children in the same way I have directed as to the land itself.

In case my wife shall marry again I will and direct that the interest I have given her above in my lands or real estate, or proceeds of the sale thereof, shall cease from the time of her marriage, and said lands or proceeds shall at once thereafter go to my said two children.

I further will and direct that my said wife and Executrix may, at any time she sees fit and proper, or thinks it necessary for the interest of my said children, divide the land or proceeds among them equally, share and share alike.

I nominate and appoint my wife Amelia Homan Executrix of this my last Will and Testament, and desire and direct that she shall be allowed to act as such without bond from any Court whatever.

And she shall have full authority to [Page 342] execute this will without any bond.

I also constitute her testamentary guardian of my said two children, to act as such without bond from any Court.

My executrix shall qualify and execute all the all the provisions of this will without giving any bond or bonds, whatever.
Chattanooga, Tenn. June 16, 1887
Christian Homan

Signed and executed in our presence and in the presence of each other by the testator, and we attest the same as his last will at his request on this June 16, 1887.
Robt. P. Woodard
Saml. Straus

SAMUEL CASTLE

Last Will of Samuel Castle

I Samuel Castle being of sound mind do constitute this my last Will and testament.

I direct that my Executor sell my land on Chickamauga Creek containing 72 Acres as soon after my death as it will bring a fair price and proceeds to be used as follows:

    1st To pay all my debts and funeral expenses.

    2nd   To pay my daughter Sally Castle one sixth of the remainder.

    3rd To my son Willie Castle when he becomes of age one sixth.

    4th To my Wife Margaret Castle the remaining four sixths for the support of herself and minor children.

    5th All the rest of my real estate I give to my wife Margarett [sic] Castle for her life time and at her death it to be divided equally among my living heirs.

    5th I give to my wife Margarett Castle all the personal property which I own at my death.
[Page 343]

    And I hereby apoint [sic] W. P. Ford as Executor of this my last will and testament.

                    Samuel Castle

August the 5th 1888
We the undersigned witness the signing of the above will
             John I. Durand
             I. E. Spangler

[Page 343]

JOHN P. LONG

Last Will of John P. Long

    Know all men by these present that I John P. Long of Chattanooga, Tennessee being of Sound Mind and disposing Memory, in view of the uncertainty of life and the certainty of death do hereby make and ordain this as my last will and testament, no other will having here to fore ever been made, I hereby testify to the love and devotion of my wife Mrs. Eliza Long who has been a loving companing, a helper and prudent councellor [sic] in the making and saving of what property we have, It is therefore my desire and I so will and bequeath to my said wife Eliza Long if she should out live me the entire estate that I may die seized and possessed of both real and personal of every kind and description in her own right absolutely and unqualifiedly [sic] to be disposed of by her as she may deem proper and out of which she will pay all the debts I may owe at the time of my death.

    This ___ day of ___ 1883
             John P. Long

[Note - No witnesses named. No date given in this will except for year 1883.]

[Page 344]

J. A. CRUMLEY

Last Will of J. A. Crumley

    Know all men by these present, that I J. A. Crumley of the 6th Civil District in the County of Hamilton and State of Tennessee being in ill health and of sound mind, and memory, do make and publish this my last will and testament, hereby revoking all former wills by me made.

    First I hereby constitute and appoint my wife Ann Crumley to be my sole Executrix of this my last Will, without bond, directing my said executrix to pay all my just debts, and funeral expenses.

    Second After the payment of my debts, and funeral expenses I give and bequeath to my wife, all my personal property and real estate that I may possess at the time of my death, for her sole use, and to aid her in raising my children. It is my request that the first sale of real Estate made by be [sic] made from the east end of the homeplace and the proceeds thereoff [sic] first be used to pay my debts and funeral expences [sic].

    Second to build a more comfortable home for my wife and children, and the remainder for their support, all after sales to be left to her discression [sic].

    In testamony whereof I hereunto set my hand and seal, and publish and declare this to be my last will and testament in the presence of the witnesses named below this 21 day of September in the year 1888.

             J. A. Crumley {Seal}

    The within instrument was signed by the testator in our presence and signed the same in his presence and the presence of each other at his request as witnesses to his last will and testament. This 21 day of September 1888.

             J. J. Durand
             Geo. W. Fuller

[Page 345]

PHOEBE CROWELL

Last Will of Phoebe Crowell

The State of Tennessee)
Hamilton County SS   )

    I Phoebe L. Crowel [sic], residing at present at

No. 503 East 5th Street Chattanooga in said County and State; do make and publish the following as my last will and testament; to wit:

Item 1st: That all just debts and obligation against my estate; including especially expenses of last sickness, funeral expenses and the cost of a tombstone to my memory be first paid out of the assetts [sic] of my said estate.

Item 2d: That out of said assetts [sic], there be paid to the First Baptist Church of South Pittsburgh in said State Thirty five dollars ($35.00) which payment shall include and be in full satisfaction of my subscription to the funds of said Church of Twenty three ($23.00) Dollars.

Item 3d: I give and bequeath to Henry H. Souder of the City of Chattanooga in said County and State, my gold watch,; also Two Hundred and Fifty ($250.00) with which to purchase a horse.

Item 4th: I give and bequeath to Harriet E. Souder, wife of said Henry H. Souder One hundred Dollars ($100.00).

Item 5th: I give and bequeath to my sister, Mrs. C. L. Mallee of the town of Alexander in the state of Minnessota [sic], all my remaining apparrel [sic] beds and bedding and sewing machine, and direct my executor hereinafter named ship said articles to my said Sister at his earliest convenience after my decease, and pay all expenses of such shipment out of my estate.

Item 6th: All the rest and residue of my estate both real and personal I give devise and bequeath to my said sister Mrs. C. L. Mallee.
[Page 346]

Item 7th: I nominate and appoint the said Henry H. Souder to be the executor of this my last Will and testament, and request that he be not required to give bonds or any security whatever for the faithful discharge of his duties as such; and I hereby authorize and empower him, as such executor to sell, either at private or public sale all of such real estate as I may be seized of at my decease, and to execute all necessary deeds of conveyance of the same; without any order of any Court authorizing the same.

Phoebe L. Crowell

The foregoing paper [blank] was subscribed by the said Phoebe L. Crowell in our presence and by her declared to be her last will and testament and we have subscribed our names as witnesses to the same, in her presence, and at her request this 7 day of May A. D. 1888.
Mrs. C. S. Selover
C. S. Selover

[Page 347]

PRYOR BURNET

Last Will of Pryor Burnet

State of Tennessee)
Hamilton County) We Richard Collins, George Hunter, and Charles Williams were present, the second day of August 1885, at the residence of Pryor Burnet, in Chattanooga, Hamilton County, Tennessee, About thirteen hours before his death, in perfect possession of his mental faculties as appeared to us, said Burnet called upon the bystanders, and especially on us to remember and take notice of what he was about to say: when he said "That he had desired to make his Will in writing, thereby to dispose of his property, but had neglected to carry his intention into execution, and that now it was not practicable.

That he wished us to understand that his Will and desire was that all his property should be equally divided between his Mother, Clara Thomas, and Joseph Burnet an infant child of Mary Thomas, about six years old. He said he owed Mr. White One Hundred dollars and Morgan Fryar fifty dollars, which debts he desired should be paid. He said he wanted his bar business to be run by Hamnes Burnet and also Wanted Mary Thomas to have a living out of it.

The said Pryor Burnet died about thirteen hours after he made the above statements, and the same were made in his last sickness.
This August 5th, 1885
C. H. Williams
Richard X Collins
his mark
George X Hunter
his mark

Probated Aug. 29th, 1885
J. H. Messick
D. C.

[Page 348]

CONSTANTINE BRAUSE

Last Will and Testament of Constantine Brause

In the name of God! Amen!
I Constantine Brause, formerly of Kingston, Roane County, Tennessee, but now residing in the City of Chattanooga, of same State, do make and declare this my

solemn Will and Testament revoking any previously made: to Wit:

(1) I Will and direct that my Executors shall pay my just debts, if any, and my funeral expenses, before distribution.

2) I will and direct that my property, real, personal and mixed of which I shall die seized and possessed of whatsoever kind or wheresoever situated shall be equally divided, after collating [sic] and charging advancements, between my children.

3) All my children being now of age, and trusting to their brotherly and sisterly love and integrity, I leave it to their volition as to the disposition to be made of the real estate in and about Chattanooga and Kingston, hoping they will agree on a plan of distribution best adapted for their mutual benefit.

4) In addition to the share falling due upon distribution to my daughter, Mary, I give to her the benefit that may be realized on one certificate for Two thousand Dollars, in Custer Commandary No. 9. United Order of the Golden Cross and also the sum of Five hundred Dollars, which I hold in Trust for her, to Wit $200-- a Legacy from my deceased mother as expressed in her last Will and $300-- Received for her from my deceased sister, Ottilie, all of which shall belong to her, outside of her proper share on distribution of the balance of the Estate.

5) I also hold in trust for my younger son George C. the sum [Page 349] of Two hundred Dollars, a gift from my deceased sister aforesaid, which is to be paid to him outside and independant [sic] of his proper share in the Estate.

6) I have already advanced to my older Son Charles F. a considerable amount of money, for which he signed and gave his acknowledgement, as also to my daughter, Lizzie, Wife of Dr. A. M. Palmer, for which also acknowledgement, was signed and given, which, advancements will be chargeable, to the two resp. parties and to be accounted for to the other children on final distribution and settlement.

7) I request and appoint my son Charles F. and Son in law Dr. A. M. Palmer, executors of this my last Will and Testament and having full faith in their integrity, I hereby release them from obligation of Bond and Security.

In testimony whereof I have hereunto set my hand seal on the 29th day of November 1887.

Constantine Brause
{Seal}

State of Tennessee)
Hamilton County   ) Personally appeared before me, Charles E. Stivers, Notary Public of said County - Constantine Brause, the within named bargainor, with whom I am personally acquainted, and who acknolwedged that He executed the within instrument of the purpose therein contained.

Witness my hand & official seal this 5th day of December 1887.

Chas. E. Stivers
Notary Public

[Page 350]

JOHN T. CAHILL

Last Will and Testament of
John T. Cahill of Chattanogoa, Tenn.

In the name of the Father, and of the Son and of the Holy Ghost, Amen.

1. I, John T. Cahill, being of sound mind, although in delicate health and knowing the uncertainty of life, do make this my last Will and testament, hereby revoking and annulling any will heretofore made by me.

My present assets consist of running accts. of $2000.00 more or less in First National Bank of Chattanooga, A policy in C. K. A. of $2000.00. The plant with ground lot on Boyce & Hooke Streets, Chattanooga, Tenn. known as Cahills Iron & Brass Foundry, vacant lot adjoining my present residence, bounded on West by College & South by Hook Streets; my present residence on College Street, one & half shares of Stoner property adjoining Cravens place on Lookout Mountain, one lot on Depot Street in Knoxville, Tenn.

I have lately sold two thirds interest in Foundry business to Caldwell & Whiteside on account of necessary delays, I have not received at this writing (July 15th 1887) payment from said Caldwell & Whiteside. I expect payment for same tomorrow, out of the money and notes to be paid me by said Caldwell & Whiteside, I will pay off all claims on my property, and if through any accident I fail to do so, I direct my executor, hereinafter to be named to pay off all claims on said property so as to make good and valid titles to same.

2. I hereby appoint my pastor Rev. P. J. Gleeson, executor of this my Will and testament, to be appointed and received as such by Court without bond or security.
[Page 351]

3. I give, bequeath and devise to my beloved Wife Ellen Cahill, our residence on College Street free from all indebtedness, which my executor will see to. I also bequeath to my beloved wife the lot on Depot Street, Knoxville, Tenn.. and direct my executor to pay all claims if any, on said lot. I also give and bequeath to said

beloved wife the remaining third interest in the Cahill Iron & Brass Foundry.

4. I direct my executor to pay all funeral expenses such as he shall think proper.

5. I give and bequeath to my beloved mother the rent of lot in which Foundry is built on Hooke & Boyce Streets for the joint use of herself and my father. In case she dies before my father I intrust the collection of rent & proper application of same for benefit of my father to my executor, and when both are dead, I direct the same ground lot of Foundry to be divided among my wife Ellen sister Mary, brothers William & Mike - and I hereby empower my executor Rev. P. J. Gleeson to use his judgment as to the time and manner of selling same.

6. I give and bequeath and devise the vacant lot adjoining my reisdence to my beloved sister Mary.

7. I give bequeath and devise my one & half shares of the Stoner property on Lookout Mountain to my sister Mary & brothers William & Mike to be equally divided between them.

8. I give and bequeath my policy of $2000.00 (two thousand dollars) in Catholic Knights of America, to Rev. P. J. Gleeson my executor to be used for the education of my brother William's two children.

9. I give and bequeath One thousand dollars to be used in building new Catholic Church in Chattanooga, Tenn. to Rev. P.J. Gleeson for same.
[Page 352]

10. I direct my executor to apply three hundred (300.00 dollars for Masses for my soul.

11. I direct my executor to purchase a lot of one thousand dollars value, and give deed of same to my brother James, with the proviso in deed that only his children shall have power to dispose of it, and that in case he does not marry or has no children said lot shall revert to my brothers and sister.

12. Any moneys remaining after above bequests are complied with I direct my executor to hand over to my beloved wife having first paid himself the ordinary Commission.

Signed in our presence and acknowledged as his signature this 16th day of July 1887.
J. T. Cahill

The undersigned
Witnesses witnessed
the execution of this
Will at the request
of J. T. Cahill & signed
the same in the presence
of each other, & in
his presence.
July 16th 1887. H. C. Squire

Theodore G. Montague
Chattanooga, Tenn.

[Page 353]

HANNAH KANE

Last Will and Testament of Hannah Kane

In the presence of God, Amen:

I Hannah Kane of Chattanooga, Hamilton County, Tennessee, being weak and feeble in body but of sound and disposing mind and memory do make and publish this my last Will and Testament -I Will my soul to God who gave it and my body to be buried in a christian-like manner according to the rites of the Church of my faith: And as to my property which may be left after my death -

After first paying all funeral expenses physicians bills &c. in which is to be included one hundred dollars for masses for souls of myself, mother, sister and brother, I give and bequeath One hundred dollars for erection of new Roman Catholic Church in Chattanooga - five hundred dollars for an alter [sic] to be placed in said church.

Three hundred dollars toward erection of a Monument in the Mount Olivet Cemetery to memory of my Step-father, Mr. Enright, Mother, sister and other relatives in said Cemetery.

And then I want all the remainder of my effects to go to my brother William Walsh - but should he die without issue or heirs before he reaches twenty one years of age - I will said residue to my Aunt Bridget Harrington of Nashville, Tennessee.

And lastly I nominate and appoint my friend William Cotter, Executor of this my last Will and Testament, but no bond and surety need be required from him but he is to manage my affairs to the best interest of the legatess and should my estate go to my Aunt Bridgett as provided above her husband, John Harrington shall have no power, authority or control over it in any shape [Page 354] or form - nor is one cent of said money to be paid to said John Harrington but is intended for my aunt and her Children to be paid to and used by them in the manner my said Executor shall deem best.

In testimony whereof I hereunto sign my name, this tenth of February A. D. 1888.

Signed and Executed in   )   her
our presence and we have   ) Hannah X Kane
attested it in presence of the)   mark
Testatrix, and in presence of)
each other   )

Jno. Crimmons
W. A. White

[Page 355]

MRS. MARGARET SHEPHERD

Last Will and Testament of Mrs. Margaret Shepherd

State of Tennessee)
Hamilton County) Know all men by these presents that I, Margaret Shepherd of the City of Chattanooga, County of Hamilton, State of Tennessee, being of sound mind and memory and recognizing the uncertainties of this life, do make and constitute this my last Will and Testament, regarding the disposition of my property, and hereby revoke and repeal any & all previous Wills.

Firstly - I desire that after my death I be buried in a decent, christian like manner by the side of my beloved husband who is now lying in the family graveyard on my old homestead near Chickamauga, Tenn. My executor who is hereinafter named shall with what Cash I have on hands [sic] at the time of my death, as is necessary, defray all my burial expenses and pay all debts, I may owe at the time of my death.

Secondly - I give and bequeath unto my beloved daughter, Temperance Moore, One hundred dollars in Cash, and the prorata share of my personal goods not hereinafter mentioned.

Thirdly - I give and bequeath unto my beloved daughter, Mary M. Robertson, One hundred dollars in Cash and her prorata share of my personal effects not hereinafter mentioned and I charge my said daughter, Mary to see that my grave, together [Page 356] with that of her dear fathers is constantly kept in proper shape.

Fourthly - I give and bequeath to my beloved daughter Maria Anderson One Hundred Dollars, and her prorata share of what personal effects I die possessed of. The large picture in my room belongs to my grand daughter Mollie Carroll whose name I believe now is Mollie Scroggins. I consign unto the care and keeping of my Picture of my beloved husband to my beloved son Lewis Shepherd. It is distinctly understood that no one comes in for a share of my personal goods except my daughters Maria, Mary, and Temperance, except as hereinafter mentioned.

Fourthly [sic] - I give and bequeath to my beloved son Lewis Shepherd the large walnut wardrobe in my room.

Fifthly - I give and bequeath unto my grandsons William Bishops, Lewis Roberson, and David S. Anderson, each One Hundred Dollars, and I reserve $50.$\underline{00}$ to be used by my Executor in keeping and maintaining my family grave yard.

Sixthly - If any money should be remaining in possession of my Executor, after he has fully complied with my wishes hereinbefore stated, I bequeath and give it to my executor hereinafter named in payment for his work in closing up my estate.
[Page 357]
Seventhly - I hereby constitute and appoint my grandson, D. S. Anderson my Executor, and vest him with full power to close up my affairs, without having to make any bond whatever.

Witness my hand and seal This Apr. 10th 1888.
Witnesses
Frank M. Walker
A. Y. Whitman Margaret Shepherd {Seal}

CHRISTINA STERCHI

Last Will and Testament of Christina Sterchi

The State of Tennessee
I, Christina Sterchi wife of Nicholas Sterchi of Hamilton County Tennessee, being of sound mind and disposing memory hereby revoking all former Wills and Codicils thereto heretofore made by me, do hereby make and publish this my last Will and Testament.

1st I direct that all my just debts and funeral expenses by paid out of any means that I may die possessed of, or out of the first money that may come to the hands of my Executor hereinafter named, from any portion of my estate.

2nd I do hereby Will and bequeath to my beloved husband, Nicholas Sterchi, absolutely, and forever, all the property which I am seized and possessed of at the time of my death, both real and personal wherever situated and located, clothing him with full power and authority to sell, convey, or bequeath the same at his pleasure, (including all notes, accounts and choses in action) - I am moved to this, in justice to my said husband [Page 358] Nicholas Sterchi, as nearly all the property in my name was accumulated by and through the hard work, thrift and diligence of my said husband.

3rd I hereby nominate and appoint said Nicholas Sterchi Executor of this my last Will and Testament in whom I have the utmost confidence and it is my request, that he be not required to give bond or file an Inventory of said property, the same being expressly waived by me.

Signed, Sealed and published in the presence of

[blank space] who I have registered to Witness this my Last Will and Testament in my presence, and in the presence of each other this 21st day of June 1887.

Christina Sterchi

We the undersigned in the presence of the Testatrix and at her express request, and in the presence of each other, Subscribe our names as Witnesses to the above Will - This 21st day of June 1887.
H. C. Beck
J. P. Smartt

[Page 359]

ADELINE C. GARRETT

Last Will and Testament of Adeline C. Garrett
Fairmount, Tenn. Sept 4, 1888
In the name of God, Amen

I, Adeline C. Garrett, of Fairmount, Hamilton County, Tennessee, being of sound mind and desiring to make due and proper disposition of my property in the event of my death do make this my last Will and testament.

I do hereby devise and bequeath to my daughter, Gracie Elma Whittaker my son Amos Jay Whittaker and my daughter, Blanch May Whittaker, all my property, personal and Real, except so much as may be necessary for the payment of my lawful debts, the expenses of Physicians attendance for funeral expenses and the legacy herein after provided. It is my desire that my Real estate and personal property should be sold as soon after my death as may be done, without sacrifice and the proceeds distributed to my three children before named in equal parts, share and share alike.

I do hereby give and bequeath to my daughter Myrtle M. Jackson of the city of Chattanooga, state of Tennessee, the sum of $10.00 (Ten Dollars) to be paid out of the proceeds of the sale of my property as before mentioned.

It is my desire that Mr. H. B. Hulse of the City of Chattanooga, State of Tennessee, shall be guardian of the persons and property of my three Minor children, Gracie, Elma Whittaker, Amos Jay Whittaker and Blanch May Whittaker.

Adeline C. Garrett

Fairmount, Tennessee
Sept. 4, 1888
We the undersigned have this day [Page 360] witnessed the signing of the above and have heard the declaration of Mrs. A. C. Garrett that it is her Will and testament.
W. A. Ervin
Mrs. Jas. R. Taylor
Mrs. E. E. Loomis

ANNIE JONES

Last Will and Testament of Annie Jones

I, Annie Jones, being of sound mind, do make this my last Will & testament, hereby revoking any Will by me at any time made.

1st I direct that my body be decently burried [sic] and out of any money on hand or first collected that my funeral expenses & just debts be paid.

2d I give devise and bequeath to my only living daughter Mrs. Catharine Anne Buckell, all my estate both real and personal, consisting among other things of debts due me and the tract of land where I now live with my said daughter in district No 1. Hamilton County, Tennessee it being my intention that my said daughter shall take exclusively every thing I may own at my death.

This January 29th 1884.
Anne [sic] Jones
Witness
W. H. McLenere
J. C. Hanna

[Page 361]

JAMES COTTER

Last Will and Testament of James Cotter

In the name of God, Amen.

I, James Cotter, of the City of Chattanooga Hamilton County, State of Tennessee, being of feeble body but of sound and disposing mind do make and publish this my last Will and Tesatment.

Item 1st I Will and bequeath my soul to God who gave it and my body to be burried [sic] in a decent Christian manner.

Item 2nd I will and desire that all my burial and funeral expences [sic] be paid as soon after my death as possible out of any means I may die possessed - I owe no debts.

Item 3rd The house and lot where I now and

have for years lived on North east Corner of Gilmer and "B" Streets in the City of Chattanooga fronting on each of said streets one hundred feet - I will and bequeath to my wife Bridget Cotter for and during her natural life and at her death I will and bequeath the same to my youngest son; James Cotter -

Item 4th Having given to all my other children their share of my estate and James Cotter the home lot as his share - all the rest and residue of my estate both real and personal, I give and bequeath to my said wife Bridget Cotter on which to live and support herself and dispose of in just such manner as she sees proper.

Lastly I nominate and appoint my son William Cotter my executor of this my last Will and testament requiring no bond and security from him and giving him and his mother full power and [Page 362] authority to sell and make title to any and all of said property devised to her.

Witness my hand and Seal
This 28th day of September 1886

James X Cotter {seal}
his mark

Signed sealed and　　　）
executed in our presence　）
and we have in presence of）
the Testator signed our　　）
names as witnesses at）
his request　　　　　　）
　Thos. McMahon
　James Hogan

MARGARET GILASPIE

Last Will and Testament of Margaret Gilaspie, of Hamilton County and state of Tennessee.

Considering the uncertainty of life and being of sound mind and memory, do make this my last Will and Testament in manor [sic] and form following.

I give and bequeath to my Sister Sarah and brother William Castle, the following piece and parcel of land which was set apart as my interest by Commissioners appointed for the purpose of dividing the Dady land among the legal heirs of my Grandfather Dady, said land as shown by the plat filed in Hamilton County Court of Tennessee, is said to contain Seventeen Acres, lying and being on the East side of the Dady lands.

I give the North half eight and one half Acres to my Sister Sarah Castle, and the South half [Page 363] eight

and one half Acres to my brother William Castle, to have and to hold the same or dispose of and apply the proceeds to their own personal use as they may deem best.

In Testimony [sic] hereoff [sic] I hereunto set my hand and Seal this 12th day of January 1888.

Margaret Gilaspie {Seal}

The above instrument consisting of one sheet of paper now hereby Subscribed Margaret Gilaspie the testator in presence of each of us, and was at the time declared to be her last Will and testament. And we at her request sign our names hereunto as attesting Witnesses.
J. J. Durand　Residence Hamilton Co. Tenn.
Ellen Forel　Residence Hamilton Co. Tenn.

JOSEPH JOHN

Last Will and Testament of Joseph John

I, Joseph John of Hamilton County, Tennessee, being of sound mind and disposing memory, and being desirous of settling all my worldly affairs, while I have strength and capacity to do so, do make publish and declare this my last Will and testament, hereby revoking any and all former Wills by me made, that is to say:

First: I will and direct that all of my debts existing against me at my decease be settled and paid.

Second: I give and bequeath to my beloved wife, Mary John, all my personal property of every description. [Page 364]

Third: I give and devise to my beloved wife, Mary John, all my real estate wheresoever situated, including two and one half (2 1/2) acres of land in the 6" Civil District of Hamilton County Tennessee, one house and lot on Harrison Ave. in the City of Chattanooga, Tennessee, being the same conveyed to me by George T. White two houses and lots in Dayton Tennessee, Six hundred and Fifty (650) Acres in Lawrence County, Tennessee, and any other lands of which I may die seized, to her and her heirs forever.

Fourth: I hereby appoint my beloved wife, Mary John, sole Executrix of this my last Will and Testament and direct that she may act as such Executrix, without giving bond.

In witness whereof I have hereunto set my hand and Seal this 30" day of November 1888.
Joseph X John
his mark

Signed and sealed by Joseph　　）

John who at the same time, pub-   )
lished and declared the same as   ) John F. Taylor
and for his last Will and testament) Martin M.
in the presence of us, who in his   )   Wetzel
presence and in the presence of   ) W. H. Burgess
each other and at his request have)
hereunto subscribed our   )
names as Witnesses.   )

[Page 365]

PATRICK BYRNE

Last Will and Testament of Patrick Byrne

In the name of God, Amen! I Patrick Byrne, being of sound mind, do make and publish this my last Will and Testament, never having heretofore made or published any Will, whatever.

Item First It is my Will that my funeral expenses and all my just debts be paid out of any moneys of which may be possessed at the time of my death, or out of the first moneys that may come to the hands of my representative.

Item Second I do hereby give and bequeath and devise, all my property real and personal, of every nature whatever that may remain, after the payment of my funeral expenses and just debts, to my beloved wife Mary Byrne, absolutely and free from all restrictions, but with confident hope, and my dying request, that she will use it all in support and maintainance [sic] of herself and all our children, looking to their care, education, and cultivation as best she can, and as she may be given strength to do until she too, is parted from them forever and that whatever of said property or its proceeds, if any, may or shall remain: she will distribute equally and justly among them, share and share alike, but this request is not intended to prevent her from selling or disposing of said property real or personal herein devised or bequeathed to her.

Item Third I do hereby appoint my beloved wife, my sole Executrix [Page 366] of my estate, with full power to sell any portion of my estate, real or personal, for the payment of debts, provided that if she sell any real estate, three fourths of the purchase price shall be upon a credit of from six months to two years, taking notes, bearing interest with two good securities and retaining a lien for the purchase money until it is fully paid. She is authorized to execute a deed for any land she may sell, when the purchase money is all paid, or where the sale is made, retaining a lien in the face of the deed, for purchase

money. She is not required to give bond for the execution of this trust.

Item Fourth I do hereby select and constitute and appoint W. L. Eakin the Attorney and Solicitor for my estate & make it his duty to defend any suits that may be pending against me at the time of my death, or that may be brought against my estate and to give my said executrix all such legal advice, and to do all such acts as may be necessary as an attorney or solicitor, for the purpose of carrying out the true intention of this Will.

It is not intended by the second Item of this Will to request my wife to contribute to the support or maintainance [sic] of any of my children after they have married or after they have ceased to be members of her family [Page 367] unless they are absent by her consent and under her direction. Should any one or more of them marry during her lifetime then it is my request that she give them only such part of my estate, as she may deem right in justice to herself and the remainder of my children, always having it in view to make them equal.

In testimony whereof I have hereunto subscribed my name on this [blank] day of November on [sic] the year of Lord Eighteen hundred and Eighty eight (1888).

Pat Byrne
Signed and ackowleldged)
in our presence the day)
and date last   )
above written.   )
W. L. Eakin
C. R. Fawkes

JOHN F. COUNCIL

Last Will and Testament of John F. Council

State of Tennessee)
Hamilton County)   I, John F. Council, being of sound mind and disposing memory, do hereby make and publish this my last will and testament hereby revoking all others that may have been heretofore made.

First: I hereby will and bequeath to each of my daughters Twenty Five Dollars, to be paid out of my estate which amount, paid to each is to be in full satisfaction of all their interest in or claim against my estate.

Second: I will and bequeath to my son Frank, my silver Watch.
[Page 368]
Third: All the remainder of my property of every kind and character, I will and bequeath to my Wife Anna M. Council should she survive me but should she not survive me, then to my son, Frank.

John F. Council

The foregoing Will was signed by the testator in our presence and at his request we hereto subscribe our names as witnesses on this the 14th day of December 1887.

H. C. Beck
W. S. Beck

GEORGE FOSTER BROWN

Last Will and Testament of George Foster Brown.
Chattanooga, Aug. 10
Unto all whom it may concern.
Chattanooga, Hamilton Co. Tenn.

I, George Foster Brown sen [sic] being of sound Mind and Health.

Doo Hear [sic] by Will & Bequeath all my Real Estate, Money, Personaly [sic] Property to my Wife Jane Brown to have and to hold during her Life to use in watever [sic] way she see [sic] Proper and at her Death wat ever [sic] property Money or Effects Remain shall be Equally Divided Between my children that is to say Mary Elizabeth Saunders George Foster Brown Sarah Jane Brown Mathew Alexander Brown they shall all Receive their share except Mary Elizabeth Saunders whose shaire [sic] shall be put to Interest For the Benefit of her children so long [Page 369] as her Husband John T. Saunders liveth. At his Death her being is [sic] widow, she shall Resume her share the same as the Rest of the children, For here [sic] use in watever [sic] way she thinks proper and during that time I request that George F. Brown Sen [sic] be appointed Guarding [sic] for her children.

This 10th Day of August 1873.
George Foster Brown Sen.
{Seal}

NATHAN DAVIS

Last Will and Testament of Nathan Davis

I, Nathan Davis of Chattanooga, Tenn. do make and publish this as my last Will and Testament, hereby revoking & making void all other Wills by me at any time made.

First: I direct that my funeral expenses and all my just debts be paid as soon as possible after my death out of any money I may have at my death or which may first come to the hands of my Executrix.

Secondly: I give and bequeath to my beloved wife, Mary E. Davis, all my property, real, personal and mixed of any and every kind and description and wherever situated, it being my Will and desire that she take and hold absolutely and free from the control of any future husband, all property of which I may die seized and possessed or to which I may be in any way entitled or to which I would have been entitled if I had lived.

Lastly: I do hereby nominate and [page 370] appoint said Mary E. Davis my Executrix with full power over my estate and to execute this my last Will and I hereby releive [sic] and release her from the execution of any bond required by law of an executor.

In Witness whereof I hereto subscribe my name and Seal at Chattanooga, Tennessee.
This 15th day of May 1882
Nathan Davis {Seal}

Signed, sealed and published in our presence and we have subscribed our name hereto in the presence and at the request of the testator.
This 15th day of May 1882
J. A. Caldwell
James B. Ingram

HANNAH SHEHAN

Last Will and Testament of Hannah Shehan.

Hereby revoking all former Wills or codicils by me at any time heretofore made I Hannah Shehan hereby make publish and declare my last Will and testament to be as follows:

Item First. My Executor hereinafter named shall pay all my just debts, funeral expenses and for a suitable monument over my grave, and to do so she may sell and convey any part or the whole of the property of which I may die seized and possesssed without the order of any Court, advertisement or other notice at public or private Sale as she thinks best.

Item Second. The remainder and residue of property of which I may die seized and possessed or in which I may [Page 371] have or acquire any interest I hereby Will and bequeath to my Sister Catherine Driscoll for and during the term of her natural life and after her death to my brother William Driscoll the remainder in fee.

Item Third. I hereby nominate and appoint my said Sister Catherine Driscoll Sole executrix of this my last Will and testament, she shall not be required to execute any bond or such or make any report or such unless requested to do so by said William Driscoll. This Oct. 2, 1886.

Hannah X Shehan {Seal}
her mark

Signed, Sealed and published in our presence and as subscribed our names hereto in the presence of the testator Oct. 2, 1886.

Tom Fort
A. S. DeLong
C. P. Jones

HUGH McNEAL

Last Will and Testament of Hugh McNeal.

Feeling the infirmities of age and the uncertainty of life, I make this my last Will and Testament as follows:

I give and bequeath to my beloved wife, Mary C. McNeal, all the property, real estate, and personal of which I may be possessed at the time of my death, including my interest in the Barton Iron Works, Ga. and the E. P. Cooke & Co. property in the 6th District, Hamilton Co. Tenn. and all other property of which I may die seized and possessed. The said M. C. McNeal to have full title in her own right and absolute [Page 372] power to control and dispose of said property as she may see proper. I also appoint her my executrix and direct that no bond be required of her. She shall not be required to make any reports, nor account to any Court for any part of my estate.

H. McNeal

Signed, Sealed, declared and published as the last Will and Testament of Hugh McNeal in the presence of the undersigned Witnesses who have subscribed the same as Witnesses at the request of said Testator, in his presence and in the presence of each other.

This 8th September, 1886.

O. H. Pennock
S. P. Dodson
E. M. Dodson

POLLY BOYCE

Last Will and Testament of Polly Boyce

State of Tenn. Hamilton Co.
Jan. 10, 1888.

Be it known to all men whom it may concern, That this is my last Will and testament. All my personal property I give and bequeath to my son Wylie Sagus, who is my only heir, of the one half acre of real estate will [sic] to me by my husband Bosen Boyce, deceased, lying in the State and Co. aforesaid and in the 6th Civil District. I most earnestly pray that the following disposition be made of it, to wit: To my son Wylie Sagus, 1/2 of the parcel of land [Page 373] to be his unconditionly [sic], to controll [sic] and dispose of as he desires and the remaining 1/2 I give and bequeath to Benevolent Order No. 88. as in apreciation [sic] of care taken of me during my sickness providing they continue to take care of me till the day of my death and honorably dispose of my body. I furthermore give to the said Benevolent Order No. 88. what ever technical claim I have on the school house situated on said parcel of land. The foregoing statement of this Will I pray to be carried out on condition that my doctors bill be paid by the person concerned otherwise the doctors to be paid and then I pray that the directions given in this instrument be applied to that portion of the land that remain.

To all which do I sign my name to my only and last Will and Testament.

Polly X Boyce
her mark

Witnesses
(W. H. Tilman
(Joseph X Pryor
(his mark
(Y. N. Wordsworth

LOUISE H. GOODSON

Last Will and Testament of Louise H. Goodson

I, Louise H. Goodson, of Marion County Tennessee, do make this my last Will & Testament & hereby give, devise & bequeath to Andrew Farrand my father & Phebe Farrand my mother all of my estate & property, real personal & mixed in fee simple absolute.

I appoint my said father executor of this my last Will [Page 374] and Testament & desire that he be not required to give security as such.

I hereby revoke all other Wills heretofore made by me.

Witness my hand this sixtennth day of July 1889. at Chattanooga, Tenn.

Louise H. Goodson

In presence of
Lillie M. Wright
Sephronica Argue
Harry L. Kirk

E. A. COULTER

Last Will and Testament of E. A. Coulter

In the name of God. Amen.

I, E. A. Coulter, being in feeble health but of sound and disposing mind, do make and publish this my last Will and testament, as follows, to wit:

1st I will that all of my just debts be paid, and to this and do hereby Will and direct that the growing crop upon the farm, known as the Horse Shoe, be set aside and devoted to an indebtedness due to D. R. Griffith & Son, or so much there of as may be necessary for that purpose except such part of said crop as may be necessary to the gathering and taking care of the same, and any further indebtedness to be such and satisfied from incomes and proceeds from my general estate.

2nd I give grant and devise to my beloved daughters, Mary Ann McDonald & Louisa Elizabeth Coulter, and to my beloved son Joseph A. Coulter, jointly and severally share and share alike the house now used and occupied [Page 375] by me, and the land the same is situated upon and immediately surrounding the same included between the roads on the North West and South East of the house, that is to say, with the road leading from the Creek, below J. E. McDonald's Mill across the heel of the Horse Shoe to the Creek, thence down the Creek to a point where another road crossing the Creek above said Mill and leading in the direction of my house clears the fense [sic] on the right, thence with said road to the creek at the Bridge, thence down the Creek to the beginning together with all of my household and kitchen furniture of every character and description, together with all live stock such as horses cattle, hogs &c. except the Bay Mare, Moll, which is given to the said Joseph A. as a seperate [sic] and individual inheritance together with all poultry that may be upon the said premises at my decease, and I especially desire that no public sale of said property shall be made but used as a possession in Common by said Mary A. Louisa L. and Joseph A. as dutiful and affectionate children.

3rd All of my other estate, including lands, incomes, notes &c after the liquidation of my just debts, I will and bequeath to my several children the issue of my body including those mentioned in the special bequest No. 2 share and share alike to be managed and disposed of to the equal advantage and profit of each.
[Page 376]

4th I hereby nominate and appoint my friend and Brother J. W. Clift the sole Executor of this my last Will and Testament who shall execute such bond as the Court having conizance [sic] of the matter may require.

Signed and acknowledged after being real [sic] and understood, in the presence of   July 12, 1889.

J. W. Clift   E. A. Coulter
Jane Henderson

MARGARET CASTLE

Last Will and Testament of Margaret Castle

In the name of God Amen: I, Margaret Castle Widow of Samuel Castle, being of sound mind, but weak of body, and mindful that it is appointed to, all to die, at some time, do make and publish this my last Will and Testament not heretofore having made or published any Will.

Item First. It is my Will that all my just debts and funeral expenses be first paid.

Item Second. I do will, bequeath and devise unto my children, John Richard Castle, Samuel J. Castle and Minnie May Castle the sum of ten thousand dollars, which I expect to receive or that may be received after my death, the proceeds of a piece of parcel of land, I recently conveyed to M. F. Penfield Trustee as I remember his name, for the price of ten thousand dollars, being a piece or parcel of land situated in the 6th Civil [Page 377] District of Hamilton County, Tennessee, and which was allotted or set apart to me out of the estate of my father John Dady, deceased, but because my daughter Minnie May, is younger than both her brothers, and because boys are usually better able to care for themselves than girls, It is my will that my said daughter receive One Thousand dollars more from said fund than her brothers on the final division of this fund. In the event this fund should not be all realized, then the One thousand dollars herein bequeathed to my said daughter will sustain its part of the top of the whole fund. But my said children are not to receive any part of this fund until they respectively arrive at the age of twenty one years except the interest arising therein which I direct shall be applied to supporting and maintaining them and giving them a good liberal education and it is my express Will that they all have a good and liberal education, but especially my daughter the said Minnie and I desire that she shall have the means and facilities of acquiring a musical education and if necessary she have instruments for that purpose. Should my said daughter Minnie Mary marry before she arrives at the age of twenty one years, in that event my executor may in his discretion pay her a reasonable marriage portion, but he is to be the judge of the amount, to be so paid and the remainder that may come to her under this Will [Page 378] will be paid to her on her arriving at twenty one years old and she will take it for her own use and benefit and free from the marital rights of any future husband, and free from all his debts & all liabilities he may incur, and should my death occur before the Sale of said land is fully consumated, then my executor is fully authorized and empowered to complete said sale at the price of ten thousand dollars by the delivery of the deed I have executed to said Penfield or to make another deed or do any other thing necessary to carry out or complete said sale.

Should any of my children die without issue before they arrive at the age of twenty one years, then the share of such deceased child will go in equal proportion to my children then living or their children if they should be dead leaving children.

In the event all my children should die before coming to the age of twenty one years and without issue living then in that event the money or other thing derived from said land will go to my Sister Ellen Ford if living and if not living then to her children.

Item Third: I give the Sulky now on Lands [sic] at my residence, with the harness and bay Colt, called Maud, to my step son William Henry Castle. He is also to have the bed clothes of his two Sisters Sallie and Maggie.

I also will that each of my children have a bed and bed clothes [Page 379] and that all my bed clothing shall be equally divided between my three children.

Item Fourth: I desire that all the stock on hands [sic] at my death except the Colt bequeathed to my Stepson Wm. H. Castle & the wagon and loose effects on hands [sic] be sold and the proceeds divided equally among my said children.

I give Minnie May my rocking chair and burea and the other furniture in my house and kitchen. I give equally to my three children.

Item Fifth: My executor is authorized to spend one hundred dollars for tombstones to make the graves of my husband, myself and our children and taking care of the family grave yard where my husband is buried.

Item Sixth: I desire that all money arising from my estate and bequeathed to my children be kept constantly on interest until it is disbributed under the terms of this will.

Item Seventh: I hereby constitute and appoint W. P. Ford executor of this my last will and testament, and it is also my desire that he take the care, control and guardianship of all my children and look after their education as well as teaching them habits of industry, so that they may become honorable and useful members of society, where ever they may be.

Signed and published on this 24th day of July 1889.

Mrs. Margaret Castle [Signed]

Page 380

The foregoing six pages were signed by Margaret Castle in our presence on this 24th day of July 1889.
Mrs. Mary E. Robertson
W. L. Eakin

WILL OF JACOB KUNZ

Last Will and Testament of Jacob Kunz

In the name of God Amen. I, Jacob Kunz being of sound mind and disposing memory, do make and publish this my last will and testament hereby revoking any former wills if any.

Item 1st: It is my will that any personal expenses, and should I owe any just debts, that they be paid out of the first money that may come to the hands of my executor hereinafter designated and appointed by this will.

Item 2nd: I do hereby devise and bequeath all my property real and personal to my five children, namely, John C. Kunz, Walter E. Kunz, Arnold A. Kunz, Bertha Kunz, and Jacob E. Kunz, subject, however to the terms and limitations, herein after stated.

Item 3rd: It is my will that upon my decease my Executor shall take possession of all my property, personal and real and all moneys I may die possessed of, except that he shall suffer and furnish such of my minor children as desire to do so, to remain and live in the house where I now reside until the youngest child arrives at the age of [Page 381] twenty-one years without charge or the payment of any rent, place the money coming to his hands from any source upon interest, payable semi-annually or annually, and the rent all my real estate to the best advantage from time to time until the youngest child herein before mentioned become of age and he will at the end of each year, pay the net income from interest, rent and all sources, share and share alike to my said children taking their receipts therefore, which receipts from any of my said children shall be a full and complete acquittance to him whether such child is of age or not, unless such child should haave a regularly appointed guardian, but before he shall make any annual distribution from the income of any estate he is authorized and directed to apply so much of said fund as he deems necessary to keep my youngest son Jacob E. Kunz, in school at St. Louis where he now is, or a similar school for the period of three years, and I also authorized my said Executor to use such portions of the income as he may deem necessary to the support, maintainance and education of my other children as long as they may remain minors and in sending my so Jacob or any of my other children to school he will be governed in expending money in the same measure and only expend such sums as he believes. I would have done under like circumstances had I been alive. I think he is familiar with my notions of the manner [Page 382] of educatiing my children, and the habits of industry I have sought to teach them. I desire that all my children pursue habits of industry & economy.

Item 4th: When my youngest child becomes of age or when he would become of age if living, it is my will that my executor divide all the money that may remain in or have come to his hands as such equally among all my said children if living; and if any one of them should die leaving a child or children then such child or children will take the share of the parent would have taken if living, And my said children if living or if any one should die leaving children, the child or children of such deceased child shall be entitled to take possession of all my real estate share and share alike.

I prefer that they shall if it becomes necessary to partition it, that they make partition themselves, or that they select three or more friends to divide it among them without any litigation and without the aid of any Court. The sums that my Executor shall pay for the education and support of my minor children from time to time, shall not be taken into the accounts. Upon the last distribution of the corpus of my personal estate, as I desire that my minor children shall in this way be as equal with my children who have arrived at the age of twenty-one years. My Executor shall allow any my minor children who remain in [Page 383] the house where I now reside to retain such household and kitchen furniture as may be on hands at my death if they desire to do so and they will not be charged with its value or for its use or lose.

I now and direct that my Executor out of any income arising from my estate real or personal before making any annual distribution of the income arising from my estate pay to my daughter Bertha in addition to the foregoing provision of this will, one hundred dollars per annum until she marries or until the final distribution of all my estate, and she will not be charged with any sum she may receive under this clause of this will but will on the final distribution of my estate take an equal share with her brothers as if this bequest had not been made.

I hereby direct that my mother-in-law Mrs. Anna Scheveiger at my house, shall be paid one hundred dollars where ever she desires to return home and that she shall, then be paid One hundred dollars each year as long as she may live, out of my estate.

My Executor may sell any personal property or household furniture my minor children may not desire to

release or use.

I do constitute and appoint my friend Samuel Geismar of Chattanooga, Tennessee. Executor of this my last will and testament and hope he will accept the trust I ask him [Page 384] to accept and I do relieve him from giving any bond as such Executor, except in the same and for the amount of money that will actually come to his hands as such Executor.

In testimony whereof I do make and publish this my last will & testament and have signed my name in the presence of two witnesses on this 31st day of October 1889.

                                    Jacob Kunz

Signed by the Testator}
in our presence and and}
witnessed by us at his}
request and in his pre-}
sence and in presence of}
each other this 31st day}
of October 1889 }
        W. Leakin
        A. Fassnacht

WILL OF T. J. PINION

Last Will and testament of T. J. Pinion

In the name of God. Amen.

I T. J. Pinion, of the County of Hamilton, being of sound mind and disposing memory but conscious of the uncertainty of life and wishing to dispose of my earthly matters before my death do make, publish and declare this to be my last will and testament hereby revoking and making void all other wills by me at any time made that is to say:

1st: I direct that all my just debts be paid out of any property which [Page 385] I may own at the time of my death.

2nd: To my children, Letitia Lankford and husband Sylvester Lankford, W. D. Pinion and wife Alice Pinion, Henry R. Pinion and wife Cynthia Pinion, Emily D. Skipper and husband John W. Skipper, Fanny Lankford and husband Taut Lankford and T. J. Pinion, Jr., I give and bequeath my tract of land containing one hundred acres situated in Greenville County in the state of South Carolina on the north side of Grove Creek adjoining the lands of the Garrison heirs on the west and the Yoer lands on the north and Grove Creek and the Evans land on the south & east said land to be divided into six shares equally between them share and share alike each child and their husband and wife taking one share.

3rd: To my son Henry K. Pinion I give and bequeath two acres of land out of fifteen acres which fifteen acres are situated in Hamilton County, Tennessee, near the Georgia state line in the 17th Civil District of said County the Georgia State line adjoining said land on the south and land owned by the City of Chattanooga on the east, said two acres to be set apart to him off of the south west corner of said fifteen acre tract adjoining each other taking one square acre as a base the width to be one acre running north and south and the length two acres running east and west.

4th: To my son Thomas J. Pinion, Jr., I give and bequeath the remainder of said fifteen acre tract of land acres of which I have [Page 386] in the foregoing third clause give to my son Henry K. Pinion, leaving to said Thomas about thirteen acres with the bridge and right of way to said thirteen acres but encumbered as hereafter stated.

5th: As the afore mentioned thirteen acres of land given to my son Thomas J. Pinion, Jr. in the fourth clause of said will are valuable as a sand bank and same is now being hauled from the same by numbers of my family I hereby give and bequeath to my son in law Taut Lankford the right and privilege of hauling same from said thirteen acres so as not to interfere with the right and title of the said Thomas, this right to haul sand to continue as long as my wife Sarah H. Pinion shall live and no longer and the bequeath to the said Thomas J. Pinion, Jr. in the fourth clause herein is encumbered with this right.

6th: To my wife, Sarah Ann Pinion, I give and bequeath the house and lot upon which I now live including the barn out houses and all tenements said lot fronting sixty eight feet on Mountain Avenue and running back of uniform width five hundred and twenty four feet to Doak Street to have and to hold the same during her natural life and at her death to go to my son Thomas J. Pinion, Jr. in fee simple.

7th: To my wife Sarah Ann Pinion, I also give and bequeath my house and lot adjoining to one upon which I now live on the East fronting fifty six feet on Mountain [Page 387] Avenue and run-ning back of uniform width five hundred and twenty four feet to Doak Street to have and hold the same during her natural life and at her death to go to my daughter Fanny Lankford and to the sole and separate use of the said Fanny in fee simple.

8th: To my wife Sarah Ann Pinion, I also give and bequeath all the household and kitchen furniture and all the stock upon the place including cows and calves mules and poultry and other personal property to use and every while she lives and whatever is not consumed in the using of said personal property to go to my son Thomas J. Pinion, Jr. except two mules and one wagon.

9th: To my daughter Fanny Lankford. I give and bequeath at the death of my wife two mules and one wagon if the same shall remain of the personal property which I have heretofore given to my wife.

10th: It is my will that at the death of my wife Sarah Ann Pinion each one of my six children or their heirs shall have the sum of twenty five dollars in money provided my wife shall in her discretion be able to provide the same for them without financially embarrassing herself if more then this amount shall be on hand the remainder to go to my son Thomas J. Pinion.

I hereby appoint my son Thomas J. Pinion, Jr. and my friend James A. Caldwell, executors of this my last will and testament. [Page 388] In Testimony where of I have hereunto set my hand and Seal this Sixth day of January 1890.

T. J. Pinion X Sr.[seal]
his mark

The foregoing instrument was signed by the said Thomas J. Pinion in our presence and ac-knowledged by him to be his last will and testament and we at his request and in his presence and in the presence of each other have signed our names as witnesses hereto this 6th day of January 1890.

C. O. Hunt
W. C. Payne

WILL OF THANKFUL A. JOHNSON

Last Will and Testament of Thankful A. Johnson

State of Tennessee}
Hamilton County }

Know all men by these present that I Thankful A. Johnson being of sound mind and disposing memory do make and constitute this my last will and testament.

First: I give and bequeath unto my beloved daughters Fannie A., Helen R. and Annie M. all my solid silver ware, my cut glass Tea and water set to be divided among them by my daughter Fannie A. as nearly equally as may becone.

Seond: I give and bequath unto my beloved children James W., Fannie A., Helen R., Annie M. [Page 398] and Ephraim Foster all the real estate which I now own and possess or to which I may be entitled at my death, wherever situated to be shared by them equally share and share alike, but it is my desire and I so will that my executor, hereinafter named, shall have full power and authority to manage, control and sell said real estate, either in whole or in part or parcels at public or private sale, for cash or on time. He shall exercise his discretion and do as he thinks best for my children in the premises. The income & proceeds of such land shall be equally divided among my children by my Executor.

Third: I give and bequeath unto my said five children to be shared by them equally, share and share alike all my personal property not herein before disposed of in the First Item hereof. To wit, fifteen (15) shares of stock in the Piney Creek Coal and Land Company and a note on the M. H. Clift for Ten Thousand ($10,000.00) Dollars, also my and all other personal property which I may own at my death. I authorize at public or private sale I authorize him to collect the note on M. H. Clift at maturity and pay one fifth thereof to said James W. and one fifth thereof to said Fannie A. and the other three fifths of said note he shall invest in loans secured by real estate for the use and benefit of the said [Page 390] Helen R., Annie M. and Ephraim Foster, the loans to draw interest payable quarterly. The principal shall be paid to each child according to his or her share, when such child shall become Twenty-one years old or marry. I authorize & instruct my Executor to pay the interest quarterly on Helen R. and Annie M. shares to my daughter Fannie A. for their respective benefit and use.

Fourth: I hereby give my son Epraim Foster to my daughter Fannie A.

Fifth: I nominate and appoint my husband A. M. Johnson, Executor of this my will and testament and excuse him from giving bond as required of executors under the law.

In witness whereof I here unto set my hand and Seal this 15th day of January 1890.

Thankful A. Johnson [seal]

Signed, sealed, declared and published by the said Thankful A. Johnson as and for her last will and Testament in presence of us, who at her request and in her presence, and in presence of each other have subscribed our names as witnesses hereto.

C. P. Goree
Tom Jones

[Page 391]

WILL OF DAVID A. STEVICK

Last Will and Testament of David A. Stevick

I, David A. Stevick, being of sound and disposing mind do make and publish this as my last will &

testament.

After the payment of all my just debts, I give and bequeath to my beloved wife Margaret A. Stevick all my property and effects of every description what so ever, real estate, personal and mixed, and every interest therein, wheresoever situated.

I nominate and appoint my said wife my executor and direct that she shall not be required to make any bond for the execution of this trust.

In testimony whereof I have hereunto signed my name in the presence of my friends Cyrus Snyder and Catherine L. Phillips on this 13th January 1890.

David A. Stevick

Witnessed and signed by us at the request and in the presence of the testator and in the presence of each other.

Cyrus Snyder
Catherine L. Phillips

[Page 392]

WILL OF ROSANNAH A. WILSON

Last Will and Testament of Rosannah A. Wilson

I, Rosannah A. Wilson of the City of Chattanooga, State of Tennessee being of sound mind and memory and considering the uncertainity of this frail and transitory life, do therefore, make, publish and declare this to be my last Will and testament, that is to say:

First: After all my lawful debts are paid and necessary funeral expenses satisfied, I give, devise, bequeath unto, J. J. Wilson, J. R. Wilson, G. W. Wilson and to the children of my deceased son W. B. Wilson, Ruth Heywood, A. E. Chumby and Mattie L. Rogers, all the real estate that I may die siezed and possessed of, which consists of certain land situated lying and being in Crawford County, Arkansas, adjoining the land of J. R. Wilson on the west, on the south by the lands of Ensiminger, North by J. M. Rogers, East Tolbert and Wright lands. Each of above named heirs to take equally in said land, except the heirs of W. B. Wilson who are to jointly receive one share that is one seventh part said land to be sold by my Executor hereinafter appointed, for distribution when he in his judgement may determine it to be to the interest of the legatees.

Second: I hereby appoint G. W. Wilson to be Executor of this my last will and testament. Releasing him from giving any bond in the case what ever and I do hereby declare and publish this as my last will and testament hereby revoking all former wills by [Page 393] me made.

In witness whereof I have hereunto subscribed my name on this the --- day Mar. 1, 1890.

The above written insturment was subscribed by the said Rosannah A. Wilson in our ---**

I have not left M. E. Moore my daughter now A. F. Wilson's childring any thing, I have giving them already more than I have to give the rest.

Rosannah A. Wilson
her X mark

** presence. And acknowledged by her to each of us, and She at the same time declared the above instrument to be her last will and testament. And we at her request signed our names as Witnesses hereto in her presence and in the presence of each other.

Sallie C. Price
Delphine Black
Mary Campbell

[Page 394]

JOHN POWERS

Last Will and testament of John Powers

I, John Powers, being of sound and disposing mind, memory and understanding, do make, publish and declare this to be my last Will and testament.

I hereby authorize & direct my Executor hereinafter named, to have my body burried [sic] in Mt. Olivet Cemetery, in a proper and becoming manner, to expend a sum, not exceeding Two Hundred Dollars ($200) in erecting a monument on the dividing line of the lot in Mt. Olivet Cemetery. Chattanooga, Tenn. which lot is now owned by Miles Kelley and myself, the understanding between said Kelley and myself being that he will expend a like sum in conjunction with my Executor in erecting said monument and to give to the pastor of the Catholic Church of this City the sum of $30.00 in consideration of said pastor offering up the Sacrifice of the Mass for the repose of my soul.

After paying, my funeral expenses and all my just debts, I will and devise the rest & residue of my property, as follows:

I will the sum of one hundred & fifty ($150) Dollars to the pastor of the Catholic Church of Chattanooga, Tenn, to be appropriated by him to the building fund of the new Sts. Peter & Paul Church, now in process of erection.

In thirds of the rest & residue of my property of

whatsoever kinds and where ever situated will & devise to my brother Patrick Powers and the remaining one third of my property I will to be divided between my three Sisters, [Page 395] Annie Powers, of Chicago, Margaret Flynn of Newark, New Jersey & Mary Flynn of Ireland, share & share alike.

I consititute and appoint "Doc" Mitchell, a member of the police force of Chattanooga as my executor.

Commending my soul to Almighty God, I hereby declare this my last testament.

Witness my hand this 11th March 1890.
John Powers.

Witnessed by us who in the presence of the testator & in the presence of each other and at the request of the Testator, signed our names as witnesses to the execution of the aforesaid Will.

This 11th March 1890.
P. F. O'brien
Pat. Maloney
G. D. Lancaster.

[Page 395 con't]

PATRICK FLEMMING

Last Will and Testament of Patrick Flemming.

In the name of God, Amen! I Patrick Flemming of Chattanooga, Tennessee being of sound mind and disposing memory, but afflicted in body and mindful, that all must die, do make and publish this my last Will & Testament revoking all former Wills if any are found, or pretended to be found.

Item 1st - It is my will that my just debts be paid out of my money coming to the hands of my Executors or either of them who may qualify as such from my business or the [Page 396] proceeds, not having reference to my policies of Insurance upon my life.

Item 2nd. - I have heretofore by an agreement made between me and my Sister Nora F. Kernes, leased to her my life estate in the lot of land where I now reside described in said agreement which is dated August 24th 1889 and to which I refer said, agreement also conveyed to her my said sister any claim I might have for betterments on said lot in the event of my death, the principal object of said agreeemnt being to secure my said Sister against certain notes executed by me to Frank P. Marquet amounting in all to about $--- and which are made a Vendor's lien upon a certain lot, I conveyed to her situate on A Street north of Brammer on East 9th Street in the City of Chattanooga, Tennessee. I desire that said lease and agreement be carried out but if in the event of my death or from my after cause said case is terminated by my death before said notes are paid and my claim for betterments on said lot is not available for that purpose I desire that said notes be paid out of the proceeds of a Policy of Insurance I hold upon my life, in the order of "the Catholic Knights of America" branch 71 for two thousand dollars which policy of Insurance or the proceeds hereby bequeath to my said [Page 397] Sister, Nora F. Kernes, free from the control and the debts of her present or any future husband together with the sum of five hundred dollars the balance that will be due on a policy of insurance I hold on my life in Order of the Fraternal Mystic Circle No. --- for fifteen hundred dollars, after paying a bequest to my mother Mary Kenedy, for the purpose of securing my said Sister against my said Notes to said Marquet and to better enable her to care for and educate my son Andrew Martin Flemming for whom I make her testamentary Guardian, and desire that he remain in her care and control as such Guardian and request that she have control of his estate as such Guardian without bond if it can be cone lawfully.

Item 3 - I devise & bequeath to my beloved mother Mary Kenedy one thousand dollars, to be collected from said policy of Insurance I hold on my life in the order of the Fraternial Mystic Circle No. Chattanooga, Tenn. for $1500.00 I direct that my executors shall collect said policy of Insurance as soon as possible after after [sic] my death and place one thousand dollars on interest payable semi-annually with security by mortgage of real estate or undoubted personal securing and to collect and pay the interest on said sum if collected at the end of each consecutive six months to my said mother as long as she may live. She resides in Ireland and my [Page 398] Executors are authorized to remit said interest in the usual way of transmitting money to that Country and on the death of my mother said thousand dollars will be equally divided among all her children then living and giving to the children of any deceased child or children the share that the parent would have taken if living.

Item 4 - I give and bequeath to my Sister Nora F. Kernes for her own separate use and benefit & free from the control and debts of her present or any future husband all my household and kitchen furniture of every nature whatever including pictures books and all other things including all bedding now in the house, where I reside on East 9th or Brammer street in the City of Chattanooga, Tennessee and expect my son Andrew Martin Flemming to remain with her as his guardian.

Item 5th - I direct that my Executors herein appointed or either of them that may qualify shall within twelve months sell and dispose of all the goods in my Store on Market Street and shop on A street upon Credit of not more than twelve months taking notes bearing interest with approved Security. I would suggest that their sales should in most instances be upon 60 or 90 days time.

They will have the right to complete all contracts entered into by me in my lifetime with the foreman and employees I now have if practicable & they will [Page 399] not renew the lease, I now have upon the house on Market Street but if they have not sold the goods & tools on hands by the time it expires they will store the tools & goods on hand in the house where my shop now is on A Street until sold and keep them. My said acting executor or executors is authorized in the event they can make any advantage in a sale of my stock of goods & tools & good will at private sale to do so. We or they may sell upon a credit taking in every insurance notes with ample Security. My said executors will after paying my debts that are found just first apply the sum of $5-- five hundred and --- dollars to placing a memorial window in the Saint Peters and Saint Pauls Roman Catholic Church in Chat-tanooga, Tennessee in memory of my beloved wife Anna now deceased & in memory of myself with the consent of the proper authorities of the church.

The remainder of any said estate be equally divided between my sister Nora F. Kernes and my brother William Flemming. I desire & direct that a portion of whatever my brother William shall received from my estate shall be invested in a home for my brother and family free from his debts and [Page 400] liability so that his children may have a home so long as they or any of them are minors.

Item 6 - I have subscribed $1000.00 Stock in the O'Brien Grocery Company, and have paid $100.00 or more my Executors may sell said Stock at private sale and relieve my estate if they can do so at a loss of one hundred dollars if necessary in their judgement.

Item 7th - I bequeath to P. D. Colter and Thomas S. Wilcox the sum of five hundred dollars each to be paid out of the residue of my estate after the payment of my just debts and the bequest to my mother and sister Bridget, provided they shall continue to conduct my business faithfully and and [sic] shall give their time and best and faithful service to my executors in winding up my estate, in addition to their Salaries, which they are now receiving but this sum only be paid to them on condition that they faithfully perform the service herein required and my Executors are made the sole judges on how they have performed their duty and their decision shall be final.

Item 8 - I give my nephew Samuel Kernes one gray pony called Queen now in my possession and to my son Andrew Martin Felmming one mare colt named Dolly Varden and the pony that was awarded to him by the

[Page 401] Catholic Fair and to Wm. Kernes the mare Fannie the mother of the colt Dolly Varden.

Item 9 - I give and bequeath to my sister Nora F. Kearnes on like condition one Pheaton and cow in my possession also other live stock and wagons now in my possession are part of my Stock of Goods and business and will be so treated and used by my Executors so long as necessary.

My Executors are required to consult my sister Nora F. Kernes and the other beneficaries if practicable in regard to disposing of any and all my estate and be governed by their advice so far as consistent with the duties as such.

Item 10th - Lastly I appoint Creed F. Bates and W. L. Eakin my Executors of this my last will & Testament.

P. Flemming.

Signed in our presence and witnessed by us at the request of the Testator in his presence and the presence of each of us on this 26th day of April 1890.

T. A. Mulligan
James Hickson

[Page 402]

JOHN BRENNER

Last Will & Testament of John Brenner of the City of Covington, County of Kenton, State of Kentucky.

In the name of the Benevolent Father of all. I the said John Brenner, being of sound and disposing mind and memory considering the uncertainity of continuance in life, and desiring to make such disposition of my wordly estate as I deem best, do make publish and declare this to be my last will and testament hereby revoking and annuling any and all forever will or wills which soever by me made.

First, I desire all my just debts and funeral expenses to be paid, as soon as possible after my decease.

Secondly, I give and bequeath my beloved wife, Caroline Brenner, her heirs, executors administrative and assigns for her and their own use and benefit forever; all my estate, real, personal and mixed of whatever kind and nature and wherever the same may be located.

I nominate and appoint my said wife, Caroline Brenner to be the sole executrix of this will and testament, and desire that no bond be required from her as such.

In witness whereof, I have hereunto set my hand and seal this twenty-first day of November, in the year eighteen hundred and eighty nine,

John Brenner, {Seal}

Sealed, Signed and acknowledged by John Brenner as and for his last will and testament in our presence [Page 403] and subscribed and attested by us as witnesses, in his presence, and in the presence of each other, and at his request.

C. H. Bramlage
W. J. Munster

[Page 403 con't]

JOHN LEARY

Last will & Testament of John Leary

I, John Leary, being of sound mind and disposing memory, do make and publish this my last will and Testament.

1. I desire that all my just debts be paid.
2. After paying all debts and just obligations I will and bequeath to my Sister Catharine Collins, formerly Catherine Leary of Boston, Mass. The sum of five dollars.
3. After paying said debts and paying said $5.00 to my said Sister, I will and bequeath to Mrs. Ellen Murphy of Chattanooga, Tennessee all the rest and residue of my property of every kind and wherever it may be found or situated.
4. I appoint and constitute P. A. Brenner, Sr. as the executor of this my last will & testament and I hereby revoke any and all former wills, I may have made and declare the foregoing as my last will.

Witness my hand this May 13th 1890.

John X Leary
his mark

Signed by us in the presence of each other and in the presence of the testator and at the request of the testator. This May 13th 1890.

H. L. McCorkle
Fannie X Strickland
her mark
J. H. Cantrell

[Page 404]

JOHANNA SHIELDS

Last Will and testament of Johanna Shields.

In the name of God, Amen! I, Johanna Shields wife, of Wm Shields, formerly Johanna Malony well knowing the uncertainty of life & the certainty of Death & being now of sound mind & disposing memory though in failing health, do make this my last will & testament hereby revoking all others.

I. - I commend my body to the Earth from whence it came & my Soul to God who gave it relying on the attoning sacrifice of our Lord & Savior, the Lord Jesus Christ.

II. - It is my will and desire that at my death my dearly beloved moth Mrs. Johanna Maloney shall have & become the absolute & unconditional power of all the property of every kind, real, personal & mixed. I die seized & possessed of or have any interest in & I desire her to have said property free from the marital rights of my husband.

III. - I have one little Girl named Mary Shields, now three years old, It is my earnest wish & desire that at my death my mother Mrs. Johanna Maloney have the custody, care, education & bring up of my said child Mary.

IV. - I bequeath to my Husband Wm Shields One Dollar & no more. I am led to this dispose of my effects & child because of the conduct of my said husband. For several years he has been very dissipated & wholly neglected to provide for me & my child & has been very unkind to us both. Some time ago he willfully & without cause abandoned me and for a long time has refused to cohabit with me as a husband & left me on a sickbed not able to help myself & wholly [Page 405] destitute & I have for a long time been & now am a charge of my mothers bounty. My husband is so dissipated and for other reasons is not suitable to have the custody of my child & for all these reasons & many more of like import it is my will & desire that my mother at my death have all I own & my child.

V. - I appoint my mother Johanna Maloney the sole Executrix of this my last will & testament & excuse her from giving bond. Witness my hand this the 8th day of May 1890.

Johanna X Shields
her mark

Signed in our presence and we were requested to witness the same as the last will & testament of Johanna Shields and signed as witnessed in the presence of the Testatrix & the presence of each other this May 8, 1890.
J. W. Pickens
Mrs. Mary E. Robertson

[Page 406]

ELIZABETH M. YORK

Last Will and Testament Elizabeth M. York

I, Elizabeth M. York of Chattanooga Hamilton Co., Tenn. Being of sound mind and understanding do make this my last will & testament, revoking all other wills made by me. After defraying my funeral expenses, I make the following bequests.

Of my one third interest in house & lot on Canal Street in Towanda, Bradford Co., Penna. Of the one third interest I I [sic] give to Helen M. Burbank, one hundred dollars to Hiram C. Myers, one hundred dollars & all that remains of my one third interest in said house & lot, I give to my Sister in law Mrs. Philomene P. Myer. The three persons heretofore named to have and dispose of said property at their own discretion. I further give & bequeath the sum of two hundred dollars & my mantle looking glass to Louise M. Gearhart. To Clarence G. York & wife two hundred dollars. To Annie F. Johnson, my black lace shawl & two hundred dollars. To Margaret E. Grove, my white Catherine shawl & two hundred dollars. To S. Augustus York two hundred dollars.

All the rest of my property with all I may inherit & money shall be equally divided between my three sisters & the three children of my niece Mary Pratt (now deceased). The first fourth part to Catherine H., Joseph G. & Susan M. Pratt of Towanda, Penna. The second fourth part to Sallie V. Giles & her heirs. The third fourth part to Elizabeth M. Parker & her heirs. The fourth part [Page 407] to Helen M. Weide & her heirs. My gold watch & chain to Mary Elizabeth Johnson for her name daughter of Annie F. Johnson.

I herein appoint as executors of my Estate Miss Susan A. Myer, & Dr. J. J. Durand, to execute this my last will & testament.

All my personal property, my Sister Susan (consisting of household articles & jewelry) A. Myer, shall dispose of as she may think best.

Whereunto I set my hand & seal this twentieth day of May 1890.
Elizabeth M. York

Witness:
Martha S. Durand
C. S. Durand.

CODICIL

Aug. 7th 1890.
I bequeath to my Sister Susan A. Myer the house in Chattanooga, on Moon Street and the house on Mission Ridge to have and to hold or sell during her natural Life and then to be distributed as designated in the above Will.
Elizabeth M. York

Martha S. Durand
Bessie E. Acosta

[Page 408]

W. J. BLACKWELL

Last Will and Testament of W. J. Blackwell

State of Tennessee }
Hamilton County   }

Know all men by these presents. That I, W. J. Blackwell do this day make my last will & Testament. I bequeath unto my son O. L. Blackwell a certain piece or parsal [sic] of land lying in 15th fifteenth Civil District of Hamilton County, State of Tenn. known as my house place, that portion of of [sic] the north west fractional quarter of Section Twenty-five all so that portion of land lying in the north east quarter of Section twenty-five that was transfered to me by M. R. Julian. Sixth Fractional Township Range 3 West Basis line Ocoe[e] District conmencing on the State line at a large wild cherry tree in a swag thence running north Parallel with the dividing line between my lands and the lands of M. R. Julian to the line of J. L. Blackwell farm thence east with said line the corner of my lands and the lands of M. R. Julian thence south with the dividing line between my lands and the lands of M. R. Julian to the south side of the W. & A. R. R. thence the east with said R. Road to the State line thence west with the State line to the beginning corner now I bind my son O. L. Blackwell in this will to suport [sic] and take care of my wife E. E. Blackwell during her life time. I further bequeath with my son O. L. Blackwell all the growing crop on my entire farm that grow in the year 1890. I further bequeath to my son A. L. Blackwell [Page 409] one hors[e] well known by name as Mike. I all so bequeath to A. L. Blackwell two yearlings known by name as Mary and Maud and all my farming implements including waggon and harness and all other uten:ils [sic] and on the farm I bequeath to my wife E. E. Blackwell two Milch cows known by name as Roseand Mag.

I further bequeath to my wife E. E. Blackwell and my son O. L. Blackwell jointly all my Stock, hogs and all my Hous[e]hold & kitchen furniture.

I further request that the rest of my stock, one mare, one mul[e] and two cows, be sold to pay my Due Bill and other expences that ma[y] occur[e]. Now I further bequeath that the rest of my real estate be soled [sic] and divided equaly between my children Mattie Angly, May Angly, Elizabeth Stricland, Cicero Blackwell, Young

Blackwell and James J. Blackwell all of my bodly [sic] Heirs.

I hereby appoint W. T. Walker to act as my Executor this the 6th day of August 1890.
W. J. Blackwell

A. M. Harris
Thos. S. Lane
Sam'l Julian

[Page 410]

J. R. FRAKER

Last Will and Testament of J. R. Fraker

I, J. R. Fraker, citizen of Hamilton County, Tennessee being sixty five years old do make and declare this to be my last Will and testament hereby revoking all wills made prior to this date.

Article 1
I desire that my executrix here in after named shall pay all my just debts.

Article 2nd
I hereby bequeath unto my wife Mariana B. Fraker and my daughter Louise L. Fraker all my interest in the firm of Fraker and Trimble and all my interest in the firm of Fraker and Trimble [sic] and all my interest in any lands, mining interests or property of any kind that may belong to said Fraker and Trimble. They to enjoy the same share and share alike.

Article 3rd
All the rest, residue and remainder of my estate real, personal and mixed I devise & bequeath unto my beloved wife, Mariana B. Fraker, to have and to hold the same unto the said Mariana B. Fraker to her sole and seperate use.

I hereby appoint my beloved wife Mariana B. Fraker executrix of this my last will of whom no bond shall be required.

In witness whereof I have hereunto set my hand & seal this 6th day of August 1890.
J. R. Fraker {seal}

Signed and sealed by J. R. Franker and by him declared to be [Page 411] his last will in our presence who have hereunto subscribed our names as witnesses in his presence and in the presence of each other and at his request.

Glennie Davies
J. Hodge McLean

[Page 411 con't]

LUCY A. ALLEN

Last Will and Testament of Lucy A. Allen

Life is short. We know not how soon we may be called to our long house. Therefore I (Miss) Lucy A. Allen do make the following statement as to disposing of what little I possess should I be taken away within the coming year.

I have two lots at Summit City, James Co., Tenn. hold deed for the same. Lot No. 14 Block 2 - I wish Dr. H. S. Chase (my Physician) to have the disposal of. He having made no charges for services rendered me. I wish him to have $35.00 or $40.00 as he deems best for services. The balance the lot brings to apply on indebtness of Walnut St. Christian Church at Chattanooga, Tenn. Wish Dr. Chase to see this is done.

Lot No. 12 Block Two, $20.00 (twenty dollars) of it to apply on Church Buildings at Highland Park, $20.00 to the Church Extension Fund with Proviso that in coming future it be applied on Erection of Christian Church at Summitt City, James Co., Tenn. Which said lots are and are now (July 14th 1890) valued at $60.00 (sixty dollars). This Mission Work, I wish bro. J. H. Garvin of Sherman Heights to take [Page 412] charge of Remaining $20.00. I wish applied towards a small plain stone to mark my resting place & service - suitable place, at Forest Hills Cemetery, togather [sic] with which I may have laid aside in City Savings Bank, wish this work taken charge of by bro. Isreal Hoover.

I have an Esty Organ - rented to Christian Church at Hartford, Croton P.O. Licking Cr., Ohio. I wish them to keep in kindly rememberance of my humble self.

My sewing machine (Singer Improved) bed & bedstead, chairs, rocker, table, mirror and stove can be sold funds applied on expences incurred. I wish Mr & Mrs. J.W. Agey to see to these things particularly assisted by -

Other smaller articles, dishes &c dispose of as they see fit, i.e. Give to any needy member of Walnut St. Christian Church or any of my friends also Elena to take such things as they wish.

My Magie Scole for dress making with book of instructions, for same give to our Pastor's wife, Mrs. S. B. Moore also Dress form if she wishes.

My watch and chain give to little niece Jessie G. Brown, at Wellsville, Allegany Co., N. Y.

Cameo Pin with head - and writing desk to niece, Jessie A. Willis, Keysville Charlotte Co., Virginia. [Page

413] Lace Pin with small cameo set, to niece Georgia A. Blynn at Utica Ohio, also beaded chair made by her (Georgia's) grandmother, for Aunt Lucy Johnson for whom I was named in part also a rug, I have partly embroidered.

Hair, Ring, give to niece, Jennie T.Allen Angelico, Allegany Co., N.Y. said ring, made of Oldest sister, Jane & sister Elizabeth hair, also give her my Bagsters Teacher's Bible.

What things, I have in form of relics, i.e. minerals, war relics, old coins, book &c send to my nephew George S. Brown, Wellsville, Allegany Co., N.Y. also a worsted Tidy you will find to his wife niece Millie, Relics, old fashioned china cup & saucer, teapot & the china creamer.

A green worsted mat to Parma Brown's wife, niece Stella at Wellsville, N.Y.

Marbleized Slate, bracked shelf, I wish Mrs. J. W. Agey to have Paper weights with name Lucy thereon to any member of Mrs. D. W. Chases family that wishes. Think Miss Bessie or Miss Hollis give paper weight to Miss Hollie. Design for Painting & an unpainted plaque to Miss Bessie.

Small bracket shelf in corner of room to Mrs. Rolston, Oil painting court case, small vase and Bible Dictionary to Mrs. R's children as they like.

Picture, Milton at 12 years of age to Parma Brown & photo album to [Page 414] Willie Brown (nephews) at Wellesville, N.Y.

Carrie Stevens, photo in frame to Fred P. Allen - Angelina, N.Y. also, what picture & paintings I have Tidy on black, Jara Canvass, to his wife, niece Millie.

China cup & Saucer, large "Present" on cup to Prof. J. W. Agey.

My Furs give to my niece, Jennie Brown, Wellesville, N.Y. Ring on my finger to my little Friend Florence Susanch at Newalle, O. No. 17 1/2 South Side the Square, and white silk kerchief, satin border & stamped corner to Jennie L. Dersonch same place.

Patchwork pieces to mother Agey & mother Hoover - also to Carrie Damber & Lula if they wish & send some to my sister Lucinda at Wellsville, N.Y. to dispose of as they best, if Elena thinks best.

Contents of my Trunks, things I've not disposed of do good with them to the needy worthy ones. A white apron, therein with narrow torclion edge, give to my true friend Miss Alice M. Hooke, #515 West Minthe, City.

Should Mr. & Mrs. Stettions be here or in City, please give her little book. Guide to Washington City, D.C. and any other articles not specified here, should she wish.

I have a few things at Utica, Ohio my former house, one book, "A Place in Thy Memory" wish that sent our Pastor. S. B. Moore #625 Cypress St. Chattanooga, Tenn. Another [Page 415] "Mistress of the Mouse" by J. G. Holland please sent to Allen E. Willis, Keysville, Charlotte Co., Virginia wish my niece Georgia A. Blynn to attend to these things other things there she (Georgia) can keep what she wishes or all r'd dispose of them as she sees fit.

Send Bro. Samuel White silk kerchief, blue border - Sis Lucinda linen kerchief with my initials or name in corner. Mrs. Samuel H. Brown, Wellsville, Allegany Co., N.Y. (Address)

Send bro. Willard Black & White silk kerchief & a linen handkerchief, lily etched with blue in corner - my work. Sis. Alina, Give Collar of feather edge my work to Sister Alena Address Mr. Willard Allen, Angelica, Allegany Co., N.Y.

I have $350 (three hundred & fifty dollars) from which I have been wrongfully deprived. Have no note or writing to show for it, my sister Elizabeth Allen & bro. in law, P.C. Allen. M. D. at Utica, Licking Co., Ohio have included it in their will (unbeknown to me) to this effect. Should they outlive me. They were to have it, for giving me a house and caretaker of me while sick should I outlive them I was to have it, I have four great nieces viz: Georgia A. Blynn, Utica, Licking Co., Ohio, Jessie A. Willis, Keysville, Charlotte Co, Virginia, Jessie G. Brown, Wellsville, Allegany Co., N. Y. and Marian L. Brown, Wellsville, N. Y. or make them to find out about her, she is Georgia's S. Brown [Pager 416] little girl,. Give to each $75.00 (seventy five dollars) remaining $50.00 (fifty dollars) to Mrs. Carrie L. Allen East Hubbardton, Rutland Co., Vermont, For care while sick at her house fall of 1880.

I appoint Mr. & Mrs. J. W. Agey administrators &c.

[Page 416]

HARRY W. DURAND

Last Will and Testament of Harry W. Durand

I, Harry W. Durand being in ill health but of sound and disposing mind and memory do make and publish this my last will and Testament hereby revoking and making null and void all other last wills and Testaments by me heretofore made.

Imprimis my will is that all my just debts and funeral charges shall by my Executors hereinafter named be paid out of my estate as soon after my decease as shall by them be convenient.

Item 1st. - The furniture, wareing [sic] appearel, books &c now in the house (near the E.T V & G. Railway at the Tunnel on Missionary Ridge, Hamilton County, Tenn.) shall be for the use of my wife and children and need not be entered up as a part of the estate but shall be theirs from my decease.

Item 2nd. - I give unto my Executors hereinafter named, full power and authority whenever in their mutual opinion [Page 417] it may seem best for the estate to sell any piece or pieces of real estate, I may die seized of passed of, and reinvest the same as may be best for the estate and they shall make good and sufficient Deed or Deeds for said real estate, to the purchaser thereof.

Item 3rd - In investing any money or monies, my Executors shall have no power to loan the same on personal Security or on personal property. And the same is expressly forbidden, and said loan shall be void, but all money loaned if any therebe, must be on first class paying. Real Estate not to exceed Forty (40) per cent of its real value, on a low valuation. Secured by first Deed of Trust and then must be an Abstract certified to by a reliable Abstract Company showing title to the property to be free and unencumbered.

Item 4th. - If my wife should marry before the date hereinafter set out she shall receive from the Estate in lieu of all other claims One thousand Dollars and this shall be in full of all claims of homestead, Dower or any other claims, she might make, but if she should remain a widow until the oldest child become of age, then she shall share equally with my children in the division of the Estate. No Dower or homestead to be allowd her, she to share alike with the children instead of receiving Dower or Homestead.

[Page 418]   Item 5th. - The rents and proffits arising from said Estate, shall be used to support and care for my wife and children, but no part of said estate itself shall be used for said purpose save money now on hands or in Bank unless in case of Absolute necessity any upon the Mutual agreement of both the acting Executors.

Item 6th. - I hereby appoint my wife, Jessie V. Durand and Dr. J. J. Durand and Dr. Charlie S. Durand as Executors of this my last will and Testament without bond. My wife Jessie V. Durand and Dr. J. J. Durand shall first qualify as executors of this will and upon the death of either of said Executors said Dr. Charles S. Durand shall immediately qualify as Executor and from that time on have equal rights and power as Executors as if he had qualified upon the filing of this will.

In witness whereof I have hereunto set my hands This the 31st day of October 1890.

Harry W. Durand.

The above will and Testament was signed by the testator in our presence and we at his request signed the same in his presence and in the presence of each other as witnesses thereof.

Ed. W. Borcharding
Jesse D. Trueblood

J. F. Bryan
J. A. Caldwell

[Page 421]

[Page 419]

MARIA A. DARRELL

Last Will and Testament of Maria A. Darrell

I, Maria A. Darrell, widow, resident of Chattanooga, Tenn. being in feeble health and knowing that at most I have not long to live - and being now of sound mind and disposing memory do make and publish this as my last will and testament hereby revoking and making void all other wills heretofore by me at any time made.

First, I give and bequeath to my daguther Mrs. Margaret L. McFarland, wife of James McFarland the sum of five dollars to be paid by my Executor after my debts & funeral expenses have all be fully paid.

Second - I give devise and bequeath to my other daughter Mrs. Ann Hedge, wife of William Hedge, one half of all the rest and residue of my property real, personal and mixed whenever and wherever situate[d] and found and to my son Alexander F. Walker the other half of all my said property real, personal and mixed after the payment of my funeral expenses and just debts of every kind.

Third - I hereby nominate and appoint my said son, Alexander Farris Walker sole executor of this my last will and testament and I desire that he shall, as soon after my death as practicable pay and satisfy all of my funeral expenses, debts and obligations of every character. Then pay to my daughter Margaret the legacy herein before mentioned and then [Page 420] divide the residue of my property and effects, equally between his said sister Ann Hedge and himself. The division of real estate to be made between them in such manner as may be agreeable to them and if not then in the manner provided by law. In testamony whereof I sign my name in the presence of the subscribing witnesses at my residence on Whiteside Street in Chattanooga, Tennessee on this eighth day of December 1890.

Maria A. Darrell

We have witnessed the foregoing signature at the request of the Testator & in the presence and the presence of each other - this 8th Dec. 1890.

Miss Nellie Garvin

GEORGE J. BRIMBLE

Last Will and Testament of Geo. J. Brimble

Be it remembered that I George J. Brimble of the village of Saint Elmo, County of Hamilton and State of Tennessee do make this my last will and testament in the manner following.

That is to say: I order that my just debts and funeral expenses shall be paid with convenient speed.

I devise to Lottie Hohnes Patten, wife of George W. Patten, of the village of Saint Elmo, County of Hamilton, State of Tennessee, and her heirs a tract of land owned by me, known as "lot Number Forty (40) in Wallace addition to Saint Elmo" and located in the Seventeenth Civil District of Hamilton County, Tennessee as a token of my appreciation of her love and kindness in providing the comforts and enjoyments of a good home for me.

I bequeath my trunk and contents and all my personal effects not otherwise disposed of by this will to my dear cousin Charles Coward of the City of Pittston, County of Luzerne, State of Pennsylvania.

In case the amount of cash turned over to my Executor amounts to $3000, it is my will and order and direct that $500 of the same be paid to my uncle, George Coward, of the City of Pittston, County of Luzerne, State of Pennsylvania, if he is alive at my death. If George Coward, does not survive me, this legacy is to be paid to Mrs. Mary Coward, his wife, if she is alive at that time.

It is my will and I order and direct that after my debts and the [Page 422] legacies and expenditure herein provided for are made and expenses of probate of this will and Executors fees shall have all been paid, that the amount remaining in custody of Executor belonging to my estate, shall be paid to my Father Henry Brimble, of the City of Pittston, County of Luzerne, State of Pennsylvania, provided he is alive at my death; if my father does not survive me, the funds that would otherwise be paid to him shall be equally divided among the children then living of my Uncles, George and Harry Coward of the City of Pittston County of Luzerne, State of Pennsylvania.

It is my will and I order and direct that J. A. Patten herein after named as Executor of my estate shall collect the policy #1384 Class A. which I hold in the U.S. Railway Mail Service Mutual Benefit Association for $2000 same being payable to my estate also in case of my death resulting from accident that said Patten shall also collect policy #1512 Class 2 in New York Accident Insurance Company for $3000 same being payable to J. A. Patten "in trust," the amounts received from these policies to be applied as directed in the will.

I wish my Executor to purchase a suitable lot in the Forest Hill Cemetery near Chattanooga, Tenn. for permanent interment of my remains; the title of this lot to be in the J. A. Patten's name and the same to be used by the family of [Page 423] G. W. Patten if so desired by them. I wish my Executor to have a small suitable head stone erected, marking the resting place of my remains in the final settlement of my estate he will also retain an amount sufficient to keep the lot in Forest Hill Cemetery in good condition for a time of twenty-five (25) years.

I also direct that my Executor have a suitable monument placed over my mother Mrs. Martha Brimble's grave in the Odd Fellows Cemetery, Pittston, PA.

I request that J. A. Patten here-to-fore referred to as my Executor, see that this request is carried out in person and if possible visit Pittston, PA for that purpose; his expenses on said trip, in case he goes there, are to be defrayed from my estate.

I appoint J. A. Patten of the village of Saint Elmo, County of Hamilton, State of Tennessee Executor of this my will. No bond, to be required of him.

In witness whereof I have signed and sealed and published and declared this instrument as my will, at St. Elmo, Tennessee on the 6th day of September A.D. 1890.

Geo. J. Brimble

The said George J. Brimble at the above mentioned place and on the above mentioned date, signed and sealed this instrument and published and declared [Page 424] the same as and for his last will and we at his request and in his presence and in the presence of each other, have hereunto written our names as subscribing witnesses.

Richard A. Conner
Thos. K. Bostick
E. Kirklin

I certify the above names are true this 6th Sept. 1890

E. Kirklin, J. P.

[Page 424 con't]

ROBERT HUNTER

Last Will and Testament of Robert Hunter

Know all men by these presents that I Robert Hunter of Ridgedale, County of Hamilton and State of Tennessee mindful of the uncertainites of Human life, and being of sound mind and memory do make publish and declare this my last will and testament.

First. I hereby direct that my Executrix herein named shall out of the proceeds of my estate pay all of my just debts including the expenses of my last sickness and funeral.

Second. I hereby give, devise and bequeath unto my loved wife Sarah Hunter all of my property real, personal and mixed of what ever description - excepting only so much as will pay my debts, funeral expenses &c as recited in items first, to have and to hold the same and the use thereof unto her the said Sarah Hunter for the term and during her natural life.

Third. Subject to the use and [Page 425] enjoyment of the same by my said wife during her natural life.

I hereby give devise and bequeath unto my son David William Hunter the house and about seven acres of land in and on which I now reside on Missionary Ridge near Ridgedale in the Fifth Civil District of Hamilton County, and State of Ten-nessee. I also give, devise and bequeath unto my said son David William Hunter all of my personal property, goods & chattels which may remain at the death of my said wife, not intending however, to restrict my said wife in the use and enjoyment of said property principal & interest should she so desire.

Fourth. The residue of my property Real, personal and mixed I hereby give devise and bequeath in equal portions to my three children, David William Hunter, Ann Elizabeth Hunter and Mary Jane Milligan Hunter - share and share alike.

And should either of my said children die without issue living, before my death then the portion of such deceased child shall go to the survivors share and share alike. And should any of my said children die before I do leaving legitimate issue, then such child or children of such deceased child or children shall receive the share that such parent would have received if living, share and share alike.

Fifth. I hereby nominate, constitute and appoint my wife Sarah Hunter as executrix of this my last will and testament with [Page 426] full power to settle, compromise and adjust all of my business & settle my estate and should it be necessary to sell any of my property for the purpose of the payment of my Debts or the settlement of my estate. I hereby authorize and empower my said executrix to sell, transfer and convey so much thereof as may be sufficient for the purpose either at public or private sale as she may decree best without resort to any court for the purpose, and I hereby request the Court having jurisdiction of administration to issue full authority to my said execurtrix without requiring bond under the Statute. In witness whereof I have hereunto signed my name in the presence of Halbert B. Case and W. E. Garvin who have signed their names hereto as witnessess in my presence and in the presence of each other at my request the the 30th day of March A.D. 1889.

R. Hunter

The forgoing will was signed by Robert Hunter in our presence and we have signed the same as witnesses in his presence, and in the presence of each other at the request of said Robert Hunter on this the 30th Day of March A.D. 1889 and the said Robert Hunter acknowledged that he executed the same as his last will and testament to us.

Halbert B. Case
Walter B. Garvin

[Page 427]

ROBERT HUNTER - Continued

Being desirous of changing my will, the original not being present but of which the above is a true copy. I, Robert Hunter of Ridgedale, Hamilton County, Tennessee do change my said will in the following respects: viz:

1st - Since making the above deed of testament a small portion of the land on which my house stands a small piece right in the V has been sold to the Southern Land and Loan Co. I desire mention of this to be made that no contest may arise in respect to this piece of property and this portion of the land is excepted from the bequest to my son David William Hunter.

Second. In the third section of the foregoing will there are the words "I also give devise and bequeath unto my said son David William Hunter all of my personal property goods and chattel which may remain at the death of my said wife," I desire to change this so that it shall not include the bank accounts that may be to the credit of the estate, but that there shall be equally divided among my three children at the death of my wife.

Third. The property upon which my house on Mission Ridge stands I devise, give and bequeath unto my said son David William Hunter after the death of my said wife, except that there is to be deducted from it the following property viz: Bourded on the East by the [Page 428] crest road on the south by the small portion of land deeded the Southern Land and Loan Company, on the west by the continuation of the Montgomery Avenue road up the ridge and on the north by the present lane running from Montgomery Avenue which said piece of property I

desire to be divided equally betwen my two daughters Ann Elizabeth Hunter and Mary Jane Milligan Hunter, after the death of my said wife Sarah Hunter.

In witness whereof I have hereunto signed my name in the presence of Melancthon Carey and Frank L. Case, who have signed their names hereto as witnesses, in my presence and in the presence of each other, at my request this the 13th day of October A. D. 1890.

Robert Hunter

The foregoing codicil was signed by Robert Hunter in our presence and we have signed the same as witnesses in his presence and in the presence of each other at the request of said Robert Hunter, on this the 13th day of October, A.D. 1890.

M. Carey
Frank L. Case

[Page 429]

D. C. TREWHITT

Last Will and Testament of D. C. Trewhitt

I, D. C. Trewhitt of Hill City, Hamilton Co., Tenn. do make ordain and publish this as my last will and testament.

First, I have advanced to Thomas L. Trewhitt in land and cash at one time Five Hundred Dollars ($500) when he was keeping Grocery at Harrison, Tenn. I paid for him to Cheatem & Co. Four Hundred Dollars ($400.00) & to Dau. Temples Fifty Dollars ($50.00) to George Flynn Eighty Dollars ($80.00) & to Kuntz & Bohr, One Hundred & seventy Five Dollars ($175.00) & the Gardenhire House One Hundred Dollars less Ten & the Kimbrough Pony ($65.00) & the Farris debts $37.50 & the Thatcher order $20.00 & to R. M. Taukiely $7.00 & Rent on Fox McAbb land $140.00 & the Jennie Ring House $40.00 & the Saunders debt $50.00. I might put down much more, but it is unecessary.

He isn't entitled to anything more but I give & bequeath to him one hundred Dollars $100.00 as a child.

I have advanced to May J. Fry, in land $800.00 & have paid a security debt to Thomas Trewhitt for her of $150.00 & I now give & bequeath to her One Hundred & Fifty Dollars ($150.00)

I give & bequeath to the heirs of Peter Holtsham deceased, Five Hundred Dollars ($500.00) Grand children taking the shares of their parents.

I will & devise that my Frazier Ave. property be sold on six, Twelve & Eighteen months time taking notes with security bearing interest from date & a vendou lein retained on said land to secure the purchase money. [Page 430] That part of the land conveyed to me by Mary Miller, upon which A. P. Hunter now lives I will & bequeath to Mrs. A. P. Hunter for & during her natural life & no longer.

The Carden Land lying immediately north of the Mary Miller land order & direct sold in the same manner & time as the Frazier Ave. property.

The fee simple title to the land I give Miss Hunter will be sold at the same time & upon the same terms as the Carden land.

Out of the proceeds of the sale of the Frazier Ave. Property & the Soddy lands will first be paid all my debts & bequeats herein. The remainder will be equally divided between my wife Mary & her four children, A. H. & Alonzo S. & P. W. & Ellen G. Trewhitt.

All my interst in the Duck Town, Copper property I give & bequeath to Thos. L. Trewhitt & Mary J. Fry share & share alike. Mary J. Fry will take all the interests she has under this will to her sole & separate use excluding the marrital [sic] rights of any husband.

The house property where I live & the lot adjoining on the north east & the west half of the Chambliss lot opposite my residence I give & bequeath to my wife, Mary M. Trewhitt for & during her natural life, for the joint use & benefit of herself & four children, A. H., Alonzo S., P. W. & Ellen G. Trewhitt. [Page 431] The fee simple title of all said property to go to said four children share & share alike.

The East half of the Chambliss lot in quantity & including the House I give & devise to my Daughter Ellen G. Trewhitt for her sole & separate use excluding the marital rights of any husband at $1250.00

If any one of my four younger children above named should die without issue, then such share or shares shall go to their whole brothers & sisters, share & share alike. In such event Thos. Trewhitt & Mary J. Fry shall have no part.

All the rest & residue of my property Real, Personal & mixed & money not disposed of in the former part of this will I give & bequeath to my wife & her said four children whose names have been mentioned share & share alike excluding the marital rights of any husband, or females.

Ellen G. Trewhitt at the age of sixteen, or sooner if she should marry takes full possession of the house & lot willed to her.

A. H. Trewhitt, Alonzo S. & Paul W. Trewhitt each must be made up to $1250.00 before Ellen gets any more. After this they share equally.

I will & direct that Thos. Trewhitt shall keep away & not in any way bother or trouble my wife, Mary M. &

her four children, whose names have been mentioned.

[Page 432] The Executor of this my last will & Testament is not required to give any bond & security for the discharge of his duties, but if an Executor of the will annexed should be appointed then he must give bond & security. A. H. Trewhitt has been advanced in money & Law Book's $1000.00, Alonzo S. & Paul W. Trewhitt must each have $1000.00 before A. H. Trewhitt gets any more.

I give & bequeath $100.00 to pay my Executor for his services.

I nominate & Appoint Dr. G. L. Abernathy executor of this my last will & Testament.

D. C. Trewhitt {seal}

Signed, sealed & published in our presence & we have subscribed our names hereto at the request of the Testator & in his presence & in the presence of each other. This the 16th day of Dec. 1890.

Attest: G. L. Abernathy
Cora B. Jones
Caroline Trewhitt

[Page 433]

SAMUEL EDWIN BURNS

Last Will and Testament of Samuel Edwin Burns

Made this first day of January 1891 in Hill City, Hamilton County, State of Tennessee as follows. I bequeath all my lands, tenements, ready money, securities for money goods, chattles and all other parts of my real and personal estate and effects whatsoever and wheresoever unto my wife Hariett Eliza Burns for her own absolute use and benefit subject only to the payment of my just debts, funeral and testamentary expenses and I appoint my said wife executrix of my will. My will is that my said wife shall not be required to give any bonds or security to the Judge of Probate for the faithful execution of the duties of Executrix.

In witness whereof I have hereunto set my hand and seal this first day of January 1891.
S. E. Burns {seal}

Signed and sealed by the above named Samuel E. Burns as and for his last will and testament in the presence of us who have hereunto subscribed our names at his request as witnesses thereunto in the presence of said testator and of each other.

F. W. Dauchy Hill City
M. E. Dauchy Hill City

This 27th day of Dec. 1890
A. A. Stong
T. P. Chamlee

CHARLES H. KISSINGER

Last Will and Testament of Chas. H. Kissenger

State of Tennessee }
Hamilton County   }   In the name of God. Amen. I Charles H. Kissinger of said State and county being of sound and disposing mind and memory Knowing that I must sooner or later depart this life deem it right and proper both as respects my family and myself that I should make a dis-positon of the property with which a kind providence has blessed me I do therefore make this my last will and testament hereby revoking and annullling all others by me heretofore made.

I desire and direct that my body be buried in a decent and Christian like manner suitable to my circumstances and conditions [Page 434] in life. My soul I trust shall return to rest with God who gave it as I hope for salvation through the merits and atonement of the blessed lord and Saviour Jesus Christ.

I desire and direct that all my just debts be paid without delay by my Executors herein after named and appointed. I give bequeath and devise to my beloved wife Ellie to have and to hold to herself, her heirs assigns and personal repre-senatives forever the following described property.

To wit: Lot of land number (27) Twenty Seven in Block Number (6) Six Montague's addition to Chattanooga, State and County aforesaid said lot fronts the south line of said block (46) Forty Six feet and extends northwardly of uniform width (114) onehundred and fourteen feet to a twelve foot alley also the north (55) fifty five feet of lot Number (25) twenty five in Montague's Addition to the city of Chattanooga, Tenn. Also the residence of my property both real and personal whereever and whatever it may be of every variety and descripton to have and to hold to have if her heirs assigns and personal represenatives forever in fee simple and I hereby constitute and appoint my friend John T. Cotter Executor of this my last will and Testament.
This 27th day of December 1890
C. H. Kissenger

Signed, sealed declared and published by Charles H. Kissinger as his last will and Testament in the presence of us undersigned who subscribed our names hereuto in the presence of said Testator at his special instance and request.

[Page 435]

LOUISA B. SMILEY

Last Will and Testament of Louisa B. Smiley

Chattanooga, Tenn Nov. 11th 1890.
Realizing the uncertainties of earth life, I being of sound mind do make my last will and Testament for those to who it may concern.

1st - I will that all my debts be paid and the medical and funeral expenses of my husband Robert W. Smiley from the proceeds of my estate.

2nd - I will that my Executors shall erect a low monument on the graves of myself and husband to be made out of Tennessee marble.

3rd - I will that the surplus after paying these expenses out of the proceeds of my estate shall be given as follows. "A" One hundred Dollars to and [sic] old womans Home as soon as the same shall be established in Hamilton County, Tennessee. "B" Fifty Dollars to the Working Girls Home, "C" One Hundred Dollars to Irma Bennett. If the said Irme Bennett should die before my estate is sold then this one hundred dollars shall go to the aforesaid Old Woman Home. "D" The balance of the surplus of my estate to be divided equally between Sallie Shaffer, Louisa B. Reynolds and Mrs. C. M. Stewart. Thankful for my experiences in earth life I step unto the other room of my Existance leaving Sallie Shaffer as my executors to act without bond.
Louisa B. Smiley

The above foregoing instrument was at the date above set forth signed sealed published and declared by the said Louisa B. Smiley as and for her last Will and Testament in the presence of us who at her request and in her presence and in the presence of each other have subscribed our names as witnesses.
D. G. Curtis - Chattanooga, Tenn.
J. W. Lerch - Ridgedale, Tenn.

Jan. 19, 1891 - Seeing that Sallie Shafer has been so faithful to my wants I hereby change Section "A" so as to read Fifty Dollars to an Old Woman's Home, also so much of [Pagee 436] Section "D" as to give Sallie Shafer double the amount of the Surplus that is to be divided between her and Louisa B. Reynolds and Mrs. C. M. Stewart.

Louisa B. Smiley

Witnesse

Miss Kate Winn
D. G. Curtis

[Page 436 con't]

MICHAEL B. CAHILL

Last Will and Testament of Michael B. Cahill

State of Tennessee }
Hamilton County   }   I Michael B. Cahill of said State and County being of sound and disposing mind and memory do make this my last will and testament.

Item 1st - I give bequeath and devise to my beloved father William Cahill of said State and County all my property both real and personal whereever the same may be situated of which I may be possessed or entitled to either either [sic] in law or at equity at the time of my death. It being my intention and desire to give and bequeath to my beloved father all the property which I now have or may hereafter acquire of which I am possessed or to which I may be entitled either in law or equity. Including real estate notes choses in action and cash as well as all other kinds of real or personal property I do not own any real estate but may acquire some hereafter.

Iten 2 - I hereby constitute and appoint my father Wm. Cahill executor of this my last will and testament and request that he be excused from taking oath and giving bond and making settlement or accounting to the court as required by law. This 26th day of Nov. 1890.

M. B. Cahill

[Page 437]

Signed declared and published by M. B. Cahill as his last will and testament in the presence of us the subscribers who subscribe our names hereto in the presence of said testator at his instance and request and each others he signing in our presence and we signing in his presence.

C. P. Goree
H. L. McReynolds, M. D.

[Page 437 con't]

ADELLA CLEVELAND RAMSAY

Last Will and Testament of Adella Cleveland Ramsay

I, Adella Cleveland Ramsay realizing the uncertainty of life and being now of sound mind and of disposing memory and also desiring that my present plans and wishes may be fully carried out and perfected after my death with reference to the disposition of all my effects both real and personal of which I may be possessed do publish this as my last will and testament revoking all others and annulling the same.

Item 1st - I do yield and return unto God and command unto him my immortal soul fully imbued with the utmost faith in the redeeming care and power of his blessed and begotten son our Lord and Saviour Jesus Christ.

Item 2nd - I do will and bequeath unto my two oldest female children Mary Addella Stock and Hetta M. Fletcher the sum of five (5) dollars to be paid them and of the residence of my estate both real and personal after all my just debts have been paid.

Item 3rd - I do will and bequeath unto my eldest son Wilburn B. Ramsay and unto my daughter. Lorena A. Phillips jointly all of the property of which I may die possessed and described as follows to wit: my house and lot on East Ninth Street in the City [Page 438] of Chattanooga Tenn. together with all my personal property whatsoever including household furniture &etc to be divided equally between them.

Item 4 - It is my will and especial request that my youngest daughter Lorena A. Phillips shall have to her own separate use and ownership the Piano now in her possession at her home also.

Item 5 - There is now a mortgage on my house and lot above described and referred to on East 9th Street, Chattanooga, and I do will and desire that my two children afore mentioned Wilburn B. Ramsay and Lorena A. Phillips shall pay off and cancel said mortgage in equal payments between them as they are bequeathed the lot jointly it is but just and equaitable they should bear equally the encumberance.

Item 6 - I do hereby constitute and appoint Dr. W. G. Bogart in whom I repose the most unqualified confidence and esteem as my Executor under this my last Will and testament and request that he Executes this trust without bond and desire that he carry out the provisions of this my last will with as little expense as practical. Witness my signature

This 20th day of dec. 1890

A. C. Ramsay {seal}

Witnessed and signed by us in the presence of the testator the foregoing will and testament being read to testator Mrs. Adella C. Ramsay before signing and signal by her and in our presence and signed and witnessed by using her presence and in the presence of each other Dec. 20th 1890.

J. W. Bennett
Sam'l L. Egelston

[Page 439]

PAT POWERS

Last Will and Testament of Pat Powers

Hereby revoking all former wills or codicils by me at any time heretofore made. I, Patrick Powers hereby make publish and declare my last will and testament to be as follows:

1st Item - after payment of my just debts and funeral expenses I hereby will bequeath and devise the residence and remainder of my estate real and personal to my wife Maggie Powers without condition or limitation in fee simple.

2nd Item - I hereby nominate and appoint my said wife Maggie Powers sole executrix of this my last will and testament without bond or such and authorize her to lease, sell and convey or otherwise dispose of all property of which I may die seized in as full and ample a manner as I could do if living. Words "real and personal" 7 line interlined before signing.

This Jan'y 11, 1891.
Pat Powers {seal}

Signed sealed and acknowledge and published in his last will and testament by the testator in our presence and we have signed the same in the presence of each other at the request of the Testator.

This 11 day of January 1891
Tomilson Fort
John O'Donohule
J. P. Light
G. W. Reese
P. J. Neligan

[Page 440]

W. S. MARSHALL

Last Will and Testament of W. S. Marshall

I, W. S. Marshall of Chattanooga, Tennessee do make publish and declare this my last will and testament as follows: To Wit: 1st I direct that all my just debts be paid. 2nd I devise and bequest to my sister Mrs. A. M. Boggs my brother Jno. P. Marshall and my niece Mrs. Adele Lasley each the sum of one thousand dollars in the event they shall each live until said bequests are paid as follows to be paid to each of them in installments running through a period of not more than five years after my death not less than one hundred dollars to be paid in any one year during said five years except that if no funds may be in the hands of my Executor during the first year after my death out of which to make any of said payments no payment need to be made upon any of said bequests during the first year after my death such payments to either bequests being intended for them personally and not for their heirs or others.

All the rest and residue of my estate real and personal I wish to be divided equally between my wife Kate M. and my son Stanhope Stewart Marshall and to this end I devise and bequeath the undivided one half interest in and to all the remainder of my estate both real and personal after payment of debts and bequests as above stated to my wife Kate M. for her sole and separate use free from the control debts and contracts of any future husband to be by her disposed of by deed gift will or any other manner. She may see proper and the little to the other undivided one half of all my estate both real and personal remaining after payment of debts and bequests as above stated in items one and two I direct shall pass [Page 441] to and vest in my said wife Kate M. as trustee to be by her held in trust for my said son Stanhope S. to be her held and controlled or disposed of as she as such trustee may deem for the best interests of my said son and she shall have full power and authority to sell or dispose of said undivided one half interest in any of said real Estate or personal property either together with her own undivided interest in the same or separately and either re-invest the proceeds thereof in any other property as she may in her discretion deem for the best interests of the said due trust or loan the same upon good real estate or personal secuirty until such time or times as the same is required to be paid out to my said son as here in after stated or she as such trustee may hold any or all of siad property and convey the undivided one half interest in the same to my said son as here in after stated that is to say the expenses of his support and education will be paid by said trustee out of his one half interest in said estate and for this purpose the the [sic] trustee will have full power and authority to sell or dispose of so much of said estate as will be necessary to raise money to pay for his support and education in such manner and to such extent as said trustee may deed best for the interests of my and her said son and upon his arrival at majority the third part of what remains of his share or interest together with its profits and increase if any shall be paid over or conveyed to him one third part when he arrives at the age of 24 years and the other third or all the balance when he arrives at the age of 27 years.

I appoint my said wife Kate M. sole Executrix of this my last will and request [Page 442] that she be not required to give bond either as such executrix or as trustee for my son. As such executrix she shall have full power and authority and authority to sell and convey any property necessary to raise money with which to pay the debts and bequests named in items one and two above and as trustee for my son she shall have full power and authority to make full and complete deeds and titles to any part of the one half interest which she holds as trustee for him either to raise money to pay for his support and education as above stated or when in the full control and management of his interest as above stated she may deem it best that a sale or sales of any part of his interest be made. The money or property received by my wife from her mothers estate she holds as her separate estate by my request and consent and no disposition of the same or any part there of is attempted in this will but left to her full and free disposition and control. In the event of the death of my said wife before a full and complete execution of the trust imposed upon her in favor of my son then it is my will and desire that T. Y. Montague succeed her in the execution of said trust in whom at her death the title to said trust property shall vest and who shall have the same power and authority over said trust property that may remain undisposed of as is herein conferred upon the original trustee.

Witness my hand and seal this 16th day of June 1890.

W. S. Marshall {seal}

The above instrument consisting of three pages was by the said W. S. Marshall on the day the same bears date signed sealed published and declared by him as and for his last will and testament in our [Page 443] presence and we at his request and in his presence and in the presence of each other have subscribed our names as witnesses thereto.

L. W. Montague, Chattanooga, Tenn
James M. Trimble, Chattanooga, Tenn.

[Page 443 con't]

DAVID T. CARPENTER

Last Will and Testament of David T. Carpenter

Mission Ridge Hamilton County and State of Tennessee September 17th 1890. I, David T. Carpenter a resident of the above State and County and being at this time in poor health but of a sound mind and fully competent to make known my wishes and desires in regard to the disposition of what little property I have and shall still be the possesser of when I shall pass on to a higher life which I have at this time full faith will be my future destiny when I shall lay aside the old body that is now racked with pains and aches and join those that are gone before which to me is a pleasant thought the first piece of property I will dispose of or direct to be disposed of when I am through with it is the Foundry property at the time of the organizing of what is known known as the Phoenix Foundry Co. I furnished the money for two thirds of the Capital Stock then paid in to start the business up and get it to running the amount was $1500. one half of that amount I intended for Clarence A. Carpenter my oldest son but never transfered it to him but I now transfer it to him by my own free act in this proper to be his to hold sell or do as he may wish with it but subject to his one third of the expense of two promisory notes that I hold against said company if not paid while I live must be paid at my death the disposition [Page 444] of said notes will be stated as I advance in the disposition of my effects. My own one third interest in said Foundry I give and bequeath to my youngest son George E. Carpenter to be his at my death or it is to be his when he shall have become of the age of 21 years old, the same one third interest is subject to the payment of one third of the Expense of the said two notes mentioned above the other one third interest in the Foundry is held by Walter S. French my son in law but subject to his one third of the expense of the two notes mentioned above now if the said two notes are not paid before I pass out of the body then they must be paid to the ones that I shall name in this paper and the proceeds to be applied to the paying of the expenses of the children that shall be living together and trying to keep together which is my wish that they will do as long as they can but I know it is natural as they advance in years first one then another will get married and the home circle will get less but I want them to stay together as long as they can. The house and lot on Prospect Street if not sold before my death I will leave in this way to be a home for the children that shall remain single as long as they wish to be together but they shall have the right [it] sell it through the two that I shall name in this as the executors of these my last wishes and requests but if they choose to sell at any time and divide the proceeds with the rest of the children and all consent to the sale then I want the proceeds to be divided equally among all seven of them or all that shall be living at the time they being Ella C. French, Clarence A. Carpenter, Clara E. Carpenter, Flora B. Carpenter, Grace L. Carpenter, Jettie A. Carpenter, [Page 445] and Geo. E. Carpenter now living at this date the property is subject to a note of $600 if not paid before my death or when due must be paid then the reason I specify it to be divided equally among them all from early youth up as I might say and I want them all to share in the proceeds of it. If sold as I have deem best. Now comes my one half interest in the ridge land Clarence being the owner of the one half I want my undivided one half interest disposed of this way as Clarence has one third in the Foundry and Edgar one third I want my half of the Ridge divided equally among my five daughters or among those that may survive me at this date there for five of them Mrs. Ella. C. French, Clara E. Carpenter, Flora B. Carpenter, Grace L. Carpenter, Jettie A. Carpenter. I think it is right in view that Edgar has my interest in the Foundry and he also owns a lot on the Ridge that I should try and help the girls as much as I can with the little that may be realized from my share of the Ridge and hope they may do well by keeping it if not sold before I pass away it is good property to hold if you can't sell it at a good price. The piece of land in Andova, Vermont known as the Joe Parkhurst place if not sold before I pass away I want disposed of and the proceeds divided equally among my Grandchildren that shall be living then that are living now, their names now living are Fredrick C. French, Reginald. M. French, John Leon French, Lillie Virginia French all personal property is to go for the benefit of the family that shall be living at the time I mean stock wagons, farming tools to be sold and the proceeds to be used in house expenses all the furniture and utensils used in the house that they wish to use to be kept for that the piano is a piece of furniture belonging [Pager 446] to the house in one sense and I wished it used in common for that purpose I have other remarks to make but must defer till another time. I will mention here there is in my undivided half interest in the Mission Ridge lands a Mortgage for some money I revised of F. F. Morrell which if not paid before I pass on must be paid out of the proceeds of my half interest of course I had to have some money to use the Foundry did not begin to pay my expenses and never has and a part of the money I spent in a pleasure trip for myself and four of the children which done me good to see them enjoy this although not of much benefit to me I think and if or can't take some comfort of a little of our means while here I am sure we can't after we pass on all I have got I worked hard to get and hope the children will remember that and try and make good use of the little I leave them I had nothing to start with when thrown on my own resources but had to work hard at that time and for a good many years that followed it was hard pulling for your mother and myself to bring up so large a family and meet all their wants you children know but little of that struggles of life to raise a family but you may experience to some extent before you pass on.

Now, I do designate and appoint as the lawfulness to settle up and carry out my wishes my oldest son Clarence A. Carpenter and my oldest unmarried daughter now living Clara E. Carpenter to have full power to carry out my wishes and desires as expressed in this paper. I have full confidence in them to do it and that without any extra expense and would say now that I have asked legal advise and find that I am carrying out the full meaning of the law in [Page 447] in these instructions laid down in the of this paper I am not obliged to let any one know of my wishes in regard to the disposition of my effects but I can leave this where my children can find it and it is fully sworn to and attested to before witnesses that this is my own free act and writing and that makes it a lawful paper without any further trouble or investigation I have tried to do what was right by all concerned in the disposal of my effects and request that you all abide by my wishes and requests. I wish to make a few suggestions to the two I have named above as the executors of these the wishes I have made above. I would advise as to my interest in the Mission Ridge land that if possible you get it into money as soon as the times will admit of a good price and divide the proceeds as designated above equally among the five daughters or if any of them should pass on before I do then to be divided equally among those that may be left as to the homestead on Prospect Street if still in my possession where I pass on I would suggest in addition to my wishes recorded above that if you all decide it would be better to sell it and fix up a home on the Ridge for these that may with [?wish?] to stay together then sell and divide the proceeds as stated above equally among the seven children and those not want to stay together as a family club together with your share of the proceeds and fix your self a home on the ridge for I want all to stay together as long as they can of course I want you all to share on your old home where disposed of now Clarence and Clara having full confidence in your ability integrity and a desire to carry out this my last wishes I do leave this whole matter in your hands to fullfill and enjoin on all concerned to accept this decision of your father as final one little change [Page 448] is my decision as to the Piano. I will give that to my youngest daughter Jettie A. Carpenter if she should be living when these papers are opened and an in hopes no one will object to the change if she should not be living then decide among yourselves whose property it shall be and I will be satisfied.

David F. Carpenter

Signed and acknowledged in our presence and we signed the same as witnesses in the presence of the maker and at his request.

This 18th of December 1890.

L. B. Headrick
Thos. Giffee

[Page 448 con't]

THOMAS CREAN

Last Will and Testament of Thos. Crean

In the name of the Father and of the Son and the Holy Ghost Amen.

I, Thomas Crean do hereby make this my last will and testament.

1st - I here by revoke any previous last will or testament I may have made.

2nd - I direct that my papers, moneys etc. (Now in the hands of Geo. D. Lancaster, Att'y at Law) be immediately after my death delivered to my executor named below.

3rd - I will and direct that my remains be buried in Mt. Olivet Cemetery after celebration of Holy Mass for the repose of my soul and that a memorial slab to cost about $50. be placed on my grave.

4th - I will and direct that all my lawful debts be paid.

5th - Having no living kinsfolk or others dependent on me. I will and bequeath all I now own or may own or inherit to my death be disposed of as follows: 'A' in defraying above named expenses 3 and 4. 'B' In promoting any work of charity in Chattanooga or vicinity according to the desire of my executor, below named. 'C' In having Masses and prayers offered up for the repose of my soul; 'D' In assisting the building of our new church of S. S. Peter and Paul and in [Page 449] erecting in it some memorial to perpetuate prayers and masses for the repose of my soul.

6th - I leave it to my executor to use his discretion in making division of foregoing bequests in accordance with my desires and now known or as may hereafter be made known to him.

7th - I appoint Rev. William Walsh, my pastor as my said executor and I direct that no bond be exacted or required of him.

Witness my hand at Chattanooga, Tennessee this 21st day of August 1889.

Thomas Crean

Witnesses:

Thos. McMahan
J. P. Thornburg
W. E. Debill

[Page 449 con't]

CYNTHIA L. HAIR

Last Will and Testament of Mrs. Cynthia L. Hair

I, Cynthia L. Hair wife of Larkin Hair of Hamilton County, Tenn. do make and publish this as my last will and testament hereby revoking all other wills by me at any time made or published.

1. First I direct that all my just debts if any and my funeral expenses be paid by my executor hereinafter named as soon as convenient after my death by or and with the property or money of which I may die seized and possessed.

2 Second - I give devise and bequeath to my beloved husband Larkin Hair for and during his natural life all the rest residue of my property real personal mixed (after payment of said debts & funeral expenses) which I may own or be entitled to at my death and I give to my said husband full, absolute and perfect possession and contrive thereof with the right and authority to use, occupy, rent, lease, sell, and convey or otherwise dispose of the same or any part thereof in any manner he may wish.

3 Third - It is my will and desire that after the death of my said Husband all the residue of my said property not consumed under the first and second [Page 450] items or clauses of this will, shall be equally divided among my legatees herein after named and I hereby direct my executor to divide the same in such manner as he may think best for the interests of all concerned and give to each in the following proportion to wit: To N. R. Hair of Soddy, Tenn, one sixth; To John Hair of Soddy, Tenn, one sixth; To Mrs. Isabella Hair Carter former wife of John Carter of Soddy, Tenn, one sixth; To W. H. Barnes of Coal Creek, Tenn, one sixth; To George R. Barnes of Retro, Tenn. one sixth; and to my good friend and companion Miss Carrie Blanch Basinger the remaining one sixth of all my said property.

4 Fourth - I nominate and appoint James A. Caldwell of Chattanooga, Tenn. Executor of this my last will and Testament and hereby release and relieve him from executing bond for the faithful performance of the duties of Executor. In testimony whereof I hereto sign my name and affix my seal this 7th Feb'y 1890.

Cynthia L. Hair {Seal}

The foregoing paper was signed by the testator in our presence and at her request we sign our names as witnesses to her signature in her presence and in the presence of each other this 11th day of Feb'y 1890.

J. B. Nicklin

L. M. Clark

[Page 451]

D. A. REID

Last Will and Testament of D. A. Reid

Hot Springs Arkansas
June 19/1888

I, D. A. Reid being in my sound mind do hereby give bequeath and bequest at my death all my entire property consisting of lands, money and notes to my beloved wife Ella C. Reid of Chattanooga, Tenn.

D. A. Reid

Witnesses: Jerry M. Sullivan
                    Sam H. Amis
Done at Hot Springs, Arkansas June 19, 1888.

ALBERTA L. STUTENWROTH

Last Will and Testament of Alberta L. Stutenwroth

I, Alberta L. Stutenwroth of the City of Watertown in the County of Codington and Territory of Dekota, declare this to be my last will and Testament.

1. I give and bequeath to my mother Acquennette E. Walker an annuity of fifty ($50.00) Dollars to be paid her on the 1st of January of each and every year so long as she may live.

2. I give and bequeath to my son Charles William, the sum of one thousand ($1000.00) Dollars, the said sum to be paid him at his maturity, with the wish that the same be used for furthering his education or toward the attainment of a profession.

3. I give and bequeath to each of my two brothers Adelbert and Charles P. and my sister Elizabeth Susan the sum of one hundred ($100.00) Dollars, the same to be expended by my executor in the purchase of suitable mementos of my love for them.

4. All the rest, residue and remainder of my real estate, I devise and bequeath to my husband Charles [Page 452] W. Stutenwroth, his heirs Executors Administrator and assigns absolutely forever.

5. I appoint my husband Charles W. Stutenwroth executor of this my will this 26 day of April 1889.

Alberta L. Stutenwroth

Acknowledged by the testator to each of us to have been subscribed by her, and at the same time declared by her to us to be her last will and Testament and thereupon we at the request of the Testator sign our names hereto as witnesses, this 26 day of April 1889 at 2:30 PM

Jessie M. Barnard - Watertown Dakota

Nellie E. Dodds - Watrtown Dakota

Filed May 28th A.D. 1889 in the Office of the Probate Court for Codington County D.T.

J. M. Weedon

Judge of Probate

Recorded in Will Record Page 14

J. M. Weedon Probate Judge

[Page 452 con't]

ISAAC LOWENBURG

Last Will and testament of Isaac Lowenburg

I, Isaac Lowenburg of the City of Natchez, County of Adams and State of Mississippi, being of sound and disposing mind and memory and being aware of the uncertainity of this life, do make ordain and publish this my last will and Testament.

First I appoint Henry Frank, Col. Tillman and my son Simeon H. Lowenburg executors of this my last will and testament, and it is my last will and testament wish that they be not required to give any bond.

Second, I desire that my just debts be paid as speedily as possible.

Third, being indebted to my three children by my first wife, viz: Clara, Simeon H. and Helen in the sum of fifteen thousand Dollars principal and interest, on amount of the Legacy left them [Page 453] by John Hill. I give and bequeath to each of them the sum of Five Thousand Dollars. Five Thousand of this amount to be paid them out of my life insurance in the Manhattan Life Insurance Company which policy was taken out in the name of my first wife Ophelia, the mother of said children and its balance of Ten Thousand Dollars to be paid out of my estate, but if it should be detrimental to the business of I. Lowenburg & Co. to pay this amount then it is my desire that this amount of ten Thousand Dollars be not paid until the business of I. Lowenburg & Co. be wound up.

Fourth. In as much as the firm of I. Lowenburg & Co. which firm is composed of myself and C. L. Tillman. I owning two thirds the said C. L. Tillman one third cannot be wound up and closed at once in the event of my death, without great loss and sacrifice, therefore in order that said business may be carried on after my death, until such time as the said business can be safely and without sacrifice or loss wound up, I give and bequeath to the said C. L. Tillman, all my interest in said business for that purpose, hereby authorizing and empowering him to carry on said business in the name of I. Lowenburg, & Co. and to that end to buy and sell and receive and receipt and to pay all debts contracted in said name until such time as said business can be closed without injury or loss to my estate but said time is not to extend beyond two years from the date of my death, and after my death if it should occur before this first of June 1889, the profits of said business to be equally divided between said Tillman and my estate, notwith-standing the capital of each is not equal, the date from which the equal division of the profits is to be made is the 1st of June 1888, this difference of profits being allowed the said Tillman for his services in managing the business and he is not required to give any bond.

Fifth I give and bequeath to my beloved wife Molcie Lowenburg my life [Page 454] Insurance in the Commecticut Mutual Life for five Thousand dollars represented by policy 122,647.

Sixth I give and devise to my beloved wife Molcie Lowenburg the Store house now occupied by I. Lowenburg & Co. No. 503 Franklin Street in said City of Natchez, subject to the debt of about Three Thousand five hundred dollars due on it and I wish her to pay said debt outof the money coming to her from my life Insuracne policy in Connecticut Mutual Life and not to be paid out of any other part of my estate.

Seventh I give and bequeath to my four children Clara, Simeon H., Helen and Jack in equal parts between them, all my interest in the business of I. Lowenthal & Co. [sic] to be ascertained and paid over to them when said business is wound up. But if it should take any portion of my interest in said business to pay any debts due by me, or to pay any portion of ten Thousand Dollars bequeathed in the third clause of the will to my said Children Clara, Simeon H., & Helen, in settlement of the amount due them on account of the Legacy left them by John Hill, then said debts and said Legacy of ten thousand dollars are to be paid in full out of said interest and the residue of said interest if any is to be equally divided beween my

four children above named. It is intended that the interest in said business of I. Lowenburg & Co. shall include all personal property and assetts of every kind belonging to said firm when the same is wound up.

Eight I give and devise and bequeath the rest and residue of my personal estate if any to my four children above named in equal parts between them.

Ninth All the rest and residue of my real estate wheresoever situated situated [sic] I give and devise to my Executor in Trust for my four children above named giving my said Executors full power and [Page 455] athority [sic] to sell any and all of my said Real Estate at their discretion for cash, or on credit and to execute warranty deeds therefore and to pay over their portion of this proceeds of said sales to those who are of age, and that portion belonging to the minors to be paid over to their legal guardian and if any portion of said Real Estate should remain unsold when the youngest child becomes of age, then said Executors or the Survivors of them shall convey said property to said children or their heirs or assigns. Witness my hand the 9th day of July 1888.

Isaac Lowenburg

Signed, published and declared by the said Isaac Lowenburg as and for his last will and testament, in the presence of us the undersigned who in his presence and at his request and in the presence of each other have hereto subscribed our names as witnesses hereto this 9th day of July 1888.

Isaac Lowe
Claude Purlard

Filed in my office September 10, 1888 for probate.
Allison H. Foster, Clerk.

[Page 455 con't]

HARRIET E. BAILEY

Last Will and Testament of Harriet E. Bailey

Hereby revoking all wills or codicils by me at anytime heretofore made I Harriet E. Bailey hereby make publish and declare my last will and Testament to be as follows:

Item 1st - My executor herein after named shall pay all my just debts including funeral expenses.

Item 2nd - The residue of my Estate I hereby devise and bequeath to Charles & Kelsey Starks, children of my brother Charles Starks. I think the correct names are Charles & Kelsey but entered the two oldest children of my said brother, who were living with me when my brother [Page 456] was living with me about two years since.

Item 3 - I hereby appoint James P. Fyffe my Executor of this will waive bond and affidavit as such and empower him to sell all property of which I may die seized without advertisement at private or public sale, authorize him as such to make a deed or deeds take notes or otherwise as he thinks to be interest of my said legatees & pay over the proceeds to such guardian or guardians as may be appointed for said children after paying himself the legal fees for his Services.

This May 20, 1889

Harriet E. X Bailey {seal}
her mark

Signed Sealed published and declared to be her last will and Testament by Mrs. Harriet E. Bailey in our presence & we sign this in her presence & that of each other at her request this May 20th 1889.

Giles Adams
Will X Lawrence
his mark
Mandy X Bowlin
her mark

Attest Tom Fort

[Page 456 con't]

SUSAN NEWBY

Last Will and Testament of Susan Newby

I, Susan Newby of Ridgedale, Hamilton Co. Tenn. being aware of the uncertainty of life and in failing health, but of sound mind and memory do make and declare this to be my last will and testament in manor following to wit:

First, I devise and bequeath I give devise and bequeath to Katie Lauter The parlour furniture, vases and carpet. I give devise and bequeath to Mrs. Sarah Lauter all my dishes and china ware.

I give devise and bequeath to Charles Whitcomb The bed and Bedding and all the furniture belonging to his room also the two clocks and refrigerator.

[Page 457] I give devise and bequeath to R. P. Johnson all my medical books.

I give devise and bequeath to Amandus Lauter Three hundred Dollars credit on the seven hundred Dollars I loaned him some weeks ago from the money received from the Hurst note left at First National Bank.

The remaining four hundred dollars to be paid to my Executor. I devise my house sold soon as thought best by my Executor after all just debts and funeral expenses are paid. I give to Ida Carlie one hundred Dollars I give and bequeath to Mary after the above bequeaths are satisfied. I give and bequeath to my brother F. A. Mariner one third of the money in hands of my Executor. I give and bequeath to Sarah Lauter one third of the money and I give and bequeath to Chas. Whitcomb the remaining one third.

Of the many articles not mentioned in this instrument I devise my Executor to have entire control and to distribute as he thinks just to those already mention in this will.

I nominate and appoint Dr. R. P. Johnson as Executor of this my last will and Testament.

In witness whereof I Susan Newby in this my last will and testament have hereunto set my hand and seal this 25th day of April 1889.

Susan E. X Newby {seal}
her mark

Signed Sealed and declivered by Susan Newby as and for her last will and Testament in presence of us who at her request and in her presence and each others presence have subscribed our names as witnesses.

R. P. Johnson
Mrs. Mary Klassie
Mariana H. Johnson

[Page 458]

NANCY P. HOUSE

Last Will and testament of Nancy P. House

State of Tennessee)
Hamilton County) Know all men by these presents. That I Nancy Presley House do this day make my last will and Testament. I give and bequeath to my colored Mrs. Mary Coffin one bed and one quilt with the same. I further give and bequeath unto my s^d nurs [sic] Mary Coffin, one hundred dollars out of my estate besides her wages. I allso [sic] give and bequeath well to the the [sic] associate reform In. Macl. Church in North Carolina Two hundred Dollars to be pade [sic] out of the proceed of my farm when sold, for the benefit of any that is in nede [sic]. I give and bequeath unto my daughter Jane Roberson one bed and necessary bed clothing and I further bequeath that all my real estate and household and kitchen furniture and all personal property be sold after my death for the

benefit of my afflicted daughter Jane Roberson during her natural life and at her death the remainder to go to my People after all necessary expenses is pade [sic]. I futher desire and do appoint W. T. Walker as executor of my estate. I further appoint W. T. Walker as guardian of my afflicted daguther Jane Roberson knowing that she is not competent to take care of herself and to take care of her own interest. I further desire that he W. T. Walker provide a suitable house for her and see that she is treated well in every way. I desire that W. T. Walker as gardin [sic] place my daughter Jane in the care of Cyntha House wife of G. W. House, make that her hirue[sic] as long as treated well and that he W. T. Walker, pay them for ther troubles a resonable compensation. I place all confidence in W. T. Walker, believing he will act faithfully in the discharge of his duty as Executor of my estate and guardian for my daughter Jane Roberson. I hereby release him from any bond and trust to his honor to act faithfully and the he be allowed a resal [sic] compensation for his service. Signed in the presence of --- this this the first day of January 1891

Nancy P. X House {seal}
her mark

Witness: T. O. Hawley
            Hez. House

[Page 459]

Codicil to Will of Nancy P. House.

State of Tennessee)
Hamilton County) Know all persons by these present that I Nancy P. House did on the first day of January 1891 make my last will and Testament. I now desire to change a part of said will - first - that part in said will that I bequeathed Two Hundred Dollars to the Associated Reform Due West Church in North Carolina. I now revoke that portion of said will and I give and bequeath unto G. W. House Two hundred Dollars out of my estate, and and I further change said will I desire that my daughter Jane Roberson kape [sic] for her benefit while living my milch cow, one trunk, one rocker, one carpet and after her death I bequeath the same to Cynthia House the rest of said will. I desire to stand as the being all change I desire to make.

Witness my hand and seal this the 30th day of March 1891

Nancy P. X House
her mark

Witness: John X Dukes
                his mark

May Cefon.
Will probated May 1891.

[Page 459 con't]

SARAH McKAHNN

Copy of will of Sarah McKahnn - Deceased

In the name of the benevolent Father of all, I, Sarah McKahnn being of sound mind and memory do hereby make and publish this as my last will and testament.

Whereas William McKahnn my late husband now deceased, did on the 27th day of August 1862, make and publish his last will and Testament and did thereby devise and bequeath to myself and our son Thomas McKahnn the west half of northwest quarter of Section 33 Town 12 Range 2 East containing eighty (80) acres of land in Darke County Ohio, and also all his personal property goods and chattel (reference here being made to said will of Wm. Kahnn Dec^d) for and during the period of my natural life, and after my death to pass to our said son Thomas McKahnn [Page 460] and to his heirs forever. And whereas myself and my said Thomas joined in selling and conveying by deed in fee simple said lands to one David Noggle, which deed was executed on the 28th day of July 1875 and recorded in Book 68 page 12 of the records of deeds in said county and whereas it is the desire of myself and my said son Thomas that said David Noggle nor his grantees shall ever be disturbed with regard to the Title to said lands, for which he has heretofore paid us the full value therefore to wit, the full sum of $5000.00 and whereas it is my desire that after my decease, my said son Thomas shall have all my estate after my just debts if any should then exist therefore.

Item 1st I give and devise to my said son Thomas McKahnn at my decease all the estate both personal and real of every kind and character to be his absolutely to him and to his heirs forever.

Item 2nd. That in order to husband and protect my estate if any should remain after my decease I hereby declare that I am not indebted at this date to any of my other children or to any of my legal heirs or sons in law, in any sum of money whatever. I do hereby nominate and appoint my esteemed friend George W. Moore to be executor of this my last will and Testament this Jan. 18th 1883.

Sarah X McKahnn
her mark

Signed and acknowledged by Sarah McKahnn as her last will and testament in our presence and signed by us in her presence]

                        John Beers
                        L. E. Chenoiveth

Certificate to Will of Sarah McKahnn deceased. The State of Ohio, Darke County S.S.
                        J. L. C. Anderson S.Cle

[Page 461] Judge and Ex-officio Clerk of the Probate Court within and for the said County, do hereby certify that this foregoing is a true copy of the last will and Testament of Sarah McKahnn late of said Darke County, Ohio deceased as the same remains on file and probate (and record) in said Court, and in my custody. In witness whereof I have hereunto set my hand and affixed the seal of said Probate Court at Greenville Ohio, this 11th day of May A.D. 1891

                        L. C. Anderson
                        Probate Jude & Ex Officio Clerk

By C. W. Perry Deputy Clerk Will Probated May 8th 1891
Will recorded Vol F page 206
Filed May 19/91 Ent. Vol 8 page 271

[Page 461 con't]

LAURA L. CHAMBERS

Last Will and testament of Laura L. Chambers

I, Laura L. Chambers do hereby will, that at my death my husband Henry A. Chambers shall have during his life all of my property both real and personal.

At the death of Henry A. Chambers all the property of every kind shall go to our son and only child Joseph P. Chambers.

I give said Henry A. Chambers the control of the property, because of my belief that he will do what is best for our child.

If he the said Henry A. Chambers desires to give any of my personal property to any relative or friend of his or ours he is at liberty to do so and I will suggest that my piano be sold. I desire that my wearing appearel be utelized in some way. That is such as my immediate family do not care particularly for. "The poor ye have always with you."

                        Laura L. Chambers

At the request of Mrs. Laura L. Chambers [Page 462] and

in her presence and in the presence of each other we hereto sign our names as witnesses to her will.
                        Kate Key
                        Margaret Key

Chattanooga, Tennessee June 2nd 1890

                        - Codicil -

I, Laura L. Chambers do make this codicil to to [sic] the will by me heretofore made. That is, I make my husband Henry A. Chambers the Trustee to take charge of and manage my real estate in the full authority to sell the same and convey it to the purchasers but he is charged with the duty of reinvesting the proceeds according to his best judgment and discretion, said Chambers is to have the remain use and and [sic] profits thereof during his natural life, and at his death the entire interest and estate therein shall go to our son Joseph P. Chambers in fee simple sales and reinvestments may be made as after by said Chambers trustee as aforesaid as after as he may deem necessary for his interest and the interest of our said son Joseph P. Chambers.

                        Laura L. Chambers

At the request of Mrs. Laura L. Chambers and in her presence and in the presence of each other we hereto sign our names as witnesses to this codicil to her will.
This 34rd day of June 1891
                        Kate Key
                        Margaret Key

Probated June 8, 1891

[Page 463]

GEORGE E. STEPHENS

Will of Geo. E. Stephens

I, George E. Stephens of Hamilton County, State of Tennessee do make and publish my last will and Testament.

First - To my children Hattie May, Myra Claire, Mildred and Marian, I give nothing but either of chattels or realty but commend them to the care of their mother.

Second To my wife Emma Elizabeth I give bequeath & devise all of my property whether real or personal to be hers absolutely in fee simple and to be held or conveyed by her and her heirs & assigns forever.

Third I hereby appoint and nominate my said wife to be the Executrix of this my last will.

Fourth I hereby revoke all other wills made by me.

Signed, published and declared by the said testator Geo. E. Stephens to be his last will in our presence and hearing and we have signed our names hereto as witnesses thereof in his presence & at his request. Done at East End Hamilton County, Tennessee this April A.D. 1891.

Geo. E. Stephens

Witnesses:
J. D. McPherson
W. T. Tyler

[Page 463 con't]

MAGGIE HAGERTY

Will of Mrs. Maggie Hagerty

State of Tennessee }
Hamilton County   }   Know all men by these presents that I, Maggie Hagerty widow of Chattanooga in the County and State aforesaid, do hereby make this my last will and testament, hereby revoking any and all other wills, that I may have heretofore made.

Item I give devise and bequeath all my estate and property of every kind and description, real and personal whereever located to my beloved son Johnnie Hagerty, he being my only child to him and his heirs forever. But if my said son should die before attaining [page 464] his majority or 21 years of age, then it is my wish that said property or so much as may remain thereof go to my beloved mother Mary O'Rourke and I so will and devise.

Item, I hereby appoint my sister Mrs Mary Hagerty Executor of this my last will and testament & guardian of my son Johnnie.

In witness whereof I have signed and sealed and published and declare this instrument as my last will and testament at Chattanooga this 14th day of November 1890.

Mrs. Maggie Hagerty {seal}

The said Maggie Hagerty at Chattanooga on said 14th day of November 1890 signed & sealed this Instrument and published and declared the same as and for her last will and Testament, and we at her request and in her presence and in the presence of each other have hereunto written our names as subscribing witnesses.

W. T. Capehart
Cecilia Capehart

Filed June 22, 1891

[Page 464 con't]

ANN LEONORA WEAVER

Will of Ann Leonora Weaver

In the name of God Amen. I Ann Leonora Weaver being of sound mind and memory do make this my last will and Testament.

Unto my beloved sister Claudia W. McCall (formerly Weaver) I give and bequeath one half of my undivided on[e] third interest in the following described property lying and being in the City of Chattanooga County of Hamilton and State of Tennessee by the North twenty six feet of the north half lot (45) forty five on Cypress Street in the City of Chattanooga, said lot fronting Twenty six feet on Cypress Street, and receiving back of uniform width westwardly to the line of the North east quarter of Sec. (29) twenty nine, dividing said [Page 465] quarter of said section. The north line of said lot being about (140) one hundred and forty feet and the south line (150 2/5) one hundred and fifty and two fifth feet respectively. I also give to my said sister Claudia W. McCall one-half of my widowed one third interest in all the furniture and personal property contained in said house and lot above described.

Unto to my beloved sister Florida G. Weaver I give and queath [sic] during her natural life and at her decease unto my sister Claudia W. McCall forever in fee simple one-half of my undivided one third interest in all of the above described real estate and personal property.

The property named in this my last will and testament shall not be appropriated to the payment of any debt or liability of the present or future husband of either of my sisters named in this instrument.

I nominate and appoint my newphew [sic] Howard E. W. Palmer executor of this my last will and testament. I appoint my newphew [sic] H. E. W. Palmer Trustee of my aforesaid sister F. G. Weaver.

Given under my hand and seal this 30th day of December 1886 - in the presence of D. G. Curtis, Alice Willingham, Maggie McBrown.

Ann L. Weaver

D. G. Curtis   }
Alice Willingham }   Witnesses
Maggie Mc Brown }

I Ann Leonora Weaver, also will that one-third interest of a tract of land, lying in the City of

Greenesboro, GA bounded on the north by land of Mrs. Mary Tunison, on the south by the land of James L. Brown, on the east by land of W. M. Weaver and on the west by GA. R. R. to be sold & the proceeds of the sale to be given to Francis R. Williams, W. D. & Mary Greenwood Weaver, the widow & children of my deceased brother Henry C. Weaver.

[Page 466] Given under my hand & seal this 30th day December 1886 in the presence of D. G. Curtis, Alice Willingham & Maggie McBrown

Anna L. Weaver {L.S.}

D. G. Curtis }
Alice Willingham } Witnesses
Maggie McBroom }

[Page 466 con't]

MATTIE SLAUGHTER

Will of Mattie Slaughter

State of Tennessee - Hamilton County
May 1st 1891

I, Martha Slaughter do make and publish this as my last will & testament hereby revoking and making void all other wills by me at any time made.

First - I direct that my funeral expenses and all my debts be paid as soon after my death as possible out of any moneys that I may die possessed of or every first came into the hands of my executor.

Secondly - I give and bequeath to my son Wm. Melvin Selcer all of my property both real and personal and he to have from my death all the income that may arrive from said property until he is twenty three years old and at the time he becomes twenty three years old he is to have full controll of said property.

Thirdly - The Executor may pay out of said incomes, for any providential occurances that may happen to said Wm. Melvin Selcer.

Fourthly - If my son Wm. Melvin Selcer should die without bodily heirs. I then bequeath said property to my brothers & sisters.

Lastly - I do hereby nominate & appoint W. J. Moore my executor in witness here of I do to this my will set my hand & seal this 9th day of may 1891.

Mattie Slaughter

Signed, Sealed & published in my presence and we have

subscribed our names hereto in the presence of the testator. This 9th day of May 1891.

A. W. Duncan
T. B. McKinley

[Page 467]

HIRAM PENDERGRASS

Will of Hiram Pendergrass

I, Hiram Pendergrass, of Sale Creek in the County of Hamilton, and State of Tennessee, being of sound and disposing mind and memory, do make, publish, and declare, this, to be my last will and testament hereby revoking all former wills by me at any time heretofore made.

As as to my wordly estate and all the property, real, personal or mixed, of which I shall die seized and possessed, or to which I shall be entitled at the time of my decease. I devise, bequeath and dispose thereof in the manner following to wit:

My will is, that all my just debts and funeral expenses shall by executors hereinafter named be paid out of my estate as soon after my decease as shall by them be found convenient.

I give devise and bequeath to my beloved wife Mary Pendergrass, all my household furniture and also one hundred dollars in money to be paid her by my executors hereinafter named within six months after my decease. To have and to hold this same to her and her executors administrators and assigns forever.

All the real and residue of my estate, real, personal and mixed of which I shall die seized and possessed or to which I shall be entitled at my decease - I give devise and bequeath - after my executors herein after named shall have sold all my real, personal and mixed property, that the money be equally divided between or amongst these my children.

And lastly I do nominate and appoint William Griffiths and William M. Beene to be the executors of this my last will and testament.

In witness whereof I the said Hiram Pendergrass have to this my last will and testament, consisting [Page 468] of one sheet of paper, subscribed my name this the 26th day of February in the year of our Lord one thousand eight hundred and ninety one.

H. Pendergrass {seal}

Signed, published and declared by the said Hiram Pendergrass as and for his last will and Testament in the presence of us who at his request and in his presence and in the presence of each other, have subscribed our names as witnesses thereto:

Peter Bolton
David R. Griffiths

[Page 468 con't]

JOHN S. DEAN

Will of John S. Dean

Know all men by these presents That I, John S. Dean of the City of Chattanooga, Hamilton County Tennessee, considering the uncertainty of this life, and being of sound mind and memory do make, declare and publish this my last will and Testament.

First - I direct that all my just debts and obligations may be paid and discharged in full.

Second - I give and bequeath to my mother Mrs. J. Dean of Penkridge, Stafford England all of my estate both real and personal of every kind and description whatsoever of which I may die seized and possessed or to which I may be in any way entitled to have and to hold to her in fee simple for her full and sole use and behoof to dispose of as she may deem best excepting and provided always that my partnership agreement entered into with my partner F. C. Cotton regarding the settlement of our partnership affairs is not to be disturbed affected or in any way changed by this bequest but She shall take said property here by bequeath her subject to the conditions of said agreement.

Third - I nominate and appoint [Page 469] E. Y Chapin Attorney at law of Chattanooga, Tennessee to be the Executor of this my last will and Testament. In testimony whereof I have hereunto this my last will and Testament, contained on three pages of legal cap paper including the attestation by witnesses thereto affixed my hand and seal this 7th day of July 1891.

John S. Dean
By W. C. Aull

Signed sealed and declared published by the said John S. Dean as and for his last will and Testament, in the presence of us who at his request and in his presence and in the presence of each other have subscribed our names as witnesses hereto this 7th day of July 1391.

D. C. Warner
W. C. Aull

[Page 469 con't]

MARY JANE WILLIAMS

I Mary Jane Williams, of Hamilton County, Tennessee do make and publish this my last will and Testament.

1st - I direct that my body be decently buried in a becoming way of Christian manner.

2 - I direct that my funeral expenses and debts of any are owing be paid out of any money which may be on hand at the time of my death or which may thereafter be realized from collections of any debts due me, or the Sale of any of my personal property. Should my personal assets be insufficient to pay my debts, funeral expenses and the expenses of administration then I give to my executor in order to raise money to pay the same the power to sell any other property of which I may die seized and possessed except that herein given to my grand daughter.

The Executor shall be the sole judge as to which it is best to sell, and the purchaser shall take a good title to any which he may decide to sell with the execution above stated.

3 - All my personal effects of every character and description, including money debts due me [Page 470] or any other kind of personal property assets and effects which I may own at my death, and which are not consumed in the payment of debts funeral expenses or expenses of adminis-tration and any real estate not herein specifically devised, of any I may own. I give to B. F. Fritts of Chattanooga, Tennessee in Trust for my daughter Sallie Pope Stewart to her sole and separate use, free from the debts, contracts control or marital rights of her present or any future husbands. Said Trustee shall have power to use the interest or other income arising from the property described in this clause of this will or to use the corpus as he sees fit for the use and benefit of my said daughter, and that of her children living with her and constitute along part of her family.

4 - I hereby give to said B. F. Fritts, Trustee the following real estate situated in Hamilton County, Tennessee in Range four (4) Township one (1) North and west of the basis line in the Ocoee District and north of south Chickamauga Creek Viz First - one hundred and forty (140) acres more or less of land being the north west fractional quarter of Section Thirty-five (35).

Secondly - Two (2) acres, being the south west fractional quarter of section twenty Six (26) except about Twenty-five acres of the two above tracts which is taken by the Cincinnati Southern Railway.

Thirdly - Forty two (42) acres of land more or less being the north east fractional of Section (34) Thirty-four.

Fourthly - Fifty two and one half (52 1/2) acres

being the west half of the south west fractional quarter of Section Twenty-Five (25) being of upper bottom.

Fifthly - One hundred & sixty (160) acres of land more or less being the north west quarter of Section Thirty Six (36) on which my dwelling house is situated, except the lot containing about (5) five acres given my grand daughter Mary Webb wife of George W. Webb and in which they are now living.

Sixthly - Eighty (80) acres of land more or less [Page 471] being the west half of the northeast quarter of Section Thirty Six (36) and known as the MilliReic [sic] fifty one (51) acres.

Seventhly - A strip of land on the lap line of about Fifty (50) or Sixty (60) acres extending from Sively's line to John Rings line half a mile, and it is it lies broad side of the MiliReic Eighty (50) [sic] acre tract and is the east fractional quarter of section thirty six (36) it being made a fraction by the lap line lapping over on it.

The parcels containing respectively one hundred amd forty (140) - Two (2) - Forty-two (42) - and one hundred and sixty (160) acres, in all, three hundred and forty four (344) acres, constituted the original Wayland farm, and descended to me from my Father Thomas Crutchfield and was allotted to me in the partition of his estate. Fifty-two and one half (52 1/2) acres were purchased with my money from James A. Whitesides. The MilliRiec tract containing eighty (80) acres was acquired with other lands descended to my. The Fifty (50) acres or Sixty (60) acres was a part of the Callaway lands and was allotted to me as a part of my interest in my father's Estate.

All of the lands described in this (the fourth) clause of this will are given in trust to said Fritts together with the rents profits and proceeds and exclusive use and benefit of my said daughter for and during her natural life, free from the debts, contracts, maratal [sic] rights and control of her present or any future husband. The fee simple title or accumulated interest on said lands I devise to all of the children which said Sallie Pope Stewart now has or may hereafter have born of her body, share and share alike as herewith in common. Should any of said children die during the lifetime of said Sallie Pope Stewart, leaving a child or children, such child or children shall step in the shoes of and represent his, her or their parents. Should any of said children marry and die childless [Page 472] before the death of said Sallie Pope Stewart, it is not my intention that the husband or wife of such married child shall take any interest in the share of the deceased husband or wife but such share shall go exclusively to the person or persons, sustaining the relations of heir or heirs at law to such deceased husband and wife. Said Trustee being thereunto authorized by a proper decree of a court of Chancery shall have the power to sell any property

herein devised and reinvest the proceeds, the new investment to be held in trust in like manner as the property sold. The purchaser shall not be responsible for the application of the purchase money but it shall be the duty of the Court to see that the same is invested, so as to provide an income for the life tenant and preserve the corpus for the remainder in all. Should B. F. Fritts fail or refuse to accept the position of Executor and Trustee under this will or if the position should thereafter become vacant by death, resignation or otherwise then a Court of Competent jurisdiction, shall appoint an Executor or Trustee and when so appointed and qualified the title to the trust property shall vest in him and he shall possess and exercise all the powers and be charged with all the duties herein conferred and imposed on the original Trustee.

5 - I have given to my grand-daughter Mary Webb wife of George W. Webb a parcel of about five (5) acres of land on which to build a house but have not yet conveyed the same should it not be laid off and conveyed before my death. I hereby authorized my executor or Trustee Mr. B. F. Fritts to have laid off five (5) acres including said house, in the most suitable shape and I hereby authorize my Executor and Trustee to convey the same to her sole and separate use free from the debts, contracts or marital rights of her present or any future husband. The land to be thus conveyed [Page 473] in excepted out of the land herein devised to Mrs. Stewart.

6 - This Instrument occupying two pages in type writing and concluding on the third, the two pages being identified by my signature written on the margin. I do hereby declare to be my last will and Testament and do subscribe my name thereto as such in the presence of witnessess who witness the same at my special instance and request this the day ___ of January 1891.

Mary Jane Williams

The foregoing last will and testament of Mary Jane Williams was signed by the testatrix in our presence when she acknowledged the same to be her last will and testament and specially requested us to witness the same and as such witnesses we do hereunto subscribe our names in her presence and in presence of each other this the 11th day of March 1891.

Thomas W. Crutchfield
Sarah L. Crutchfield
Ismar Noa
Dr. H. Berlin

[Page 474]

JOHN WILLIAM BANKS

Will of John William Banks

I, John William Banks, being mindful of the uncertainty of life and the certainty of death, and being of sound mind and disposing memory do make and publish this as my last will and Testament.

It is my will that after my death, my body be buried at Forsythe GA, with as little expense as possible. After payment of Funeral Expenses and such small sums as I may owe.

It is my will and desire that my wife Ellas W. Banks, shall have all my property of every character, wherever situated and I devise and bequeath the same to her. I desire that she be appointed executor of this my last will and Testament without bond which she will not be required to give. It is also my will and desire that she be appointed guardian of our children who on my death will be entitled to the benefits of certain Insurance Policies which I have carried for their benefit and in their names.

It is also my will desire and direction that she be excused from and not required to give bond as such guardian.

Witness my hand this June 20th 1891. The Insurance money left my wife and children is not to be used to pay and [sic] debts.

John William Bankes**

We the undersigned witnesses in the presence of the testator and of each other and at his request have signed this will as witnesses he signing it in our presence and acknowledging it to be his las will and Testament this June 20th 1891.

R. M. Barton, Jr.
W. A. Willlingham
M. J. Willingham

** both Banks and Bankes spellings are used here.

[Page 475]

JAMES A. WARDER

Will of James A. Warder

I James A. Warder do make & publish this my last will & Testament.
1st - I desire all my debts paid.

2nd - I will and hereby bequeath all of my property real and personal and mixed to my my [sic] wife Laura D. Warder.

I appoint Laura D. Warder my executor without bond.

I have signed this & placed it among my valuable papers. June 4, 1891

Jas. A. Warder

Probated Augt 3, 1891

ALICE PATTERSON

Will of Alice Patterson

State of Tennessee }
Hamilton County } I, Alice Patterson, do hereby make this my last will and Testament. I am of sound mind but sick and know that I cannot live but a short time. I want Newton Smith to take charge of my remains and all my personal property as he has been very kind to me in my last sickness. I want him to be first paid, then pay to A. G. S. Rhodes & Co. the amount I owe for furniture and if anything be left, I want my little grandaughter Frankie Cannon to have my wearing clothes, sewing machine and trunk if possible.

Signed this 12 day of Augt 1891

Alice X Patterson

Witnessed by :   Henry C. Collins
                    Has. Hurd
                    Wilson Lea

Probated Augt 24, 1891

[Page 476]

DRURY SCRUGGS

Certified Copy of Will of Drury Scruggs

I, Drury Scruggs of the County of Rutherford North Carolina, considering the uncertainity of my earthly existence, do make and declare this my last will and Testament in the manner and form following to wit: -

That is to say, First - That my executor hereinafter named shall provide for my body a decent burial suitable to the wishes of my relatives and friends, and pay all funeral expenses together with my just debts howsoever and to whomsoever owing out of the money that may first come to hand as part and parcel of my estate.

item: I wish the moneys gotten for my land, the three Thousand Dollar notes left with Lewis Shepherd**, shall be equally divided between my eight Legatees to wit: - Between C. S. W. Scruggs heirs S. C.; Chesterfield Scruggs S. C.; Thomas Scruggs Texas; Judson Scruggs, Ala; M. H. Camp, N. C.; heirs of C. C. Scruggs, Texas; Luther Scruggs Texas; P. E. McMath, Tex.; as my son D. D. Scruggs has had his part of my landed estate my personal estate I wish divided equally between my nine legatees - D. D. Scruggs getting his equal part of all except the notes for the land which is the three one thousand dollar notes left in the hands of L. Shepherd.

And lastly - I do hereby constitute and appoint my trusty friend Louis Shepherd my lawful executor to all interests and purposes to execute this my last will and Testament according to the true interest and receiving of the same and every part and clause thereof hereby revoking and declaring utterly void all former wills and Testaments by me herotofore [sic] made. Lewis Shepherd is my executor. In witness whereof I the said D. Scruggs do hereunto set my hand and seal this the 2nd day of December 1890.

D. Scruggs, {seal}

**Lewis and Louis are both used as spellings in this instrument.

[Page 477]

Signed, sealed, published and declared by the said D. S. to be his last will and Testament in the presence of us, who at his request and in his presence do subscribe our names.

John Philips
D. F. Wood
J. W. Camp

North Carolina }
Rutherford County } It is adjudged that the foregoing last will of Drury Scruggs has been duly proved it is ordered to be filed and recorded this May 20th 1891
J. F. Flack
Clerk Superior Court**

North Carolina }
Rutherford County } In the Supreme Court in action August 11th 1891 I, J. F. Flack, Clerk of the Supreme

Court of Rutherford County & State of North Carolina do hereby certify that the foregoing copy as contained and written on pages 2, 3 & 4 is a true and perfect copy of the last will & testament of Drury Scruggs as recorded on the Will Book in my office and the original of which is filed in my office & I further certify that the foregoing written on pages 1 & 2 is a true and perfect copy of the record of probate of said will as recorded in said office.

Witness my hand and seal of office this 11th day of August 1891.

{seal}　　　　J. F. Flack
　　　　　　　Clerk Supreme Court
　　　　　　　Rutherford County
　　　　　　　North Carolina

** Both Superior and Supreme Court are given in this instrument.

[Page 478]

B. B. BELL

Will of B. B. Bell

Know all men by these presents, That I Benjamin B. Bell of Chattanooga, Hamilton County, Tennessee being in sound mind and memory and mindful of the uncertainties of human life, do make and publish and declare this my last will and Testament, hereby revoking and making void all others by me at anytime made.

First - I direct that my funeral expenses and all my debts be paid as soon after my death as possible, out of any moneys, that I may die possessed of, or may first come unto the hands of my executors.

Second - I give devise and bequeath unto my beloved wife Martha Ann Bell all the residue of my property real, personal and mixed during her natural life or so long as she may remain my widow, with full authority to use and enjoy the same for her comfort or pleasure, and if necessary to her comfort and maintenance, she is authorized to use such portion of the principal or income as may be required to comfortably support & care for her during her natural life or so long as she shall remain my widow.

Third - It is my desire that my said wife Martha Ann Bell shall out of the income derived from my property devote such sums as may be necessary to educate my adopted son Willie B. Bell if he shall desire such education, but this request is not designed to deprive my said wife of a reasonable amount for her comfort and proper support.

Fourth - On the death of my wife Martha Ann Bell, or in the event of her marriage I give devise and bequeath all the residue of my property real and personal and mixed, unto my said adopted son Willie B. Bell and his heirs forever should he die leaving lawful heirs, but should he die without lawful issue, then at his death and the death of [Page 479] my wife Martha Ann Bell - I give devise and bequeath all and singular the residue of my property, real, personal and mixed unto the Woman Christian Association of Chattanooga and it successors as Trustee to be kept as a permanent fund and invested so as to produce the largest income possible consistent with safe investment and the income to be used perpetually for the support and maintenance of The Orphan Home for White Children. Said Orphan's Home being now owned and controlled by said Woman's Christian Association, my intention being to establish a permanent fund or endowment the income of which shall be forever devoted to the support of said Orphans Home.

Fifth - My said adopted son Willie B. Bell will be sixteen (16) years old on the 16th day of September 1891. I do not desire it best, that he should have possession and control of the property herein bequeathed to him in the event of my wife's death or marriage until he shall arrive at such mature years as to give full guarantee of his ability to manage and care for it successfully.

I therefore, hereby nominate constitute and appoint my friend Halbert B. Case as Trustee, to take possession of the property, real, personal and mixed as herein before bequeathed to my said adopted son, in the event of the death or marriage of my said wife Martha Ann Bell including all accumulation not used by her and to hold the same until my said adopted son Willie B. Bell shall arrive at the age of Twenty-five years.

And I hereby authorize and empower said Halbert B. Case as such Trustee to hold control improve and use said property and invest the money derived therefrom, or to sell and convey the same and reinvest the proceeds thereof if in his judgment it shall be for the interest of my said estate, and generally to do with said estate what in his judgement may be for the best interest of [Page 480-481 are blank - Page 482] said estate, and out of the income to be derived therefrom, he will pay from time to time to my said adopted son Willie B. Bell such sums as shall be necessary for his reasonable maintenance should he at anytime be unable to comfortably support himself, my object being to provide him a reasonable estate to enable him to carry on business with, when he arrives at such mature years as to enable him properly to manage the estate. Should my said adopted son desire to be educated, and show himself studious my said Trustee is hereby authorized and directed to devote such portions of the income from my said estate, as he may deem necessary to the payment of the expenses of such education. When my said adopted son Willie B. Bell shall arrive at the age of Twenty-five years it is made the duty of the said Halbert B. Case Trustee to deliver possession of said property, less the amounts then already paid him, together with the accumulations thereof, after deducting reasonable compensation for his services, to my said adopted son Willie B. Bell or to his heirs should he die leaving lawful issue before he arrives at said age of Twenty-five years.

Sixth - I hereby nominate constitute and appoint my wife Martha Ann Bell as the Executrix of this my last will and Testament and direct that no bond shall be required of her.

In witness whereof I do to this my will set my hand this the 16th day July AD 1891 and signed in the presence of Andrew J. Gahagan and Frank L. Case whom I have called to sign as witnesses in my presence and in the presence of each other.

B. B. Bell

Signed and published in our presence and we have subscribed our names hereto in the presence of the testator at his request and in the presence of each other this the 16th day of July AD 1891.

Andrew J. Gahagan
Frank L. Case

[Page 483]

SAVELDA HALLUM

Will of Savelda Hallum

I Savelda** Hallum being of sound mind and disposing memory, realizing the uncertainty of life, and the certainty of death and being desirous of disposing of my property & effects & giving and giving direction in regard thereto. Do hereby make and publish this my last will and Testament.

First - It is my will that my body be nicely buried in a neat case.

Second - I will and direct that my just debts & expenses be paid out of my estate, including furneral expenses.

Third - I will and bequeath to my husband Robert Hallum all my property real & personal wherever situate of every character of which I may die seized or possessed of, absolutely & in fee [sic].

Fourth - I hereby nominate my said husband Robert Hallum my executor with full power to collect & receive my personal property & debts due me as such executor or in his own right, either, and he will not be required to give bond or make settlement as Executor, the same being expressly waived.

In witness where of I have hereunto set my hand in the presence of ----- who witness this will at my request and in my presence and in the presence of each other they having been called by me to witness the same as my will this the 16th day of July 1891.

Sevrelda** Hallum

We witnessed the signature of Mrs. Sarelda** Hallum to the foregoing will at her request & in the presence of each other as stated above This July 16th 1891.

J. J. Clift
W. L. Templeton

Probated Sept. 8th 1891.

** Spelling varied on the name.

[Page 484]

BARNA POWELL

Will of Barna Powell

I Barna Powell of Parkersburg, West Va. being of lawful age, of sound mind and disposing memory do make and publish this my last will and Testament, hereby and expressly revoking all former wills and codicils heretofore made by me.

First - It is my will that my just debts be paid.

Second - I give and bequeath to my wife Anna, all my real and personal estate of every kind and description situated in West. VA., Tennessee and elsewhere, to have and to hold during her natural life, and with the power of selling the same and conveying any part thereof with covenants of general warranty and I desire that she may invest the proceeds thereof in other desirable estate, in the name of my estate and have the power of selling and conveying such real estate in the same manner and with convenants as above directed.

Third - After the death of my said wife, I give and devise all my estate both real and personal to my son Barna absolutely and in fee simple with the express provision that he enter into the possession thereof immediately upon the decease of his mother and without the intervention of a guardian in case he may still be a minor under the age of twenty-one years.

Fourth -In case my said son Barna should die

before his mother, I further bequeath to her all my real and personal estate absolutely in case she remains my widow subject to her disposal by will, and in case she should so survive, and my estate or any part of it should become invested in her by the terms of this will. I request that she dispose of it to suitable public use as the erecting of a public Hall, where reputable persons of liberal education and intelligence may be free to discuss all subjects of public interest, free and clear of all sectional bias or religious training so called and where the stage may be open for dramatic performances of all kinds calculated to promote sound morality and intel-lectual growth. but I do not impose these or any other condition [Page 485] for her disposal, as the amount of my estate, or other condition might make such a disposal thereof unadvisable and in much as this disposal contemplates a public benefit, she is at liberty to annex a condition or conditions, that the Town of [sic] City favored with such bequeast may manifest its interest by a generous aid to the object. One condition to any such bequest I recommend that is, that persons born in America without regard to race be first permitted to enjoy its benefits, where from any circumstances   some must be excluded from participating therein.

Fifth - I desire that my wife, as soon as the condition of my estate will warrant it and her judgment may approve it, purchase a farm and have the same conveyed to Rowena Holty such expenditure to be in the neighborhood of two thousand dollars, more or less according to my wife's judgment but this provision is not imperative but is wholly a matter of discretion on the part of my said wife and subject to her judgment.

Sixth - I hereby constitute and appoint my said wife Anna, executor of this my last will and Testament and direct that she may qualify as such without giving any bond or security without having any appraisal of my property without being required to make any settlement with the Probate board or other authority having jurisdiction of probate matters. The true interest and meaning of this provision being that my said wife is to succeed to and manage my estate without any hinderance or interference while she remains my widow, but in case she remarries I direct that all powers herein conferred shall cease, and in that event all powers herein conferred on her I expressly confer on my son Barna including the appointment as executor subject to the same conditions I have attached to and relating to my wife, and this appointment as executor is to take effect whether he he [sic] is under twenty one year or not.

Seventh - I desposing of my estate to my son [Page 486] Barna, under the third paragraph, above written. I further provide, that he shall have no power to sell, convey or incumber said Real Estate herein bequeathed or encumber the same or in any way make the same liable for any debts or obligations, until he shall have arrived at the full age of thirty-five years.

Eighth - In case I become the owner of other estate either real or personal before my death. I hereby bequeath and dispose of the same to my wife Anna and son Barna respectedy in the same manner and subject to the same restrictions and conditions, as I have and do herein bequeath the real and personal estate I now possess and this without regard to where it may be located, or its nature or character.

This paper is wholly in my own handwrite [sic] and deliberately considered before being reduced to writing and is believed to be plain and unequivocal in its provisions and written on one sheet.

Given under my hand as my last will and testament this 8th day of April 1889 at Parkersberg, [sic] W. VA.

Barna Powell

WILLIAM WALSH

Last Will and Testament of Wm Walsh

In the name of God. Amen. I William Walsh in the view of the uncertainty of life and the certainty of death, being now confined to my bed by sickness but of sound mind & disposing memory, do make and publish this my last Will and Testament revoking all others heretofore made by me.

Item 1 - I do give & bequeath to my beloved wife Mary E. Walsh all my property of every nature & kind, real, personal & mixed and I do hereby appoint my wife executrix of this my last will & testament and do also appoint her as Guardian of my little girl Katie Walsh and I also direct that she shall be relieved of giving bond either as Executrix or Guardian. Given under my hand & seal this September 21st 1891.

William Walsh

[Page 487]

We James Kickson & James W. Conroy & Pat Reeves do sign our name hereto as witnesses, in the presence of each other & the Testator William Walsh being called to witness this as the last will & Testament of said Wm Walsh by himself. This Sept. 21st 1891.

Witnesses: Pat Reeves
                    James Hickson
                    J. W. Conroy

Probated Oct. 14, 1891

AMOS GALLUPE

Will of Amos Gallupe

I A. R. Gallupe of Hamilton County, Tenn. being both of sound mind & body & of disposing memory do hereby make this my last will and Testament.

1st - I will & bequeath that all my debts be first paid out of any moneys I die possessed of or that may first come into the hands of my Executor.

2nd - I will & bequeath all the remainder of my property real & personal or mixed after my debts are paid to my beloved wife Sallie A. Gallupe during her life & at her death to Miss Maggie L. Campbell.

3 - I request that my Executor or Executrix employ Messrs. Clift & Clift Attorney to see that this my last will is carried out & to represent her in looking after my estate.

And I hereby appoint my beloved wife Sallie A. Gallupe my Executrix & in event of her death before me or the execution of this will then I appoint Miss Maggie L. Campbell my executrix and having full confidence in both neither will be required to vie bond as Executrix.

This the 9th day of Oct. 1878. Signed & sealed the day & date above written in the present of R. M. Tankesley & O. R. Lane who witness the same at my request.

                A. R. Gallupie**
      ** both spelllings used
Witness: R. M. Tankesley
                   O. R. Lane

Probated Oct. 23, 1891.

[Page 488]

JAMES H. DONAHUE

Will of James H. Donahue

I, James H. Donahue being feeble in body, but of sound and disposing mind, do make this my last will and Testament.

First - It is my desire, that I shall be decently buried, in a manner becoming my station in life and in keeping with my estate which I shall leave behind me.

Second - I desire that all my just debts, including

my funeral expenses & all debts of every kind & character, that I justly owe or for which my estate may be or become liable after my death, shall be first paid.

Third - After the payment of my just indebtedness, I will and bequeath all of my remaining property of every character & kind to my brothers Thomas Donahue & Stephen Donahue & my sisters Mary & Bessie both of whom are now married, but to who I am now enable to State in equal portions. That is to say, one fourth of my estate to each of my said brothers and sisters. If any one of my said brothers and or sisters be dead, then and in that event, I will and bequeath the portion that should go to them, to their or his or her heirs first to their children if any and then to my brothers and sisters to be equally divided between them.

Fourth - I nominate and appoint John E. Connor of Chattanooga, Tennessee as the Executor of this my last will and Testament & direct him to carry out the same as herein before devised and bequeathed.

Done in the City of Chattanooga, Tennessee on the 7th day of November 1891

J. H. Donahue

[Signed for him] J. H. Donahue by S. M. Adams by direction of the Testator. The above last will & Testament of James H. Donahue was signed in our presence by James H. Donahue & we here sign the same as witnesses in his presence and in presence of each other. This November 7, 1891.

S. M. Adams
C. P. Jones
Wm P. White

Probated Nov. 9th 1891

[Page 489]

RUTH AMELIA SHATTUCK

Will of Ruth Amelia Shattuck

I Ruth Amelia Shattuck being of sound and disposing mind, make this my last will and Testament. I will, devise and bequeath to my daughter Ruth Amelia Derr and husband George O. Shuttuck my house and lot, situate in Mount Pleasant Issabelle [Isabella] County, State of Michigan: Lot 1 Block S in Halls addition to said town of Mount Pleasant, to be jointly and equally their own property, to be sold at the option of the Executor of this my last will and Testament and the proceeds to be equally divided between my said husband and Daughter. I also will and bequeath my said daughter Ruth Amelia Derr, Lot No. 3 Block No. 3 in Barkster's Sub-division of

Ridgedale in the 5th Civil District of Hamilton County, Tennessee and this I desire to be considered in full liqudation of all dues to her as her guardian. In the event of my daughters death before her majority, then I desire that all of the foregoing property shall become the property of my said husband, except such part as shall be found due my daughter as her pension clause. I also will and bequeath to my said daughter my organ and sewing machine. I also hereby appoint my husband Geo. O. Shattuck the executor of this my last will and Testament without bond.

Witness my hand this 4th day of November 1891.

Ruth Amelia Shattuck

Witnesses: J. P. Smith
                 A. J. Cox

Probated Nov. 23, 1891

[Page 490]

J. M. FRAER

Will of J. M. Fraer

I J. M. Fraer of the City of Chattanooga in the State of Tennessee have this day and do hereby make publish and declare this to be my true lawful & only Will & testament all others being hereby revoked.

First - I want my debts paid by my Executor.

Second - I give and bequeath the sum of Two hundred Dollars to J. C. Deuslon of Wellsville, Ohio & direct the same to be paid him out of my estate.

Third - I give and bequeath the sum of one hundred & fifty dollars to the Cleveland Homeaepathic Hospital College of Cleveland, Ohio & direct the same to be paid out of my estate.

Fourth - I give and bequeath to my wife Julia S. Fraer all the balance of my property of any and every kind and nominate and appoint her Executrix of this will & ask that she be not required to give bond for the discharge of her duties as such.

Given under my hand on this 30th day of September 1887.

J. M. Fraer

Signed in our presence & we subscribe our names as witnesses in the presence of the Testator & at his reqest.

W. H. Converse
Jas. P. McMillin

Probated Dec 12th 1891.

[Page 491]

A. L. DeLONG

Will of A. L. DeLong

Hereby revoking all former wills or codicils by me at any time heretofore made I hereby make publish and declare my last will and Testament to be as follows, viz:

All my just debts, funeral expenses and cost of a suitable memorial over my remains shall be first paid, the residue and rest of my estate, consisting of all property real personal or mixed of which I die seized and possessed or to which I may be or become entitled - I hereby will, bequeath and devise to my mother Mrs. Sophronia R. DeLong absolutely without any reservation or limitation whatever. I hereby nominate and appoint my mother said Mrs. Sophronia R. DeLong sole executrix of this my last will and testament. I authorize her as such to act without bond. I require her to make no report as such to any person or Court further than to show that as such she has paid my debts. I authorize and empower her as such to borrow money on such levies as she thinks best and to mortgage, execute a mortgage or mortgages or deed or deeds of Trust conveying any part or the whole of the property of which I may die seized and possessed to secure any such sums or sums of money so borrowed by her as such. I authorize and empower her as such to sell, transfer and convey by deed or deeds at private sale on such terms as she deems best or to lease any part or the whole of the property of which I may die seized and possessed. This the 8th day of Febry 1888

A. L. DeLong {seal}

Signed, Sealed and Published in our presence and we have subscribed our names hereto in the presence of the testator and of each other at the request of the Testator this 8th day of Febry 1888.

Tom Fort
A. H. Pettibone
W. B. Garvin

Probated Dec. 18th 1891.

[Page 492]

EVAN D. EVANS

Will of Evan D. Evans

My last will and Testament. In the name of God, Amen.

I Evan D. Evans Orchard Knob, Hamilton County - State of Tennessee being of sound mind and memory do hereby make publish and declare this to be my last will and testament hereby revoking and making void all former wills by me at anytime heretofore made.

First - I order and direct my Executors as soon after my decease as practicable to pay off and discharge all the debts dues and liabilities that may exist against me at the time of my decease.

Second - I give and bequeath unto my wife Martha Evans, my whole interest in the Chattanooga Sash Weight Co. and all real and personal belonging to me at my decease.

Third - I hereby appoint my wife Martha Evans to be my Executor.

In witness whereof I have hereunto subscribed my name this 3rd day of Sept. 1890.

The above and foregoing instrument was at the date thereof signed sealed and published and declared by the said Evan D. Evans as and for his last will and testament in presence of us who at his request and in his presence and in the presence of each other have subscribed our names as witnesses.

Evan D. Evans

S. L. Williams
F. Rees Woolford

Probated Jan^ry 9th 1892

[Page 493]

HARRIET FLOWERS

Will of Harriet Flowers

I Harriet Flowers, being of sound mind & desiring to make provision for my children according to what I consider just and right do make & publish this my last will and testament hereby revoking all wills at any time made by us. I am at present owner of Lot No. (3) three on Gilmer St. in Kaylor's addition to Chattanooga, Hamilton County, Tennessee and some household & kitchen property.

My youngest son, Manson Flowers, has for a number of years contributed largely to my support has helped to pay off an encumbrance on said lot and has at his own expense built two houses on said lot, therefore I will and desire:

1st - That out of my personal effects, all my just debts shall be paid and as soon after my death as may be convenient.

2nd - I desire that the residue of my personal property shall be distributed between my five children Joseph Andrew Flowers, Roxanna Law, Cornelius Flowers, Mary H. Flowers & said Manson Flowers share and share alike.

3rd - I will and devise that my said son Manson Flowers shall have in fee simple and undivided one half interest in and to said lot No. 3 Gilmer Street and that the other one half interest in said lot shall be vested in my other four children, above named in equal proportions giving to each one undivided one eighth interest in said lot.

4th - In the event of the death of either of said children his or her heirs to take the interest of such deceased child.

5th - I nominate and appoint my said son Manson Flowers, Executor of this will and desire that he wind up and settle my estate without being required to give bond and I desire that he confer with and be advised by J. A. Caldwell attorney at law in regard to any matters arrising in the adjustment and settlement of my estate and the disbribution of said property.

[Page 494] In testimony whereof I hereto affix my signature in the presence of the subscribing witnesses at Chattanooga Tennessee this 28th June 1888.

Harriet X Flowers
her mark

Signed Sealed and Delivered}
in our presence this the   }
28 June 1888   }
    J. A. Caldwell
    Henry Daugherty

[Page 494 con't]

D. T. DODDS

Will of D. T. Dodds

I D. T. Dodds being of sound and disposing mind, and hereby revoking all former wills, do make this my last will and Testament.

I hereby devise, will and bequeath to my dear wife Mary W. Dodds, all my estate, both real and personal. The real estate consisting chiefly of town lots in the City of Chattanooga, Highland Park and Ridgedale, Hamilton County State of Tennessee. Also of lots on Lookout Mountain, Dade County, State of Georgia and my personally consisting mostly of notes in my possession and in bank, also some money in Bank. Also all other real and personal property of which I shall die seized and possessed.

I hereby appoint my wife Mary W. Dodds and my son William L. Dodds Co-Executors of this my last will and Testament. Made and signed this 13th day February 1891.

D. F. Dodds

Signed in our presence }
by D. T. Dodds this   }
13th day of February 1891}
    M. H. Fetts
    J. P. Smith

Probated Jan. 11th 1892

[Page 495]

J. P. SMITH

Will of J. P. Smith

On the 25th day of December 1891 Jas. P. Smith in his last sickness, at his own house in Ridgedale, Hamilton County, Tenn. declared in the presence of the undersigned whom he especially requested to bear witness thereto that his will was as follows to wit: -

That his wife Julia Smith should have all of his property both real and personal, and that she is to have full power to control and dispose of the same, as she may deem best and that the Real estate included the following property to wit. - The House and lot in Ridgedale occupied as a house, the lot in front of said house, used as a garden, his two lots on Ringold Road, and his real Estate, consisting of 8 lots in Salt Lake City, Utah and his lots on Lookout Mountain.

Of his personal property he included what money he had in First National Bank of Chattanooga, and a claim he had against the Burn's Estate.

It was further his request, that his wife give to Grace G. Smith, his unmarried daughter two Hundred Dollars more than any of his other children with interest from this date, this is to be done whenever she might make a distribution of the Estate or at any other time that she desired to carry out the request. He also requested that his wife Julia Smith act as Executrix of his estate with out bond.

The said J. P. Smith died on the 31st day of December 1891 - written and signed by us this 4th day of Jan. 1892.

Henry Rothwert
H. L. Dayton

[Page 496]

NANCY G. EATON

Will of Nancy G. Eaton

I Nancy G. Eaton, make and publish this my last will and Testament.

1. - My debts and funeral expenses will be paid out of any assets of my estate not specially bequeathed. If insufficient then out of the property mentioned in the following real clause.

2 - My house and lot on the corner of Cowart Street and Montgomery Avenue in Chattanooga, or its proceeds after my debts are paid as provided in the proceeding clause, will be divided into six equal parts. My sons, Eugene G., Albert C., Elbridge M. and Edwin H. Eaton, and my daughter Mary C. Payne, wife of T. H. Payne each to have one sixth's interest absolutely.

3 - The remaining one sixths interest will be held by my sons Eugene G., Albert C., and Elbridge M. Eaton or the survivor or surviors of these in trust for the benefit of Susie M. Eaton, wife of my son Frank H. Eaton to this interest and purpose, namely that the rents issued and profits of said one sixth interest or share will be paid Susie M. so long as he may live as the wife of Frank and so long as she remains his widow should she survive him. At her death, or in the event she should marry again then this trust will contine for the benefit of their children with the discretionary power however in the Trustees to pay to those or anyone or more of said children their proportionable share after arriving at age or such seem bes[t] their shares as the Trustees may deem best or to pay all to the minor or minors until the last one is of age when the youngest child arrives at the age of Twenty-one years this trust will cease and terminate and the said one sixth interest will then be the estate or property of my son Frank H. Eaton if living, if not living, the property will be equally divided between said children.

4 - Any two of said trustees shall have power to act with power to sell and convey said property mentioned in the second clause of this will in conjunction with the others holding their respective absolute interests and with the proceed of sale of said one sixth interest as mentioned in the third clause and invest its proceed and again sell and reinvest [Page 497] as often as they may think proper.

5 - The property known as the Brown & Carver tract of Mountain land in Hamilton County to which I hold a certain interest by title as a purchaser at a tax sale together with all rents issues and profits. I bequeath to my son Eugene G. Eaton, to whom in equity the same belongs.

6 - Whatever other estate I may die seized and possessed of - after paying my debts and funeral expenses as heretofore provicded, should there be any, will be equally divided between my six children share and share alike.

7 - I nominate and appoint my sons Eugene G., Albert C. and Elbridge M. Eaton or any one or more who shall qualify my Executor or Executors.

8 - I require no bond of either said trustees or Executors or Executor as provided by Statute.

In witness whereof I do to this my last will set my hand seal this the 4th day of August 1891.

Nancy G. Eaton {Seal}

Signed sealed and published in our presence and in this we have subscribed our names hereto in the presence of the Testatrix this 4th day of August 1891.

N. Werver Meyer
Marion E. Meyer

Probated Jan. 29, 1892.

[Page 498]

MAGDALENA WIRZ

Will of Magdalena Wirz

Chattanooga, tenn. sept. 12th 1891

I the undersigned Magdalena Wirz being of sound mind herewith declare in my last will and Testament that in case I should die I bequeath all my Property Real & personal being at No. 9 Grove St. in the City of Chattanooga, Tenn. to my husband Fredrich August Wirz who shall be the only rightfull owner and possessor of all said property Real & Personal, he shall be the only Exeuctor of all said property and shall have full control thereof.

Signed by me in presence of Witnesses this 12th Day of September 1891.

Wirz, Margila [?]

Witnessed by: Chat Theodore Mayer
                 Cubert Shuylon

J. J. Strecker, M. D.

Probated Feby. 22, 1892

SARAH RYMAN

Will of Sarah Ryman

This writing is to witness that I Sarah Ryman, being of sound mind and disposing memory and desiring to dispose of my property and designate to whom it shall go and belong when I am dead and gone make this my last will and testament concerning the same.

It is my desire and will that all of my property of every kind real personal & mixed whether now in possession or hereafter acquired consisting now chiefly of my undivided one-sixth (1/6) interest in lots Nos. Six (6), Eighteen (18) and Twenty (20) on High Street, Chattanooga, Tennessee and some personal effects shall go to and belong on my decease to my oldest daughter Mary Allie Mansfield and my son John Charles Ryman in equal proportions each one receiving one half of the same.

I make this disposition of my property giving it to my daughter Mary Allie and son John Charles aforesaid not that I love them more than my other children but because of the peculair circumstances and need of my daughter Mary Allie & Son John Charles, they needing it more than the others.

[Page 499] This Nov. 27th 1890.

Sarah X Ryman
her mark

Witnesses: B. F. Cickman
Jno. R. Dean

Probated March 12th 1892.

[Page 499 con't]

DANIEL A. HOUSER

Will of Daniel A. Houser

State of Tenn. }
Hamilton County }   Be it remembered that I, Daniel A. Houser of the County and State afore-said, being of sound mind and memory, do make this my last will and Testament.

First - I give and bequeath all my house hold effects and personal property to my beloved wife, Katie Houser and further bequeath and devise to my wife Katie Houser, my real estate consisting of Sixty four and one half acres in the 18th Dist. of Hamilton County, Tenn. to have said personally and real estate during her life. Then at the death of my wife, Katie Houser I give and bequeath to my oldest son Adolphus Houser all the personal property and household goods that belongs to the place at the time. And further bequeath and devise my real estate (64 1/2) Sixty four and one half acres to my oldest son Adolphus Houser his heirs and assigns forever.

Second - I give and bequeath to my second son, Return Houser One dollar to be paid after the death of his mother.

Third - I give and bequeath to my 3^d & and youngest son, Clabore Houser one dollar to be paid after the death of his mother Katie Houser.

In testimony wherof I have unto set my hand and seal and published and decree this to be my last will and Testament in the presence of the witnesses named below. This the 3^d day of August in the year of our Lord 1891.

Daniel A. X Houser
his mark {seal}

Witness: W. H. Benton
Signed sealed declared and published by Daniel A. Houser Testator as and for his last will [Page 500] and testament in presence of us, who at his request and in his presence and in presence of each other have this day subscribed our names as witnesses hereto.
N. L. Rawlings, Tyner, Tenn.
F. B. Varnell, Tyner, Tenn.

Probated March 24, 1892.

[Page 500 con't]

GREEN B. CUMMINGS
Will of Green B. Cummings

I Green B. Cummings, a resident of the 4th Dist. of Hamilton County, Tennessee being of sound mind and disposing memory do make and publish this as my last will and testament hereby revoking all other Wills by me heretofore made.

First - I direct that all my just debts and all expenses incident to my death burial be paid.

2nd - I will and bequeath to each of my four children, viz: Susan Evans, Carlina Light, John Cumming

[sic] and William Thomas Cummings each the sum of Five Dollars which shall be in full of all claim they or either of them shall have against my estate.

3rd - I will and bequeath to my grand daughter Ada Cummings, only heir of Alex Cummings dec'd who was a son of mine the sum of Fifty Dollars which shall be in full of all claims she could have against my estate.

4th - All of the remainder of my estate both real and personal after paying the bequeat set out above, I will and bequeath to my wife Sarah Elizabeth for life with remainder in fee to our child Ida May Cummings.

Witness my hand this 29 Day of Dec. 1888.

Green B. X Cummings
his mark

Signed and sealed by the Testator in our presence and in the presence of each other at the request of the Testator we hereby witness this same.
H. C. Beck
W. S. Beck

Probated March 26, 1892.

[Page 501]

FREDRICK A. NEBHUT

Will of Fredrick A. Nebhut

I, Fredrick A. Nebhut of Chattanooga, Tennessee, being of sound mind and disposing memory, do hereby make publish and declare this my last will and testament, as follows, to wit:

First - I direct that all of my just debts be paid when due.

Second - I will and bequeath to Mrs. E. Nebhut, Mrs. Jennie C. Lowe and Mrs. Jessie N. Caldwell, each, the sum of Fifty Dollars, the former being my adopted mother, and the latter two being my adopted sisters.

Third - I will and bequeath to my sister Mrs. Nettie Dunbar the sum of One hundred Dollars.

Fourt - I will and bequeath to my sister Mrs. Elizabeth Hackett the sum of Two Hundred Dollars.

Fifth - I will and bequeath to Fredrick A. Lowe son of my said adopted sister, Mrs. Jennie C. Lowe, the sum of One hundred Dollars.

I direct that none of the above bequests be paid until after all of my just debts be paid, and then not until such time as the same can be paid without sacrificing any of my effects or estate.

Sixth - I will devise and bequeath all the rest and residue of my property real, personal and mixed, of every name and nature and wherever situated to my beloved wife, Mrs. M. M. Nebhut for her sole and separate use, free from the control, debts and contracts of any future husband to have and to hold the same to herself, her heirs and assigns forever.

I nominate and appoint my said wife M. M. Nebhut sole executrix of this my last will and testament and direct that she shall not be required to execute any bond as such.

In testimony whereof I have hereunto set my hand and seal this 21st day of June A.D. 1888.

Frederick A. Nebhut {seal}

The above instrument was at the date thereof signed, sealed published and declared by the said Fredrick A. Nebhut as and for his last will and testament in presence of us, who at his request and in his presence and in the presence of each other have subscribed our names as witnesses thereto.
Harry W. Durand
James M. Trimble
W. S. Marshall

Probated Apl. 30, 1892

[Page 502]

LEONARD MANGOLD

Will of Leonard Mangold

State of Tennessee }
Hamilton County } Know all men by these presents that I, Leonard Mangold being of sound and disposing mind, memory and understanding for the purpose of disposing of what Almighty God has been pleased to endow me, and especially for the disposal of my six children that they may have and receive the best care possible under the circumstances in which I may and am about to leave them do make publish and declare this as and for my last Will & Testament, hereby revoking all others that I may have made.

Item - I will and bequeath to my children being six in number all the property of every kind that I may die seized and possessed of remaining after payment of my funeral expenses and debts justly owing and due.

Item 2nd - I hereby nominate and constitute my friend Michael Oscar Roesslein of Chattanooga executor of this my last Will & Testament with power to act without being required to give Bond and I also hereby appoint him Testamentary Guardian of my six children Viz: Leonard Cickey Mangold, Gaward Nicholas Mangold, Adoff Mangold, Louis Alfos Mangold, Maria Antonette Mangold and Lille Estreva Mangold and believing that he will do for them all that can reasonably be expected and in accordance with my wish that they be placed with as little delay as possible in the Orphan Assyulm St. Mary's at Nashville in charge of the good sisters I hereby release him as far as I can from Oath or Bond and request that neither be required of him. In witness hereto I hereunto set my hand and seal and make publish and declare this instrument to be and as and for my last Will and Testament.

Leonard Mangold XXX {seal}

The said Testator Leonard Mangold signed, sealed, published and declared the foregoing as and for his last will and testament in our presence who at his request and in his presence and in the presence of each other have subscribed our names as witnesses thereto.
Louis Bischof
Frank Sweet

Porbated May 23, 1892

[Page 503]

GEORGE LEVI

Will of George Levi

The State of Tennessee: In the name of God, Amen.

I, George Levi of the County of Hamilton and State of Tennessee Having been blessed to live to a ripe age in life and blessed in some of the goods of this World and of sound mind and disposing memory. And knowing that at most I cannot live many years longer. And desiring to avoid litigation about any of my property or effects after my death. And to designate clearly myself the objects of my bounty and the persons to enjoy it and the manner and proportion of such enjoyment. do make ordain and publish this as my last will and Testament. Viz:

1st - I commend my spirit to God Who gave it And pray its acceptance in Peace.

2nd - I desire that my boddy [sic] be plainly but decently buried.

3rd - That all my just debts be paid if any owing.

4th - I give bequeath and devise my Estate and property as follows, Viz: To my beloved Wife Mary A. Levi, my present wife and the mother of our little daughter Martha A. Levi who is young and of tender years And the only issue of mine by my wife aforesaid (50) Fifty acres of land Which is more fully described as follows. Beginning on the top of the hill in the corner of the Widow Gann or Wm. & Kale Gann land at the three bushes chesnut I think near a poplar on the Gann line. Thence a north West direction along James Adams line. So as to include about one half of my old home place apple orchard to a rock and walnut tree thence south some degrees West a few polls Still with James Adams line to the top of the spur of the mountain to a rock thence with some degrees East to the Pickett and Levi line, thence with this line a South West coarse to the corner in the old Original line of Levi and Hixon. Then along said line to a lynn and Beach at the foot of a steep ridge thence across the point of the Ridge, along Mrs. Gann's line to the Beginnning. The same to contain Fifty acres more or less. The dwelling house out buildings and Part of the orchard as above desclribed I devise all the above described land and improvements thereon to my Beloved wife aforesaid during her natural life, and also all the present growing crops of every kind and character for his year 1889.

5th - I bequeath to my beloved child Martha A. Levi, aforesaid one note on hand which I now hold on B. M. Brown and Nancy Brown for one hundred and two dollars [Page 504] dated the 1st day of April, 1889 and due 15th Nov. 1889. And also Two Hundred Dollars cash to be used for her by her mother in raising and educating her.

6th - And I bequeath to my Beloved Wife Mary A. Levi three milk cows, Two calves all the hogs now on hand. One old sorrel mare and one old sorrel horse. And all my house hold goods and house hold furniture of every kind and character. Such as all the beds, bed clothing, bed steads, chairs, Trunks, spinning wheels, cooking utensils, table ware, knives & forks, clock & Bookcase and all the Books. This bequest is to include everying in the hosue of a house hold character. And all the farming utensils gearing &c.

7th - I bequeath to my step son John H. McClary the son of my present wife by D. W. McClary dec[d] and which I have the care and custody of and he is working for me and waiting on me in my old age, one Clay Bank filly which is one year old past.

8th - And lastly I hereby appoint my true and trusty Wife, Mary A. Levi my Executrix to to [sic] this my last and only Will and Testament Without Bonds to carry out the same to the letter and spirit thereof. And that she act as guardian for and have the care and custody and training of one minor child Martha A. Levi. And that she use the funds set apart to her for the purpose of educating her and for her sup[p]ort. This 28th day of June A.D. 1889.

George Levi

The above instrument as the last Will and Testament of George Levi was read over to him and fully explained to him and understood by him to be his last will and testament. And signed by him in our presence and each of us as subscribing witnesses thereto in the presence of each of us on the day it bears date.

A. P. Hunter
R. M. Brown

Probated June 6, 1892

[Page 505]

JESSE FREEMAN

Will of Jesse Freeman

Know all men by these presents that I, Jesse Freeman of the City of Chattanooga, Hamilton County, Tennessee realizing the uncertainty of human existance, but being of sound mind, do make, declare and publish this my last will and testament:

1st - I direct that all my just debts shall be paid and satisfied in full.

2nd - I give and bequeath unto my beloved daughter Minnie Freeman the following real estate in the City of Chattanooga, Hamilton County, Tennessee, viz: The West half of lot Eighteen (18) and the East half of Lot Seventeen (17) in Fade's Addition to Chattanooga, being the premisis on the North East corner of Strait and Palmetto streets in said city, on which I now reside. To have and to hold unto my beloved daughter Minnie Freeman and her heirs and assigns forever in fee simple.

3rd - I give and bequeath unto my beloved wife Mary J. Freeman all the residue of my estate of every kind and description whatsoever, embracing all my property both real, personal and mixed except the bequest above recited of which I may be seized and possessed or to which I may be in any way entitled and including among other things Lot Number Sixteen (16) in Block Number One (1) in Weihl & Patten's Addition to Chattanooga, Tennessee and a five acre tract of land in James County, Tennessee to have and to hold to the said Mary J. Freeman and her heirs and assigns forever in fee simple.

4th - I nominate and appoint my beloved wife Mary J. Freeman to be the executrix of this my last will and testament, and direct that she be allowed to serve without giving bond. In witness of all which presents I have hereunto set my hand and seal and caused this my last will and testament to be published (same being written on two pages of legal cap paper) at Chattanooga, Tennessee this 8th day of March, 1892.

Jess Freeman {seal}

Signed, sealed and declared published by said Jesse Freeman as and for his last will and testament in the presence of the undersigned who in his presence and in the presence of each other, at his request hereunto subscribe so witnessed [Page 506] at Chattanooga, Tennessee, this 8th day of March 1892.

Witness: J. W. White
                 H. Daugherty

Probated June 11, 1892

[Page 506 con't]

MAHALA EMILY NICHOLS

Will of Mahala Emily Nichols

I, Mahala Emily Nichols being of sound mind and disposing memory but feeble in body do make and publish this, my last will and Testament hereby revoking and make void all others by me at any time made.

First - I direct that my funeral expenses and all my debts be paid as soon after my death as practicable out of any money I may die seized and possessed of or that may first come into the hands of my executor.

Secondly - I give and bequeath to my son Oliver Elijah Ellison the North (25) Twenty-five feet of a (50) Fifty foot lot that I own on Williams Street in the City of Chattanooga, Hamilton County, Tennessee and which is fully described in a deed from J. B. Weaver to me, dated March 8th 1870 and registered on the 26th day of April 1872 in the Register's Office of Hamilton County, Tennessee, in Book W Page 111 and which deed is now among my papers.

Thirdly - The other 25 feet of this lot mentioned in the last paragraph of my will above together with one other 50 foot lot on said Williams Street and which lies along side of the first mentioned lot and which was conveyed to me and my husband Charles W. Nichols jointly by J. B. Weaver on the 17th day of January 1872 and which deed was registered in the Register's office of Hamilton County, Tennessee, on the 26th day of April 1872 in Book "W" Pages 108 and 109 and which deed is now among my papers and to which I here refer for a perfect description my husband having died since that date. I give and bequeath to my four children Oliver Elijah Ellison, Henry Thomas Ellison, Mary Susan Miller wife of W. C. Miller and Octavia Iler wife of C. J. Iler share and share alike.

Fourthly - I give and bequeath to my four children [Page 507] named in the last paragraph to wit: my two sons, Oliver Elijah Ellision and Henry Thomas Ellison, and my two daughters Mary Susan Miller and Octavia Iler share and share alike my undivided one third interest in the following real estate on Lookout Mountain to wit: Situated lying and being in the 11th District and 4th Section of Dade County, Georgia Number (282) containing two hundred and sixty acres more or less.

It is my intention in this will to divide all my property equally between my four children above named except the North 20 feet of the 50 foot lot on Williams Street this lot is given or intended to be given at my death to my son Oliver Elijah Ellison in addition to his one fourth interest hereto fore given and bequested with my other children jointly. After my decease it is my will that the foregoing real estate be sold, except the 25 feet bequeathed to Oliver Elijah Ellison and the proceeds divided equally between my four children herein named in proportion as the same is herein bequeathed.

Lastly - I do hereby nominate and appoint my son Oliver Elijah Ellison Executor of this my last will and testament. In witness whereof I do to this my will set my hand this the 30th day of March 1892.

Mahal Emily X Nichols
her mark

Signed and published in our presence and we have subscribed our names and in the presence of the other and in the presence and at the request of the maker of this gorefoing will. This March 30th 1892.

S. M. Ellis
W. A. Ellis
Cooper Holtzclaw

Probated June 13, 1892.

[Page 508]

THOMAS JOSEPH

Will of Thomas Joseph

I, Thomas Joseph of Soddy in the County Hamilton, State of Tennessee being of sound and disposing mind and memory, do make, publish and declare this to be my last will and testament hereby revoking all other wills by me at any time heretofore made.

And as to my worldly estate and all the Property, real, personal or mixed of which I shall die seized and possessed or to which I shall be entitled at the time of my Decease I devise, bequeath and dispose thereof in the following manner. My will is that all my just debts and funeral expenses shall by my executor hereinafter named be paid out of my estate as soon after my decease as shall by them be found convenient.

I give devise and bequeath to my beloved wife Mary Joseph all my household furniture I also give to her the use, improvement and income of my dwelling house, Land and it appurtenances situated in Soddy, Hamilton County, Tennnessee and my House and Lot where W. B. Thomasson lives fronting the C.N.O. & P. Rail Road and adjoining the lot where I now live. She is to have the use of and income from both houses and Lots with their appurtenances as long as she remains unmarried, and in case she remains my widow untill her death then she is to have and to hold the same to her during the term of her natural life. And after her death Said Property is to be sold and the proceed divided Equally between my natural Heirs provided further that my wife pay a debt of [blank] that is now against the house, or cause it to be paid. I give devise and bequath to my Daughter Mary Jones the Home and Land where she now lives it being the South west corner Lot joined on the North by Wm Joseph and on the East by the Lot where I now live to have and to hold the same to her and her heirs forever provided, however, that she pay or cause to be paid a debt of One Hundred Dollars that is against the Home of the Said debt is not paid before my Decease.

I give to my Son William Joseph Ten Dollars to be paid as herein after provided by my Executors to be named hereafter.

I give to my Daughter Elizabeth Davis Ten Dollars to be paid by my Executors to be named hereinafter.

I give to Dan Joseph my watch & chain and to Jimmie Jones my chest and carpenter tools.

[Page 509] I give to the heirs of my Daughters Ann Davis five Dollars and to my Daughter Anna R. Williams, I give Ten Dollars for the use of her heirs to be paid to them by my executors to be hereafter named.

And lastly I do nominate and appoint W. H. Cord

of Soddy Hamilton County, Tenn. and Wm B. Thomas of Soddy Hamilton County, Tenn. to be the executors of this my last Will and testament.

In witness whereof I the said Thomas Joseph have to this my last will and testament, consisting of two sheets of paper subscribed my name and affixed my seal this -- day of -- in the year of our Lord one Thousand Eight hundred and Ninety one.

Thomas Joseph {seal}

Signed sealed published and declared by Thomas Joseph as and for his last will and testament in the presence of us who at his request and in his presence and in the presence of each other have subscribed our names as witnesses thereto.

T. Morgan, Residing at
Soddy, Tenn.
J. M. Bowman, Residing at
Soddy, Tenn.

Probated Oct. 18, 1892

[Page 509 con't]

MILES KELLY

Will of Miles Kelly

I, Miles Kelly being of sound mind and disposing memory do hereby make and publish this as my last will and testament.

First. - I devise that my body be decently buried on the lot owned by me and John Powers in Mount Olivet Cemetary near Chattanooga, Tennessee.

Second. - I direct that all my debts including funeral expenses be first paid by my executors out of any money which I may leave at the time of my death.

Third. - I direct my executors to expend a sum not exceeding Two hundred dollars out of the money now deposited in the Chattanooga Savings Bank, together with a like sum devised for that purpose by John Powers dec[d] in erecting a joint monument for the families of both on the lot jointly owned by said [Page 510] Powers and myself in Mount Olivet Cemetary. And to expend not exceeding fifty dollars in marking the graves and dividing the lot and in lettering said Joint monument. If for any reason the two hundred dollars, devised for that purpose by John Powers dec[d] should not be furnished to help erect said joint monument, then, in that event, my Executors after having said lot partitioned so as to separate my part for his, will expend not exceeding four hundred and fifty

dollars, out of the money now in said Chattanooga Savings Bank in erecting a monument on my part of said lot to mark the graves of myself and family.

Fourth. - I will and bequeath unto the Pastor of the Catholic Church at Chattanooga, known as Sts. Peter & Paul Church, fifty dollars to be used and expended by said Pastor as trustee in such way as he may think for the best interest of said Church, and my executors will pay said sum out of the cash now deposited in said Chattanooga Savings Bank. I also will and bequeath to my daughter Mrs. Margaret Mitchell, wife of D. F. Mitchell, one hundred dollars in cash, to be paid out of said money in said Bank.

The balance of said money, after paying off the said foregoing bequeath and debts, I bequeath one half to my son John Kelly and the other half to my son-in-law D. F. Mitchell.

Fifth., - I will and bequeath to my daughter Mrs. Margaret Mitchell, all my other personal property of whatever kind or description, except said nine hundred cash now deposited in said Chattanooga Savings Bank, all of the money thus deposited I want expended and delivered as herein before directed, and do not intend my [by?] this fifth clause to change said provisions.

Sixth. - My home place where I now live on "C" Street, I will and bequeath as follows, to wit: The north half of said lot next to the Byrne and McGuire lot, fronting fifty feet on "C" Street and running through of uniform width to an alley known as Warren's Alley I will and bequeath unto my daughter Mrs. Margaret Mitchell and here husband D. F. Mitchell jointly and in fee simple. The South half of said lot, fronting fifty feet on "C" Street and running through of uniform width to said Warren's Alley, I will and bequeath unto my son John Kelly. The whole lot fronts about 100 feet on "C" St. in [Page 511] Chattanooga and runs through the alley and I devise it one half to each as above Stated, including the houses and improvements, which go with the land those on the North half with it and those on the South half with it.

My one half interest in a lot fronting twenty-five feet on Congress Street in the 10th District of Hamilton County and known as the McDowell lot, the other half being owned by D. F. Mitchell, I devise to my son John Kelly, in fee simple.

My one third interest in a tract or piece of land owned jointly, or as tenants in common by me, D. F. Mitchell and John Kelly, which has laid off into lots, there being about 14 of said lots, situated in East End Syndicate and on or near Harrison Avenue in --- District of Hamilton County, Tennessee which land is described fully in a deed executed by W. R. Hall and wife Adaline Hall to said D. F. Mitchell, John Kelly and myself on the 10th day of April 1888 and now of record in Book I Vol. 3 page

334 of the Registers office of Hamilton County, Tennessee, to which reference is here made for a perfect description, I give and bequeath equally to my said son John Kelly and my son-in-law D. F. Mitchell, that is one half of said third interest to each in fee simple. I give and bequeaath to my daughter Mrs. Margaret Mitchell in fee simple the lot fronting on an alley in the rear of a lot sold by me to Abner Bradley which latter lot fronts on Congress St. in the 10th District of Hamilton County and being a part of the North half of lot 55 Congress St. East End Addition to Chattanooga, Tennessee.

Said lot fronts 51 1/4 feet on said alley and runs back of uniform width one hundred feet.

My half interest in a lot owned in common by myself and D. F. Mitchell, in Fort Cheatam Addition to Ridgedale fully described in a deed dated January 24th 1889 and signed by J. F. Hall and wife Fannie Hall and of record in Book P Vol. 3 pages 266 and 267 Register's Office Hamilton County, Tennessee to which reference is heremade I bequeath to my son John Kelly in fee simple.

[Page 512] Seventh. - I hereby nominate and appint my son John Kelly and my son-in-law D. F. Mitchell my executors of this my last will and testament, having confidence in their honesty and integrity, I desire both of them to qualify and to faithfully carry out and dishcarge the trusts in this will imposed upon them.

In witness whereof I do here and now, in the presence of the undersigned witnesses, set my hand and seal to this my last will and testament.

This August 29th 1892
Miles X Kelly
his mark

The foregoing will was signed, sealed and published in our presence, and was witnessed by us and we have subscribed our names hereto in the presence of the testator and of each other, and we are not related to any of the parties or beneficiaries, under said will nor interest in the same.

This August 29th 1892
Jno. Crimmins
M. J. Murphy
J. B. Frazier

[Page 512 con't]

MARIA DANNEBERG

Will of Maria Danneberg

I, Maria Danneberg, of the County of Hamilton

and State of Tennessee, being of sane mind and disposeing memory do make and publish this my last will and testament, hereby revoking and makeing void all other Wills, by me at any time made.

I will and bequeath to my beloved Husband, Louis Danneberg, my lot and all improvements thereon, in the city of Chattanooga, State of Tennessee , herein after described, to have and to hold all the profits and benefits that may be derived from said estate, the rest of his natural live, then at his death the property to be equally divided between the four children of Maria Danneberg and Louis Danneberg, the eldest being Mrs. Sophia Rand, next eldest Eliza Geilor, next Albert R. Danneberg, next Mrs. Annie Norman, and the said Louis Danneberg, husband of Maria Danneberg [Pager 513] can not dispose of said estate only as herein mentioned. Said estate being on "E" St. fronting 50 ft. on said street and running back 100 feet, and now being occupied by ourselves.

Maria   X   Danneberg
her mark

Signed, sealed and published in our presence and we have subscribed our names hereto in the presence of the testator, this the twenty-first day of April 1891.

Maria   X   Danneberg
her mark

Witnesses   W. H. Lessly {seal}
J. A. Foster {seal}
John Geiler, Jr. {seal}

The reason I, Maria Danneberg alter my will is the following explanation:

During last summer I made a will, and after due consieration I decided it unjust, the Will referred to is in the hands of Henry B. Knauff, a resident of James County, State of Tennessee. Where it was executed and where it is hereby revoked, with all previous Wills. Date above.

Maria   X   Danneberg
her mark

W. H. Lessly {seal}
J. A. Foster {seal}
John Geiler, Jr. {seal}

Probated. Nov. 7/92

[Page 514]

JAMES W. BALL

Will of Jas. W. Ball
Chattanooga, Tenn.
June 16, 1892

This is to certify that I Jas. W. Ball, being of sound mind, make this my last will and Testament. I do hereby will to my wife, Alice J. Ball, one House and Lot with all improvements, situated on Lot 89 Blk 5 in T. J. Lattner's Sub-division of the Sixth Civil District of Hamilton Co. Tenn. Also 14 acres in the Fourth Civil district of Hamilton Co. Tenn. situated in the Twenty-fifth Section of Township one North, Range Five, west of the base line, in the Ocoee district.

Also one real estate note on Celestia Gaston and J. L. Gaston, Given on Lots 197 & 198 Block 20 of T. J. Lattner's sub-division of Hamilton County, Tenn. Also Two Lots No. 17 & 18 Block 95 in Livingston, Montana. I also appoint my beloved wife Alce [sic] J. Ball sole executrix of this my last will and testament.

Jas. W. Ball

Witness: Ed. F. Sisson
                  H. Bond

Probated Oct. 28/92

[Page 514 con't]

MILLIE ADAMS

Will of Millie Adams

State of Tennessee
Hamilton Co.
Aug. 20, 1891

I, Millie Adams of Hamilton Co. Tenn., make this my last will and Testament.

I give and bequeath to Jessie Redmon, One Thousand Dollars ($1,000). I give and bequeath to Armistrad** Redmon One Thousand Dollars ($1,000). I give and bequeath to Matilda Smalley Five Hundred Dollars ($500.00) I give and bequeath to Furgesson Redmon Five Hundred Dollars ($500.00) I give and bequeath to John Redmon of Hamilton Co. One Hundred Dollars ($100.00). I give and bequeath to Philip S. Smalley, Four Thousand Dollars ($4,000.).

All the remainder of my property, Real, Personal, [Page 515] Mixed, money and Notes I give and bequeath to Sevier S. Smalley. After paying all my debts and the sum of Two Hundred Dollars ($200.00) to my Executor for winding up the business of my Estate.

I know nothing of the whereabouts of any of the parties mentioned above excepting Philip S. Smalley, Sevier S. Smalley and John Redmon. Have heard nothing from them since long before the War. Don't know that any of them are living. They are scattered over the west I suppose. Don't even know what State any of them reside in.

I want my Executor to use ordinary diligence to find the parties mentioned. I want him to advertise one week in some two Chattanooga Papers, making inquiry for them and if within twelve months from the date of advertising the parties cannot be found, then I want the various sums mentioned to be given to Sevier S. Smalley.

I make and appoint Y. L. Abernathy. Executor of this my last will and Testament and require that he shall give bond in the sum of Two Thousand Dollars $2,000. for the faithful performance of his duties as such.

Millie   X   Adams
her mark

Signed in our presence and we sign our names in the presence of each other and the testator.
Y. L. Abernathy
Lizzie Carter
W. M. Carter

Codicil to the within Will
State of Tennessee, Hamilton Co.
July 1st, 1892

I, Millie Adams, do this day make this codicil to my last Will and Testament.

On account of not knowing the whereabouts of some of the parties mentioned therein and believing it doubtful about their ever being found and not wanting to have the slightest chance for littigation [sic] and expense after my death. And on account of the kind care and attention given my by Sevier S. Smalley, I give and bequeath to him the $1,000 mentioned as going [Page 516] to Jessie Redmon. Also the $1000 mentioned as going to Armstead** Redmon. Also the $500.00 mentioned as going to Matilda Smalley. Also $500.00 mentioned as going to Furgesson Redmon.

I have given Philip S. Smalley $1,000 of the $4,000 mentioned and have this day given my check for the remaining $3,000 payable at my death. This leaves $1737.37 cts besides interest that has accrued and I cover this amount $1739.37 cts with my check payable at my death to Sevier S. Smalley. I also want all other money and property of every kind to go to Sevier S. Smalley at my death, after all debts are paid.

Millie X Adams
her mark

Signed in our presence and we sign our names in the presence of each other and the testator.
Y. L. Abernathy
Mrs. M. M. Smith
W. H. Dills

** various spellings used in this account

Probated Nov 21st 1892

[Page 516 con't]

RETURN HOUSER
Will of Return Houser, Dec'd

Fairmount, Tenn
Nov. 11, 1892

I, Return Houser, being of sound mind, do will and bequeath to my beloved wife, Nancy C. Houser, all my real estate and personal property to sell and control during her widowhood, for the benefit of my children. This is not for the benefit of any future husband in the case of her marrying.
E. K. Smith to be executor of this will.
Return Houser

Witnesses: J. M. Brown
Alice McGuffey
E. K. Smith

[Page 517]

ELIZA KIRKE

Will of Mrs. Eliza Kirke**

The last Will and Testament of Eliza Kirk** of Hamilton County, Tennessee.
I, Eliza Kirk, being of sound mind and memory, do make and publish this my last will and testament, hereby revoking and making void all former wills by me at any time made, in manner and form following, that is to say:

1. - After all my just debts are paid. I give and devise all my property, both real and personal, to my son Karl Q. Kirk but not so as to interfere with the rights of my husband W. A. L. Kirk and family to occupy and enjoy my real estate for and during the term of his natural life.

2. - I appoint my husband, W. A. L. Kirk sole executor of this my last will and testament and sole trustee for my said son Karl Q. Kirk, and expressly excuse him from giving bond and security in either capacity.

3. - I hereby expressly authorize and empower my said husband as executor and trustee, or in either capacity to sell, convey, mortgage or otherwise dispose of any or all of said real estate at such time and in such manner as he may see proper or deem best, the proceeds to be held according to the time of this will, that is my said husband to be entitled to the use of the proceeds for life, the principal to belong to my said son. Karl, but to be held by my said husband as trustee until my son shall attain the age of twenty-one years.

4. - I own lots 13 and 14 in Block 1 in Boyce Town Company Plat at Boyce Station, Tennessee and a half interest in lot 12 adjoining the above, which are fully paid for. But I owe a balance of purchase money on our home place which is lots 633 and 634 in Mission Ridge Land Co's Addition to east Lake. My said husband may, if he sees proper as executor or trustee, sell said property at Boyce and apply the proceeds to payments of the amount due on the home place but shall not be bound to do so, it being my intention to leave this to his discretion. If my husband, or the brothers and sisters of my son shall, at the request of my husband, make any payments [Page 518] on the home place, they shall be interested in the place to the extent of such payments.
This 17th day of September, 1892

Eliza X Kirk
her mark

Signed by the said Eliza Kirk, as and for her last will and testament, in the presence of us, the undersigned, who at her request and in her sight and presence, have subscribed our names as attesting witnesses, the day and date above written.
Lizzie F. Vetter
Harvey W. Bayley

** both spellings given in this document

Probated Nov. 22/92 J. H. Messick, Clerk

[Page 518 con't]

WILSON HIXSON

Last Will and Testament of Wilson Hixson

State of Tennessee }
Hamilton County   }   In the name of God, Amen.

I Wilson Hix[s]on of the County of Hamilton in the State of Tennessee, Having been blessed to live to a ripe age in life, and blessed in Some of the goods of the World, And of sound Mind and disposing memory, And knowing that at most I cannot live many years longer. And being desirous to avoid litigation about any of my property or effects after my death. And to designate clearly myself the objects of my bounty, the persons to enjoy it and the remainer and proportion of such enjoyment. Do make, ordain and publish this as my last Will and Testament, viz:

1st - I comend my soul to God who gave it and pray its acceptance in peace.

2nd - That my earthly remains be plainly but decently burried.

3rd - I am now owner and seized and possessed of the following land in addition to other lands which will be hereafter fully explained and set forth in this my will:

[Page 519] Three hundred and Forty acres (340). This is known as my Old home tract where I now live. Also my Ridge Place.

4th - I Devise to my beloved wife Nancy Hixson should she be the longest live, Forty acres of land, out of the above described lands. Which is bounded as follows, Viz: on the East by the lands of Washington Hixson, Sr., on the North by P. M. Rogers, on the west by R. A. Anderson's Heirs and James Hixson and on the South by Pleasant Rogers. I Devise that my wife's share in the above described lands comence in the center of the dwelling house where we now live and extend from that point each way so as to give her a square lot of land including the dwelling house all out buildings &c containing 40 Acres, and that she have full control and peaceable possession of the Same during her natural life. And at her death I devise that my beloved wife's life estate as above specified revert back to the lot or lots of land from which her life estate was taken from so as to give each heir Equal Justice.

5th - I devise and set apart to my son G. W. Hixson (10) Ten acres of land commencing on a postrak marked (A) East of his dwelling house, which he now lives, So as to include his dwellling house and out buildings, Where he now lives. This 10 acres of land is out of the home tract. I also devise to my son, G. W. Hixson, the following additional lands viz: - Sixty acres

more or less adjoining his lands in the bend of the creek. And also one Seventh interest in what is termed my Ridge lands adjoining R. A. Anderson' Heirs and Rufus Chadwick, he shall take his interest in said lands on the South end, And I also devise to him one seventh interest in a tract of land 44 Acres of land on Walden's Ridge that descended to me of my Father's estate [son of Ephraim and Margaret (Hixson) Hixson]. All of the above described lands to the said G. W. Hixson and his bodily heirs during their natural lives.

6th - I also bequeath to my son G. W. Hixson aforesaid $25.00 Twenty-five dollars in money [Page 520] that accrued from the sale of a colt that his Grandmother gave him when he was a little boy. I sold the colt and desire that he should be paid for the same. And direct that my executor pay him the above sum out of any means that may come into his hands from my personal estate.

4th clause of this my will completed as to who are the remaining beneficiaries in the old home tract of land of (340) Acres. I devise to my beloved Sons and Daughters, Viz:" E. F. Hixson, Rebecca Hixson, Samuel Hixson, Elizabeth Hixson & Margaret Holcomb.

That the above named five heirs have their interest in the above mentioned tract of land. And also 1/7 interest each in the 44 Acres mountain tract Share and share alike And also 1/7 interest each in my Ridge tract of land, as to no. of acres to them and each of them and their bodily heirs during their natural lives.

7th - I devise to my Grandchildren, the Heirs of my deceased son John Hixson the following described tract of land containing 38 Acres at the bald hill and adjoining on the West & South by the lands of Henry Hixson on the East by Thomas Cansinger, on the north by their own lands. And one 7th Interest in what is termed my ridge tract of lands, also one 7th interest in my 47 Acre piece of mountainlands heretofore spoken of I had advanced to my son John Hixson in his lifetime $247.65 - 20th Aug. 1872. Also advanced to him $75.00 - 10th January 1873. For which I hold his notes as above stated, this will account for a lack in amount of value in lands devised to said heirs. The above lands is devised to the above Heirs to and through their Guardian, during their natural lives and their bodily heirs after them, share and share allike, equal in valuation.

8th - I devise that my son E. F. Hixson have his share in the remaining portion of the Old home tract off of the uper end of said tract of land adjoining the land of P. M. Rogers.

9th And that Samuel Hixson take his interest in said land at the East end of the old home tract [Page 521] adjoining the lands of Huston Hixson, Jr. on the East.

10th Rebecca Hixson. She will take her share in said lands in the South east corner of said home tract.

11th - Margaret Holcomb take her share in said lands in the the South west corner of the home place adjoining the lands of Anderson's Heirs, Washington and James Hixson.

12th - That Elizabeth Hixson have her share in the old home place assigned her, adjoining the lands of E. F. Hixson and G. W. Hixson and Margaret Holcomb.

13th - I have made advancements to the following heirs to this my last will, to Samuel Hixson $189.80 - 8 February 1882. And to G. W. Hixson 2 notes for $135.00 dated 23^d January 1884. And to E. F. Hixson $300.00 in land deeded to him about January 1889. I desire the above named heirs to account to the other heirs so as to make all the Heirs equal.

14th - I Bequeath that all the personal property or effects that I may die Seized and possessed of off every kind or character if any there be at my death. I direct that my Executor sell the Same. At Such time and place and such times as he thinks best so as to realize the most for it. And divide the proceeds equally among my heirs. Share and share alike so as to make all equal.

15th - In order that my executor may be more fully able and authorized to carry out my will as above Stated, employ a Suveyor and two disinterested neighbors who are acquainted with the lands who he may select to partition said lands according to the stipulation of this my will so as to give each heir Justice as near as can be done.

And I further appeal to my executor and all my children. If their mother should be the longest liver to see that she never wants for anything.

16th - I hereby nominate and appoint my son-in-[Page 522] law H. G. Hixson, Guardian for the minor children of my deceased Son John Hixson, and to see that their rights are protected under this my will.

17th - And lastly I nominate and appoint my true and trusty son, Ephraim F. Hixson my Executor to carry out this my last will and testament to the true letter and speech of the same. And I here further add and repeat my former words, that my principal object in making this will is to avoid that dreaded monster litigation and that fair and impartial Justice may be meeted out to all my children.

This 26th day of March A.D. 1891.

Wilson Hixson

The foregoing was at the date thereof signed published and delivered by the said Wilson Hixson as and for his last will and Testament in the presence of us and each of us at his request and in his presence and in the presence of each other. have subscribed our names as Witnesses thereto.

Addison P. Hunter
John Hughes

[Page 523]

ANNA D. LIPES

Will of Anna D. Lipes

I, Anna D. Lipes of Allen County in the State of Indiana, being of full legal age and of sound mind and memory, do make and publish this my last will and Testament, hereby revoking all other wills by me at anytime made.

1st - It is my Will that all my just and legal indebtedness, including my last sickness and funeral expenses be paid out of my estate.

2nd - I give, bequeath and devise to my daughter Anna M. Lipes, all my real and personal property of every description whatever belonging to me at the date of my deceases to be hers to dispose of as she may deem proper.

3rd - I hereby nominate and appoint my husband Robert F. Lipes Executor of this my last will and Testament, he to act in said capacity without bond.

In witness whereof I hereby set my hand and seal this 7th day of June 1892.

Anna D. Lipes {seal}

Signed by said Anna D. Lipes as her last will and Testament in our presence and signed by us in her presence.

John Gieseking
Stanley Brown

[Page 524]

JAMES W. OLIVER

Will of James W. Oliver

In the name of God, Amen.

I, James W. Oliver of the City of Chattanooga State of Tennessee being of sound mind, do make and publish this my last will and Testament revoking all other wills by me made.

First - I give and bequeath all my estate real and personal to my beloved wife Louisa Oliver, in trust for my beloved daughter Pearl Oliver, especially that estate which

I derived from my son Edwin S. Oliver by descent at his death, said Estate is situated in and near Los Angolos in the State of California.

Second - I give to my said wife Louisa Oliver full power to sell mortgage or exchange any or all, of my said Estate as she may deem best, without any proceedings in Court giving her full power in regard to any of my estate whereever situated as I would have myself.

Third - I direct that my said wife shall out of my estate, first pay all my just debts and expense of administration, and the residue of my estate of every description shall be paid to my daughter Pearl Oliver, upon her arriving at the age of Twenty-one years.

Third - I hereby appoint my beloved wife Louisa Oliver the Exercutrix of this will who will not be required to give bond or sworn as such.

In witness I have set my hand and Seal this 3rd day of November 1892.

James W. Oliver

Witnessed by Theodore Richmond, Rachael Divine & Charles T. Divine at the request of James W. Oliver, who signed and acknowledged the Same in their presence and in the presence of each other on the 3rd day of November 1892.

Theodore Richmond
Rachael Divine
Chas. T. Divine

Probated & filed the 10th day of December 1892.
J. H. Messick, Clerk

[Page 525]

JOHN L. DIVINE

Will of John L. Divine

I, John L. Divine of Chattanooga, Hamilton County, Tennessee being of sound mind and disposing memory, and bearing in mind my duties and responsibilities as a husband and the father of children, some of whom are of tender years. do make and publish this my last will and Testament.

Item 1st - It is my desire that my funeral expenses and all just debts I may owe, if any at the time of my decease, be paid out of the first moneys coming to the hands of my executrix.

Item 2nd - Having, as I believe, provided amply and liberally for my son Samuel W. Divine and my daughter Mary M. Key by advancing and giving them in money or other things which I estimate to be an equal and fair proportions, to what my other children, will be likely to receive under this will. I do bequeath and devise unto my beloved wife Rachael V. Divine, should she survive me, all my entered estate, real and personal, including all stocks in banks and other incorporated companies, notes, accounts, all debts due me, and all other property of every nature and character whatever and vest her with the absolute legal title thereto, with full power and authority to use and dispose of the same, or any part thereof nor shall she be required to account for the use or disposition she may make of it to any one. I make this disposition of all my estate, so that my said wife may have full power to use and dispose of any portion of my real or personal estate, not only for her own use, comfort and maintenance, but that she may use it, for the comfort, support maintenance and deducation of all my children of whom she is the mother and that she may have power and authority to make advancements to anyone or more of my said children, and so that she may distribute any portion of my estate, among any one or more of my said children. But she is to be the sole judge and is to determine to whom, when, and what money or other thing shall be advanced or distributed, and [Page 526] whether and advancement or distribution shall be made at all, during her natural life, looking to the condition, circumstances and character of the child or children before making such advancement or distribution.

I confide this trust to her with full confidence, that she will do that which she believes just to all our children. My said wife is also empowered to dispose of any property or other thing by will belonging to or growing out of my estate, that may remain in her hands at the time of her death among my said children in such manner, as she may deem right and just, in view of any Advancement or distribution she may have made to any child or children, in her lifetime and in view of the condition of anyone or more of said children.

But should my said wife die without having disposed of all the property herein bequeathed and devised to her, either in her lifetime or by will, then in that event, the money, property or other thing so remaining at the death of my said wife, shall be equally divided among all of my said children born of my said wife, looking to and estimating all advances, that my said wife may have then made to any child or children out of my estate, herein bequeathed and devised to her, the child or children of any deceased child taking the share that the parent would have taken if living.

It is my request that my said wife retain the house where I now reside, as a residence and as a house for such of my children as may require it and as a place where all my children may meet each other and meet together, but if in her judgment it becoming to valuable for a residence or in any way unsuitable for a residence in her opinion, she may sell it and convey it to the purchaser or make such disposition of it as she deems best and invest the proceeds in another house or make some other disposition thereof.

My said wife is fully empowered [Page 527] and authorized to make advances to my said son Samuel W. Divine or to my said daughter the said Mary M. Key should there necessities at anytimes in her opinion require it, but she will be governed in this by her own best judgement and descretion.

My said son Samuel W. Divine and my daughter Mary M. Key do not otherwise participate in the benefits this will simply and above from the consciensious I feel heretofore contioned that I have already given each of them a full share of my estate.

Witness my signature this 16th day of march 1889.
Jno. L. Divine.

The foregoing will written upon this and four other pages, was signed by the Testator John L. Divine in our presence and witnessed by each of us, at his request and in his presence and in the presence of each other on this 16th day of March 1889.
H. C. Beck
L. M. Clark

Filed this 14th day of Dec. 1892.
J. H. Messick, Clerk

[Page 528]

PETER PERKINS

Will of Peter Perkins

In the name of God. Amen.

I, Peter Perkins, being of sound mind but feeble in body & expecting soon to leave this world for an other. I do make this my last will and Testament.

First - I commend my soul to Almighty God from whom I got it.

Second - I direct that all my just debts be paid out of my estate.

Third - All the rest & residue of my estate both real and personal I give & bequeath to my beloved wife Jane Perkins including my lot & house deeded to me by E. O. Tade in a certain deed dated Oct. 7th 1870.
Peter X Perkins
his mark

Witnesses: P. J. Hale
                  Peter X Duff
                    his mark - attest A. C. Downs
                  A. C. Downs

Probated & filed this 15th day of Decr 1892
J. H. Messick, Clerk

[Page 529]

A. S. MANNING

Will of A. S. Manning

State of Tennessee }
Hamilton County   }   Third District -

Know all men by these presents I, A. S. Manning of the third District in the above mentioned State & County farmer. Considering the uncertainty of this life and being of sound mind and memory and in good health. Do make declare and publish this my last will and Testament.

First - I give and bequeath unto my beloved niece Eliza Ellen Manning daughter of Thomas Manning and Eliza Keller his wife both deceased late of Dayton, Ohio, said legatee now residing in Chattanooga, Tenn., all the real estate, money goods and chattles that I may be possessed of at my death, after all my just debts are paid the above mentioned Legatee to have and possess and to hold the said estate money goods and chattles in her own name and right, and to do any and all things therewith that I might do if living. I do further appoint the above named Legatee to be the Sole Executrix of this my last will and Testament.

In testimony whereof I hereunto set my hand and seal and publish and decree this to be my last will and Testmaent in the presence of the witnesses named below this 31st day of July in the year A.D. one thousand eight hundred and Eighty-five. Signed sealed declared and published by the said A. S. Manning as a[nd] for his last will and Testament in presence of us who at his request and in his presence and in presence of each other have subscribed our names as witnesses hereto revoking all forever wills of whatever kind that might be presented written and signed with my own hand this the 31^d of July 1885.

A. S. Manning

Witnesses: A. M. Rogers
                  J. A. Conner

Probated 7th day of Janry 1893

J. H. Messick, Clerk

[Page 530]

JAMES LAMON

Will of James Lamon

Chattanooga, Tenn. Nov. 21st 1892

I, Dr. J. Lamon** of No. 217 Magnolia St., Chattanooga, Tennessee, being of sound mind and good understanding do hereby make this my last Will and Testament. After my demise I will and decree, that my wife Amelia Laman** shall have all my effects of every kind, all monies in Bank, also all my notes, Books and valuable papers, all my furniture, also my watch and chain after first paying my funeral expenses, except fifty dollars to each of my Grandsons Fred and Harry Gaston to be paid them when they shall have attained the age of Eighteen years and two hundred and fifty Dollars I direct paid to my brother Joseph Laman of Burwick. PA.

I do also make constitute and appoint my wife Amelia Laman Executrix of this my last will. I also direct that if desired by my wife, that my body be cremated.

Dr. J. Laman

Witnesses:

J. M. Ellis
W. A. Ellis

** both spellings used

Filed Jan^ry 31, 1893

J. H. Messick, Clerk

[Page 531]

LIZZIE C. WILSON

Will of Lizzie C. Wilson

I, Lizzie C. Wilson, a resident of the City of Chattanooga and State of Tennessee, do hereby make my last will and Testament which is as follows:

First - I hereby will and direct, that all expenses which may be incident to, and which may be incurred my funeral and the proper burial of my remains, to be paid out of any funds which I may leave, or if no funds are left by me, then that Said expenses be paid from the proceeds of the sale of such real estate as I may leave at my death.

Second - I further will and direct that all my just debts be paid out of any funds that may remain after the payment of the expenses attending my funeral and burial or if there be no funds or an insufficient amount thereof for the payment of said Debts, then the same shall be paid out of the proceeds arising or that may arise from the sale of the real Estate left by me.

Third - I further will and bequeath to my two children Jennie S. and John H. equal amounts of such of the proceeds arising from the Sale of all of my property, which includes the lot on Gillespie Street, on which I now reside and which was conveyed to me by deed executed by J. S. Gillespie and wife which deed is recorded in Book "I" Vol 2 pages 603 and 604 of the records of Hamilton County. Also a house and lot on Cherry Stret, which was covnveyed to my late husband W. H. Wilson and myself by deed executed by John Kesterson, which deed is of record in Book "T" Vol 2 and page 241 of the records of said County, as may be left after the payment therefrom of such an amount as may be necessary to carry out the provisions contained in the first and second Sections of this Will and also the payment of such expenses as may be occurred in making the sale of the property or otherwise incurred in executing the terms of this will, the portion due my daughter Jennie S. shall be paid over to her to be used and controlled by her, as her own judgement may dictate but that portion due my son John H. shall be invested by my Executor in such manner as his best judgment may dicatate [Page 532] until my said son shall become 21 years of age when the principal as such of the interest as may have been acrued thereto, or that may have been derived therefrom and remaining unexpended shall be paid over to him; provided that the interest that may be derived from the investment aforesaid or so much thereof as may be necessary shall be applied by my Executor or paid over to the Guardian of my son, should a Guardian be appinted to the payment of Educational expenses, and for the support of my said son.

Fourth - I hereby name and appoint Robt Hooke, a resident of Hamilton County and State of Tennessee as the Executor of this will and I hereby authorize and empower him to sell and convey by deed, the property mentioned in the third Section of this will and for the purpose therein set forth, and I further authorize and empower and direct hiim to apply the proceeds derived from the sale thereof, as is therein specified.

In testimony whereof I have hereunto subscribed my name this the 25th day of March A.D. one Thousand Eight hundred and nienety-two.

Lizzie C. Wilson

We the undersigned at the request of the Testatrix Lizzie C. Wilson, have witnessed her signature to the foregoing will, in which we have no interest whatever and in witness to said signature we hereby subscribe our names this the 25 day of March 1892.

R. B. Stegall
Mary J. Stegall

[Page 533]

JANE HOWDEN

Will of Jane Howden

I, Jane Howden resident of St. Elmo, Hamilton County, Tennessee, being weak in body, but of sound mind and memory do make and publish this my last will and Testament.

First - I direct that my body shall have proper and decently burial and that all my funeral expenses shall be paid out of my estate, and after the payment of all my just debts I make the following disposition of my property. That is to say:

Item - I give and bequeath to my only Daughter Caroline M. Braden all my property, Real, Personal or mixed, consisting in part of the house and lot on which I now reside. Also a Lot I hold in Walker County, Georgia, all my household goods, one hundred shares of stock in the Dowlin & Rush Cattle Company in the State of Wyoming all the Stocks I hold or may at the time of my death hold in the Bank of Seward County, Kansas, all monies coming on a judgment I hold against Doctor D. W. Braden, now in process of collection, and all my property of whatsoever kind, that I may hold claim or possess at time of my death.

Item - If I should be living at the time of my daughter Caroline M. Braden's death. Then or in that event I give and bequeath to my Grand Daughter Belle Braden Foster, now living in Lebanon, Tennessee all my property of whatsoever kind real personal or mixed, that I may possess or claim at the time of my death to be hers only.

I hereby revoke all former wills and appoint Doctor D. W. Braden to be my executor and to attend to all my business in Settlement of my estate, and to be paid a proper compensation for the same, and not to be required to give bonds and to have all authority to sell any and all property belonging to my estate If it be necessary to liquidate claims, or my heir should so desire. Witness my hand and seal this seventh day of March 1891.

Jane Howden

Witness Present: R. L. Bice
C. S. Mason

Probated 6th Mch 1893

[Page 534]

JOHN GEILER, SR.

Will of John Geiler, Sr.

Hereby revoking all former Wills or codicils by me at any time heretofore made, I John Geiler, Senior do hereby make, publish and declare my last Will & testament to be as follows:

1 - Item - My just debts & funeral Expenses shall be first paid out of rents accuring and to accrue out of real estate of which I may die seized & possessed.

2 - Item - I bequeath to my daughter Emma Geiler Five hundred Dollars in full of her distribution share of my estate, to be paid out of rents accruing or to accrue as herein before set forth in Item No. 1.

3 - Item - I bequeath to the Trustees of the Imanuel Lutheran Church, located at No. 22 State Street, Chattanooga, Tenn. Two hundred dollars to be paid out of rents accruing & to accrue as set forth in Item No. 1.

4 - Item - I bequeath to the Chattanooga Orphans Home located at No.2 - 40 Vine Street in said City one hundred Dollars to be paid out of rents accruing and to accrue as set forth in Item No. 1.

5 - Item - My Executor hereinafter shall next pay to my son John Geiler Junior my promissory note dated Feb. 5th 1889 payable to him on or before my death for one Thousand Dollars & interest. Said note is not to be chargeable aginst the distribution share of my said son as herein after set forth in Item No. 1.

6 - Item - The residue of my estate I bequeath to my said son John Geiler Junior or his heirs an undivided one half and to my Grand daughter Constance Duckwity, the use of the other undivided one half until she arrives at the age of Eighteen years or shall sooner marry and here [have?] living issue then and in that event I bequeath & devise to my said Grand Daughter Constance Duckwity, free from the control, management or debts of any husband she may marry the other undivided one half of my estate provided that if my said Grand Daughter Constance Duckwity shall die before I do or before arriving at the age of Eighteen years, without leaving issue her surviving then & in that event I will & bequeath to my said son John Geiler, Junior the share of my estate to which my said Grand Daughter would otherwise have been entitled.

7 - Item - I appoint my son John Geiler, Junior sole [Page 535] Executor of this my last will & Testament and authorize him to lease the real Estate of which I shall die seized & possessed until my said Grand daughter Constance Duckwity shall arrive at the age of Eighteen years, out of which shall be paid my debts & legacies in the order received in this will & he may erect a suitable monument over my grave out of this same as part of my funeral expenses.

8 - Item - My said Executor is authorized to act without bond as such.

In testimony whereof I have hereunto signed my name and affixed my seal this the -- day of July 1891.

John Geiler, Sr. {seal}

Signed sealed & published in our presence and we have subscribed our names hereto at the request of the testator, in his presence & in the presence of each other this the -- day of July 1891.

Sam Geismar
Casper Saffer
Tomlinson Fort

Filed by John Geiler, Jr. March 13/93 and probated Mch 14/93 in presence of John Geiler, Jr., Emma Geiler and witness Tomlinson Fort.

J. H. Messick, Clerk

[Page 536]

PATRICK PAUL McMAHAN

Will of Patrick Paul McMahan

State of Tennessee }
Hamilton County } I, Patrick Paul McMahan of said State and county, do make and publish this as my last will and Testament, hereby revoking, annulling and making void all others by me at anytime made.

1st - I will and direct that my funeral expenses and all my debts be paid as soon after my death as possible out of any moneys that I may die possessed of or may first come into the hands of my Executrix.

2nd - I will give and bequeath to my beloved wife Jennie McMahan Lots of land Nos 29-31 & 33 of the Subdivision of the Lyones property to the City of Atlanta, Fulton County, Ga as shown and described by deed recorded in Book A3 page 466 in the Clerk Superior Court Office of said County and State.

Also lot of land No. 32 of the Sub-division of the Johnson property in the City of Atlanta Fulton County

Georgia as shown and described by deed recorded in Book ZZ page 92 in the Clerk Office of said State and County. Provided however that John S. Johnson of said City of Atlanta shall have the privilege of buying said lot 32 at the agreed price of Three hundred & seventy five Dollars ($375.00) of which Seventy dollars have been paid to me, on agreement that when $100.00 shall have been so paid Bond for title to said lot shall be executed to said John S. Johnson, and when the balance of said price shall have been paid the proper deed shall be executed to said Johnson, in the event of my death before the final payment and execution of said papers.

3rd - I will, give and bequeath to my said wife Jennie McMahan, all of my one half interest in and to the Patent right on what is known as the McMahan and Wilcoson Spring Box for Coupling Cars Patented Mch 1st 1892.

4th - I will, give and bequeath to my said wife Jennie McMahan all such other property of which I may die possessed of every kind, variety and description, Real, Personal and mixed to hold and enjoy to her own use and benefit forever.

Lastly - I do hereby nominate and appoint my said wife Jennie McMahan my Executrix.

In witness whereof I do to this my will set my hand this the 18th day of November 1892.

Patrick Paul McMahan

[Page 537]
Signed, sealed and published by Patrick Paul McMahan as his last will and Testament in the presence of us the undersigned, who subscribed our names hereto in the presence of said Testator, at his special request and in the presence of each other.

This 18 day of November 1892.

D. W. Miller
T. P. Chumlee

Probated Mch 24, 1893

[Page 537 con't]

D. CAL McMILLIN

Will of D. Cal McMillin

I, D. Cal McMillin of Chattanooga, Hamilton County, Tenn. make this my last Will and Testament.

I give and bequeath my Estate and property both real and personal to my wife Minnie to be used by her for the support and benefit of herself and our children. Douglas Newman and Edwin West when the children shall respectively come of age, I direct my wife to give unto their hands for their own use such part of the estate as her judgment may dictate, reserving however to herself enough for a comfortable support during her life. But at her death the balance of the estate shall be equally divided between our two children above mentioned. I appoint my wife Minnie Executrix of this my last will and testament, without bond, and with full authority to make whatever disposition of any of the property she may think best for the interest of herself and our children including authority to Sell and make Title to real Estate.

But I direct that she keep a careful record of such transactions so that she may be able to show what disposition has been made of property and funds. In case of the death of my wife before the children come of age, I appoint Dr. Geo. R. West Executor in her stead. He shall manage the estate for the children receiving such compensation for his service as is fair and right and shall divide the estate equally between them when they respectively come of age, giving each his share.

In witness where of I have signed and signed [sic] and sealed this my last [Page 538] will and Testament.
This Dec. 16th 1892
D. Cal. McMillin

Attest: Atwell Thompson
                 Kate Lyle West

[page 538 con't]

GEORGE P. KARR

Will of George P. Karr

I, George P. Karr of Chattanooga, Tennessee, being of sound mind and disposing memory do make and publish this my last Will and Testament.

First - I give and bequeath to my son Lewis Karr the following Real Estate in Chattanooga, Tenn. to wit: Situated on the corner of East Fourth and Moon Streets in said City fronting one hundred feet on the East side of Moon Street and running back of uniform width to the middle of the alley and one hudnred feet.

Second - I give and bequeath to my daughter Mrs. Annie Forstner the followingh Real Estate in Chattanooga, Tenn. described as a lot fronting on the south side of East Fourth Street fronting about 25 or 30 feet on East Fourth Street and extending back Southwardly one hundred feet. I also give and bequeath her my said daughter a note made and signed by her husband Joseph Forstner and

payable to my order dated Jany 2, 1888 for $1800.00 due and payable one year after date, which note is a lien on the Real Estate herein given to my said daughter.

Third - I will that my just debts be paid as soon as practicable after my death.

Fourth - I make and appoint Martin Becker the Executor of this my last will and Testament and that he said Martin Becker as Executor shall not be required to give the usual bond with security required in such cases.

Witness my hand this April 1st 1893

George P. Karr {seal}

Signed and sealed in the presence of us & in the prensence of each other April 1st 1893.

S. P. Stover
Thos Rowell

[Page 539]

ELI WILLIAMS

Will of Eli Williams

State of Tennessee }
Hamilton County   }   In the name of God. Amen.

I Eli Williams of Stanley Town, Hamilton County, Tennessee being of sound mind and disposing mind and memory do make publish and declare this to be my last Will and Testament, hereby revoking all other wills by me heretofore made.

First - I desire that my body be buried in a decent and Christian like manner, according to my circumstances in life and desire further that the expenses of the same be paid by my Executor herein after named out of my estate.

Second - I desire that out of my Estate my Executor pay all my just debts and liabilities.

Third - I desire that out of the rents of my property my executor herein after named pay off the debt due by me to the National Home Building & Loan Association of Chattanooga, Tennessee.

Fourth - I desire that my Executor take charge of all my real and personal property of every description whatever and out of any debts due me or rents of my property that he may collect to pay off my indebtedness that may be just and due.

Fifth - I further give and bequeath to my daughter Mattie Lou Williams of Sharp's Station, Georgia, the property whereon I have been living to wit: lots number one hudnred and one hundred and one (100-101) in Stanleys subdivision of the DeLong tract in the town of Churchville as shown by plat recorded in Registers plat Book No. 2 page 14 and all other property that I may have of every discription after my debts are paid.

Sixth - I further desire that my Executor be paid what is reasonable and proper for his services and I hereby name and constitute and appoint H. W. Lynch and George McGill of Hamilton County, Tennessee as my executors to carry out this my last will and Testament.

Seventh - I further desire that my Executor sell if necessary to pay my debts the property whereon I have been living & upon which there are unfinished two story houses and also my last lot at Sherman Heights, being the East half of lot no. 7 in Spring place addition to Sherman Heights (Glass farm) and when this is done. if my Executor think it is necessary to pay my debts, I desire that after all my debts are paid, the balance to go to my daughter Mattie Lou Williams. I desire my Executors to take care of and manage my property as they think best calculated [Page 540] to carry out my wishes herein expressed.

Signed Sealed published & declared as the last will & Testament of Eli Williams.

Eli X Williams
his mark

[Witnesses]

C. C. Green
A. F. Perry M.D.
Seth M. Walker

Probated April 1893.

[Page 540 con't]

ELIZABETH W. WARNE

Will of Elizabeth W. Warne

It is my will that at my death my niece Lizzie W. Crump shall have all my property, both real and personal and mixed. My Real Estate consists in a lot at Ridgedale Hamilton County, Tennessee, the same purchased by me of Mrs. Cordelia A. Kirshner. I appoint the said Lizzie W. Crump my Executrix and no bond is required of her, upon her qualification as such. Said Executrix will of course pay all my debts.

This Sept. 28th 1889

Elizabeth W. Warne {seal}

Signed, sealed and published in our presence and we have subscribed our names hereto in the presences of the testator and of each other.

R. M. Barton, Jr.
N. H. Burl

Probated April 19/93

See Record #9 pages 60 E. Sig.

[Page 541]

ELLEN H. WEER

Will of Ellen H. Weer

I, Ellen H. Weer widow of John Weer deceased, being of sound and disposing memory do make and publish this my last will and testament, hereby revoking and making void any and all other wills by me at any time made.

First - I direct that my funeral Expenses and all my debts to be paid as soon after my death as possible out of any moneys, that I may die possessed of or that may first come into the hands of my Executrix.

Second - I give, devise, and bequeath to my five children - Nellie, Edith, Fred, Ben and Ethel, all my estate both real and personal and whereever Situated. Said property and Estate being described as follows viz: The house and lot now occupied by me as a residence being known as Lot 463 of Block 40 of the Mission Ridge Land Cos addition or sub-division known as East Lake; also Lots 9 and 10 of Block 1 of the Mutual Real Estate and Home Building Associations Addition or subdivision known as Eden Park all in Hamilton County, Tennessee State, also all my personal effects and property in the House aforesaid also my Stock in the merchants & Merchants Building & Loan Association, each of said five children to have an equal share in my Estate share and share alike. In case of the death of either of my said children before or after my decease, it is my will that the surviving children shall share equally in my Estate. It is my wish that the estate be held intact until the youngest child shall arrive at the age of 21 years, but if necessary for the suppoort of the said children, or if in the judgment of my executrix it appears for their interest it may be sold at anytime, if in the opinion of the Executrix it is necessary to do so, and she is hereby given full power and authority to dispose of said Estate as her best judgment suggests.

Lastly - I hereby nominate and appcint my eldest daughter Nellie Weer my Executrix and in the event of her death or disability before the closing up of the Estate and distribution of the proceeds among the children there and in that event I apppoint my second daughter Edith Weer, my executrix and having full faith in their integrity and good faith, she and each of them are excused from giving bond as Executrix. In witness whereof I have here unto set my hand and seal this 12th day of May 1893.

Ellen H. Weer

[Page 542]
Signed, Sealed and published and acknowledged in our presence and we have subscribed our names hereto in presence of the testator and at her request. This 12th day of May 1893.
Walter K. Newport
C. V. Brown

Filed and probated June 25, 1893
J. H. Messick, Clerk

PATTIE V. PRYOR

Will of Pattie V. Pryor

I, Pattie Pryor of Hamilton County, Tennessee, being of sound mind and disposing memory, do hereby make publish and declare this my last will and Testament that is to say.
First - I direct that all my just debts be paid.
Second - I give, devise and bequeath to my beloved mother E. F. Pryor, all my estate, real, personal and mixed wheresoever located and of every descripton whatsoever.
Third - I appoint my beloved mother E. F. Pryor, sole Executrix of this my last Will & Testament and desire that she administer without giving bond.
In witness whereof I hereunto set my hand and seal, this 17th day of March 1893.

Pattie V. Pryor {Seal}

Signed and sealed by said Pattie Pryor, who at the same time published and declared the same, as for her last will & Testament in the presence of us who in her presence, and in the presence of each other, and at her request have hereunto subscribed our names as witnesses.
Mrs. C. E. Hunter
Miss Jennie Terrell
Mrs. A. W. Goines

Filed and probated June 6, 1893
J. H. Messick, Clk
By A. Shelton D. C.

[Page 543]

REBECCA EVANS

Will of Rebecca Evans

I, Rebecca Evans being mindful of the uncertainties of life & the sureness of death do hereby publish this my Last will and Testament.
I hereby give devise and bequeath to my husband Jessee Evans, all my property real personal or mixed, the real Estate is more particularily set out in a deed made by Zed & Jordan Lucas to me on the 21st Dec. 1882 and Registered in the Registers Office of Hamilton County, Tennessee in Book M Vol 2 page 574 to which reference is here made.
Witness my hand 8th Sept. 1885
Rebecca Evans

Signed sealed and acknowledged in our presence and witnessed by us in the presence of the Testator, and of each other at the request of the Testator on this 8th Sept. 1885.

Attest: H. G. Hixson
P. A. Rogers

Filed 18 April 1893
Probated April 29th 1893.

E. H. KUYKENDALL

Will of E. H. Kuykendall

I, E. H. Kuykendall of Chattanooga, Tennessee, do hereby declare this to be my last Will and Testament.
I hereby devise and bequeath unto my beloved wife M. G. Kuykendall all my property, real, personal and mixed and wherever situated.
I appoint my beloved wife M. G. Kuykendall Executrix of this my last will and Testament of whom no bond shall be required.
Witness my hand this the 14th day of April 1893.
E. H. Kuykendall

In witness whereof we have hereunto set our hands in the presence of E. H. Kuykendall who declared this to be his last will and Testament and the same is witnessed at his request and in the presence of each other and in his presence who signed the same in our presence.

J. H. McLean
G. Manning Ellis

Filed & probated May 8th 1893.

[Page 544]

ELLEN SMITH

Will of Ellen Smith

I, Ellen Smith, do make and publish this as my last will and Testament hereby revoking and making void all others by me at any time made.

1st - I direct that my funeral expenses and all my debts be paid as soon after my death as possible out of any moneys that I may die possessor of or may first come into the hand of my Executor.

2nd - I direct that my executor will offer for sale as soon as convenient my house and lot in Cleveland, Bradley Co. Tenn. in 6th Ward of said City bounded on the South by Bates road, on the North by a lot owned by Mrs. Ford, on the West by Clark & Payne. Also sell my lot at Sumit in James Co., Tennessee.

3rd - I want my two daughters to peaceably divide equally between themselves all my clothing, furniture and other Household articles I may have.

4th - When my property is sold, and all lawful debts are paid, then the balance of the money is to be divided equally among my 3 children, Richard Nelson, Lizzie Thompson, Nelly Smith.

5th - And lastly - I do hereby nominate and appoint my Executor John Trunk of Cleveland, Bradley Co. Tenn to act as such as my last will and Testament.

In witness whereof I do this day set my hand and mark the X mark this the 8th day of May 1893.

Ellen X Smith
her mark

Witness: Samuel Hunt
                 Annie A. Smith

Signed sealed in our presence of the Testator the 8th day of May 1893.

[Page 545]

SARAH C. WROE

Will of Sarah C. Wroe

In the name of God. Amen.

I, Sarah C. Wroe of the County of Hamilton in the State of Tennessee being of sound and disposing memory and wishing to arrange all my wordly matters before my death, do hereby make, publish and declare this to be my last Will and Testament hereby revoking and making void all other wills by me at anytime heretofore made. That is to say:

1s - I direct that my funeral Expenses and all my debts be paid out of any money or property which I may own at the time of my death.

2n - All the residue of my property of every character and descripton, real, personal and mixed, wherever situated, and particularly all my right tile and interest in the estate of my Uncle William O. Wroe who died in the City of New Orleans, but who owned large landed Estates in Travis and adjoining counties in the state of Texas and perhaps in other counties in said State of Texas, but whether in Travis or any County is said State of Texas, I hereby will and bequeath to my cousin Joseph F. Thompson and his wife Lydia Ann Thompson of Hamilton County, Tennessee jointly in fee simple forever.

I hereby nominate and appoint my said Cousin Joseph F. Thompson Executor to this my last will and Testament and direct that he execute the same without giving bond therefor.

In testimony whereof I hereuto signed my name and affixed my seal this the 25th day of May 1893.

Sarah X C. Wroe {seal}
her mark

The foregoing instrument was subscribed by Sarah C. Wroe the Testator in our presence and declared by her to be her last will and Testament and we at her request and in her presence have signed our names as witness hereto the day and date above written.

W. C. Payne
J. E. Montgomery

Filed July 29, 1893.

[Page 546]

WILLIAM CAHILL

Will of William Cahill

Know all men by these presents That I, William Cahill of Chattanooga in Hamilton County, Tennessee, being of sound and disposing mind, in view of the certainty of death and uncertainty of the time thereof Do make this my last Will as follows: -

Item First - I give, bequeath and devise to my beloved wife Margaret Cahill, for and during her natural life, all my estate and property, real and personal, except a Lot fifty by one hundred and fifty feet, on South Side of Gillespie Street and being the second East of College, which I give and devise to her in fee simple.

Item Second - I give and bequeath and devise to our Son James Cahill, upon the death and termination of the life estate of Said Margaret Cahill therein. The lot on which we now reside on corner of Pine and Fourth Streets in Chattanooga being one hundred and ten feet on Pine and running back of uniform width to Poplar, and all the furniture household and kitchen and effects in and about the premises and also one half share in the Cloudland Subdivision formerly Stover property on Lookout Mountain, to him and his heirs forever.

Item Third - I give and devise to our Son William Cahill, upon the death and termination of the life Estate of said Margaret Cahill therein, All of the Lot on Whiteside and Missionary Ave. not hereto conveyed to him, Said lot originally being one hundred feet on Whiteside Street and Two hundred and eighty feet on Missionary Avenue to have and his Heirs forever.

Item Fourth - I give and bequeath to our daughter Mary Connelly at the death and termination of Life Estate of said Margaret Cahill - one half share in the Cloudland Subdivision formerly Stover property on Lookout Mountain.

Item Fifth - I hereby nominate and appoint the said Margaret Cahill Executrix of this my last will, without Bond which is hereby excused.

In witness whereof I have signed and sealed and published and declared this as my will at Chattanooga this Seventh day of March 1893.

William Cahill

[Page 547]   The said William Cahill at Chattanooga, Tenn. on said seventh day of March 1893 signed and sealed this Instrument and published and declared the same as and for his last will and we at his request, and in his presence and in the presence of each other, have hereunto written our names as subscribing witnesses.

J. J. Bencler

P. A. Brawner

Filed and probated Augt 9th 1893
J. H. Messick, Clerk

[Page 548]

JULIA SOUTHGATE FRAER

Will of Julia Southgate Fraer

I, Julia Southgate Fraer being in sound health of body, and disposing mind and memory, do make and publish this my last Will and Testament, hereby revoking all former wills by me at anytime made.

I.

I direct, that all my just debts, including funeral Expenses, and the expense of Administration be paid by my executors.

II.

I devise and bequeath all the residue and remainder of my Estate, both real and personal to Chas. Edward Hamlin and George Clifford Steward Trustees, and their Successors, in trust, for the benefit of my two daughters Florence Clement Hamlin and Carrie Watson Steward, and their legal issue in the manner hereinafter provided. My said two daughters are to share the said residue of my estate equally between them, each taking one half thereof, and said Trustees who are the husbands of my said daughters, are to manage the property herein devised and bequeathed, for my daughters. But I hereby direct, that the share of each daughter shall not absolutely vest in her, but shall be retained by the Trustees herein appointed, and shall be put at interest or upon rent, and only the income thereof paid annually to her during her natural life, unless said life estate is terminated and merged into an estate in fee simple as hereinafter provided. The powers and duties of the said Trustees shall be as follows: As to the personal property, the said Trustees shall have the right to sell and convert the same into money, except each articles as may be hereinafter specifically devised. The process arising from the Sale of such personal property as they may sell, they are authorized and empowered to invest for the benefit of my said daughters and the said Trustees are given full power and authority to select the manner and the property in which the proceed of said property shall be invested. The Real Estate herein devised shall be managed in such a manner as may be said Trustees seem best. In case the same is rented, then the net amounts received from said rents, shall be at least once in each year, equally divided between my two daughters, and the said Trustees are given full power to make leases of said real Estate. Although the title to said Real Estate is by the terms of this will, vested in the Said Trustees and their successors in trust, nevertheless they have no authority to sell and convey said real estate [Page 549] without the consent of both my daughters and said property shall not be sold while both my daughters are living unless both of said daughters consent to said sale and sign the deed of conveyance. If one daughter dies, then the consent of the other, shall be necessary before the Trustees can, during her lifetime, sell said property.

III.

My two Sons in law, George Clifford Steward and Charles Edward Hamlin are now engaged in paying off a mortgage of Five Thousand Dollars on my home property, situated on Gilmer Street in Chattanooga, Tenn. and it is my desire that each be protected to the extent of the amount, which he has paid out in discharing said mortgage.

I therefore direct that said Trustees pay to themselves out of the personal property of which I die seized, the amount or amounts which may be respectively due to them on account of said mortgage. In case there is not sufficient personal property to re-emburse them for the amounts thus expended, then upon the final sale of said Gilmer Street property, I direct that out of the proceeds of the sale of said property they pay themselves the amounts which they have expended as above set out.

IV.

In case of the death of either of my daughters herein named, leaving surviving heirs, her present husband and legal issue of their marriage then the whole of the share of said daughter, shall be equally distributed among said children. But the trust herein created shall as to the share of said daughter then become vested in her said surviving husband as sole trustee of said share, and the said trust as to said share shall not terminate until the youngest of her living children attains it majority when said share shall be equally distributed among said children. In the event the Trustee herein named shall die after the death of his wife and before said period of final distribution then let a Successor be appointed under the laws of the land.

But nothing in this paragraph con- [Page 550] tained shall terminate the Trusteeship herein created so far as the share of the surviving daughter is concerned.

V.

In case of the death of either of my daughters herein named without legal issue, leaving her present husband surviving her, then in that case, it is my wish and I so devise, that such husband shall be entitled to such proportion of my Estate as his wife would have being entitled to under the terms of this will. And said husband

shall take said wife's portion free from control of the Trust herein created and said Trusteeship as to his portion shall thereupon cease. He shall have full power to use, and expend said property as he desires, the same as I could do were I living and enjoying same. But if any part remains unexpended at his death, then I direct and devise that such portion shall pass to my legal heirs. But the death of said daughter shall not terminate the trust herein created so far as the share of the surviving daughter may be concerned and during the contiuance of the life of said surviving daughter her present husband shall be sole Trustee of his wife share.

VI.

In case of the death of my son in law George Clifford Steward one of the Trustees herinbefore named before the death of his wife Carrie Watson Steward, then his said wife is to become the holder in her own right of all her portion of my Estate and herein fixed by this will, free and clear from the control of any Trustee.

VII.

But in case Charles Edward Hamlin my other son-in-law and one of the Trustees herein before named, should die leaving surviving him his wife Florence Clement Hamlin, then in that event I nominate W. H. Converse of Chattanooga, Tennessee to succeed the said Charles Edward Hamlin as Trustee under the terms of the trust herein created and said Trust shall continue until she is Twenty-five years of age. In case she dies during the trusteeship of said Converse, then I devise her share to her heirs.

{Page 551}   ### VIII.

I hereby appoint my said Sons-in-law George Clifford Steward and Charles Edward Hamlin as Executors of this my last will and Testament. I desire that they be required to give bond as Executors as required by law and that they also be required to give such bonds as the law may require as Trustees under this will and in case the said W. H. Converse should become Trustee as hereinbefore provided, then let him also give bond as required by law for such purposes.

In Testimony whereof I have hereunto signed my name this 5th day of April 1892 - and have also signed the margin on the four preceeding sheets.

Julia S. Fraer.

Signed by the Said Testatrix Julia S. Fraer as and for her last will and Testament in the presence of us who at her request and in our sight and presence and in the presence of each other have subscribed our names as attesting witnesses, both on this sheet and on each of the four preceeding sheets.

Maud Liteheser
Francis Martin

Filed and probated August 28, 1893
J. H. Messick, Clerk

[Page 552]

MARGARET SULLIVAN

Will of Margaret Sullivan

I, Margaret Sullivan of the City of Chattanooga Hamilton County, Tennessee being now far advanced in life, do make this my last Will and Testament.

Item 1 - I desire to be burried on my lot in Mount Olivet Cemetery, Hamilton County Tennessee in accordance with the usages of the Holy Catholic Church.

Item 2 - I direct that my Executor herein after named sell my house and lot known as Number 14 Porter Street in the City of Chattanooga, in such manner and on such terms, at public or private sale in his discretion, so as to make it sell for the best attainable price, and that he convey the same by proper deed to the purchaser, all of which is hereby empower him to do out of the proceeds he shall erect a suitable monument on my lot in Mount Olivet Cemetery.

Item 3 - I hereby set apart the sum of Fifty Dollars, the first money coming to the hands of my Executor from any source, to be paid by him for the offering up of Holy Sacrifice of the mass, for the repose of my Soul.

Item 4 - I give to my three grand children, Mary, Annie and Katie Mulvey children of my deceased daughter Ellen Mulvey my house and lot on the corner of Vaughn and Porter Streets in the City of Chattanooga known as No. 16 and if any one of my said grand children should die before I do, said lot shall belong to the survivors of them unless such deceased grand child should leave a living child or children, in which event such child or children will take the share of its mother.

Item 5 - My house and lot known as lot Number 12 Porter Street in the City of Chattanooga I give to my daughter Mrs. Mary Dowling during her lifetime with remainder in fee to her three children James, Nellie and Kate Dowling, but if any one of her said children should die in her lifetime without issue the survivors shall take the share of the one so dying. But if anyone of her said children dies before she dies before she does, [sic] and leaves living child children or decendents such child, children or decendents shall take the share of the deceased parent. And on the death of my said Daughter my Executor is hereby authorized to sell and convey said lot and divide the proceeds as herein indicated.

Item 6 - My house and lot number ten (10) Porter Street in the City of Chattanooga, I give to my grand child [Page 553] Margaret Sullivan, daughter of my deceased son Michael.

Item 7 - To my son James J. Sullivan I give my two houses and lots known as Number 115 and 117 Florence Street in the City of Chattanooga, on condition that he pays all my funeral expenses, including the sum of fifty dollars herein set apart for the Sacrifice of the Mass and that he also pay to my grandson James Dowling the sum of Three Hundred Dollars, all of which are made a charge on said two houses and lots.

Mrs. Margaret Sullivan

Signed, Sealed Declared and published by Margaret Sullivan as and for her last Will and Testament, and we have at her special request signed our names hereto as witnesses in the presence of the Testator and in the presence of each other this 17 July 1893.

Joseph Mety
E. M. Dodson

[Page 554]

W. D. POSEY

Last Will and Testament of W. D. Posey

I, W. D. Posey being of Sound mind and disposing memory do make and publish this my last will and Testament.

First - I give and bequeath to my son Oliver N. Posey one acre in the north east corner of my farm, and the same will be laid off and set apart to him by my Executor.

Second - I give and bequeath to my daughter Polly Margaret Gillem, one acre and a half where she now lives and which is also to be laid off and set apart to her by my Executor.

Third - I give and bequeath all the balance of my farm, after taking out the above bequests to my Son Wiley D. Posey, Jr. said property is described as follows to wit: lying in the 12 District of Hamilton County, Tennessee - Beginnning on Black Oak John Brown Sr. corner thence South 30 West with his line about ninety poles to a white oak in Said line. Thence north 60 west with Wm Brown's line to his corner a Black oak and post oak. Thence north 30 East with W. R. Browns & Madison Varner line to a Stake in Jack Brown's line. Thence with Jack Brown's line South wardly to the beginning, to contain Fifty acres. Said property was conveyed to my by Robt C. McRee, Sr. by deed dated the 18th day of February 1859 and Registered in the Registers Office of Hamilton County, Tennessee in Book "O" page 282 on the 29th day of Sept. 1862.

Fourth - I nominate and appoint my son J. C. Posey, my Executor of this my last will and request that he qualify without bond.

Signed, Sealed and executed in the presence of the Subscribing witnesses, who witness this will in my presence and in the presence of each other and at my request on this the 22nd day of September 1891.

Wiley D. Posey {Seal}

Witness: R. C. McRee
            M. B. McRee

Probated December 4th 1893.

[Page 555 - blank]

[Page 556]

MRS. MARY THOMSON

Last Will and Testament of Mrs. Mary Thomson

I, Mrs. Mary Thomson being of sound mind, and disposing memory, do make and publish this my last will and Testament revoking any and all wills by me at anytime heretofore made.

1st - I direct the payment of my funeral expenses and any just debts that I may owe out of any money on hand or due me at the time of my death.

2nd - I give my son Harry A. Thomson and to Mrs. Charles Lewis, formerly Emma L. Thomson my daughter five Dollars each.

3rd - The entire residue of my Estate both real and personal of every kind, and whereever situated I give and devise to my daughter Mrs. Fanny McKenny, and refer to my title deeds and papers alway kept and designated "Valuable Papers" Said property at present is situated in the City of Chattanooga, Hamilton County, Tennessee and consists of:

1. One lot on Early Street 50 X 116 1/2 feet with improvements, described in deed from Eliza J. Paxton & husband to me dated August 13, 1885 and registered in the Registers Office for said County Book S Vol 2 page 275 to which reference is made.

2nd - One lot No. 43 Block one (1) Stautons

addition to Chattanooga described in deed from James McClarin to me dated June 23 1884 and registered in the Office of Register aforesaid Book 2 Vol 2 page 33, which is also refered to.

3rd - 5 Shares of Stock in the Lookout Homestead Association.

4th - All other personal property of every kind whatever, such as household goods, money, notes accounts & in a word everything whether here in enumerated or not, it been [sic] my intention that it shall pass hereunder to said Mrs. McKenny.

5th - All of said property both real and personal is devised to said Mrs. McKenny to have and to hold to her Sole & separate use free from the debts contracts, obligation and control of her present or [Page 557] and future husband and in express exclusion of any and all marital rights whatever of her present or any future husband but with full power and authority to my said daughter Mrs. McKenny to sell, charge & convey and & all of said property by deed or otherwise as fully & in the same manner as a single woman may do & without the concurrence, consent or knowledge of her husband and without his joining in deed.

5th Lastly - I name and appoint my son in law Charles Lewis Executor of this my last will and Testament.

In testimony whereof I hereto set my hand this July 23rd 1892.

Mrs. Mary Thomson

Attest: Signed, Sealed & acknowledge in our presence & witnessed by us in presence of Testatrix & at her request this July 23, 1892.

Foster E. Brown, Chattanooga, Tenn
Ruth Millington, Chattanooga, Tenn.

Filed and probated November 23, 1893
J. H. Messick, Clerk

[Page 558]

FRED DEVINE

Last Will of Fred Devine

To whom it may concern greeting:

I, Fred Devine, being of Sound mind and memory, and mindful of the uncertainies of human life, do hereby make publish and declare this my Last Will and Testament hereby revoking all former wills by me made.

First, I direct that all my just debts and the expenses of my last Sickness and funeral expenses be first paid and out of any money that may come to the hands of my Executors.

Second - I will and direct that my Executors shall cause to be erected, upon a lot Forrest Hill Cemetery, to be purchased by them for that purpose in some suitable place where the sun will shine upon it. A vault somewhat similar to those now in said Cemetery, containing but one compartment in which to lay my body and coffin, Said lot and Vault to cost not more than one Thousand Dollars.

Third - After the payment of my just debts and funeral expenses and for the said vault and cemetery lot and of the administration of my Estate. I will devise and bequeath all the residue of my Estate, real personal and mixed unto my nephew Gus D. Devine of Lawrence Massachusetts except as devised in item Sixth.

Fourth - I hereby nominate constitute and appoint my Comrades A. J. Gahagan and Halbert B. Case as Executors of this my last will and Testament.

Fifth - For the information and guidance of my said Executors I hereby record the following: (1) It is my desire to be buried by my Comrades of the Grand Army of the Republic.

(2) My Executors are requested to secure some temporary resting place for my body during the time they are creating the vault above directed.

(3) - The ready funds which I have are in the First National Bank and in the Chattanooga Savings Bank and in the City Savings Bank of Chattanooga.

(4) My bank Books for the First National Bank and for the Chattanooga Savings Bank are in the drawer at my office.

[Page 559] (5) My certificates of Deposit for the City Savings Bank are in a Tin box along with my Tax receipts in my Bureau at my residence in Chattanooga.

Sixth - In addition to the Special bequests made above, I hereby will devise and bequeath unto Father Walsh, the Priest in charge of the Roman Catholic Church in Chattanooga, the sum of One hundred Dollars, and direct my Executors to pay the same, and I request that Father Walsh shall cause masses to be said for the repose of my soul.

In witness whereof I have hereunto set my hand in the presnece of J. B. Woolson & John Englehardt** whom I have called to witness my signature and they have signed the same as witnesses at my request in my presence and in the presence of each other this the 6th day of December 1893.

Fred Devine

The foregoing instrument was signed by Fred Devine who declared it to be his last will and testament in our presence and we have signed the same as witnesses in his presence at his request and in the presence of each

other on this the 6th day of December A. D. 1893.

J. B. Woolson
John Englehard**

** both spellings used in this instrument

Filed and probated Dec. 16th 1893.

J. H. Messick - Clerk

END OF WILL BOOK 1

CLARA, 5
ELIZA, 5(3)
JOHN, 5
MICHAEL, 5(4)
PATRICK, 5(5)
TIMOTHY, 5
GARRETT
A.C., MRS., 135
ADELINE C., 135(4)
GARVIN
ELLEN, 80
J.H., 150
NELLIE, 152
PATRICK, 80
W.B., 116, 177
W.E., 154
WALTER B., 154
GASKILLS
MRS., 53
GASTON
CELESTIA, 187
FRED, 193
HARRY, 193
J.L., 187
GEARHART
LOUISE M., 148
GEILER
EMMA, 194, 195
JOHN, 115
JOHN, JR., 186(2),
194(3), 195(3)
JOHN, SR., 115(2),
194(3), 195
GEILOR
ELIZA, 186
GEISMAR
SAM, 195
SAMUEL, 142
GEISMER
. S., 40
GEORGE
MACON, 77, 78
SOCIAL CIRCLE, 21(3)
GEORGIA, 51, 83
ATLANTA, 195(2)
FORSYTHE, 171
GREENESBORO, 168
MACON, 81(2)
ROME, 58(3)
SHARP'S STATION, 196
SOCIAL CIRCLE,
19(2), 20(4)
TUNNEL HILL, 72
GERMANY, 5
GIBBS
LOUIS C., 97
GIBSON
JULAS, 110
GIESEKING
JOHN, 190
GIFFE

THOS., 94
GIFFEE
THOS., 161
GILASPIE
MARGARET, 136(3)
GILES
CORA JANE, 97
R.A., 52, 97(2)
ROBERT A., 97(3)
SALLIE V., 148
SARAH J., 97
SARAH JANE, 97
THOMAS, 21
GILLASPIE
MARGARET, 136
GILLEM
POLLY MARGARET, 202
GILLESPIE
GEORGE L., 114
J.C., 17, 33
J.K., 114
J.S., 14, 33(2), 36,
193
J.T., 1
JNO. M., 114
JOHN C., 32(2)
JOHN K., 114(2)
JOHN M., 114(3)
MARGARET J., 33(2)
GILLILAND
JAMES R.W., 96(2)
JAMES W., 96
LADY BLANCE, 96(3)
N.J., 96(5)
GIMINARD
PHILLIP, 109
GLASS
ELBERT A., 3(4),
4(4), 6
F.M., 10
J.G., 4, 7
JOHN BELL, 6
JOHN G., 3, 6(4)
JOHN H., 3
LEWIS, 4
M.E., 4
MARY E., 3, 6
WILLY BLOUNT, 6, 7
GLEENSON
P.J., REV., 133
GLEESON
JOSEPH, 50
P.J., REV., 109,
132, 133(2)
GOANS
T.A., 60
GOIN
ESTER, 17
GOINES
A.W., 198
GOINS

ESTHER, 17
O.C., 17
GOODSON
LOUISE H., 139(4)
GOODWIN
F.H., DR., 119
GORCE
C.P., 67
GORDEN
DENIS B., 73
JAMES, 9
GORDON
CICRO N., 10
JAMES, 9(2), 10(3)
JAMES C., 10
SARAH, 10
THOMAS M., 10(4)
WILLIAM L., 10(2)
GOREE
C.P., 81, 112, 144,
157
GORMAN
CHARLES H., 67
MARGRETT, 110
GOTCHER
HENRY, 1(4), 8
J.L., 1
J.T., 1
MARGARET, 1
W.P., 1(2)
GOTHARD
ELIZABETH, 106(2)
IRA, 106
JAMES, 105(2), 106
JOHN, 106
LARKIN, 106
LEWIS, 106
GOWIN
G.A., DR., 13
GRAFTON
D.R., 29, 50
JANNEY, 50
GRANT
ANNA C., 104
WILLIAM, SR., 11
GRANVILLE
BURL, 41
GRAVES
RICHARD, 95
GRAY
DINA, 73
DINAH, 72
DINNAH, 73
W.R., 22
GRAYN
ZION, 107
GREEN
A.P., 28, 57, 58(4)
AUGUSTUS P., 57(2),
58
C.C., 197

EMILY J., 57
JANE, 28
L.Y., 14(2), 53
LEB., 28
M.W., 28
MARSHALL W., 28(4)
MARY ANN, 57(2)
MARY E., 57
SAMUEL E., 57, 58
SARAH H., 57
WILLIAM, 42, 72
WILLIAM T., 57,
58(3)
GREY
CHAS., 98
GRIFFIS
J.C., JR., 114(2)
GRIFFISS
JOHN C., 104
GRIFFITHS
DAVID R., 169
WILLIAM, 168
GRISCOM
FANNIE J., 116
FANNY J., 116
H.F., 90(2)
HARRY F., 116(6)
GROSS
JOHN, 18
GROVE
MARGARET E., 148
GUDSEY
ALTI, 17
GUTHRIE
L., 43
LAWSON, 43
NARCISSA M., 43(2)
R.H., 1, 2(2), 4,
5(2), 6, 7, 9(3),
10, 11(2), 12,
13(2), 14(2),
15(2), 16(2)

-H-

H.C. SQUIRES & CO., 94
HACKETT
ELIZABETH, 181
HAGERTY
JOHNNIE, 167
MAGGIE, 167(5)
MARY, 167
HAGGIE
JACK, 120
HAIGAR
JOHN F., 107
HAINEY
HIRAM, 9
W.R., 9
HAIR
CYNTHIA L., 161(4)

DOC, 42
ROBT., 193
HOOVER
GEORGE M., 4, 5
ISREAL, 150
SAMUEL, 123(7)
HOPE
M.M., 70, 114(2)
W.F., 103
W.T., 122
W.T., DR., 114(2)
HOPKINS
EUPHRANIA, 119
HORAN
W.L., 67
HORD
A.C., 85
B.M., 104
ELLA S., 85
ELLEN S., 85(2)
J.K., 85(3)
HOREHAN
D., 120
HORN
BETSY, 18
HORTON
IBBY, 106
HOTEL
WALDENS RIDGE, 112
HOUSE
CYNTHA, 165
CYNTHIA, 165
G.W., 64, 165(2)
HEZ., 165
NANCY P., 164(2), 165(4)
NANCY PRESLEY, 164
HOUSER
ADOLPHUS, 180(2)
CLABORE, 180
DANIEL A., 180(5)
KATIE, 180(4)
NANCY C., 188
RETURN, 180, 188(4)
HOUSERS
SUSAN, 15
HOUSTON
H., 27
HOWARD
EDWARD, 51
EMILEY J., 57
HOWARDS
OBEDIENCE, 15
HOWDEN
JANE, 194(4)
HOWLETT
T.S., 60
HUDDLE
N., 95
NOAH, 95
O.P., 95

HUEGENIN
EDWARD D., 77
EDWARD D., MRS., 78
JULIA D., 77
JULIA E., 77
LEILA V., 77
MARTHA F., 77
HUEGININ
JULIA E., 77
HUFF
JOHN THOMAS, 44
HUGENIN
EDWARD D., 77
HUGHES
ANN, 92
BRIDGET, 80, 116
DAVID W., 92(2)
JOHN, 190
JOSEPH, 92
WILLIAM, 18
HULBERT
ORIEN, 37
ORION, 37
HULSE
A.J., 112
ALEXANDER B., 112
BRUCE, 112
H.B., 135
H.C., MRS., 112
HERBERT C., 112
HULSEA
A., 17
HUMPHREY
SALLY, 34
HUMPHREYS
P. [T.?] M., 17
SALLY, 33(2)
HUMPHRIES
J.W., 26
HUNNICUTT
D.M., 67
EVA, 67(2)
Z.T., 67(4)
HUNT
C.O., 143
MR. & MRS., 119
SAMUEL, 199
THOS. H., 10
HUNTER
A.P., 155, 183
A.P., MRS., 155
ADDISON P., 75, 190
ANN ELIZABETH, 153
C.E., MRS., 198
DAVID WILLIAM, 153(3), 154(3)
ELIZABETH, 154
GEORGE, 131(2)
MARY JANE, 26
MARY JANE MILLIGAN, 153, 154

R., 154
R.A., 61
ROBERT, 153(3), 154(8)
SARAH, 153(3), 154
HURD
HAS., 171
HUTCHESON
J.C., 105(2)
W.L., 29
HUTCHISON
WILLIAM, 1
HYDE
A.A., 75(3), 76(2)
ALBERT E., 75
CHAS. R., 75
F.G., 75
F.S., 75(2), 76
MARTHA A., 75
WILLIAM A., 75

-I-

I. LOWENBURG & CO., 163(4)
I. LOWENTHAL & CO. [SIC], 163
ILER
C.J., 184
OCTAVIA, 184(2)
ILES
ELENDER, 17, 18(2)
JAMES, 17(2), 18
JOHN, 18(4)
L.J., 18
LEANAGHER J., 18
LEANAHER J., 17, 18
NANCY, 18
ILLINOIS
CHICAGO, 119(2), 145
MORRIS, 120, 121(2)
INDIANA
INDIANAPOLIS, 93(2)
INGRAM
JAMES B., 138
IOWA, 112
IRELAND, 42(2), 145, 146
COUNTY DONEGAL, 61
COUNTY KERRY, 23
IRVIN
PERRY, 112
IRVING
MARY ANN, 104(2)
PERRY, 88
ISLAND
SODDY, 47
ISOM
JAMES EDWARD, 103
WM., 103

-J-

J. LOWENBURG & CO. [SIC], 163
JACK
BELL, 9
ELIZABETH H., 54(2), 55
JAMES, 54
JACKSON
BURL, 41(2)
BURL, SR., 42
CHARLOTTE, 41(2)
EMILY S., 121
GRANVILLE, 41
JAMES L., 121(3), 122
MYRTLE M., 135
SAMUEL, 41(2)
JACOB
LEWIS, 45
JACQUET
ANTHONY, 26
JAMES
FRANK, 34
THOMAS, 35(2)
JARNAGIN
G.H., 93
JOHN
JOSEPH, 136(4), 137
MARY, 136(3)
JOHNSON
A.M., 6, 24, 73, 144
ALBERT O., 118(6)
ALTA, 26
ANNIE F., 148(2)
DOLLY, 101, 105
E.W., 118(2)
EDWIN W., 118(5), 119
ELIZA, 26
FRANZINA, 26
GREEN, 72, 73(2)
J.M., 31(3)
JAMES, 26(2)
JOE, 72
JOHN, 31
JOHN S., 195(2)
LUCY, 150
MARIANA H., 164
MARTHA, 1
MARY A., 118(6)
MARY ELIZABETH, 148
MORNING, 26(4)
R.P., 164(2)
R.P., DR., 164
SARAH, 26
THANKFUL A., 143(3), 144(2)
THOMAS H., 26
WILLIAM, 26
JOHNSTON

McMANUS
  J.A., 78, 79(2)
  JOHN, 79
  JOHN A., 78
McMATH
  P.E., 172
McMILLAN
  ALEXANDER, 89(7)
  ELIZABETH, 89
  WILLIAM, 89
McMILLIAN
  J.P., 29
McMILLIN
  ANN CRAVENS, 68
  D. CAL, 68, 69
  D. CAL, 195(3), 196
  J.P., 59
  J.P., SR., 68(3)
  JAMES P., 68
  JAS. P., 176
  M.P., SR., 69
  MINNIE, 195, 196
  NANCY JANE, 69
McNABB
  ELIZA ANN, 12
  R.L., 15, 38
  ROBERT L., 12
McNALLY
  PATT., 32
McNEAL
  H., 139
  HUGH, 139(3)
  M.C., 139
  MARY C., 139
McPHERSON
  J.B., 5
  J.D., 167
  JOHN B., 4(2)
McREE
  M.B., 47(5), 68, 203
  R.C., 18, 47(2), 203
  R.C., JR., 47(3)
  R.C., SR., 47(3)
  R.G., 100
  ROBT. C., SR., 203
McREYNOLDS
  H.L., M.D., 157
McROY
  J.C., 13
MADDEN
  E.J., 84(4)
  JULIA, 84(2)
MAGILL
  HUGH, 17
MAHAGAN
  A.J., 86
MAHONEY
  ELIZA, 42
  JEREMIAH D., 50
MAKER
  WM., 25

MALLEE
  C.L., MRS., 131(2)
MALONEY
  JOHANNA, 148(3)
  PAT., 145
MALONY
  JOHANNA, 147
MANGOLD
  ADOFF, 182
  GAWARD NICHOLAS, 182
  LEONARD, 181(3),
    182(2)
  LEONARD CICKEY, 182
  LILLE ESTREVA, 182
  LOUIS ALFOS, 182
  MARIA ANTONETTE, 182
MANING
  MATILDY, 120
MANN
  AMANDA, 113
  MILES, 113(3), 114
MANNEY
  FRANCIS, 49
  MARY, 49
MANNING
  A.S., 192(5)
  AMOS, 120
  ELIZA ELLEN, 192
  THOMAS, 192
  W.J., 23
MANSFIELD
  MARY ALLIE, 180
MANUM
  SARAH, 37
MARINER
  F.A., 164
MARQUET
  FRANK P., 145
MARSHALL
  JNO. P., 158
  KATE M., 158, 159
  STANHOPE STEWART,
    158
  W.S., 36, 87,
    158(3), 159(2),
    181
MARTIN
  E.R., 51
  ELIZABETH, 110
  FRANCIS, 201
  GEO. W., 109
  L.C., 92
  SAMUEL, 110(5)
  THOMAS, 110
  WILLIAM, 17
MASON
  C.S., 194
MASSACHUSETTS
  BOSTON, 87(2), 147
  LAWRENCE, 204
MASSEY

W.R., 18
MATHIS
  JAMES, 31(2), 32
  MELISSA, 31(2)
MATTHEWS
  JAMES, 18
  MILTON H., 66
MAURER
  G.L., 6
MAY
  CHARLES, 55(4)
  H.D., 55(3)
  MILTON R., DR.,
    88(2)
MAYER
  CHAT THEODORE, 179
MAYS
  N.M., 101, 105
MEACHAND
  J.E., 118
MEE
  J.F., 34
MELTON
  A.P., 27
MEREDITH
  ALBAN, 34(3), 35
  CONWAY, 35(2)
  GEORGE, 35(3)
MESSICK
  J.H., 131, 188, 191,
    192(2), 193(2),
    195, 198(2), 200,
    202, 203, 204
METTS
  CHARLES STEVEN, 44
METY
  JOSEPH, 202
MEYERS
  R.M., 118
MICHIGAN
  MOUNT PLEASANT,
    176(2)
  SUMMERTOWN, 29
MILES
  BISHOP, 24
MILL
  J.E. McDONALD'S, 140
MILLER
  A.T., 94
  D.W., 195
  MARY, 155(2)
  MARY SUSAN, 184(2)
  W.C., 184
MILLINGTON
  RUTH, 203
MILTON
  SARAH F., 79
MINNESOTA
  ALEXANDER, 131
MISSIONARY RIDGE
  BATTLE OF, 6

MISSISSIPPI
  CANTON, 48
  NATCHEZ, 162, 163
MISSOURI
  CAPE GIRARDEAU, 24
MITCHELL
  D.F., 185(6), 186(3)
  DOC, 145
  JAMES C., 15(5)
  JESSIE, 20, 21(4)
  LARY, 72
  MARGARET, 185(3),
    186
  NANCY JANE, 15
  T.C., 15
MONTAGUE
  L.W., 159
  LIZZIE, 96
  MARY, 87(3)
  T.G., 41, 57
  T.Y., 159
  THEODORE G., 133
MONTANA
  LIVINGSTON, 187
MONTGOMERY
  J.E., 199
MOON
  A.W., 8
MOONEY
  MARTHA G.W., 55
MOORE
  B., 93
  EDWARD H., 15
  FREDERIC J. 15
  GEORGE W., 165
  JAMES M., 15
  JOHN, 15
  JOHN A., 115
  M.E., 145
  MALINDA, 14(3)
  NIMROD, 15
  PETER P., 15(2)
  RICHARD J., 15
  S.B., 151
  S.B., MRS., 150
  SARAH, 14(4), 15
  TEMPERANCE, 134
  W.J., 168
MORELAND
  L.C., 1, 15, 16(2)
MORGAN
  HARRY, 93
  MAHOLY, 106
  MARTHA F., 79
  PAT, 94
  T., 185
MORRELL
  F.F., 160
MORRIS
  F.A., 127
MORRISON

LIZZIE, 132
WM., 26
PARHAM
M.B., 52
PARK
LUCY, 122
PARKER
BARNETT, 26
PARKHURST
JOE, 160
PATILLOW
W.B., 10
PATTEN
G.W., 153
GEORGE W., 152
J.A., 152, 153(4)
LIZZIE, 53(5)
LOTTIE HOHNES, 152
Z.C., 53(4), 74
PATTERSON
ALICE, 171(4)
PAXTON
ELIZA J., 203
PAYNE
G.A., 50
MARY C., 179
T.H., 119, 179
THO. H., 30
W.C., 143, 199
PEABODY
C.H., 86
MARY H., 38
PEAK
WM., 119
PEAR
DR., 73
PEARSON
ABNER, 88
JOSEPH, 88(5)
MOSES, 125(4)
NANCY M., 88
PEEPLES
S.C., 47, 128
W.O., 47
PENDERGRASS
H., 168
HIRAM, 29, 168(5)
JAMES A., 28, 29
JEFFERSON, 29
JESSE, 29
JOHN, 29(2)
MARTHA, 29
MARY, 168
NATHANIEL, 29
NIMROD, 28(2), 29(2)
PENFIELD
M.F., 140
PENNESYLVANIA
TOWANDA, 148
PENNOCK
O.H., 139

PENNSYLVANIA, 76
BURWICK, 193
PITTSTON, 152(4),
153(2)
TOWANDA, 148
PENNY
ISOM, 18
PEOPLES
S.C., 128
PERKINS
JANE, 192
PETER, 192(4)
PERRY
A.F., M.D., 197
C.W., 166
PETTIBONE
A.H., 177
PFRUMER
KATE, 67
PFRUMMER
KATE, 67
PHELAN
JNO. D., 103
PHEMER
CHARLES, 42
PHILAN
JOHN, 81
PHILIPS
JOHN, 172
PHILLIPS
CATHERINE L., 144(2)
LORENA A., 157(2)
M.M., 10
PICKENS
J.W., 148
PICKETT
MARGARET N., 35(3)
PIERSON
HELLEN TURNELL,
104(2)
JOHN, 104(5)
JOHN EDWARD, 104
THOMAS C., 104(2)
THOMAS CARTER, 104
PINION
ALICE, 142
CYNTHIA, 142
HENRY K., 143(2)
HENRY R., 142
SARAH ANN, 143(4)
SARAH H., 143
T.J., 142(3)
T.J., JR., 142
T.J., SR., 143
THOMAS J., 143(2)
THOMAS J., JR.,
143(6)
W.D., 142
PITMAN
GARY, 105(2)
PITNER

T.H., 128(2)
W.H., 129
PLANT
ROBERT H., 81(2)
POE
A.W., 13, 74
ASARIAH, 61
AZARIAH, 54
CATHERINE, 13
CHRISTOPHER, 13
H.H., 61
HASTEN, 61(4)
J.H., 61
JAMES A., 61
JAMES CALVIN, 2
JANE, 13(2)
JOHN, 1(3), 2
JOHN L., 2
MAHALY, 13
NANCY, 2
REBECCA, 1
SAML., 13(2)
SAMUEL, 13(3)
SARAH E., 61
W.H., 61
WM., 18
POSEY
J.C., 203
OLIVER N., 202
W.D., 202(3)
WILEY D., 203
WILEY D., JR., 202
POWELL
ANNA, 174, 175
BARNA, 174(4),
175(2)
MORRIS B., 89
POWERS
ANNIE, 145
JOHN, 80, 145(4),
185(3)
MAGGIE, 158(2)
PAT, 94, 158(3)
PATRICK, 80, 158
PRATCHARD
J.M., 58
PRATT
A.J., 40
CATHERINE H., 148
JOSEPH G., 148
MARY, 148
MILO, 40
SUSAN M., 148
W.H., 38(2), 39(2)
PRICE
POMPEY, 97
SALLIE C., 145
PRINTUP
D.S., COL., 58
PRYOR
E.F., 198(2)

JOSEPH, 139
PATTIE, 198(2)
PATTIE V., 198(3)
PUCKET
A.G.W., 69
PUCKETT
A.G.W., 113
ANDREW G.W., 113(3)
JULIA CANNON, 113(2)
NANCY LEE, 113
W.R., 18
PURLARD
CLAUDE, 163
PUTNAM
SARAH E., 61

-Q-

QUEENER
MITCHELL, 85(4)
QUIGBY
ANDREW, 5
QUIN
MAG, 23
THAD, 23

-R-

RAGAN
JESSE S., 18
RAGSDALE
WILLIAM F., 6(2)
WM. B., 124
RAILROAD
ATLANTIC, 19
C.N.O. & P., 184
CENTRAL, 77(2)
E. TENN. VA. & GA.,
44
GEORGIA, 19, 168
W & A, 149
RAILWAY
CINCINNATI SOUTHERN,
169
E.T.V. & G., 151
RAMSAY
A.C., 157
ADELLA C., 158
ADELLA CLEVELAND,
157(3)
WILBURN B., 157(2)
RAMSEY
SAM, 126
RAND
SOPHIA, 186
RANKIN
W.R., 48
WILLIAM, 90
RANSOM
EVA, 31(5)
PERRY, 31

121
LEWIS JESSE, 121
SUSANNAH, 121
WILLIAM STOCKSTILL,
121
WIRZ
FREDRICH AUGUST, 179
MAGDALENA, 179(3)
MARGILA (?), 179
WISCONSIN, 112
GREEN BAY, 64
WISDOM
A.J., 124(2)
WITCHER
T.A., 96(3)
WOLF
F.S., 31
FRANCIS S., 31(2)
JOHN, 94
KATE, 82
LEONARD, 82
WOLLY
THOMAS, 99
WOMBLE
PEGGIE, 49
WOOD
D.F., 172
G.A., 94
WOODARD
ROBT. P., 129
WOODBURY
A.G., 121
WOODEN
IDA, 112
ISAIAH, 112
WOODHEAD
ADAH, 121
L.J., 121(2)
LAURENCE JOHN,
121(2)
WOODRUFF
W.T., 53
WOODWARD
LOUISA E., 65
WOOLFORD
F. REES, 177
WOOLSON
J.B., 204(2)
WORDSWORTH
Y.N., 139
WORLITZER
CONSTANT, 115
WORNACUT
T.K., 23
THOS. K., 7
WORTHEY
MATTIE, 67
MATTY, 67(4)
SAMUEL H., 67
WRIGHT
CHARLIE, 67

LILLIE M., 139
WROE
SARAH C., 199(5)
WILLIAM O., 199
WYOMING, 194

-Y-

YARNELL
JOHN L, 16
YORK
CLARENCE G., 148
ELIZABETH M., 148(5)
S. AUGUSTUS, 148
YOUNG
ESSEY MAY, 95
S.J., 95(2)
W.C., 95(2)
WESLEY C., 95(3)

-Z-

ZEIGER
CAROLINE, 82(2)
HERMAN, 82(4)

www.ingramcontent.com/pod-product-compliance
Lightning Source LLC
Chambersburg PA
CBHW080419270326
41929CB00018B/3093